SEX IN VIDEO GAMES

SEX IN VIDEO GAMES

BRENDA BRATHWAITE

CHARLES
RIVER
MEDIA

CHARLES RIVER MEDIA
Boston, Massachusetts

Cover Design: Tyler Creative

CHARLES RIVER MEDIA
25 Thomson Place
Boston, Massachusetts 02210
617-757-7900
617-757-7969 (FAX)
crm.info@thomson.com
www.charlesriver.com

This book is printed on acid-free paper.

Brenda Brathwaite. *Sex in Video Games.*
ISBN: 1-58450-459-5

All brand names and product names mentioned in this book are trademarks or service marks of their respective companies. Any omission or misuse (of any kind) of service marks or trademarks should not be regarded as intent to infringe on the property of others. The publisher recognizes and respects all marks used by companies, manufacturers, and developers as a means to distinguish their products.

Library of Congress Cataloging-in-Publication Data
Brathwaite, Brenda.
  Sex in video games / Brenda Brathwaite.
    p. cm.
  Includes index.
  ISBN 1-58450-459-5 (pbk. : alk. paper)
  1. Video games--Social aspects. 2. Sex. I. Title.
  GV1469.34.S52B73 2006
  794.8--dc22
2006025163

Printed in the United States of America
06 7 6 5 4 3 2 First Edition

CHARLES RIVER MEDIA titles are available for site license or bulk purchase by institutions, user groups, corporations, etc. For additional information, please contact the Special Sales Department at 800-347-7707.

To my family, the whole extended thing.

Contents

Acknowledgments

When you read a book, you frequently skim over the list of names in sections like these. When you write a book, you know why they're there.

I am indebted to the following individuals for their help and support with this project.

Thanks first go out to Hugh Hefner and the wonderful group of people at *Playboy* who, by doing what they did, allowed me to do what I'm doing. The *Playboy: The Mansion*™ game changed the course of my career. My colleagues at the former Cyberlore Studios, where *Playboy: The Mansion* was developed, supported my somewhat absurd interest in the history of this field (600 *Playboy* magazines in my office qualifies as "absurd") and celebrated this book's milestones along with me. So, too, did my former colleagues at Sir-Tech Software and Sirtech Canada, particularly Robert F. Sirotek, Norman A. Sirotek and Linda Currie, who gave me my start and shared their support and stories with me from the dawn of the industry.

Thanks also go to those who gave this topic a respected platform within the game development community, particularly the Game Developers Conference (GDC) for allowing adult content development to be a part of the discussion, and Jason Della Rocca and the International Game Developers Association (IGDA), who took the risk and allowed for and welcomed the creation of the IGDA's Sex Special Interest Group (SIG), the contributions of which cannot be understated. You, the members of that group, have continuously provided me a wealth of material, support, and knowledge from which to work.

Following that fateful GDC, Sheri Graner Ray uttered those rather prophetic words, "I see a book in your future." Sheri, author of *Gender Inclusive Game Design*, has been a long-time industry friend and more recent source of inspiration and support. She provided and continues to provide just the right words at just the right moment.

My profound thanks and gratitude are also extended to Kyle Machulis, founder of slashdong.org and MMOrgy.com. This topic and book changed the course of his life as much as mine. Kyle has been my proverbial partner in crime through numerous conferences, uncountable emails, and even more IMs. He is a wealth of knowledge about this field, and his contribution to the IGDA Sex SIG and his friendship is invaluable to me.

Deb Solomon, a lawyer and a professor of game design at Montgomery College in Maryland wrote the chapter on obscenity for me. Thank you so much for all the research and work that was required to pull that chapter together. The knowledge provided within those pages will be useful to all game developers.

I am also grateful to all of you who provided interviews and anecdotes for this book, including such industry icons as Richard Garriott, Bob Bates, Steve Meretzky, Richard Bartle, and Neil Newell, and industry defenders like MIT's Henry Jenkins, who deserves 10 times the recognition and accolades he gets.

Thanks are also due to Patrick Wildenborg, illspirit, and the *GTA* mod community who gave me a behind-the-scenes look at the days leading up to and following the infamous Hot Coffee scandal. Despite how they've been characterized in some media, these modders are not out to destroy gaming as we know it. In fact, by creating mods, they often extend the life of games. Thank you to all of you, but particularly Patrick and illspirit, for opening up to me.

During the course of this book's production, individuals at the ESRB, the ESA, the IEMA, and the IGDA were quick to answer my many questions. Thank you for the work that you do on behalf of game developers and the general public to keep adult content out of children's hands.

Many people contributed anecdotes and interviews for this book—Patric Lagny, Greg Kasavin, Chris Oltyan, Chris Morris, Kyle Hamilton, Jason Compton, Ray Schwartz, Andrea Fryer, Catherine Smith, Noche Kandora, Patricia Vance, Eliot Mizrachi, Jeff Sloan, Dennis McCauley, Hal Halpin, Doug Lowenstein, the Administration of the GTAGarage.com, Lawrence Walters, Esq., Ed Kuehnel, Rich Carlson, Dave Taylor, Tom Forsyth, George Broussard, Matthew Ford, Kelly Rued, Gabe Zichermann, Peter Payne, David Potter, Brad Abram, Marlene, Seth Spaulding, Clarinda Merripen, Jeb Havens, Richard Cobbett, Anando Banerjee, Guido Henkel, "Jonathan Yip," Michael Hengst, and those anonymous people who were willing to tell me their stories.

I am also grateful for the tremendous support of my employer, the Savannah College of Art & Design, which gives me the freedom to pursue this topic, and my Chair, Josephine Leong, and Dean, Peter Weishar, who have been nothing but incredibly supportive.

There is also a community of game developers for which I am thankful. We failed to agree on a secret handshake by five, so I will assume you all know who you are.

Last, but above all, thank you to my husband for taking care of every last little detail of life for me while I did nothing but type for a year. You have supported this project from its inception with your own time and effort. Thanks, too, to my children, Maezza, Donovan, and Avalon, whose countless smiles, hugs, and humor make my world a wonderful place.

Games are not just for kids.

Brenda Brathwaite

About the Author

As a 24-year veteran of the video games industry, Brenda Brathwaite is a game designer and professor of game design at the Savannah College of Art & Design. She has worked on 21 published titles, including the award-winning *Wizardry®* series of role-playing games and the award-winning *Jagged Alliance®* series of strategy role-playing games. She recently completed work on an upcoming, unannounced Xbox 360/PS3 title for a major publisher and was previously lead designer on *Playboy: The Mansion™*. Brenda is the founder and chair of the International Game Developers Association's (IGDA) Sex Special Interest Group and a passionate anti-censorship advocate. She is a regular speaker at universities and conferences, including The Game Developers Exchange (GDX), Game Developers Conference (GDC) 2006, Future Play 2005, GDC 2005, and Women in Games Conference (a part of the Austin Games Conference). She writes the IGDA's Sex & Games blog at *www.igda.org/sex*.

1 Defining Sex

DEFINING SEX

The Merriam-Webster Dictionary defines sex as "1 : either of the two major forms of individuals that occur in many species and that are distinguished respectively as female or male, 2 : the sum of the structural, functional, and behavioral characteristics of living things that are involved in reproduction by two interacting parents and that distinguish males and females, 3 a : sexually motivated phenomena or behavior, b : sexual intercourse and 4 : genitalia. [Webster01]."

Not exactly a definition for sex in games.

SO WHAT IS SEX IN GAMES?

It should be an easy question to answer. Yet listening to participants at the "Sexuality in Games: What's Appropriate?" roundtable at the 2005 Game Developers

Conference, it's clear that "sex in games" means a great many things to a great many people.

"Can you show masturbation in a game?" asked one.

"Is kissing all right in an E-rated game?"

"How does one handle reproduction in a game like *Zoo Tycoon®*?"

"I'd like to talk about the portrayal of female characters in games."

"What about the booth babes?"

In its first session—roundtables run once a day for three days—the roundtable raised more questions than it answered. It also expanded the definition of "sex in games" to include more than just physical intimacy.

Sex in games includes everything from flirting to hard-core sexual simulators. It occurs when characters kiss or people "hook up" in massively multiplayer online role-playing games (MMORPGs). Models that parade the show floor at the Electronic Entertainment Expo (E3)—particularly those who appeared prior to E3's 2006 enforcement of its attire restrictions—are as much a part of sex in games as the avatars that walk through game worlds. The sexual content found in video game advertising has as strong a place in the discussions as the sexual content that happens quite by accident.

So what is sex in games?

SEXUALLY THEMED CONTENT

Sexual content in video games ranges from the completely abstracted to the explicit. With such an array of material, how does one categorize sexual content in video games? There are several ways to look at it: by use, by range, and by purpose.

Sexual Content by Use

When sexual content appears in a game, it's there for a reason, whether to carry out a specific gameplay mechanic or to convey an aesthetic, a particular feeling, to the player. In general, there are three specific uses for sexual content in games.

How is sex used in games?

Sex as Mechanic

A gameplay mechanic is a rule of a game. A barrel that blows up when it is hit is a mechanic, as is a floor pressure plate that causes a secret door to open. Throwing a die, taking a card on your turn, or advancing three spaces on a board are all mechanics of board games. For some video games, particularly those in the hard-core market, sex is a mechanic. In the online game *VirtuallyJenna*, for instance, players use a variety of tools to bring a virtual version of porn star Jenna Jameson to climax.

In *Playboy™: The Mansion™*, characters who develop a sufficiently high relationship with each other might also "get it on" in the Grotto.

When sex is used as a mechanic, it can be employed actively or passively. An active sex mechanic allows the players to directly control the action. The controversial mini-game revealed in the infamous *Grand Theft Auto: San Andreas™* "Hot Coffee" mod allows players to control the avatar's thrusting. By timing the avatar's thrusts properly, the player can please the woman. Other games like *Roboho* or *3D Sex Villa* allow the player to insert sex toys into virtual characters or, in the case of hardware-enabled virtual sex simulators, like those designed to work with the *Interactive Fleshlight*, allow a male player to insert his penis into a sleeve hooked up to a computer's ISB port. The *Interactive Fleshlight* is designed by Sinulate Entertainment. By contrast, a passive sex mechanic puts the game in control of the actual sexual content. For instance, *DreamStripper* (Figure 1.1) lets the player choose the clothing and moves of his stripper, but he cannot actually control her body directly. Likewise, in *The Sims™ 2*, the player can do all kinds of things to bring two characters together, but ultimately, when they have "woo hoo," if they have "woo hoo," it is up to them.

FIGURE 1.1   Ensign Games' *DreamStripper*. © 2005 Ensign Games, Inc. Reprinted with permission.

Sex as Reward

There are dozens of strip poker games available online, and it's in these games that sex used as a reward is most obvious. In the first such game of its type, 1982's *Artworx Strip Poker*, when a player wins a hand, his or her virtual opponent removes a piece of clothing, gradually revealing more and more. Whenever a game awards or makes sexual content available to the player as a result of his or her actions, sex is being used as a reward. *The Guy Game*™ used a similar tactic, but instead of cards, its mechanic is trivia questions. Players begin by selecting a sexy co-ed avatar. Then, players watch brief film clips of women being asked trivia questions. The player must guess the answers to these questions, and further, guess whether the women will answer them correctly. The better the player does, the more his in-game avatar reveals. The amount of nudity the player sees in the video clips within the game is also tied to his performance. The game initially pixelates topless nudity, allowing only top-performing players to see nonobscured video clips of the women. *The Guy Game* was eventually removed from the market when it was revealed that one of its participants was 17 when she agreed to participate. As a minor, she was legally incapable of giving her consent.

Sex as Aesthetic

Sex is an incredibly immersive experience that affects all the senses deeply. Games that hope to fully simulate this experience must affect as many senses as they possibly can to recreate a sexy aesthetic. Devices such as the *Sinulator*™, *Interactive Fleshlight*, and *SeXBox* allow players to feel sexual stimuli while playing a game. The *Sinulator* is a vibrator that can be controlled over the Internet, while the *SeXBox* is an Xbox controller whose vibration devices have been removed and inserted into sex toys. Both are covered later in this chapter. The *Scent Dome*™, a device that emits smells as directed by a program, could be used to convey the scent of a woman or a man. Visually, computers and consoles are easily capable of recreating the sights and sounds of sex, too. Video, live streaming images, and high-polygon renderings of virtual characters are all commonplace (*www.renderotica.com*) as are soundtracks, sound effects, and chat and voice between systems. While this technology currently exists, none compares to that of a real human being.

In some cases, that's actually key. For those who desire sex with things that are impossible on this earth, computerized images and the artists who create them are a proverbial saving grace. In online worlds where anything goes, dragons can have sex with foxes, and people can pleasure themselves while on fire . . . or dead.

Of course, most of today's games, particularly the mainstream ones, don't go that far. Instead, they use sexual content to make the game more appealing to convey a somewhat sexy aesthetic. The aesthetic the developers wish to convey often reveals itself even before the game's opening screen. Games with names like *Roboho*™, *Rapture Online*™, and *Do You Like Horny Bunnies?* suggest the game to come. The aesthetic can be carried out into the game's interfaces, HUD ("heads up display," the interface that overlays the main gameplay screen), options, minigames, animations, and even the loading screens. For instance, *Leisure Suit Larry:*

Magna Cum Laude™ features a conversation mini-game in which a sperm attempts to avoid obstacles in a side-scrolling maze of sorts. *7 Sins* is also full of similar sexually themed mini-games. *Playboy: The Mansion* features *Playboy* trivia and quotes on its loading screens, and unlockable centerfold photos.

The way a game's camera is used also reveals its aesthetic. Games occasionally zoom in on a particular character or show him or her from a sexually flattering angle that accentuates some feature of the character's body, like the buxom barmaid in *Baldur's Gate: Dark Alliance*. Some games even allow players to control the camera. *Dead or Alive: Xtreme Beach Volleyball* features a voyeuristic mode that lets players watch the women from multiple angles and zoom in for a closer look.

As an aesthetic, sexual content also appears as "window dressing," whether it's the breasts of a bartender, the relationship between in-game characters, or the setting of the game. *Phantasmagoria™ 2: A Puzzle of Flesh™*, for instance, sets some of its scenes in a fictional S&M club called "The Borderline." *Playboy: The Mansion* allowed players to recreate Hugh Hefner's famous home right down to its steamy grotto.

Sex by Range

The range of sex content found in video games is as wide as that found in any other medium. It ranges from the hard core to the fully abstracted. Even within individual categories, there is great variety. Early text-based games, particularly the early online worlds, featured hard-core scenes that could only be imagined by the player, while more recent games feature avatars with buxom, bouncing breasts that steal the scene. Some avatars appear to be on their way to a stripping engagement instead of a day in the dungeon.

What is the range of sex in games?

Abstracted Sex

When asked to point out the sexual content in *Zoo Tycoon™ 2*, most people aren't readily able to. "There's no sex in that game," said one. "In *Zoo Tycoon*? Are you sure you have the right game?" said another. However, breeding animals is very much a part of the game's appeal. The sexual content in the game, though, is fully abstracted.

"In order to successfully breed animals, you need to care for them properly and care for their surroundings," said Linda Currie, a designer on *Zoo Tycoon 2* and now producer at its developer, Blue Fang Games. "Happy animals make baby animals. You need to meet their basic needs like hunger, thirst, and environment, and their more advanced needs including mental stimulation, social interaction, exercise, and privacy. You must also have a male and female animal in the same exhibit" [Currie01]. If all the conditions are met, the baby animal just shows up.

The Sims™ also abstracts the actual reproductive act. Like *Zoo Tycoon 2*, specific conditions must be met, but once met, a baby arrives. *Grand Theft Auto 3* also featured abstracted sex. Although the game was much maligned for allowing players to have sex with a prostitute, the actual sexual content in the game was relatively tame. Players saw the car bounce up and down, nothing more.

Family Friendly Content

Sexual or "racy" content found in games for children, if it is found in a nonabstracted form at all, tends toward three things: clothing, comic mischief, and kissing or other gentle expressions of affection between game characters. Clothing on game characters can at times be revealing, although in games designed for a younger crowd, it is rarely more than tight-fitting outfits, the occasional bikini, or a bare-chested male character.

As the age of the game's target audience rises from children to teenagers, the sexual content found in games increases. Revealing clothing and crude jokes are more commonplace, and romantic relationships between characters may develop. In *The Sims*™ *2*, players can watch characters kiss and make out and even have "woo hoo," although the latter is far more comical than titillating. From time to time, *The Sims* characters even remove their clothing to change clothes or to shower, for instance. When *The Sims* characters are nude, the game pixel blurs their bodies so the player cannot see anything vaguely sexual. Underneath the blur, however, *The Sims* characters aren't revealing much. Anatomically, they are the video game version of Barbie® dolls.

There have been games released to a teen market that did feature partial nudity, however. Titles such as *Breath of Fire*™: *Dragon Quarter*™, *Shadow Hearts*®: *Covenant*™, and *Atlantis Evolution* all feature partial nudity, although the duration and context of the nudity is quite limited. Whenever partial nudity is found in a T-rated game title, it is always noted on the box cover in the Entertainment Software Ratings Board (ESRB) content descriptors.

The Mature Audience

As games target an older, more mature audience, those 17 and above, the amount of sexual content increases still more. A character's clothing may become far more revealing and suggestive. A character like *BloodRayne*™, from the game of the same name, is exceptionally attractive, and her clothing leaves little to the imagination, even when she's mostly covered. Within games, animations sometimes become more suggestive and sexy, particularly "idle" animations in which female characters stand still waiting for another action or those that do not directly affect the primary game (e.g., noncombat animations in a combat-intensive game). The dance of the Night Elf in *World of Warcraft*® is among the animations regularly cited as particularly sexy among gamers. Dialogue may comment on a character's attractiveness, and situational humor may become suggestive. The writers of *Leisure Suit Larry: Magna Cum Laude*, Ed Kuehnel and Matt Entin, mastered the art form within their game, which was ultimately nominated for a Game Developers Choice Award for its writing. For sexually themed games, mechanics may include soft-core sexual situations, including prolonged kissing, fondling, fetish realization, and actual, but obscured, intercourse. In such games, penetration is not seen, but rather implied. The characters may be animated, performing sex while still wearing underwear or while obscured by pixel blurs. *God of War*™, for instance, features a threesome between Kratos, the lead character, and two women. Rather than seeing any sexual action, however, the camera focuses on a bedside table and a vase wobbling thereon. Other games like *7 Sins*, *Playboy: The Mansion* and the first iteration of the "Hot Coffee" mod shows characters having sex with their underwear on.

Hard-core Sex

Hard-core sex in video games is uncensored, unashamed, and almost always un-rated. Far beyond *Grand Theft Auto: San Andreas'* "Hot Coffee" sex mini-game, hardcore games are characterized more by what's left *out* rather than what's put in. Often, a hard-core "game" is only a game in the most basic sense of the word—for instance, in *Orgasm Girl* and others like it, the player needs to get the character in the game to orgasm to "win." Other times, the game is nothing more than an adult toy that lets the player use a variety of sex toys on a simulated man, woman, or fetish object. Such games as *Soma Doll*, *VirtuallyJenna*, and *3D Slut* all fit this bill, and are often referred to as "poke the doll" games. Still other games simulate hard-core sex stories, particularly early 1980s games where it was only possible to tell, not show.

Some hard-core games do try to make a game of it, though. For instance, *Sociolotron*SM, an MMORPG, gives players a standard RPG world to play in and also allows players to explore their sexual desires. Players are free to express themselves through their clothing—or lack thereof—and their actions. Patric Lagny, developer of *Sociolotron*, designed the game with this freedom in mind. "We have put great effort into making it possible to break any taboo, as far as legally possible, and have some quite shocking and blasphemous game elements. I believe in free speech and intend to use the rights the USA takes great pride in pointing out all the time" [Lagny01]. Lagny notes that the game does have its necessary limits. While en-couraging people to explore their sexuality, the game will not allow any kind of pedophilia and goes to great lengths to insure that this type of content is impossi-ble to create or to role play in the game world. They even record a log of every action and word exchanged between players. Furthermore, notes Lagny, "We have excluded some things that are legally questionable, like sex with animals or 'furry creatures,' or the graphical description of extreme sexual torture. In fact,

Sociolotron gets away with remarkably little violence and blood, except an occasional splatter on the ground. I'm quite glad to discover that there are still some people out there who find sex more attractive than gruesome violence" [Lagny02].

Japanese "hentai" and "bishoujo" games are also frequently hard core. Known more gently as "dating sims," the more adult hentai and bishoujo games allow players to experience graphic anime sex. One company, Peach Princess, produces English-language localizations of these Japanese games. For instance, *Doushin—Same Heart* features the three characters known as the Suruga sisters. Whenever one of the girls gets sexually aroused, the other two sisters also feel the same way. Another game, *Water Closet: The Forbidden Chamber* (Figure 1.2), allows the player to choose different fetish play paths, each from a different character's perspective.

FIGURE 1.2   Peach Princess' *Water Closet: The Forbidden Chamber.* © 2006 Peach Princess, Inc. Reprinted with permission.

Sex by Purpose

Why is sex found in video games? The same reasons sex is found in art, movies, television, or books. To stimulate players sexually is just one reason. Sexual content can be used to entertain, as it is in countless television relationship dramas. It can be used to teach, just as it is in sexual education or health classes in high schools everywhere.

For what purpose is sex used in video games?

Sex to Stimulate & Entertain

At the "Sexuality in Games: What's Appropriate?" roundtable at the 2005 Game Developers Conference, one developer noted that he had no real problem with sexual content in games provided that it wasn't "just sex for sex's sake."

"What's wrong with sex for sex's sake?" asked another developer. "Why else have sex?" she continued. "That's the best use of sex."

When developers choose racy clothing, busty or beefy characters, or suggestive themes, the use of sex for sex's sake seems most obvious, but its intent in that use is questionable. Rather than stimulating, such sexual content is most often merely entertaining or pleasing in a passive way. Sometimes, the clothing or physical attributes of such characters are so over the top that they become comical. Are designers really hoping that the buxom avatar will turn a player on, are they dressing her to be pleasant to the eye or to meet the industry status quo?

There are games that feature sex for sex's sake, however. *Rapture Online*, a sex positive massively multiplayer online erotic game (MMOEG), features a player-to-player stimulation model. Games with this model enable live players to connect online and explore their sexual fantasies and fetishes with each other. Such games are, in many ways, an evolution of Internet chat rooms. Other games feature a player-to-computer stimulation model. Games like *3D SexVilla*, *Virtual Hottie*, and *VirtuallyJenna* allow players to have a sexual experience with a virtual partner.

Whether with a real or a virtual partner, games that use sexual content to stimulate provide players the freedom to explore their sexuality in a safe and healthy way alone or with other consenting adults. When games truly seek to turn players on, however, they face unique design challenges unlike those faced by any other game. The unique challenges that AO games face in development and in reaching the market are covered in Chapters 12 and 10, respectively.

Sex for Education

For some, discussing the birds and the bees is a daunting ritual of parenthood. However, sexually themed serious games aim to take some of the stress out of the process. One such game is Iser Games' *The Sex Ed Game*. It allows parents and teens to play a trivia game together, and encourages them to use the experience as a basis for more serious discussions about sexuality.

Games can also teach the value of abstinence and safe sex. One of the early *Leisure Suit Larry*™ games, in fact, required Larry to use a condom or face severe consequences. Iser Games' *The Sex Ed Game* also features a Christian version of the game that promotes abstinence.

Of course, teens are not the only ones who need to learn about sexuality. As the success of the self-help market shows, there is a demand for information that can improve the sex lives of couples. Many games that were created for sexual education purposes are covered in Chapter 5.

Sex for Realism

Developers occasionally use sexual content to convey realism. If a role-playing game uses mythical sirens, for instance, one would expect them to be topless. Likewise, a *Playboy* game that featured a monogamous, sexually conservative Hugh Hefner would seem questionable. In social simulations like *The Sims*, mild sexual content occurs to accurately and realistically convey the relationship between two characters. If a game bills itself as an MMO erotic world, but doesn't provide players the necessary actions and animations to complete those actions and fulfill their fantasies, players might question just how "real" the simulation is.

SEXY IMAGES & AVATARS

In the middle ages, women rarely went into battle. Those who did often disguised themselves as men, dressed in male armor or fought alongside men out of pure necessity. However, none wore platemail thongs. And, if they were wearing bras or what passed for medieval lingerie, it was more than likely covered in several pounds of leather, chain, or plate.

Not so in video games. Female heroines regularly venture into dungeons clad in the slightest of armor, far more interested in generating smiles from players than protection from monsters, and even games set in modern or futuristic settings frequently feature what author and designer Sheri Graner Ray refers to as "hypersexualized" females [GRay01]. In her book *Gender Inclusive Game Design: Expanding the Market*, Graner Ray notes that hypersexualized avatars are characterized by their accentuated features, the same features seen in women when they are sexually aroused. Their eyes look dreamy. Cheeks are flush. Breasts are high, and the nipples are erect. Their lips are full and red [GRay02].

Sexy avatars started to appear in video games in the early 1980s as the graphic processing power of computers evolved beyond two color choices. One such system, the Atari 2600, was home to a highly controversial game, Mystique's *Custer's Revenge*. The game featured a fully nude woman, although the nature of the system made the nudity quite abstract. However, the point was not lost on feminists and anti-gaming crusaders who lashed out at the game for this and other, far more controversial reasons. The woman was tied to a post, and as his reward for avoiding a hail of arrows, Custer raped her. This game and controversy are covered in more detail in Chapter 2.

By the mid-1980s, sexy avatars in video games had developed momentum, and an oogling in-game supporter. Sierra's landmark game, *Leisure Suit Larry in the Land of the Lounge Lizards™*, was released quietly and with little fanfare in 1987. Through word of mouth, however, the title eventually caught on. Larry Laffer, the main character in the humorous game, constantly pursued buxom beauties with mixed success. The initial release was profitable enough that its publisher released multiple sequels, however.

By the 1990s, sexy avatars were common. However, it wasn't until 1996 that a sexy avatar took the gaming world by storm. Lara Croft™ was suddenly everywhere. A buxom, gun-toting girl, Lara was loved by male and female gamers alike. She appeared on the cover of countless magazines, spawned fan sites, and inspired a wave of sexy female leads that would appear in games in the years to come. In 2001, Paramount Pictures brought the franchise to the big screen. *Lara Croft: Tomb Raider*, starring Angelina Jolie, was largely panned by critics, but was successful enough that it spawned a sequel, *Lara Croft Tomb Raider: The Cradle of Life* in 2003.

By 2004, digital beauties had become mainstream sex symbols in and of themselves and required no actor to play the part. The October 2004 issue of *Playboy* magazine featured its first ever video game photo shoot, choosing Luba Licious of *Leisure Suit Larry: Magna Cum Laude* as its centerfold. The magazine also featured nude or seminude "photos" of Dixie from *Playboy: The Mansion*, Tala from *Darkwatch: Curse of the West*™, and BloodRayne from *BloodRayne*™ (Figure 1.3). In

FIGURE 1.3 Majesco Entertainment's *BloodRayne*. © 2005 Majesco Entertainment, Inc. Reprinted with permission.

2005, G4TV hosted its first ever Video Game Vixens Awards, and handed the Vixen of the Year award to *Dead or Alive: Xtreme Beach Volleyball*'s Tina. Awards were also given for such categories as "Best Booty," "Kinkiest Accessory," and "Best Bounce" [G4TV01].

Sexy men also appear in video game worlds. Duke Nukem™ (Figure 1.4), a popular video game character and star of his own game series, is the classic, sexy action hero. His one-liners, his love of women, and his bravado proved a hit with gamers. More recently, Kratos from *God of War* has taken a top spot as one of the sexiest guys in a game.

FIGURE 1.4   3D Realm's Duke Nukem.
© 2005 3D Realms, Inc. Reprinted with permission.

Although Duke didn't make the list, Gameinatrix.com, a Web site for female gamers, featured the following top 10 list of video game hunks on its Web site [Trix01]:

10. Jin Kazama—*Tekken*™
 9. Carth—*Star Wars® Knights of the Old Republic*™
 8. Jubei Yagyu—*Onimusha*™ *2*
 7. Master Chief—*Halo*®
 6. Ryu Hayabusa—*Ninja Gaiden Yungsung—Soul Calibur*™ *II*
 5. Yungsung—*Soul Calibur II*
 4. Snake—*Metal Gear Solid*®
 3. Sam Fischer—*Splinter Cell*™
 2. Auron—*Final Fantasy*® *X*
 1. Dante—*Devil May Cry*™ *1*

The use of such sexy characters in games is not without controversy, however. Critics point to the continued unrealistic portrayal and objectification of women as sex objects. Some female players in MMORPGs say their dress provokes sexual harassment from male players, particularly if the game does not allow for or provide less provocative choices. In her book, Graner Ray cautions developers about the consequences such hypersexualized content can have. In a nutshell, if you choose to design games and avatars that are hypersexualized and attractive to a particular gender, don't be surprised if the opposite gender is turned off of your game for the exact same reasons [GRay03].

Not all players feel this way, however, and if the popularity and mimicking of super sexualized women like Britney Spears, Jennifer Lopez, and Christina Aguilera is any indication, the market may not either. Some women like the option of choosing more racy clothing. "In many games, or at least the games I play, the character is a 'hero' of sorts, and is someone who I hope would be bigger and better than I am in my real, nonfantasy life," says Linda Currie. Currie is both a veteran gamer and developer having been in the industry more than 20 years. "Given a choice, I'd rather play a female character that had some sex appeal vs. one that was homely or otherwise portrayed in a less than ideal fashion. Playing scantily clad women doesn't concern me much since I can accept that characters in games are often portrayed in a stereotypical and fantastical fashion. And this 'over-the-top', unrealistic portrayal is just as often applied to the male characters as the females."

What would Currie choose if she could design her character from the ground up? "It's probable I'd choose a little differently," Currie notes. "I'd probably still choose to have her portrayed in an athletic and sexy fashion with attire that was somewhat less than realistic compared to what you might get on a real battlefield, but still more realistic than what you get in some games. Some of the chain mail bikinis that you see in games are really too ridiculous for words. That said, I would not put her in head-to-toe 'realistic' solid plate armor either. I don't want an androgynous figure."

Ultimately, Currie notes that it comes down to a person's degree of tolerance. "Mine might be a little higher than many women because of my background and number of years in this industry," says Currie. "Ultimately, there's a balance between sexy and sexual and some games just don't get it. But then again, if you watch 100 people wandering around your local shopping mall you'll see some percentage of them who just don't get it, either. Sometimes, as the saying goes, there's just no accounting for taste" [Currie02].

SEX IN THE INDUSTRY

At game industry shows, most notably the Electronic Entertainment Expo (E3), female models are often hired to staff the booths of software and hardware publishers. Models also roam the show floor or stand outside convention centers handing out flyers that describe their client's wares and booth location to passersby. These models are frequently referred to as "booth babes."

The video game industry is hardly unique in its use of models, of course. Convention Models & Talent Inc. of Atlanta lists Pepsi Corporation, Sysco, Proctor and Gamble, and Sara Lee among its clients, and attractive models are used on television and in magazines to market everything from eye drops to automobiles.

When E3 first began in 1995, spotting models was difficult. Although rumors circulated the show floor about who was using models and who wasn't, it was difficult to tell. Models generally wore whatever the company's staff wore, be it company tee shirts or other more formal attire. Attractive staff members were occasionally brushed off as spokesmodels who, it was assumed, knew nothing about the products they were presenting.

By 1999, however, "booth babes" were standard at game industry shows and spotting them was not difficult. Industry pundits had even started asking whether the show was about games anymore. Crave Entertainment's booth featured women in bras with racing stripes, and over at the Midway booth, the model's apparel was decidedly low cut. However, Gathering of Developers, a Dallas, Texas–based publisher, took the booth babe concept to a new level—and what many called a new low. Having positioned themselves as an anti-establishment, developer-driven publisher, Gathering of Developers rented a parking lot across from the Los Angeles Convention Center where E3 was taking place. Having a booth separate from the show asserted their independence. At the booth's entrance, women dressed in schoolgirl uniforms carded people to make sure they were at least 21 years old. Inside, the booth was loud, even by E3 standards. Bands performed and competed with the sound of traffic from the street. Dwarves dressed up as members of the band Kiss strolled around the booth to promote the *Kiss Psycho Circus: The Nightmare Child* game that Gathering of Developers would be releasing later that year. The biggest surprise, the one that would be remembered for years to come, was what came to be known in the industry as "the lesbian sex show." On the final day of E3 and in a parking lot across the street, two women were broadcast kissing one another intimately on the big screen behind the main stage where bands traditionally performed. In subsequent years, the infamous Gathering booth would continue to make waves, most notably hosting pole dancing strippers in 2001. Images of these dancers can be found at *www.ritual.com/index.php?section=inside/showcavepics&id=79.*

Although people within the game industry regularly talked about the use of booth babes and expressed their distaste for it, year after year, the booth babes continued to be a fixture at industry events. Booth babe photo roundups have become standard fare for press covering industry events, and one site, *www.e3girls.com*, covers the show's models exclusively. The site has also released DVDs featuring the show's models.

At E3 2005, having had its fill of booth babes and looking for a little publicity of its own, Agetec®, a game publisher and hardware manufacturer, launched an anti-booth babe campaign in an effort to remind people that E3 is about the latest games, not the latest looks. Wearing long blonde wigs, black logo tee shirts and high-waisted, form-covering women's underwear *over* black lycra shorts, the male Agetec Anti-Babes (Figure 1.5) caused quite the stir and a fair number of smirks. Photos and further information on the anti-booth babes can be found at *www.antiboothbabes.com*.

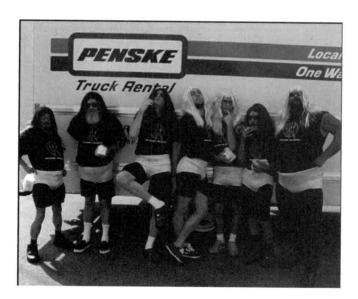

FIGURE 1.5 Agetec's Anti-Booth Babes © 2005 Agetec®. Reprinted with permission.

By 2006, the tide had turned, however. E3 indicated that it would enforce its dress code policy and fine violators $5,000. Those inappropriately dressed would be asked to leave. The policy prohibited bikini tops and other revealing attire that had become common among booth babes and furthermore excluded games with adult sexual content from the show. For developers of sexual content, it was a watershed moment, perhaps the very one in which the mainstream game industry and adult games industries went their separate ways. For booth babes, their participation in the conference was largely unchanged. They were still there, just better (or more) dressed.

Some gaming sites have also ceased publication of booth babe "news." For instance, Gamespot.com, a leading industry site, doesn't offer special coverage of show models. Greg Kasavin, the executive editor of Gamespot.com, said it's an editorial decision. "While we have significant resources available to us for coverage of E3, we nevertheless believe all those resources should be spent covering games and the show itself. We did offer our audience video booth tours and lots of other video content from the [2005] show, allowing those who couldn't attend E3 to take in all the different sights and sounds. So, we certainly didn't go out of our way to not show any E3 booth babes in our coverage, especially since they're a fairly common sight during the event. However, we gave them no special attention, because we're much more interested in the subject matter of E3 rather than the people hired to work the show, and we think our audience feels the same way. I understand why these types of pictorials exist elsewhere—they probably generate more page views than an average preview—but we're focused on game coverage" [Kasavin01].

Although criticism and celebration of booth babes has often focused on the female models and those who ogle them, male models also play a part, although that part is tiny in comparison. Previous E3s have seen an actor dressed up as Duke Nukem, various sports stars, Colby Donaldson from the *Survivor* television series, and even Vin Diesel. Chris Oltyan, a game developer and a member of the IGDA's women in game development mailing list, coined a unique phrase to describe male booth babes. "I personally like the term 'Booth Beef'," said Oltyan. "I feel it properly objectifies men, whereas 'brawn' makes me think of paper towels" [Oltyan01].

SEX IN MARKETING & ADVERTISING

Whether it's a first-person shooter (FPS), an RPG, or a social simulation, sex sells—or at least game publishers hope it does. Advertisements in video game magazines frequently feature scantily clad and busty women and buff, bare-chested handsome men. In the March 2005 issue of *Electronic Game Monthly*®, a magazine pulled randomly from a shelf containing many video game magazines, the following sexy material in advertising was found:

> Page 17—An advertisement for Sega's *Tenchu*® *Fatal Shadows*™ contains a panel that shows a computer-generated buxom fighter with large breasts and lower armor that exposes the women's hips.
>
> Pages 20, 21, and 23—A three-page advertisement for Sony's *Champions: Return to Arms*™ features a real woman wearing leather panties and a bra. She looks longingly upon the armor she has yet to put on—a platemail bra and panties with leather fringe. The third page of the advertisement features the same woman now dressed in the "armor."

Page 27—An advertisement for Lucas Arts' *Star Wars®: Knights of the Old Republic® II: The Sith Lords™* features two women with exceptionally large breasts, lipstick, and rouge.

Page 33—An advertisement for Namco's *Tekken 5®* shows a bare-chested, buff, attractive man.

Page 36—An advertisement for a company that provides Java games, wall-papers, and ring tones features 27 images of scantily dressed or topless women. The topless models use their hands, another woman's body, or their pose to obscure their nipples.

Page 51—An advertisement for Namco's *Death by Degrees™* features a woman in a tight, ripped leather body suit. Its largest rip exposes some of her left breast.

Pages 62–63—An advertisement for Capcom's *Devil May Cry® 3* features a bare-chested, buff, and attractive man.

Back Cover—An advertisement for Epic Games' *Unreal® Championship 2™: The Liandri Conflict* shows a large-breasted woman wearing a platemail bikini. Her male counterpart is heavily armored from the neck down except for a por-tion of his right upper arm, which contains an ornament.

Sometimes the sexy models have no connection to the game they're advertis-ing. For instance, a two-page advertisement for Sony's *ATV Offroad Fury® 3* in the January 2005 issue of *GMR* magazine uses a model that has no connection to the game, any of its mechanics, or even its setting. On the left-hand page is a supposed advertisement for the cologne "Fuzion." On that page, a beautiful model in lingerie kneels provocatively on a bed covered in crisp white linens in what appears to be a typical bedroom. The viewer's eye is instantly drawn to her and secondly, to the spray of mud which has begun to cover her. She looks on, oblivious. Looking at the advertisement, the viewer is initially confused. When the advertisement was shown to several people, all were puzzled, and one even asked aloud, "What's with the mud?" The answer is in the advertisement on the right-hand page. The ad for *ATV Offroad Fury® 3* shows an ATV rider as he blasts through a mud pit, spraying it across the magazine fold and onto the beautiful model in the seemingly unrelated advertisement [GMR01].

The sexual content in the advertisement is successful. Unlike others in the issue, the viewer stops, questions, contemplates, and resolves. The viewer might get a kick out of it and show it to other people. It also illustrates how sex can sell. Had it not been for the model and the oddly placed mud, the page may have been flipped, and the advertisement unnoticed.

In addition to advertisements, sex sells on box covers. One of the earliest ex-amples of sexual packaging was Sierra On-Line's 1981 release of *Softporn Adventure*.

The cover featured three nude women in a hot tub. Behind them, a waiter is poised to serve champagne. The packaging can be seen online at *www.vintage-sierra .com/other/spv1.html*. The package is also notable for its trivia value: the woman to the far right is noted game designer and co-founder of Sierra On-Line, Roberta Williams.

Sheri Graner Ray's book, *Gender Inclusive Game Design: Expanding the Market*, also discusses the use of sexy women on box covers. In one of the more extreme examples, she notes that the cover of *Tomb Raider: Angel of Darkness* is embossed, allowing one to feel Lara Croft's breasts [GRay04].

In marketing games, some go to extreme—if fitting—lengths. Publishers of the *Playboy: The Mansion* game, for instance, held two parties at Hugh Hefner's Playboy Mansion in Los Angeles to commemorate both the announcement and the launch of the video game. Playboy Bunnies, celebrities, Playmates, and numerous painted ladies (naked women whose "clothing" is painted on) were present for both parties. The event paid off, and the game's announcement and launch received substantial national and international press.

SEX IN SPITE OF...

Sometimes, sexual content becomes a part of a game through emergence, accident, hack, or modification. Such content is either unintended, unexpected, or out of the control of the game's developers and publishers.

Emergent Sex

Emergent content occurs when two or more things collide to produce content or behavior that was not scripted or otherwise programmed. These things that come together can be game systems, components, or players. When this content is sexual, it is known as emergent sex. Emergent sex can be either active, using the game's systems to create sexual content, or passive, when a game turns a player on as it is, and that stimulation was not intended by the developers.

MMORPGs frequently have issues with active emergent sex. For instance, using existing systems it is quite possible to develop an active emergent sexual system where one player can pimp others out for cash and profit and even charge others to watch. How could this happen?

All of these games feature a series of animations that allow characters to perform various actions like crouch, lie prone, or kneel, among others. These animations are necessary and normal, particularly in combat. Furthermore, these games also provide systems where players can chat with one another. Lastly, these games provide players the ability to exchange cash. By using all three systems together, emergent sexual content is possible. In fact, such content is relatively common in online games and any online medium where people can talk with one another. In worlds from *Ultima Online* to *World of Warcraft* to *Habbo Hotel* to *Second Life*, emergent sex exists. Players trade gold or Lindens or linen cloth or furniture for cyber sexual favors, none of which were intended by the game designers. The (ESRB), the group that assigns ratings to video games in the United States, requires games with user-generated content to display a warning on the product and on the game's Web site.

Other times, emergent sexual content is created in a game when a player finds a loophole at the convergence of two systems. In the original *The Sims*, a cheat allowed players to move objects. Likewise, a system removed a character's clothing when he or she entered a shower. The "nude" character was obscured by a pixel blur while entering and exiting the shower, so the player never saw any nudity. However, if the player asks a character to enter a shower, pauses the game, uses the "move object" cheat and moves the shower, the player sees his or her character nude [Eggh01]. As has been noted, under their clothes *The Sims* characters have nothing to see.

Passive emergent sex arises when players find developer-generated content in a game sexually arousing, provided arousal was not the developer's intent. For instance, if a player becomes aroused while playing *DreamStripper* (Figure 1.6) or while staring at a buxom barmaid, such behavior is expected and desired and not emergent.

FIGURE 1.6   Ensign Games' *DreamStripper*. © 2005 Ensign Games, Inc. Reprinted with permission.

If a player's character is eaten by a dinosaur and this turns the player on, such behavior is considered passive emergent sex. The Web site Vorarephile.com, for instance, lists over 300 games where something is eaten, be it the player's character or entire planets [Vore01]. The site serves the vorarephilia community—a fetish where one becomes sexually aroused by being eaten. Since the fetish is a difficult one to enjoy in real life, games are uniquely positioned to provide fetish realization.

Passive emergent sex also occurs when players are turned on by characters in video games that are clearly not designed to be in any way sexually stimulating. Some sites that target the adult market feature images of famous video game characters such as Sonic, Mario, and others. Along with these undoctored images are many more, however, that feature the same characters engaging in hard-core sex.

Emergent sex is covered in detail in Chapter 3.

Modded Sex

When shipped game content is modified and the result of that modification creates sexual content, that content is considered modded sex. "Hot Coffee," an example of modded sex, is arguably the most famous mod of all time. Discovered in June 2005 by Dutch gamer and hacker Patrick Wildenborg, the mod enables a character to have sex with his girlfriend in the game *Grand Theft Auto: San Andreas*. The mod caused a worldwide controversy and is the focus of a case study in Chapter 4.

Nude skins are the most frequent type of modded sex, however. Nude skins are simply pieces of clothing painted to make the character appear nude. There are many examples of such mods. *The Sims* and *The Sims 2*, for instance, have an active adult mod community. Players can create and download nude skins, objects, and even animations that allow their characters to perform a large range of sexual acts. Nude skins can also be found for Lara Croft in *Tomb Raider*™, Mona from *Max Payne*™ *2*, Cate from *No One Lives Forever*™, and even Britney Spears in *Britney's Dance Beat*™. Links for these mods can be found on *www.adultgamereviews.com*.

Modded content is often confused with unlockable and "Easter egg" content. Mods are to some degree created by users after the game has shipped to market by altering the game's code or content. *The Grand Theft Auto: San Andreas* "Hot Coffee" mod, while fully contained on the disc, was not accessible without external code or memory modification. Unlockable or "Easter egg" content *and* access to that content are created by developers before the game ships. Furthermore, access to unlockable and "Easter egg" content requires *standard* user action *inside* the game to reveal the content. Standard user actions include hitting a certain key or button combination or gathering enough bonus or experience points to unlock a particular feature or image. By contrast, modded content requires a user to actively alter the code base or art assets by some means *outside* of the game through a code, asset, or hardware-assisted alteration through devices such as the Action Replay™ Max. Such devices alter existing variables in the console's memory.

The difference between unlockable content and "Easter egg" content lies in prior player knowledge. Unlockable content is defined as content that is generally known to the user when the game begins but is unavailable for use or for viewing. For instance, in the game *Playboy: The Mansion*, unlockable content included centerfold images and interviews. In fighting games, new moves are frequently locked when the game begins and unlocked as play progresses. Furthermore, unlockable content is sometimes required for gameplay to progress normally. By contrast, "Easter egg" content is unknown to players, is not required to complete the game, and occasionally tips the scales absurdly in the player's favor. "Easter eggs" are often unlocked by pressing a secret series of buttons, completing a series of seemingly unrelated moves, or by finding a secret location containing the "Easter egg." For instance, in the game *Ratchet & Clank*, players can find a location in the game that offers a ridiculous amount of bolts, the currency for the game. In an old version of Microsoft's *Excel*, if the user highlighted a particular cell and pressed a series of keys, the program launched a 3D engine reminiscent of old 3D shooters.

Unlockable and "Easter egg" content is taken into consideration by the ESRB when rating a game. This alone accounts for the lack of sexual unlockables and "Easter eggs." Modded content, since it is created by users after a game is released, is generally not taken into account. This changed in 2005, however, following the Hot Coffee controversy. The ESRB now takes into account all content on the disc, even if the content is not accessible off the shelf. If there is material on the disc that may be revealed through a mod, such as the nude skin in *Oblivion*, publishers must declare this content and it will factor into the game's ratings. Complete user modifications, like the user-created nude skins for *The Sims*, are beyond the scope of the ESRB. By comparison, think of the huge array of things people could potentially paint on their cars. That creative streak, perverted as it may possibly be, is beyond the scope of GM or Ford.

Hacked Sex

Hacked sexual content arises when a product is modified by a member of the development team unbeknownst to its publisher and others. In 1996, programmer Jacques Servin modified the code of the Maxis game *SimCopter*™. The game featured numerous beautiful women, and Servin, who is gay, decided he wanted to see beautiful men in the game, too. So, he created a muscular character that appeared in a swimming suit. If another sim encountered the male character, the code made them kiss one another. The hack also created more characters on designated days like Servin's birthday. Regrettably, Servin's hack wasn't quite bulletproof. The random number generator caused more of these characters to appear than he bargained for. The hack was ultimately discovered when the game had already sold 50,000 copies [Wired03]. Servin was fired the following day.

Almost a year after the attack, a group calling itself "®™ark" (artmark) was revealed as the act's true mastermind [BPhon01]. The organization, which had remained underground until breaking its silence in 1997, offered rewards for specific public acts of corporate sabotage. Originally, Servin had claimed that he acted on his own to draw attention to the status quo of heterosexual characters in video games [Wired03]. He later admitted that he had been paid $5,000 for the act [Wired04].

Accidental Sex

When Ubisoft shipped Tom Clancy's *Rainbow Six® 3* to stores, they neglected one small piece of marketing—registering a domain name that was prominently featured on posters in a level in the game. The domain took players to a Web site filled with pornography links.

In an interview with CNN/Money℠'s Director of Content Development Chris Morris, Tony Ashcraft said he noticed the URL while playing the game and went to the link hoping to find additional game information, but instead he found it unregistered. So, he purchased the domain and filled it with porn links. He hoped to build traffic, which porn is known to do, and ultimately sell the site [CNN01].

Ubisoft was unaware of the gaffe until Morris contacted them seeking comment, and told him they thought the incident was unfortunate. Although Ashcraft expressed willingness to sell the domain to Ubisoft, the company released a statement December 31, 2003, saying that they would not be subjected to "blackmail" or those trying to "extort" money from game developers for what it deemed was an honest mistake [CNN02].

WHAT ISN'T SEX

Games have been made that allow the "player" to simulate sexual harassment, stalking, and rape. Such mechanics do not represent sex. Instead, they represent violence or the threat of violence and are therefore beyond the scope of this book.

REFERENCES

[BPhon01] Barry, Ellen, "The Dilbert Front," *The Boston Phoenix*, January 22, 1998. Available online at *www.bostonphoenix.com/archive/features/98/01/22/ARTMARK.html*. Accessed August 7, 2005.

[CNN01] Morris, Chris, "XXX . . . in a Tom Clancy Game?" *CNNMoney*^{SM}, January 7, 2004. Available online at *http://money.cnn.com/2004/01/05/commentary/game_over/column_gaming/*. Accessed August 7, 2005.

[CNN02] Ibid.

[Currie01] Currie, Linda, interview with Brenda Brathwaite, July 29, 2005.

[Currie02] Currie, Linda, interview with Brenda Brathwaite, July 15, 2005.

[Eggh01] Henderson, Cory (contributor), "Sim Porn," *Egg Heaven 2000!*. Available online at *www.eggheaven2000.com/detailed/1860.html*. Accessed August 7, 2005.

[G4TV01] *Video Game Vixens*, G4TV. Available online at *www.g4tv.com/videogamevixens/features/52011/Vixen_of_the_Year_Finalists.html* (2004). Accessed August 7, 2005.

[GGA01] jane, "Sex in Games=Rez+Vibrator," *Game+Girl=Advance*, October 26, 2002. Available online at *www.gamegirladvance.com/archives/2002/10/26/sex_in_games_rezvibrator.html*. Accessed August 7, 2005.

[GMR01] *GMR* magazine, advertisement for *ATV Offroad Fury 3*, pp. 94–95, *GMR*, January 2005.

[GRay01] Graner-Ray, Sheri, *Gender Inclusive Game Design: Expanding the Market*, p. 104, Charles River Media, Hingham, MA, 2004.

[GRay02] Graner-Ray, Sheri, *Gender Inclusive Game Design: Expanding the Market*, p. 105, Charles River Media, Hingham, MA, 2004.

[GRay03] Graner-Ray, Sheri, *Gender Inclusive Game Design: Expanding the Market*, p. 181, Charles River Media, Hingham, MA, 2004.

[GRay04] Graner-Ray, Sheri, *Gender Inclusive Game Design: Expanding the Market*, p. 33, Charles River Media, Hingham, MA, 2004.

[Kasavin01] Kasavin, Greg, interview with Brenda Brathwaite, July 7, 2005.

[Lagny01] Lagny, Patric, interview with Brenda Brathwaite, June 24, 2005.

[Lagny02] Lagny, Patric, interview with Brenda Brathwaite, June 24, 2005.

[Oltyan01] Oltyan, Chris, interview with Brenda Brathwaite, May 27, 2005.

[SD01] qDot, "SeXBox version 2, or How to Create Your Own Army," *www.slashdong.org*. Available online at*www.slashdong.org/content/projects/diy_sex_toys_and_teledildonics/sexbox_version_2_or_how_to_create_your_own_army-000229.php*. Accessed August 7, 2005.

[Trix01] "Top 10 Video Game Hunks," *Gameinatrix.com* forums, September 14, 2004, unavailable online.

[Vore01] "Vore in Video Games," *Vorarephile.com*. Available online at *www.vorarephile.com/. Accessed August 7, 2005.*

[Webster01] Definition of "Sex," *Merriam-Webster Dictionary* online. Available at *www.m-w.com/dictionary/sex.* Accessed June 29, 2006.

[Wired01] Kohler, Chris, "Better than a Joystick," *Wired*, November 5, 2003. Available online at *www.wired.com/wired/archive/11.05/play.html?pg=6*. Accessed August 7, 2005.

[Wired02] Kohler, Chris, "Better Than a Joystick," *Wired*, November 5, 2003. Available online at *www.wired.com/wired/archive/11.05/play.html?pg=6*. Accessed August 7, 2005.

[Wired03] Silberman, Steve, "Boy 'Bimbos' Too Much for Game-Maker Maxis," *Wired*, December 3, 1996. Available online at *http://wired-vig.wired.com/news/culture/0,1284,775,00.html*. Accessed August 7, 2005.

[Wired04] Frauenfelder, Matt, "Secret Prankster Fund Goes Public," *Wired*, April 8, 1997. Available online *at www.wired.com/news/culture/0,1284,2997,00.html*. Accessed August 7, 2005.

2 History of Sex in Games

In This Chapter

FROM THE BEGINNING

Sex and video games. It's always been here, right from the beginning of the computer game industry, and even earlier if one counts the emergent sexual behavior of players in multi-user dungeon (MUDs) or the alleged phallic controls on the arcade games of the 1970s. From the 1981 release *Soft Porn Adventure* to the *Leisure Suit Larry* series to 2006's *Naughty America: The Game*, sex and games have gone hand and hand. Like any other form of media, sex is a part of the human experience, and that experience works itself into all forms of entertainment, one way or another. Books, movies, art, games. Despite efforts to ban it, curtail it, censor it, and cut it, there is still always sex, no matter the medium.

Due to the prevalence of sexual content in games, every few years someone sounds the horn of alarm, usually due to a controversy of some sort. In the early 1980s, it was the sex crime in *Custer's Revenge*, a game that featured the rape of a Native American woman and rewarded the act with points. In the 1990s, it was *Night Trap*, a game that, along with *Mortal Kombat*, set the stage for the video game rating system and trade associations we have today. Most recently, it was the nude skin in *Oblivion* that caused the game to be re-rated from T to M. Of course, the biggest controversy in recent years was the Rockstar-created content unlocked by modders in *Grand Theft Auto: San Andreas*. The "Hot Coffee" mod and the controversy it created is the subject of Chapter 4.

Sex and games have always had a natural if uneasy relationship, in part fueled by the perception that games are for kids. Like comics of the 1950s, video games appeal to a wide audience, from the young to the old, and the average gamer gets older every year. In fact, the Entertainment Software Association's "Essential Facts About the Computer and Video Game Industry" from 2006 reports that the average gamer is 33 years old, and more likely than not is a man [ESA01].

In games, sex plays itself out in many forms, from romance in *The Sims* to the more modern-day flirting of *Jade Empire* to the hard-core action of *Virtual Hottie 2* and *LoveChess*. Sexual themes have appeared in literally thousands of games over the years on every platform. In the last few years, the advent of Macromedia® Flash and the independent developers that have embraced it have produced seemingly hundreds of sexually themed games every year.

This chapter focuses on the wide history of sex in games, from its highs to its lows.

"HOW COULD YOU FORGET . . ."

With thousands of sex games to choose from, mentioning every sex game ever created would require an encyclopedia in itself, particularly if it included Flash games.

Such a project is underway, in fact, at the International Game Developers Association "Sex & Games" blog written by the author of this book. The blog is located at *www.igda.org/sex*. Every day, a different sex game is featured in its "Link of the Day" feature and contributions are welcome via email at *sexingames@yahoo.com*.

In addition, although sex games are common the world over, particularly in Japan and Germany, the sex games mentioned here are largely contained to those released to the North American audience. That said, a brief discussion of Japanese bishouju games and hentai games does appear later in this chapter.

For this book, each section includes a survey of the games that are available, and some of the key games on the platform or the subject matter (e.g., the introduction of Flash or full motion video).

SEX IN THE ARCADE

Almost from the beginning, arcade machines were associated with sex, largely due to the joystick controls that would become popular in the early 1970s. In an interview with G4 TV for its special "Sex in Games: A G4 Special Report," Nolan Bushnell, founder of Atari and creator of *Pong* and the first arcade machine, *Computer Space*, says that almost everyone was talking about joysticks as phallic devices. Apart from their looks and how they're held, even the name "joystick" has subtle sexual overtones. Although many think the name is unique to games, it actually comes from the field of aeronautics and is thought to have originated in the early 20th century.

In 1973, and partly in response to the phallic nature of the joystick, Atari released *Gotcha*. *Gotcha*'s controls consisted of two soft, pink rubber mounds. On the G4 special, Bushnell noted that he and the marketing department at Atari wondered whether the breast-inspired controls would work as well as the allegedly phallic ones. *Gotcha* was their means to discovery. Ultimately, the game was a failure, but whether it was due to the controls or the gameplay itself is up for debate.

As machines of primarily public venues, there were few actual sex games produced for the arcade as compared to the computer and console games that would come in later years. Occasionally, games featured beautiful women, risqué elements, or sexual innuendo, but games based purely on sex appeal were few and far between. One such game was 1985's *Sex Trivia* released by Kinky Kit and Game Company. *Sex Trivia* posed questions to players and gave them points for the correct answer, and the speed with which they gave that answer. Although the game was rarely in arcades, it was popular in bars. In one frequented by this author in the mid-1980s, players would line up quarters on the machine and queue to play the game, even those who had played many times before. The game's questions weren't endless—players would often get repeat questions in subsequent plays—so repeat players competed for best times. An image of the game can be found on *www .arcadeflyers.net*.

Another well-known title is Comad's 1996 release *Miss Nude World 1996*. The player's job is to uncover nude and scantily dressed models while avoiding the enemies that are trying to destroy the player. *Miss Nude World 1996* was like many other Comad titles that featured nudity as a reward, including 1990's *Pushman*, 1993's *Zero Zone*, 1994's *Las Vegas Girls*, *Fantasia*, and 1996's *Gal's Pinball*.

The most notorious arcade game of all, however, is *Boong-Ga Boong-Ga* by Taff System. Although it's not a sex game, per se, it is so overwhelmingly absurd that this book would be incomplete without its mention. In *Boong-Ga Boong-Ga*, the player uses a controller shaped like a large hand complete with an extended finger. The front of the machine features the lower half of a body whose buttocks face the player. The player then uses the controller to spank or forcefully sodomize the body. On the screen, the player sees the upper half of the victim responding to the player's actions. Players can choose to victimize ex-girlfriends or boyfriends, gangsters, gold diggers, mothers-in-law, child molesters, and con artists. When the player spanks the bottom, the game shuffles various fortune cards. When the player inserts the finger, the machine detects the player's power through an internal sensor and releases a card that reveals the player's sexual behavior, according to the game's flyer. The game's flyer can be seen at *www.arcadeflyers.net*.

SEX ON THE EARLY NETWORKS

Before gaming networks emerged, computer gaming was a relatively solitary activity. Until players could connect online, by modem or by academic networks such as the PLATO system, the only multiplayer games were those where two individuals sat next to each other.

The Birth of MUD

When Richard Bartle and Roy Trubshaw created *MUD* at the University of Essex in 1978, a whole genre of games was effectively born. The undergraduates' "multi-user dungeon," a name from which its famous acronym "MUD" was formed, allowed players from all over the world to explore the environment Bartle and Trubshaw had created. Unlike previous games that could be played over networks, *MUD* was both accessible and understandable, and its community of players flourished. At the time, the only players who could access *MUD* were the few who had modems or those with access to university computers. Even so, players numbered in the thousands.

Where players get together, particularly if they have access to a chat interface, emergent sexual behavior frequently occurs. Emergent sex, like emergent gameplay, is something that happens outside the game's intended rule set or design. In modern games like *City of Heroes*®, for instance, people have met in game and later married in real life. Chapter 3, in fact, is devoted entirely to the topic of emergent sex.

According to Bartle, however, nothing of that kind happened in *MUD*, at least early on. Rather, it was in a game called *Shades* that emergent sex likely first occurred. Sex occurred in *MUD* when it reached the United States, but by then, Bartle notes, he'd already heard of it happening within *Shades*.

"*Shades* was a very early virtual world, written by a player of my own game, *MUD*," says Bartle [Bartle01]. That player was Neil Newell. His world offered players something that other worlds didn't—privacy.

"I'd say the 'cybersex' emerged on *Shades* simply because it was the first game that gave players a guaranteed private area. Back then, all other games gave high-level players unlimited power to see everything another player did," says Newell, the game's author. "*Shades*, by comparison, had 'safe areas' where fighting was disallowed and snooping was impossible (even for programmers/admins). These safe areas included a church, a pub, information center, and a hotel. The hotel naturally included bedrooms (including a bridal suite) with the feature that players could decide who entered a room with them. So, people took to locking themselves in the bedrooms for private conversations and, as became apparent after a while, rather more than that!" [Newell01].

Shades opened in December 1984. The game was written for Newell's personal programming pleasure, and as he notes, "crept out into the real world by accident" [Newell02]. *Shades* was already running when British Telecom contacted him to ask if he was the person who wrote it. They later released the game commercially in the fall of 1985.

Newell first realized sex had entered the game sometime in 1986. "That'd be around the time certain players who'd had their expectations upset started complaining." In hindsight, Newell says the signs were fairly obvious. "Naively, I figured people were hanging out in the safe areas for private chats. Cybering wasn't a well-known phenomenon back then. It only became a concrete issue when a man would occasionally be upset to discover the woman he was playing with was actually another man. Some of them got so upset by having their fantasy world upset like that that they lodged formal complaints—typically in the guise of 'my nephew innocently logged into the game and got propositioned by some old man!'" [Newell03]. Legally, Newell notes, players had to be 18 or over to have an account.

Aside from the periodic complaint, the *Shades*' player community wasn't much bothered. "It was just something players slowly realized was going on behind locked doors (i.e., in the private areas), and because those areas were so private, no one could accidentally stumble upon people cybering in the hallway, so to speak. I suppose for most people, learning that people were having sex out of sight in hotel bedrooms just never came across as a big surprise." Although it never amounted to anything, British Telecom did pressure Newell to close the private areas occasionally. According to Newell, however, "they really didn't understand the game at all, so it was easy to resist (especially as it was so successful)" [Newell04].

Bartle agrees that players and administrators of the early worlds were largely accepting of the emergent sex within the worlds, even if they didn't participate. When asked whether administrators or programmers tried to curtail or stop it, Bartle said, "Either it didn't happen, or the game designer didn't object to its happening."

"These were games played by grown-ups, not by children," Bartle adds. "If there were children involved, I dare say there would have been some attempt to control it. Also, if it happened in the open, then we might have asked them to move on, as it would have been a distraction from gameplay. However, if it were two adults doing it in private, why WOULD we want to stop it? It's not like we were control freaks or anything" [Bartle02].

It was only a matter of time before an intentionally erotic multiuser game evolved. *Zone*, short for "erogenous zone," was certainly one of first games of its kind, and it may well be the first. *Zone* was created by Chris Butterworth in response to a *Shades* player's suggestion to create a world just for adults. It went live in 1987. Players in *Zone* scored points by having sex with other players in the game, among other things, and received extra points for being someone's first. Preliminary commands such as "cuddle" eventually established a relationship, not to mention the mood, for players to "make love." Players could drink alcohol in the game to speed things up, or "stop" the action if they didn't want to "make love." *Zone* was eventually banned from the British Telecom network, but its notoriety propelled it to greater fame. As a pay-for-use service, however, *Zone*'s popularity was soon undermined by another free early multiuser adult game, *Void*.

Created by Clive Lindus, *Void* debuted in 1989 and was officially launched in 1990. Like *Zone*, *Void*'s primary purpose was a social one, although not a purely sexual one. In it, players could flirt with one another, enter commands to dress and undress themselves, and engage in cybering, but the game strongly encouraged all kinds of social interaction. As of the writing of this book, *Void* is still being played and is available at *http://void.greenfinch.com/*.

Eventually, many of the early text-based worlds gave way to the graphical environments of today, worlds like 2003's *Second Life* and 2006's *Red Light Center*. Even so, text-based worlds continue to exist, and now narrowed in numbers, thrive. Furry MUCKs like *Tapestries* or *FurryMUCK*, and erotic role-playing games like *Belariath*, are all text based, and their players enjoy the experience, graphics or not.

"Aerowolf," a gamer who played text-based games on BBSes from 1992 to 1995, before moving on to Internet-based multiplayer text-based games in 1995, outlined a typical play experience for him in a furry-based MUCK.

"A typical experience in these games is to find people who meet the criteria of what you're looking for. For example, if you're looking for a dominant leather-winged dragon for a bondage/piercing scene, you're not going to look for a submissive deer that's into being chased down and eaten by a cougar or a pack of wolves. Then, you contact the people on the list you've found, and start a conversation (sometimes directly, sometimes indirectly) about the kinds of things that you're wanting to do, and mention that you're looking for someone to do them with you."

"It depends on your personality, and your prospective partner's personality, to see whether you have compatible writing styles and interests. The interest-matching system isn't perfect, as it can't show all the shades-of-gray possibilities inherent in the human race's sex drive.

"On these places, we have a kind of 'hanky code'—a kind of shorthand list of the types of things that someone might be interested in trying with the right people. This is how you might find your prospective partners. The command for the normal version of this type of code is 'wi' –'whatiz'… to see whether someone's a rabid republican, democrat, liberal, fascist, interested in talking about certain topics and if they have an agenda regarding them, etc. The command for the sex-related one is 'wixxx'—'whatiz XXX'. Some of the identified fetishes are just out there.

"Another way to find a partner is to hang around a place where aficionados of your type of sex[ual desire] spend their time. All sorts of possibilities exist. For example, on one MUD I'm on, there's a leather bar loosely based around the Lure, in New York City. BDSM is the type of sex you'll find [in the online bar]. There are virtual bordellos (no 'actual' money exchanges hands; it's all role played), and many other places suited to your particular kink. And, if you can't find one, you can always create one."

. . .

"Sex isn't everything in any of the worlds that I take part in, even if it isn't frowned upon or even encouraged. Sometimes, you find yourself getting intimate with a partner you didn't expect [to get intimate with], upon which you can build a friendship. Sometimes, you get the one-night stands. Sometimes you get advanced players and programmers who come up with interesting ideas—such as STDs, and [they] create programs that can keep track of who's been infected with what, whether it's curable, whether it's a wasting disease, whether it's detectable by looking at them, several variables.

"The community is also a great place to find people to try things that can't be done in real life. There's more of a willingness to deal with the absurd ideas, such as transformation (changing from one body to another), transmutation (changing from one material to another—flesh-to-living rubber is a fairly common one, as is cyborgization), male pregnancy, macrophilia/microphilia, and many others" [Aero01].

Despite their obviously dated appearance, some players believe that text worlds are better than graphically enhanced worlds. Richard Bartle, who in addition to co-authoring *MUD* also authored the book *Designing Virtual Worlds*, outlines some of the likely reasons:

"1. You can animate text far more fluidly than graphics.
 2. Graphical representation of what goes on in text would be illegal.
 3. Text is more nuanced than graphics can ever be, and can cover more senses.
 4. The imagination is where all the activity is in a sexual relationship. Why do people make love with the light off?
 5. Women tend to prefer to read erotica; men prefer to look at the pictures. However, as there are fewer women in these games than men, if a man wants cybersex with a woman then he has to play by the rules.
 6. The pictures are better with text than with graphics." [Bartle03]

Aerowolf prefers text-based games. "In text, you have 1% of the communication. In tonality, you have another 10% of the communication. In body language, you have 89% of the communication. The problem with graphical worlds is that you're stuck with pre-scripted body language—you can't get the subtle cues, such as slight distaste, or being nauseated, or the small smiles you get when you do something nice for someone you care about. You can't get the small cues that you need to know that you're pleasing your partner, or boring them, or anything." For Aerowolf, the presence of graphics is actually distracting. In fact, he admits that he doesn't cyber in graphical worlds such as *Second Life* precisely because of the "eye candy." In these worlds, he notes, "you're stuck with eye-candy that's about as effective as porn at showing emotion (and let's face it, most porn doesn't show emotion, it shows a physical act with a distinct lack of connection between the people involved)." For him and other players who prefer text-based worlds, the addition of graphics is a "lose-lose situation for everyone involved" [Aero02].

BBS Door Games

As early online worlds began to form, players also used their modems to enter erotic worlds hosted by bulletin board systems, or BBSes. Frequently known as "BBS Door Games," the BBS would serve as a middleman, of sorts, allowing users to connect with an external program through the BBS. The BBS was, in effect, a door to the program. The Web site *www.doorgames.org/indexes/adult.htm* lists over such 20 adult games.

According to Jason Scott, director of the BBS Documentary, door games came into play around 1982 after BBSes had developed the ability to run external programs. However, they really took off in 1983. "It can't be overstated, no matter how obvious and silly it is, how much influence the movie *Wargames* had on the purchase of modems." *Wargames* was released in 1983. In the movie, a young man accidentally accesses a top-secret military computer and nearly sends the world into World War III. From the film's release to Christmas, Scott says, "it just starts exploding." Modems, largely the domain of the computer engineers, whiz kids, and academics, were suddenly in thousands of homes everywhere. "The BBS world is a lot different in 1983–1984 than it was before," says Scott. "So, when people reference stuff happening before then, you're talking about a very small amount of people, probably less than a few thousand, having much influence on BBSes" [Scott01]. After 1983, going online became much more common.

BBS door games are as varied as sex games are today. Some doors featured rooms that players could enter to have cybersex with one another. Still others featured trivia, adventure, and role playing. For sexually themed doors, the game elements were often secondary to the sexual narrative. For instance, one door, Bordello, allowed players to run their own bordello and to fight with other players. Matchmaking services between players were also popular early on.

"For the purposes of hooking up, there have been BBSes of that nature almost from the beginning, certainly from 1980 onward, a couple years after the first BBSes arrived," says Scott. "There's even software to facilitate dating, specifically DIAL-YOUR-MATCH software, and therefore tons of 'DYM' boards for people to go to, answer intense sexual and personal questions, and then get 'matched up' with others and send each other email messages" [Scott01]. Scott shared a list from 1982, prior to the movie *Wargames*, that featured 15 such DYM boards. The list can be found at *www.textfiles.com/bbs/BBSLISTS/PAMS/pams8212.txt*.

The Dark Side of Modems

As players connected in online worlds by the hundreds and then the thousands, the connections also spawned a dark side—virtual sex economies, professions, and even rape. The most famous of these incidents is the rape of a character in the *Lambda MOO*. An early multiuser world, Lambda MOO was founded in 1990. In the game, one character took control of others through use of a voodoo doll and forced the other characters to commit sexual acts within the game. The incident was covered in a widely publicized 1993 article in the *Village Voice* titled "A Rape in Cyberspace." Chapter 9 covers the rape in more detail. Emergent sexual economies are covered in Chapter 3.

SEX ON THE APPLE—EARLY 1980S

Released in 1977, the Apple II computer had been out for only a few years when a company known as On-line Systems (then Sierra Online and now, simply, Sierra) released a game called *Soft Porn Adventure* by Charles Benton. As was common with games released in the early 1980s, the game was completely text based. However, it shipped and sold in its own full-color folder as opposed to the Ziploc® packaging that was relatively common at the time. Although the industry had not yet developed a formalized rating system in 1981, *Soft Porn Adventure* included both a self-imposed rating, "R," and a warning on its front that the game was for adults only.

Soft Porn Adventure is notable in many ways. As the first major sex game to be released commercially for home computers, *Soft Porn Adventure* stands as a landmark all on its own. The game also featured Roberta Williams in a hot tub on its cover. Williams is a noted game designer, creator of the *King's Quest* and *Phantasmagoria* series among other notable games, and co-founder of Sierra. Titillating as it may have tried to be for its time, *Soft Porn Adventure* was mostly regarded as "cheesy." In its attempts to be seriously erotic, it ended up being comical instead. A few years later in 1987, *Soft Porn Adventure* would inspire game designer Al Lowe to create one of the best known and best loved comic sexual superstars of all time, *Leisure Suit Larry*.

Before *Larry* would enter the scene, however, another landmark product would be released for the Apple II, *Artworx Strip Poker*. Released just a year after *Soft Porn Adventure* in 1982, *Artworx Strip Poker* was the first strip poker game ever released for the home computer. In addition to that accolade, the product is the longest running, sexually themed video game series in history and is still in production today. *Artworx Strip Poker* would eventually be released for many different computers, including IBM PCs and compatibles, the Commodore 64, and the Atari ST. The company's product line can be found at *www.artworx.com*.

SEX ON THE ATARI 2600

When the Atari 2600 was released in 1977, players gravitated toward the machine. Unlike other game machines that came with a single or a few games pre-installed on them, the Atari 2600 used cartridges that players inserted into the machine. This gave the systems a tremendous variety of play experiences, and ultimately led to the most notorious sex game of all, *Custer's Revenge.*

Released in 1983, *Custer's Revenge* features a Native American woman tied to a post on its box cover. In the game, the graphics are less detailed due to the limits of the early hardware. Nonetheless, an obvious erection is present on Custer as he makes his way through a hail of arrows and rapes the woman, still tied to the post. He even gets points for doing so.

Right from its release, the game caused an outcry among women's groups, anti-pornography groups, Native American groups, and others. Picketers even appeared outside publisher Mystique's offices carrying signs protesting the game. One such sign claimed, "*Custer's Revenge* says rape is fun."

Even by the standards of the day, *Custer's Revenge* was a terrible game. In fact, numerous critics have gone so far as to call it one of the worst games of all time for its gameplay and its narrative, although either would have sufficed. Had it not been for the controversy it caused, the game would have long since been forgotten.

Custer's Revenge wasn't the only adult title released by Mystique for the 2600, however. The company also released *Beat 'Em & Eat 'Em*, a game in which women tried to catch sperm in their mouths dropped from a man masturbating above them, and *Swedish Erotica: Bachelor Party* among others. Mystique manuals claimed that the time for adult entertainment in games had at last arrived. Atari, however, disagreed with them, and sued Mystique. Atari lost the suit in court.

SEX ON THE SPECTRUM

The Sinclair ZX Spectrum was an affordable home computer released in 1982 primarily in the UK. The computer was relatively easy to program and featured color output to televisions. As such, it was only a matter of months before the first sex games were released. One group, Silver Fox, released no fewer than five games in 1983 alone, including *Cathouse Blues, Philly Flasher, Sex Invaders,* and remakes of Mystique's *Beat 'Em & Eat 'Em*, and *Gigolo.* For the most part, as it was with other home computers in the early 1980s, games were often created by a single individual and sold through small ads in the back of technical magazines or traded friend to friend. Like all games of that time, the graphics were crude, blocky representations by today's standards. At the time, however, *any* sexual content on computers was sensational regardless of how it looked.

The Spectrum Sinclair sported one of the most prolific sex content development communities. Many of the games developed for it can still be found online at *www.worldofspectrum.org/sex.html.*

SEX ON THE COMMODORE

The Commodore 64 (C64), also released in 1982, was the main rival to the Spectrum ZX in the UK and was the dominant, affordable home computer in the United States. Like the Spectrum, the C64 sported color graphic output and used the player's television set to display the graphics. The C64 was popular with gamers and had strong support from the early video game development community, sexual content developers included.

While many sex games were released for the Commodore, one of the most prominent was Avalon Hill's 1986 release of *Dr. Ruth's Computer Game of Good Sex*. It was also one of the earliest sex game licenses. Billed largely as an educational title, the software offered advice and information about good sex from famed sexologist Dr. Ruth Westheimer. That same year, Martech released another famous licensed title on the C64—*Samantha Fox's Strip Poker*. While not as famous from a game history perspective as the Artworx early *Strip Poker* on the Apple II, the game nonetheless gained a following from Samantha's many fans.

In addition to a more mainstream development community, the C64 was supported by a substantial independent game development community. Many games such as the text-based *Quest for the Whorehouse Queen* by the Odd Couple and the appropriately titled *Sex Games* by Landisoft were released for the C64. Many of these games are archived at *http://girls.c64.org/a__show.php?cat=gam&newcat=1*.

As the C64 transitioned out and made room for the superior Commodore Amiga, the sexually themed games continued to be popular on the machine, particularly with its enhanced graphical abilities. In the late 1980s and early 1990s, companies like Coktel Vision released numerous games for the system, including 1989's *Emmanuelle: A Game of Eroticism* and 1990's *Geisha*. Even Artworx, the same company that had pioneered computerized strip poker, released *Centerfold Squares* for the machine in 1988.

SEX ON THE APPLE—MID 1980S

By 1986, sexual comedies, or comedies with a good amount of sexual innuendo, started to appear on the Apple. The earliest was *Leather Goddesses of Phobos*. Created by Steve Meretzky at Infocom, *Leather Goddesses of Phobos* actually started out as a name well before it became a game. According to Meretezky, in the early days of Infocom, the company had a matrix on one wall that listed the current release version of every Infocom product on the market. Just before a company party—the first one ever and one the owners were diligently preparing for— Meretezky inked in "Leather Goddesses of Phobos" on the grid.

As Meretezky tells it, Joel Berez, Infocom's president, "noticed the addition just a few minutes before the first guests arrived and couldn't erase it fast enough. But the name lived on, and for years after that, people would jokingly refer to it as one of our games in production. At some point, when it was time for me to start working on a new game, I thought about how much everyone loved the name, and that it made sense to write a game to go along with the name. I threw the idea out there, and Mike Dornbrook, Infocom's chief marketer, loved it and helped push it through. It was certainly the only time I've started with a name, and written a game to match it, rather than vice versa" [Meretzky01].

For Meretzky, *Leather Goddesses of Phobos* was the first in a string of comedies. In 1990, he designed *Spellcasting 101: Sorcerers Get All the Girls* and worked on the 1992 release *Rex Nebular and the Cosmic Gender Bender*. For Meretzky, however, the sexual content of his games wasn't to titillate, but rather used for comedic effect. As Meretzky says, there were "[l]ots of double entendres, such as in *Leather Goddess of Phobos*, when your new Tonto-like sidekick (Trent, if you're playing as a man, or Tiffany if you're playing as a woman) says, 'We'll lick those Leather Goddesses together!'" [Meretzky02]. Meretzky also used player's sexual expectations against them. In *Spellcasting 101*, for instance, the player finds a spell of bust enlargement. "You can try casting it on every woman in the game to no avail," Meretzky says. "It turns out to be useful if you cast it on a statuette sitting on a pedestal in the library" [Meretezky03].

Meretzky acknowledges there were some literal sex scenes in his game, but notes they were still all about the comedic effect. He cites the chapter "The Island of the Amazons" in *Spellcasting 101*. "You land on this island of gorgeous Amazonian women, who have never seen a man and are all eyeing you hungrily. You are shown to your chambers, where the Amazon chief has her way with you. She's barely gone when another pops out from under your bed . . . then another comes out of the linen trunk . . . then another falls out of the air duct. If you don't escape, you'll never survive the onslaught" [Meretzky04].

The most famous sex comedy series, *Leisure Suit Larry and the Land of the Lounge Lizards*, was released in 1987. Inspired by the unintentionally comedic 1981 release *Soft Porn Adventure*, *Leisure Suit Larry and the Land of the Lounge Lizards* put players in the shoes of Larry Laffer, a 1970s kind of guy ever in search of female company. Larry was a hit with both male and female players. He was funny and unthreatening, bumbling and occasionally lucky. Like Meretzky before him, designer Al Lowe's mix of humor and sex would resonate with players. In all, the Larry series would support seven sequels, including the most recent release, *Leisure Suit Larry: Magna Cum Laude*. Lowe was not a part of the last game in the series and has frequently criticized it in interviews and on his Web site, *www.allowe.com*. Although the series was nominated for a Game Developer's Choice award for its writing, some players disliked the turn the series had taken. No longer an adventure game, *Magna Cum Laude* was instead a puzzle game whose puzzles were connected by brief story segments. The game's language had also gotten more graphic. As Sheri Graner Ray, an expert on gender inclusive game design, noted at her keynote speech at the 2006 Sex in Video Games conference, when one uses humor in sexual games, one needs to be exceptionally careful. In general, sexual innuendo and jokes that might be perfectly fine in a group of men don't fare so well among a group of women who may feel uncomfortable or, worse, offended. More than a year after the release of *Magna Cum Laude*, developer High Voltage Software laid off a significant number of its employees, many of whom had worked on the previous game in the series and hoped to be working on the next. As of the writing of this book, no future plans for the *Leisure Suit Larry* series had been announced. Meanwhile, Lowe announced his return to gaming and his new game, *Sam Suede™ in Undercover Exposure®* at the 2006 Electronic Entertainment Expo.

While many adult games featured warnings on the box, the Larry series was the first to incorporate an age verification system. The first and third games in the series required players to answer a series of questions correctly before they could begin play. The questions, which were targeted at the average American adult, weren't successful, however. Those too young to play the game or know the answers could easily look them up. Meanwhile, the questions also proved difficult for Larry's international audience, which had neither the cultural context nor the material with which to find the answers (the Internet was not in wide usage by the average gamer at the time).

In its entire run, the *Leisure Suit Larry* series would appear on the Apple and its various iterations, the Amiga, DOS-based IBM PCs and compatibles, Windows®, the PlayStation® 2, and the Xbox®.

SEX ON THE MAC

Comparatively speaking, Macintosh computers were not hotbeds of commercial computerized sex games when compared to other machines. However, two releases on the Macintosh stand as absolute landmarks in the history of sex in games: the 1986 release of *Mac Playmate* and its pseudo-sequel, the 1989 release of *Virtual Valerie*. Created by Mike Saenz of Reactor, Inc., *Mac Playmate* was the first game of its type and invented the "virtual woman" category of games. Using digitized representations of body parts or sex toys, the player attempted to bring the woman to orgasm. *Mac Playmate* inspired dozens of products in the years that followed, including games like *Orgasm Girl*, *3D Playmate*, *Virtual Hottie 1* and *2*, *Virtualfem*, and the Jenna Jameson simulator, *VirtuallyJenna*.

In a January 1992 article in *Compute! Magazine*, Saenz discussed his famous creation, noting that he created it in just three days. Saenz admitted he thought the idea of sex on the computer was essentially foolish and had intended his game to be a parody of the average man's fantasy [Compute01]. Regardless of Saenz's stated intention, however, the game went down in sex game history and created a genre all its own.

Virtual Valerie was similar to *Mac Playmate*, although it featured an expanded setting and allowed the player to first seduce Valerie before he could perform sexual actions on her. In some ways, like *Mac Playmate* before it, *Virtual Valerie* was also a trailblazer in sex and games history—it was the first adult CD-ROM product released for home computers. *Virtual Valerie* also spawned sequels, *Virtual Valerie: Director's Cut* and *Virtual Valerie 2*. In *Virtual Valerie: Director's Cut* Saenz added a sexual response meter so players could tell how turned on the woman was, and added new wardrobe items for her.

SEX ON THE NINTENDO

Launched in North America in 1985, the Nintendo Entertainment System was exceptionally popular. With its focus on quality games (the Nintendo "Seal of Quality"), the North American market eagerly gravitated toward the machine. The previous few years had seen the release of some of the worst games in the history of the industry and ultimately led to the video game crash of 1983. Nintendo was determined that its machine and games would not suffer the same fate as the systems that had come before it like the Atari 2600. The non-Atari approved sexually themed titles like *Custer's Revenge* and *Beat 'Em & Eat 'Em* that had appeared on the Atari 2600 had hurt that company's image, and Nintendo did not want to see their system suffer the same fate.

To prevent unlicensed titles from appearing on their system, each Nintendo Entertainment System (NES) shipped with a lockout chip known as the "10NES." Only officially approved Nintendo cartridges would be authenticated by the chip and be allowed to play on the system. This allowed Nintendo to have control over game quality. When this author worked on the *Wizardry* series of role-playing games in the 1980s and 1990s, for instance, various iterations of the game were ported to the NES. In one of the early ports, some of the game's content had to be changed to comply with Nintendo's requirements. The wine a Priest drank at a particular point in the game needed to be changed to juice or soda or something non-alcoholic. Furthermore, though a role-playing staple, the professions of Priest and Bishop were considered too religious, and therefore, it was requested that these be changed, too. Based on these requests, one can imagine how Nintendo would handle sexual content. In all their dealings with the North American market—particularly early on—Nintendo was exceptionally cautious about the content it would carry.

In fact, by 1988, Nintendo's Game Content Guidelines expressly prohibited sexual content, among other things. The nature of that content, however, was different depending on the market. In several cases, content was released to the Japanese market, but edited when it was brought to North American audiences. For instance, take the example of a statue in the game *Castlevania IV*—in the Japanese version, the statue is seen with a cloth covering her from the hips down. Her breasts, however, were bare. In the North American version, the cloth extends to her shoulders and covers everything. Editing games for North American release is not uncommon, of course. Recently, the game *Fahrenheit* was edited to remove nudity and scenes deemed likely to garner it an AO rating in North America. It ultimately released as the edited but M-rated *Indigo Prophecy*.

Despite all these restrictions, however, there has been some sexual content on the Nintendo in the North American market. At the tamest end, one can count well over 50 love stories within RPGs, typically those developed by Japanese companies. While romantic stories in these games are common, less common, however, are titles on the Nintendo with deliberately sexual overtones. The most famous of these is the 1991 Panesian release, *Bubble Bath Babes*. The game was a sexualized takeoff on the popular *Tetris*. Players tried to fit colored bubble shapes into the grid as they floated up from a nude model. Players were rewarded with progressively more sexy stills of pixilated women. The images, however, weren't very titillating. Panesian would release *Hot Slot* for the Nintendo the same year, a sexualized slot game, and *Peek-a-Boo Poker*. Both games rewarded the player with progressive nudity as they won. None of the Panesian releases was authorized by Nintendo.

In more recent years, it appears that Nintendo has both stood by its core "family friendly" market but cautiously expanded its horizons in a few areas. Some games, like the violent *Resident Evil® 4* and the sexually themed *BMX XXX*™ were allowed to release on the platform. On the Nintendo DS, meanwhile, quirky games like *Feel the Magic*™ *XX/XY* and *Rub Rabbits* cast players in the role of a man trying to land his dream girl, although all the content within the game remained T-rated.

SEX ON THE SEGA

Although Sega had been in the console market for several years, the company wouldn't gain solid footing in North America, long the stronghold of Nintendo, until 1989 when it released the Sega Genesis. Although more liberal in its content allowances than Nintendo, all the same, relatively few sexually themed titles were released on its various platforms. Nonetheless, it was on this system that a landmark title in sex and games history would be released.

Night Trap, a rather campy game, was released in 1992. Although the sexual material within the game was minimal and largely limited to the dress of the women in the full motion video (FMV) scenes, it sparked a phenomenal amount of controversy. The gameplay revolved around a plot of trying to save college co-eds from vampiric creatures. Rather than trying to save the co-eds, however, some said the game was about *killing* co-eds and chastised it for its scantily clad models, a criticism that would be leveled at video game characters and video game events for years to come. Along with the violent game *Mortal Kombat®*, *Night Trap* would lead to the Congressional hearings on video games in 1993 and the formation of all the key groups associated with video games, from the Entertainment Software Ratings Board (ESRB) rating system to the International Game Developers Association (IGDA).

In 1995, Sega followed up its Genesis system with the Sega Saturn. The system also had a small selection of sex games, some of which were released in Japan, but regularly found their way to the North American market. *The Yakyuken Special* was one such game. Released for the system in Japan in 1996, *The Yakyuken Special* used an old game—in this case, the classic "rock, paper, scissors"—and repurposed it into a sexually themed game by adding nudity as a reward. The game featured 12 different women who would take off a piece of clothing with each loss. By the mid-1990s, hentai (adult) titles that rose to prominence on the PC in the early 1990s began to make their way to the Saturn. While not explicitly sexual, titles such as 1995's *Eve Burst Error* contained partial nudity and sexual themes, as is common in titles of this nature. While known as games and sold as such, titles like *Eve Burst Error* are far more akin to interactive stories than video games. In this game, the player takes on alternating roles of two characters, Kojiroh, a detective, and Marina, a special agent, to solve cases. Hentai games are covered in more detail later in this chapter.

SEX ON THE PC—EARLY 1990S

As the 1980s rolled out, so too did the Apple, Amiga, Atari, and the seemingly half dozen different computers for which developers made games. In came the IBM PC, and machines compatible with it, as the development and play platform of choice. While PCs had been prominent since the mid 1980s, it was in the late 1980s and early 1990s that the great majority of game developers stopped developing titles for the other platforms, largely abandoning the machines. Titles like the popular sexually themed series *Leisure Suit Larry* and Artworx *Strip Poker* transitioned to the new machine (*Leisure Suit Larry 3*, released in 1994, would be a PC exclusive), and designers like Steve Meretzky, designer of *Leather Goddess of Phobos*, brought their talents to the new machine, too. In fact, it was on the PC that Meretzky's *Spellcasting 101: Sorcerer's Get All the Girls* was released in 1990. *Rex Nebular and the Cosmic Gender Bender*, a game he worked on, followed in 1992.

In addition to its market dominance, the PC provided improved processing power and improved graphics over computers available in the late 1980s. From CGA to EGA to VGA, the graphics processing power of the machines improved steadily throughout the 1980s, allowing users to see ever more detail within their game worlds. While previous machines like the Amiga were also known for their graphical ability, the machines did not have the processing power or wide acceptance of the IBM PC. Titles like *Wolfenstein*, *Ultima Underworld*, *Wing Commander*, and *Doom* pushed the machines to their proverbial limits, and games were more graphic and immersive than ever before.

As the North American market perfected the art of violence in video games, the Japanese were busy creating a new kind of game—the dating sim. Depending on the target audience, the title could range from a classic pre-teen story (e.g., the princess finds the prince, and they fall in love) to a deeply erotic and sexually graphic narrative. Although companies such as JASTUsa.com are making inroads in bringing English language translations of these games to the U.S. market, the games have yet to catch on in a big way. The reasons are many, but limited distribution and limited awareness are highest among them. However, given the rising popularity of anime and manga (Japanese comic books), that could change in the very near future.

Megatech's *Cobra Mission* is largely credited as the first Japanese hentai game to make it to the United States. Originally released in Japan in 1991, it was released in English in North America in 1992. Unlike traditional North American offerings that were either sexual comedies or too hard core for the mainstream market, *Cobra Mission* took its sexual content seriously and integrated it into the storyline in a natural way. While not the first time something like this had happened in North America—in fact, 1981's *Soft Porn Adventure* had tried serious integration with comedic results—the concept was largely new to North American players. The game featured the JR Knight, a private investigator, and his girlfriend, Faythe Watson. She, in turn, is searching for her friend Donna. Throughout the game, JR has an opportunity to meet and seduce numerous women. Although it's not required in order to win the game, the sexual encounters within *Cobra Mission* are what people most seem to remember and mention most often. Upon meeting a woman, the player has a limited number of moves in which to please her before their encounter ends. As with many games of this time period, the player selects from a menu of choices that allow him to do everything from lighting a candle to whispering to placing a hand in her hair, on her breasts, or in other suggestive places. Players can even select to use a vibrator on their date. The player selects an option, such as "hand," "kiss," or "vibrator" and then uses his mouse to determine where to use the selected option. Ironically, the player "hooks up" with these women by calling them from Faythe's house, having received their number as a reward for completing a map within the game.

MegaTech followed *Cobra Mission* with three other titles—*Metal & Lace: The Battle of the Robo Babes* in 1993, *Knights of Xentar* in 1994, and *Power Dolls* in 1995. *Power Dolls* was a strategy game in which beautiful, anime-style women armored themselves heavily for combat. The game rewarded players with anime style pictures of the women, minus their heavy armor. The images were placed in the game's directory.

The PC is the hands-down winner when it comes to the amount of sexual content on a machine. When one can develop, download, and play all on the same machine, it's a recipe for success. Furthermore, unlike consoles, no one needs to approve release on the platform. Therefore, provided the publisher has given the project a green light, the game is unlikely to face hurdles in its release, unless it fails to meet its publisher's expectation. Of course, getting the game into the retail channel is another matter and the subject of Chapter 10.

THE RISE OF FULL MOTION VIDEO (FMV)

Full motion video (FMV) was going to change *everything*. Although it had been around since the early 1980s, with the broad acceptance of CD-ROM drives in the early 1990s, developers now had the ability to include movies within their games. For the video game industry, the technology was novel and exciting. Some speculated that it would change the way games were made entirely. Fans hotly anticipated releases that incorporated the new technology, and actors—albeit B- and C-list actors—lined up to be a part of the latest technology. Among the most prominent early releases was the Sierra title *Phantasmagoria*. The game shipped on a then-record seven CD-ROMs, and the game's avatar was a filmed actress, not a digital recreation of one. Some years later in 1996, *Phantasmagoria 2: A Puzzle of Flesh* was released. That game also featured FMV footage and was set, in part, in Seattle's BDSM scene. Of all the FMV games created—and there were many—1993's *Night Trap* was likely the most controversial. As mentioned earlier in this chapter, *Night Trap*, in conjunction with *Mortal Kombat*, led to 1993's Congressional hearings on video games and contributed to the formation of the industry's rating system and the various groups that support the industry, including the Entertainment Software Association (ESA) and the IGDA.

With the ability to show movies, FMV was a natural platform for sexually themed games, and designers integrated the new medium into existing play mechanics. For instance, in 1994, Interplay released its first sexually themed FMV game, *Voyeur*. It was followed in 1996 by *Voyeur 2*, released by Philips Interactive Media. True to its name, the player played the role of a voyeur, spying on people for various reasons, and collecting evidence or information to solve particular quests. At the time of its release, the market was particularly sensitive, having weathered the recent Congressional hearings. Nonetheless, despite its potentially controversial content, the game never achieved the same kind of notoriety.

The FMV craze also gave rise to a new form of games—the social-sexual adventure, the most famous and likely notorious of which was *Man Enough: The Ultimate Social Adventure*. Released in 1995, players of *Man Enough* take various virtual women on dates in hopes of impressing them. Ultimately, if they are "man enough," they can get a date with the owner of the dating service in the game, Jeri. Despite its place in sexual video game history, the game was largely panned by critics. Likewise panned was *Virtual Vixens* and its sequel *Space Sirens*. Although the games featured moderately more gameplay than *Man Enough*, *Virtual Vixens* used the same mechanics—please the woman to move on to the next woman. In some respects, *Virtual Vixens* was a melding of *Mac Playmate* and *Man Enough*, mixing FMV with the "please the virtual woman" mechanic popularized by that game.

ENTER THE PORN MARKET

When FMV entered video games in the early 1990s, it was only a matter of time before the adult entertainment industry realized its potential. Armed with miles of video footage, video games offered a tremendous opportunity to sell existing content to a new market and with it, generate new profits. At the same time, the CD-ROM was making huge inroads into the home computer. On it, adult content developers could actually store the large FMV and graphic files that were their bread and butter.

Pitched as "interactive" titles within the adult market, the games allowed players to make periodic choices within the game. After a brief setup scene, the player would get to choose the path of the narrative, selecting woman A as opposed to woman B, for instance, or choosing where the star of the game would have sex. One such title was *The Interactive Adventures of Seymour Butts*, a well-known porn star. Although it and others were released in the 1990s, they're still popular today, even if they're no longer considered "games" as they once were. In fact, some adult film Web sites list over 200 such interactive titles.

Other adult industry names took more advantage of the video game medium by mixing FMV and traditional game mechanics. *Riana Rouge*, released in 1997 by Black Dragon, featured Playboy Playmate™ Gillian Bonner in an erotic adventure game. Riana, played by Bonner, finds herself in another world where she must explore more than the environment. The game uses something called an "emotivator" that determines the style of the player's responses. While the player can talk tough to other characters in the game, he or she can also attempt to seduce them. In the game's "World of Indulgences," such a mechanic may prove particularly important to the player. In that world, Riana is tempted sexually again and again. The game is still available online at *www.rianarouge.com/*.

In 1994, *Penthouse* would enter the video games market with its product, *Penthouse Virtual Photo Shoot*. Long high on the career dream list of men everywhere, the game allowed players to take on the role of a *Penthouse* photographer. The game showed FMV clips of women, and players took photographs of them. Players were allowed to select clothing choices and choose from a variety of video clips that featured the women posing in different ways. Ultimately, a virtual Bob Guccione, publisher of the magazine, judged the player's portfolio. *Penthouse*'s product was followed to the market by other virtual cameramen games in the years that followed. Recently, the mechanic was used in 2006's *Rumble Roses XX* and 2005's *Playboy: The Mansion*, although the game features computer-generated models as opposed to FMV videos.

THE FALL OF FMV

The FMV craze that had invaded video games was relatively short lived. Having lost its newness, players tired of the bad acting and canned nature of the FMV sequences, and preferred the more spectacular creations of artists who were creating purely computer-generated environments and cut scenes. With the exception of 2004's release of *The Guy Game,* FMV is largely gone from games. *The Guy Game* featured FMV sequences of women answering trivia questions or performing various nonsexual acts while topless. The game was pulled from shelves after it was discovered that one of the contestants in the game was under the age of consent when she signed her release form to appear in the game.

For the adult market and adult games, FMV and even the medium of games also had a not-so-surprising downside. By making pornography interactive, the developers necessitated player interaction with the computer or console every so often to keep the action going. Such an action was often counterproductive to the players' original purpose of stimulating themselves, however. In a nutshell, players don't like to be interrupted while watching pornography. Imagine if a pornographic movie required viewers to press "play" every few minutes to keep the movie rolling. Such movies would likely be tossed in favor of those that let the viewer concentrate on things other than the "play" button on the DVD remote.

THE RISE OF THE SEXY CHARACTER

By the mid 1990s, the big news wasn't the sex games—it was the characters within them. While games had traditionally been designed in such a way that the player could create and customize his or her own avatar, two characters were poised to change all that. In the end, they would become more famous than the games in which they appeared.

Leading the charge was one of the sexiest (and some would say sexist) video game characters to date, Duke Nukem™. Originally released in 1991 as a side-scroller, Duke hit his stride (as far as sex in games is concerned) in 1996's *Duke Nukem 3D*. He had an ever-ready one-liner for every situation, "Shake it baby" famous among them; the line was said as Duke handed over cash to a woman. The lines from the game became video game legend. Throughout the game, Duke could frequent adult shops, strip clubs, and strippers, who bared their breasts, and posters for adult films were a common site in the game. Not surprisingly, the game was criticized by anti-pornography and censorship advocates who thought its treatment of women and its inclusion of adult themes in video games was inappropriate. The game, however, treats most all subject matter equally. Fans of the series recognize the many parodies present in the game, including several targeting a competing first-person shooter franchise. As a game, *Duke Nukem 3D* took *everything* over the top. Sex was not the exception.

In 2002, *Duke Nukem's Penthouse Paradise* was released as an official *Penthouse* magazine mod for *Duke Nukem 3D*. The game chronicled the story of Duke's vacation between the release of *Duke Nukem 3D* in 1996 and the *Duke Nukem Plutonium Pak* later that same year. The mod features Penthouse Pets and photo shoots (although the player does not control the action) and the typical style of gameplay and personality for which Duke is known. Ultimately, his vacation with the Penthouse Pets gets interrupted by aliens, and Duke makes them pay.

Duke wasn't the only character that appeared in 1996, however. The same year, the fall and winter would be owned by a buxom, gun-toting heroine named Lara Croft™. Her game, *Tomb Raider™*, was an action adventure in which Lara made her way through ruinous tombs in search of various artifacts. The story of the game, however, is secondary. The story of Lara is key. Even before the game's release, Lara garnered significant attention. Before and after the game's release, Lara appeared on well over a dozen magazine covers. Unlike previous video game characters, either those the player created or those created by the designers of the game, Lara had a substantial backstory to her that her publisher continues to update regularly. Upon gamers, Lara's effect was obvious. Fan clubs and Web sites sprung up, and she became a bonafide star, reaching beyond the gaming world to the big screen. As was discussed in Chapter 1, in 2001, *Lara Croft: Tomb Raider* hit the big screen and starred real-life beauty Angelina Jolie. A sequel was released in 2003, *Lara Croft Tomb Raider: The Cradle of Life.*

On the little screen, Lara had also begun to appear in a less favorable light, at least in the eyes of her publishers. In addition to the traditional sites that offered hints and tips on gameplay, others offered nude mods, doctored nude photos, and images of Lara in compromising positions. The site at the center of the controversy, at least once Lara's publisher entered the picture, was *www.nuderaider.com*. On the site, players could access a nude patch for PC versions of the game that, not surprisingly, removed Lara's clothing. The site also hosted a Web ring that provided links to numerous others sites that offered illicit Lara content. In an article on BBC News online, the publisher cited its desire to protect not only their character but her fans, many of whom were under the age of majority. Having them stumble upon inappropriate pictures was simply not acceptable [BBC01]. The publisher sent cease and desist letters to the various sites, and nuderaider.com was eventually shut down. The site currently points to a dead URL.

Lara and Duke, an unlikely pairing if ever there was one, set off light bulbs in the minds of marketing departments throughout the industry. In the years that followed, games would deliberately craft sexy heroines and heroes in hopes of attracting a fan following like Lara and Duke had. From Luba Licious of *Leisure Suit Larry: Magna Cum Laude* to Tala from *Darkwatch: Curse of the West*™ to Blood-Rayne from *BloodRayne*™, the digital beauties appeared again and again and again. As was noted in Chapter 1, G4 TV hosted its first ever Video Game Vixens Awards in 2005, and *Playboy* magazine even featured a digital beauty as a centerfold (although she did not replace the traditional real-life centerfold in that issue).

THE ADVENT OF MACROMEDIA FLASH®

Macromedia Flash did for sex games what the printing press did for books—suddenly sex games were everywhere. Everyone had the tools they needed to produce a sex game, provided they had the technical aptitude and creativity to do so. Since its release in 1996, Flash has been used to create thousands of small games with sexual themes.

Flash sex games generally come in six varieties:

Original games: Many developers have used Flash to create new, sexually themed games. From 2006's *MILF Warriors* to the *Sack Smash* series, these games are readily playable online and consist of original designs or, in the case of *MILF Warriors*, designs inspired by other games. *MILF Warriors* was inspired, in part, by the *Grand Theft Auto: San Andreas.*

Repurposed games: Taking a classic game like Tetris®, poker, solitaire, a puzzle, or the "flip n' match" mechanic, developers use nudity as a backdrop or reward. Sometimes, the games are more elaborate. One such game recreated the arcade classic *Asteroids*, but used a penis rather than a gun to shoot at the incoming projectiles.

Advergames: Flash has been used on many occasions to create sexually themed games for all kinds of companies. Milwaukee's Best®, for instance, contracted the development of *Busted*, a game where a man looks at a woman's breasts, but can't get "busted" doing so. *Cool Condoms* has a game available on their site that lets players pick matching sexual positions. *Axe®* deodorant has several games on their site, including one of the better-known advergames, *Hide the Hottie*.

Educational games: Numerous institutions and agencies have used Flash to create games that teach people about abstinence, safe sex, and sexuality. Planned Parenthood has a series of such games on their Teenwire.com site.

Bishoujo/hentai games: Romantic and sexually charged bishoujo or hentai games are also popular with Flash designers. The games are much more common and intricate on the PC, however. The medium of bishoujo, which usually uses still images mixed with text, is relatively easy to program, although its content requires a degree of artistic talent, more so than the average online sex game.

Games that aren't games at all: Although they bill themselves as "Flash games" and frequently appear in the "adult" or "sex game" listings on many sites, some games aren't actually games at all, but rather sexually themed utilities or animated movies. For instance, one such utility allows the player to move his or her mouse over Lara Croft's body as she lies in a pool of water, removing her clothing as the mouse touches it. Other utilities let users increase a woman's breast size to impossible proportions. Still others ask users to answer a series of questions before evaluating their sexual potential, prowess, or knowledge.

Flash provides an affordable medium that gives everyone the opportunity to be a game developer on a small scale with varying degrees of success. While games like *Alien Hominid*™ have jumped the gap and gone from Flash game to commercial game, so far, no sexually themed games have had the same success.

MOBILE GAMES

In the late 1990s and early 2000s, the mobile gaming market took off. Like Flash games, mobile games were comparatively quick and inexpensive to make when compared to traditional PC or console game development, and the market was perfect for classic games or ports of games that had appeared on other systems. Nonsexualized versions of Tetris, solitaire, blackjack, and poker, among others, appeared early on. Eventually, companies like Touchlink Mobile would contribute games (and utilities) that were sexually themed. One such game, *Girls Everywhere*, allowed players to see naked women in whatever scene they selected. Touchlink Mobile also offers numerous classic games that provide nude images as a reward and sexually themed adventure/puzzle games like their *Oskar* series, which features the male character Oskar in various jobs, all of which ultimately test his prowess with women.

In 2006, adult film legend Ron Jeremy formed RJMobile to create sexually themed video, games, "groan tones," and phone wallpapers featuring the Ron Jeremy brand. For now, however, sexually themed mobile games are largely limited to non-U.S. markets. Jeremy's company RJMobile.com, in fact, is based in London, England. Later in 2006, and coinciding with the World Cup, *Sexy Soccer* was released for mobile players, although again, the game was not available for U.S. markets. Most mobile carriers in the United States, including Verizon®, Cingular®, Sprint®, and others, have decided not to carry pornographic or erotic materials, be they games or images. A news report carried on gaming blog Joystiq.com on April 27, 2006, reported that both Cingular and Verizon had created content restriction guidelines that prohibited corporate distribution of pornographic content (the company could not prohibit cell phone users from taking pictures with the cell phones that were equipped with a camera and sending them to others) [Joystiq01].

SEX ON THE PC—MODERN

The fall of FMV by no means killed the market for sex games on PCs. In fact, on today's home computers, the ready availability of broadband Internet access has created a huge and segmented market for sex in games. When it comes to sexual content, computers have two distinct differences from consoles: they have online access to thousands of games, and there is no regulatory body that says whether a game can or cannot run on their particular system. Microsoft, for instance, can keep any game it likes off the Xbox 360 simply by refusing to give it approval to release on the console. On computers, that's not the case. Therefore, sex games proliferate.

In the North American market, there are three distinct types of adult content in PC games available to players: mainstream games with sexual content, online games, and imported games.

Mainstream Games

Mainstream games are those you'd find in the average game retailer like Best Buy®, Wal-Mart®, or GameStop™. The sexual content found in the games is typically rather limited, and in some cases, it's even abstracted. Consider, for instance, *The Sims 2*. In that game, characters can develop relationships, fall in love, and have families. When characters choose to have "woo hoo," they dive under the sheets and flail around. The player never sees anything, and what he or she does see is comically abstracted. The Sims' franchise released *The Sims: Hot Date* in 2001. Despite its racy title, the game remained squarely in the family friendly zone. The game allowed *Sims'* characters to do what players had long requested—enjoy a social life with their significant other.

When sexual content—if it can even fairly be called that—appears in mainstream PC games, it often appears in the form of romance, particularly in RPGs. For instance, consider the MMO *Asheron's Call*™. Released in 1999, *Asheron's Call* included a wedding quest in which two players proceeded through a dungeon and ultimately were married upon successful completion of the quest. Likewise, launched in 2003, the *Star Wars Galaxies*® MMO also supported marriage between player characters. While not offering a specific quest like *Asheron's Call* did, the game did have an event coordinator that would make in-game weddings "events to remember." Sheri Graner Ray, who worked on the franchise, told this author that the events were really pretty spectacular for fans. Storm Troopers would be placed to line the aisles and Princess Leia would sometimes be among the guests [GRay01].

Even traditional PC games that didn't support massive online communities got in on the act. *Baldur's Gate 2* featured flirting between the player's character and another in-game character. The feature actually led to the development of an entire "flirt pack" mod. An interview with Jason Compton, one of the creators of the mod, appears at the end of this chapter. Both *Final Fantasy 7*, which featured a dating scene, and *Final Fantasy 8*, whose entire literary theme was romance, also explored the subject.

Not all games released in the mainstream channel were so light, however. In 2004, Deep Silver's *The Singles: Flirt Up Your Life* took the social simulation where it had never gone before. The game featured significant sexual content, right from its premise. Your job, as the player is to get the apartment's two residents to connect with one another intimately, and virtually every option and action in the game is geared toward this ultimate goal. The game was released in North America by Eidos Interactive as an M-rated game. An AO version was also available online. While both were flagged with the strong sexual content descriptor, the AO version featured full nudity while the M-rated version contained only partial nudity.

Other titles from somewhat unlikely sources also made their way to the PC at the turn of the century. Simon & Shuster Interactive, known more for book publishing, released *Panty Raider: From Here to Immaturity* in 2000. *Panty Raider* takes the player to Model Isle where, playing as Nelson, he must save the Earth from aliens by photographing women's bras and panties. By doing so, presumably, the testosterone charged aliens can be kept at bay. The game was shot down by critics and achieved a 21% score on GameRankings.com.

Online Games

With no retail, rating, or geographic restrictions of any kind, in the online world, anything goes . . . and often does. Online PC games generally fall into two categories: subscription service games or pay-for-play games that require a one-time purchase on the part of the user. There are also hundreds of free sexually themed games online. However, due to the sheer number of these games and their obviously low development cost, it's often a challenge to find games that are high quality and enjoyable productions. Most developers of free games have, by now, also transitioned to Flash. That said, over 200 free games can be found at the Sex & Games site at *www.igda.org/sex* in the Link of the Day section.

Subscription-based games require the user to pay a recurring fee to access the game, usually in exchange for periodic updates. Jenna Jameson's simulator, *VirtuallyJenna*, is one such game. Others include *Roboho*, the aptly named *3D Sex Games*, *3D SexVilla*, *3D Slut*, and *3D GayVilla*. Each of these games allows players access to a virtual porn set where they can experiment with the game's model in a variety of ways. Many of the upcoming MMOEGs, covered later in this chapter, will also be subscription based.

Pay-for-play games are also popular among adult software developers. Both *Leisure Suit Larry: Magna Cum Laude* and *The Singles: Flirt Up Your Life* offered downloadable AO-rated versions. Beyond rated games, however, titles like *LoveChess* and *DreamStripper* offer players a complete game for a one-time fee. *LoveChess* is a standard chess game, with a distinctly erotic twist. When two characters meet on a square, they surrender sexually and have intercourse with one another before the game progresses. *LoveChess* also released *LoveChess: Age of Egypt*, a follow up to its original game. *DreamStripper*, meanwhile, puts the player in the shoes of a virtual strip tycoon. The player manages everything from the woman's moves to her clothing. Online game *Virtual Hottie* and its sequel, *Virtual Hottie 2* are also available as one-time purchases. The developer has also expanded the brand to include other proverbial hotties, including porn actresses Mandi Rose and Terri Summers. Each of these games can be purchased for a one-time fee. The developer even offers a customized version of its game featuring the face of anyone the player desires.

Imported Games

Although not for sale in traditional retail outlets in North America, some titles, usually from Germany or Japan, make their way to North American gamers, some translated, some not.

Among all commercial producers of sexually themed game content, the Japanese are the cultural winners. Since the artform's arrival on computers in the early 1980s—Koei's *Night Life* is believed to be the first such title—hentai or bishoujo "dating sim" titles account for well over 25% of the adult commercial titles released in any given year. A quick scan of Mobygames.com adult listing reveals hentai title after hentai title from companies like G-Collections, Peach Princess, and Himeya Soft, Inc. In various discussions with those familiar with the dating sim's importance in Japanese gaming, this author has heard claims that these dating sims account for over 25% of PC software titles in any given store. In some cases, these figures gusted upward of 50%. Whatever the actual figure may be since they vary widely by store and by location, just as quantity of adult materials varies in the United States, the prominence of these titles in Japanese gaming is clear. Not all dating sim titles are "hentai," however. As with any other art form, the games span the range of human experience, from mild to wild.

For the most part, dating-sim games focus on the characters and the story rather than the physical aspects of sex like the "poke" and "touch" mechanics used in the hard-core sexually themed games. As such, the games are still mostly 2D. In North America, gamers desiring these titles can find them at comic and anime conventions, some comic shops, and from online distributors such as JASTUSA.com and PeachPrincess.com.

Titles from Germany have also made their way to North America. *Lula 3D* was released in 2005 for purchase online. The star of the game, Lula, is a producer of erotic films who finds that several of her stars have been kidnapped. Throughout the course of the game, she works to get them back. Among the game's more interesting listed features was its mention of breast bounce technology—motion capture was used to accurately model the movement of a woman's breasts. The game also noted that it was simple to operate using only the mouse, presumably leaving one hand free [Lula01].

SEX ON THE MODERN CONSOLES

Like the consoles before it, for games to play on the modern consoles like the PS2®, Xbox, and GameCube™, the game must first be approved for development and release by Sony, Microsoft, or Nintendo®, respectively. This need for approval and the possibility of not getting final, release approval after spending hundreds of thousands or millions of dollars in development—tends to keep the more risky and mundane content out. Nonetheless, with the turn of the century, several game developers decided to take that risk and develop games that were decided sexually themed. For these developers, the risk was a triple one—how would the console manufacturers, retailers, and ratings boards react to such a game? What made it tricky was that no clear precedent existed at the retail or rating level. How would ESRB raters view topless characters in a game? How about FMV of *real* topless women? What about animated sex between characters in a game? The same questions applied to retailers. Would they allow these titles to be stocked beside their other game titles or keep them off store shelves?

For the sexual content developers of the early 2000s, these questions and others loomed large.

When developing games, people often look for precedent for many reasons. With the cost of software development ever rising, developers and publishers need to know what the acceptable thresholds are. When developing a violent game, for instance, developers can look at a game like *Manhunt* and judge their own game, or the idea for their game, against retail, ESRB, and public reaction to that game, which allowed players to carry a human head around in a bag. For developers of sexual content, however, the horizon was mostly blank. At the time, the truly sexual games were online and unrated or sold through small outlets, and while there was lots of eye candy in PC games and console games alike, it didn't generally affect ratings for games in the T- and M-rated categories in which buxom babes abound. Besides, PC games don't generally require an "approval" process similar to the one console titles are subjected to, and therefore don't have to worry about being rejected at alpha, beta, or final build. In most cases, if a publisher kills a project, the wound is largely self-inflicted—they paid for the game they're killing.

Among the developers creating sexual content at the time were Cyberlore Studios with *Playboy: The Mansion*, High Voltage Software with *Leisure Suit Larry: Magna Cum Laude*, Top Heavy Studios with *The Guy Game*™, Z-Axis Games with *BMX XXX*™, and Monte Cristo Multimedia with *7 Sins*. On the PC, Deep Silver was developing *The Singles: Flirt Up Your Life*.

Adding to the confusion for these developers was the industry's tendency to keep its information close to the vest. Since secrets in the video game industry can be worth millions of dollars, it's a pattern well worth keeping. However, in this case, it actually held some developers back. For instance, in the years that followed the release of these games, this author learned of conversations developers had had in advance of release of their game with the ESRB, retailers, and first party (the name commonly used in the industry for Sony, Microsoft, and Nintendo). If shared among the developers, this information would have undoubtedly been useful to all developers concerned.

In the end, all of the games were rated M, and indeed, a precedent had at long last been set. Two of the titles, *Leisure Suit Larry: Magna Cum Laude* and *The Singles*, went on to release AO-rated PC versions that were sold online. Both of these titles reportedly sold well. All the titles did have difficulty at retail, however. Some big box stores refused to carry them—even with their M as opposed to AO rating. Ultimately, these games' inability to sell at big box retail will affect future investment in similar games. Until the distribution model of games changes to primarily online or until stores are willing to carry software with adult themes, the market will remain lukewarm.

In addition to the more sexually charged titles, mature themes also began to work their way into mainstream titles. In 2001, for instance, *Grand Theft Auto III* allowed the player's in-game character to hire a prostitute and have sex with her. No actual sex was shown; the player merely saw a car bouncing up and down. The mechanic caused quite an uproar among concerned citizens groups and politicians when it was revealed that the player could kill the prostitute when the act was completed and get his or her money back. Although the player could actually kill *any* character in the game and get his or her money, the particular emergent combination is still referenced today by censorship advocates as an example of video games gone wrong.

In 2004, sports games like *Rumble Roses* and *Dead or Alive: Beach Volleyball* gave players who had long been accustomed to sexy avatars some serious eye candy to look at by incorporating beautiful digitized women and environments with traditional sports game mechanics. The trailer for the latest *Dead or Alive: Beach Volleyball* game, in fact, was shown at the Sex in Video Games Conference on June 8, 2006, during Dave Taylor's presentation on sex and technology. Taylor caused the audience to laugh by pointing out repeatedly during the trailer that we'd yet to see an actual volleyball, although one eventually does make its appearance.

In 2005, another sexually themed title was released for the PS2, *7 Sins*. Unlike the sexually themed titles before it that rode a wave of press to market, *7 Sins* seemed to make a relatively quiet entrance, likely due to its restricted availability. It is not yet available in the United States, nor is it rated by the ESRB as of this writing. The same year also saw the release of the critically acclaimed *God of War*. Early in the game, the character approaches a bed upon which two partially nude women lie. As the women approach Kratos, the protagonist in the game, the camera pans away to a table that contains a vase. The player engages in an interactive mini-game of sorts in which Kratos purportedly has sex with the women on the bed. The player never sees anything, however. His job, instead, is to knock the wobbling vase off the table. The wobbling is presumably caused by Kratos' activity with the women.

All the sex in games in 2005 was completely and utterly eclipsed by 2005's most notorious sex-in-games scene—*Grand Theft Auto: San Andreas'* "Hot Coffee" mini-game. The mini-game, which was included on the *GTA:SA* disc, was discovered by the mod community. A patch, readily available online, allowed people to control the character in the game, CJ, as he made love to his girlfriend after the two had gone on several dates. The "Hot Coffee" mod is the subject of Chapter 4.

SEX AT THE GAME DEVELOPERS CONFERENCE

In 2005, the Game Developers Conference (GDC), the biggest conference of its type in the world, hosted the first ever "Sexuality in Games: What's Appropriate?" roundtable for developers interested in the appropriate use of sexual content within video games. The roundtable—in which participants discussed a range of issues facilitated by a moderator—was held three separate times during the conference and welcomed over 50 people each day. The roundtables were moderated by Brenda Brathwaite, the author of this book, and Sheri Pociljuko, a developer who worked with High Voltage Software on the *Leisure Suit Larry: Magna Cum Laude* game. The attendees were a diverse lot, from people who thought sex had no place in games to those who wondered if you could even have flirting in a T-rated game, to those who were creating virtual prostitution simulators. In many respects, for developers of adult content in video games, the roundtable was like a homecoming of sorts. It was the first time these developers had gathered in a room at GDC or any other conference for that matter. Business cards were exchanged, and a moderator of the roundtables collected business cards of those who wanted to stay in touch after the conference ended. It was that particular conference and those roundtables that ultimately gave rise to the formation of the International Game Developers Association's Sexuality Special Interest Group, better known as the IGDA Sex SIG.

In 2006, GDC again brought sexual content back to the proverbial table. Held under the IGDA track, the conference hosted two "Sex in Games: Hardcore" roundtables and a lecture, "Sex in Games: The Exciting Evolution of Adult Content." Unlike the roundtables held the previous year, the focus of the 2006 roundtables was limited exclusively to the more liberal end of adult content. Developers currently making and interested in making adult content were present, as were some developers who had included adult themes in more mainstream titles. As with most roundtables, discussion was varied and topics such as realism in graphics versus abstraction, distribution, diversity, and turning the player on were discussed.

THE FORMATION OF THE IGDA'S SEXUALITY SPECIAL INTEREST GROUP

Following the Game Developers Conference of 2005, one of the moderators of the "Sexuality in Games: What's Appropriate?" roundtable was left with a pile of business cards. Each of these individuals wanted to discuss the issue further and stay in contact with one another. That moderator, Brenda Brathwaite, contacted the IGDA about starting a mailing list and, ultimately, a Sexuality Special Interest Group similar to others the IGDA had for women developers, casual game developers, and educators, for instance. Jason Della Rocca, the executive director of the IGDA was receptive to the idea, and the IGDA gave it the green light. Starting with an official IGDA mailing list in late March, the work to form a SIG was begun. Developers of adult content needed a community, a group, a mailing list, and a set of resources that were unique to developers of adult content. They needed a place—if even a virtual place—where they could discuss issues associated with sexual content development freely. The IGDA's Sex SIG was launched in August of the same year after the necessary proposals and paperwork had been completed.

Although many thought the IGDA's Sex SIG was in response to the *GTA:SA* Hot Coffee scandal, it in fact was not. Work was well underway by the time the notorious code was discovered. The IGDA's Sex SIG hosts a blog at *www.igda.org/ sex*.

THE RETURN OF THE ADULT INDUSTRY

Although the adult industry would return briefly in 2002 with an official *Penthouse* mod for the FPS *Duke Nukem*, it wouldn't be until 2005 that they returned to the video game market with any kind of force. Two games bearing adult industry names were released that year: *Playboy: The Mansion* and *VirtuallyJenna*. *Playboy: The Mansion* was the first adult industry title to appear on modern day consoles. The game put players in the slippers of adult industry icon Hugh Hefner and took them through 12 missions that chronicled the evolution of the men's magazine. *VirtuallyJenna*, featuring porn icon Jenna Jameson, let players stimulate Jenna with a large variety of sex toys, and digitized anatomical representations. In many respects, the game is a virtual pornography set where players can see Jenna do the things for which she is most famous.

By 2005, the rise in popularity of MMOs, the emergent sex in them, and the wide acceptance of both broadband and online dating services encouraged porn site Naughty America to license its name to developer Eight Legs, Inc. Similar to all MMOs, *Naughty America: The Game* allowed players to create avatars and interact with other players within the world. Unlike traditional MMOs, however, the game actually welcomed and facilitated social and intimate interaction between players by providing the animations, actions, and privacy they'd need to be comfortable with intimacy. Each character in the game has an apartment that he or she can decorate according to his or her particular style. Players are even welcome to invite other players to move in with them. Massively multiplayer online erotic games, known as MMOEGs, are covered later in this chapter.

The summer of 2006 saw the first ever summit of the video game and adult industries in San Francisco, California. The appropriately titled "Sex in Videogames Conference" brought together minds on both sides of the table, from Brad Abrams of 3DXtreme, developer of *VirtuallyJenna*, to Wired.com's sex and technology columnist Regina Lynn, to sex author and Fleshbot.com reporter Violet Blue, to industry icons Sheri Graner Ray, author of *Gender Inclusive Game Design*, and Dave Taylor, one of the developers of *Doom*™ and *Quake*™. In addition to sex and technology specialists, sexologists such as the renowned Marty Klein appeared, as did prominent First Amendment lawyer Lawrence Walters and Tom Hymes of the Free Speech Coalition, the trade organization that represents the adult video industry. The conference was chaired by Brenda Brathwaite, the author of this book. At the conference, attendees discussed the current state of the sex and game industry, its more prominent issues such as distribution, keeping kids out, and diversity, and exchanged information and contacts.

SEX AND THE PLAYSTATION® PORTABLE

Released in 2005, the PlayStation Portable (PSP) was Sony's answer to the Nintendo GameBoy. While the machine certainly never achieved anywhere near the market that Nintendo claimed, it did come with two features Nintendo's platform did not have: the machine could access the Internet and play movies. As such, the format was quickly adopted by adult content producers who released movies such as *The Palace of a Virgin* and *Bouncy: Virtual Lap Dances Vol. 1* on the platform's unique UMD format. In fact, the Web site porn4psp.com features over hundreds of downloadable movie clips for the platform. Eventually, the potential for pornography on the PSP led some to dub it the "PlayStation Pornable" [Joystiq02].

THE MMOEG

By 2005, the ready availability of broadband distribution, coupled with the popularity of MMORPGs such as *World of Warcraft* and its predecessors, *Everquest*, *Asheron's Call*, *Anarchy Online*, *Ultima Online*, and others, inspired numerous developers to do for erotic content what other companies had done for role playing—namely, make it a massively multiplayer affair. Unlike the MUDs of the late 1970s and early 1980s, however, massively multiplayer online erotic games (MMOEGs) are graphical worlds complete with animations and visually appealing environments. For their developers, it stood to reason that if players were having emergent sex in worlds that didn't support such actions, players would welcome games that actually *encouraged* and facilitated sexual encounters. Able to sell subscriptions online, the developers were also freed of the traditional distribution constraints of adult content and could reach their potential consumers directly without having to go through a retail outlet or fear the effects of an AO rating.

One of the first to the market was *Sociolotron*. Released in 2005 after a public beta test, *Sociolotron* was never intended to be a mainstream game nor marketed as such. Developed by Patric Lagny, the game has a small and tight knit community of players. The game is part role-playing game—players develop characters and slay monsters, as one would expect—and part MMOEG. Although *Sociolotron* allows players to perform all kinds of sexual actions from oral sex to standard intercourse, it has achieved a measure of notoriety for allowing characters to rape other characters in the game. Players are, however, warned that this is possible before even entering the world. So, by entering the world at all, following the warning, players are, in effect, giving a modicum of consent.

By 2005, the number of announced MMOEGs had eclipsed the number of announced MMORPGs. No fewer than six announced MMOEGs were in development—*Spend the Night, Naughty America: The Game, Rapture Online, Heavenly Bodies, Red Light Center*, and *3 Feel*. Although each game had a slightly different feature set, all focused on sexual interactions between characters in the game to some degree or another. *RedLightCenter.com* even went the proverbial extra mile by allowing people to purchase sex toys and other products in game for delivery in real life. The announced games also had another thing in common—they were deliberately designing their game to target women. In fact, *Spend the Night, Naughty America: The Game, Rapture Online*, and *Heavenly Bodies* all had women in positions of power within the development team and, in some cases, as owners or co-owners of the development company. By targeting women, the games were, in effect, targeting men as well. The marketing technique has been used again and again by companies hoping to target a male clientele. From "ladies' nights" at bars to the "free for women" sex chat lines of the 1990s—shallow as it may seem, where women are, the men will follow. If the games, then, make themselves attractive to women and provide them a play style and an environment that makes them comfortable, they will also attract a male audience.

In early 2006, *Spend the Night* regrettably announced that it was suspending production, having failed to secure the necessary funding to continue development. However, the year also saw the announcement of two new MMOEGs, *Erotasy Island* by FX Interactive and *Jewel of Indra*, and another unnamed MMOEG was soliciting bids for development on the game development contract Web site at *www.project247.com*.

While many of these MMOEGs are targeting the game market, some developers are also attracted by the larger social phenomena of digital environments—one that goes beyond gaming. While knockout hits like *World of Warcraft* could boast over 6 million players at its peak, in a broader social content, MySpace.com attracted over 70 million subscribers. By shooting for the larger market, one that is interested in connecting people, developers are hoping to deliver big on their development investments.

In some respects, the games are the next logical extension—if perhaps a hyper-sexualized extension—of dating services such as Match.com and eHarmony.com, except instead of meeting at a local coffee shop, players meet online and "in world" instead. At this point, however, the success of these games remains to be seen. Will players leave the emergent sex behind in favor of worlds that facilitate cybering visually, or will they choose to stay in worlds like *Second Life*? Will the players of erotic text-based games care for the addition of graphics or stick to the tried and true—and some say more erotic—places they have already come to know?

It remains to be seen.

THE FUTURE OF SEX IN GAMES

In some respects, adult content development in video games is very much like the Wild, Wild West. For purely sexually themed games, developers are overwhelmingly small, independent outlets that publish almost exclusively online. No large game companies, and certainly no large publishers, have entered the market as of this writing. It will likely remain this way until some game or small company scores a big hit and with it big profits. Should the sales model of games change from retail distribution to online distribution, similar to the way songs are increasingly sold as MP3s as opposed to albums, tapes, or CDs, games with sexual content would most certainly have a bigger market and a better chance for profitability. The restrictions on sales of AO-rated games at retail outlets heavily curtail their chances at present.

Sexual content in games is also likely to become more normalized and less sensationalized in the future. While the majority of today's games seem to sport one extreme or the other—hyper-sexualized environments, avatars or actions, or nothing at all—games in the future will likely not be designed in such a way. Just as love scenes in movies are the norm and, with few exceptions, don't make headlines, so too will games find a comfortable medium. In 10 years, the North American market—or those who rate the games that reach it—might be ready for a game like *Fahrenheit* in its unedited form (it was released in North America as *Indigo Prophecy*). It will take something along the lines of the game equivalent of *The Brown Bunny* to draw media attention. The field of MMOEGs will also likely welcome a few entries in the less extreme range, bringing a new type of game into the fray—the massively multiple online romantic world. These games would be closer to a virtual eHarmony or Match.com than the current set of MMOEGs.

At present, the perception that games are for kids is pervasive, and video games today are under intense media and political scrutiny similar to the way *Dungeons & Dragons* and comic books were in the past. As today's gamers become tomorrow's parents and as a new technology comes along, a better understanding of the medium, its potential, and its range of offerings will develop, and the spotlight will shine on something else.

INTERVIEW WITH JASON COMPTON

Jason Compton is one of the creators of the Flirt Pack, a mod for *Baldur's Gate 2*. He is now a managing member of Planewalker Games.

Since Baldur's Gate 2 *(BG2) already had a romance system in place, what made your team take it to that next level?*

BG2 had romance, but as has been well-documented, it shipped with just one romance with a male character. So there was a lot of player outcry, both from women and from men who enjoyed playing female characters, for more than just one available romance partner. So my first efforts were addressing the disparity with Kelsey. At first, Kelsey was written as a mirror of the BG2 romances—he had about the same number of talks, about the same pacing to the relationship, and about the same results, from a storytelling perspective. I wanted to give players something they would recognize—taking it upon myself to imagine how a Bioware-penned romance with a male sorcerer might look.

The way I started writing the more in-depth "flirting" content was actually done to address a storytelling glitch while writing Kelsey content for BG2's expansion, *Throne of Bhaal*. The pattern BG2 (and BG1) used was that toward the end of the main game, the NPC would say, in effect, "Would you like to have sex now?" and the player would say "yes" or "no" and then there would be a little morning-after scene and that was that. I started thinking about how to write Kelsey in the expansion based on how this question was answered, and thinking about when he should bring it up again if he had been denied . . . and then decided that it was really, really silly that the player had no way to click on Kelsey (or any other romance partner) and say, "Hi, I've changed my mind. See me after everybody's gone to bed." So I added one.

From there, it seemed obvious that if you could click him and proposition him, that it would be nice and sweet if you could do less intense things on demand as well, such as kissing or hugging him or just saying a kind word. And then from there, it seemed only natural that he should return the favor from time to time and initiate his own flirts, rather than starting some heavy love talk where the player had to make serious choices that might affect character development or end the romance. They would just see the character come up and give their protagonist character a peck on the cheek or a pat on the butt or whatever. That way, instead of the romance simply ending when the last scripted talk had completed, there could always be this rotating, semi-random pool of mini-encounters playing back. Sure, they'd get repetitive, but when it comes down to it, a lot of real-life relationships are repetitive, too... the kisses before going off to work or bed and "I love you's" over the phone and so forth. Just because we've done them before doesn't mean it's not special to do them again.

Anyway, once Kelsey had all these neat features, I thought it would be fun to go back and add them back into the core four romance characters Bioware had provided. I did want my own creations to fit reasonably well with the rest of the game's content, after all—even if that meant helping the originals catch up with new material.

As far as "the next level" is concerned with explicitness, the very first flirts I published were extremely innocent. But as time went on, I added more and more that got more and more descriptive about sensations, or offered more outright lewd and "inappropriate in polite company" options. By and large, player response remained positive—people liked the wider range of options, and didn't mind the fact that they were reading on the screen about things they presumably assumed their characters were doing off-camera anyway as part of their normal, active sexual relationship. Admittedly, I do occasionally open the dialogue files, shake my head, and say, "Did I really write and publish that?!?" but I know that overall it's provided a lot of entertainment to a lot of people, and no digital pixels have been unduly molested in the process.

While sex in games gets a lot of attention, romance isn't given its due. What does romance add to a game that other game mechanics can't provide? How does it enhance the other mechanics?

For one thing, it gives players an extra ego boost to share through their characters that doesn't just rely on expertise with the fighting system. They each get to play a character who another character considers hot stuff. They get to play a character who can soothe another character with a well-timed compliment. They get to intersperse makeup sex with their high-level, set-piece tactical combats. RPGs are all about a player taking a character through a world that, through his/her actions, will be in some way greatly affected as a result. Usually that's on the macro level ("You saved the world!") but it's nice to do it on the micro level as well ("You saved the world, and made your new boyfriend very happy in the process!").

It also gives players a different angle to differentiate their player-characters on. Now there's an extra dimension—rather than just choosing between "an easygoing paladin" and "a reckless swashbuckler with a self-destructive streak," players can craft their alter-egos as "an easygoing paladin who likes her men simple and genuine" or "a reckless swashbuckler with a self-destructive streak, doomed to choose a co-dependent partner" and so on. And if that aspect gives them more reason to stop and consider how others might view their decisions about whether or not to aid somebody, or how to settle a dispute, or whether or not they should sacrifice themselves for the good of the world, or whatever . . . then, so much the better for an immersive experience.

How have players responded to your romance mods?

In the main, very well. We certainly didn't convert everybody who didn't like BG2's romances in the first place, of course, and there are still purists who either don't like our storytelling or don't like the more explicit content we offered and pass on installing the flirt packs even though they continue to play the stock romances.

I never receive unsolicited underwear in the mail or anything like that, but I do get a lot of positive feedback. Overall, Kelsey and the Flirt Packs have been hugely and enduringly successful. Both have enjoyed many tens of thousands of downloads, are often on people's "most recommended" lists, and I don't think it's going too far to say that they have been a tremendous part of the movement that has kept a substantial number of people playing this game almost six years after its initial release.

Somewhat by accident, we ended up setting the standard for other mods. Any time anybody announced a new character, inevitably players would quickly ask, "Will there be a romance? Will there be flirting?" to the point where it has become a wry entry in FAQs about quest mods that have nothing to do with characters or romance.

It's also worth pointing out that it was the creation of a romance mod (Solaufein, by Westley Weimer) that really kick-started Infinity Engine modding. Up until mid-2001, Infinity Engine modding was done with the proverbial stone knives and bearskins. The number of completed mods could probably be counted on two hands, none of them particularly stable. Wes needed something better to implement his story, and being a computer science Unix geek, he wrote his own flexible modding tool that enabled hundreds of mods to follow.

What's surprised you most about the reaction to these mods?

I think my biggest surprises came when we released the *Throne of Bhaal* add-on portion for Kelsey. That was a few months after he was initially released, so I knew by then that he had fans and that some players genuinely liked him. But in the expansion, we added two new storylines that both provoked responses I hadn't expected.

One was a storyline where Anomen (BG2's canonical male romance character) would proposition the PC to cheat on Kelsey. I really didn't know how this would play out when I wrote it up—would people find it believable? Would they just switch and never look back?

It was devilishly fun to read forum conversations where players would discuss just how agonizing they found the choice—either because they/their characters still did feel for Anomen, or because they were "completists" who wanted to see everything I had written. But some of them just couldn't pull the trigger, knowing that it would crush poor Kelsey. I think one player said she had to reload the game about 16 times before she could finally pick the dialogue option to succumb to Anomen's charms . . . and then was, of course, enormously ashamed when Kelsey berated her about it the next morning. I didn't expect quite that much devotion and guilt.

The other storyline involved Kelsey becoming involved with Imoen, the BG2 protagonist's "little sister," in the event that he did not have a relationship with the PC. Now, I knew full well that Imoen was a very popular character with a substantial portion of the player base and that there would be a fair amount of resistance to this idea, including from Kelsey's co-developer, Jesse Meyers, who handled most of the character's technical implementation. He made sure to point out that he recommended that people "put an axe in Kelsey's face" to prevent this from happening. So when the cries of "Keep that Kelsey away from MY IMOEN!" started up, I wasn't at all surprised.

But then I noticed that a number of players were instead saying "No! Keep Imoen away from MY KELSEY!" Players were starting to structure their parties so that Kelsey and Imoen couldn't start up their relationship—not because they were protective of Imoen, but because they were jealous of her, and felt that "If my character isn't going to have Kelsey, nobody will!"

If you had to identify a point at which I started believing that it wouldn't be patently insane to think that I could put together a bootstrap Computer role playing game (CRPG), that would probably be it. I'd successfully gotten a significant number of players to care just that much about a character in a game [Compton01].

INTERVIEW WITH PATRIC LAGNY, *SOCIOLOTRON*

Patric Lagny is a veteran game developer who has worked for companies like Blue Byte and on various games, including the *Battle Isle* Series, *The Settlers*, and *The Starfarers of Catan*. He is both developer and publisher of the sexually themed MMO *Sociolotron*.

Can you describe Sociolotron?

Sociolotron is a massively multiplayer online role-playing game, where the "massive" is relative. At the time of this writing, we have 200+ players online at peak times in the evenings and our goal is to increase this number by a few hundred, at best, over the lifetime of *Sociolotron*. We don't intend to try to reach the 1000s, because that would also cause many additional logistical problems for us.

Sociolotron offers the usual RPG gameplay like monster killing, raw materials, a production chain, spell casting, and so on, but we also have very sophisticated social mechanics in the game. For instance, there is a player-run government and a justice system that takes care of crimes committed by players, a Player vs. Player (PvP) system with some sort of permanent death that takes the characters to an afterlife, and, of course, sex. Characters can engage in sex, which is depicted in the form of explicit graphics and animation, but relies heavily on their role-playing ability [to describe what is happening in text], just like in any virtual sex chat room. The difference here is that the sexual actions have consequences for your character. For example, sex can change a character's brain values, which in turn change the way the player must play his character. There are also sexual diseases and pregnancy, which results in children that a player can take over as their main character when a parent character dies. We have set up the game so that no role playing with child characters is possible. Since the whole setting is in the future, it's easy to explain that children are taken from the mother at the time of birth, altered genetically to age to 21, and then are educated in a university until the player has a need to take over the child because a parent character died.

In fact, we have taken every possible precaution to prevent any sort of under-aged role play. The game itself does not provide any characters under 21 (since characters age virtually, we just start new characters at age 21), and we also avoid the word "child" when it comes to this aspect of sex and rather call them "offspring" so no false idea is given. Also, we keep log files on the server of everything that is said in game. In case somebody informs us of under-aged role play, we can check it here and ban the respective player. Our EULA [user agreement] makes it quite clear that this is forbidden and there is no tolerance if anybody breaks this rule.

Other than children, there are few taboos in *Sociolotron*. We have put great effort into making it possible to break any taboo (as far as legally possible) and have some quite shocking and blasphemous game elements. I believe in free speech and intend to use the rights the USA takes great pride in pointing out all the time. We have excluded some things that are legally questionable, like sex with animals or "furry creatures" or the graphical description of extreme sexual torture. In fact *Sociolotron's* graphic gets away with remarkably little violence and blood, except an occasional splatter on the ground, and I'm quite glad to discover that there are still some people out there who find sex more attractive than gruesome violence.

What was your inspiration in creating Sociolotron?

My inspiration in creating *Sociolotron* was an age-old desire to play a game like this myself. In early pre-Internet times, I discovered various chat rooms and, like most people if they are honest, got into contact with virtual sex. I always thought those online facilities lacked a set of rules like you have in RPGs and prevented people from just doing goofy stuff. Later, I kept searching for games like I thought should be out there, but didn't find any. During my time in the game development industry, I often talked to other game developers about this and most agreed: "Yep, sex sells!" However, no management level person was ready to do anything like that, so I came to the conclusion that sex and games just didn't go together. I'm not talking about those jigsaw puzzles or the Flash animation crap here, but real games. I believe it's because the money people behind each game company just don't want their company being associated with "porn stuff" since that would ruin their reputation. And perhaps they are right.

How would you break down your players (i.e., average age and percent male/female)?

Our player base is pretty much 50:50 between male and female. Today, I would even say it's more like 60:40 in favor of women players. We have an ongoing demographic poll in our forum about gender and location. I don't have exact statistics about the age, but from what I can see, it's mostly between 25 and 40 with many players above 40 years of age. The reason I have an overview here is that until quite recently, we offered an alternative way of signing up for the beta test by allowing players to send us copies of their drivers licenses or passports that I had to process manually. So, I got an approximate overview of the people that signed up, and can confirm the poll results from our forum.

Has anything about its development surprised you?

Yes, I have made some interesting observations that contradicted what I expected in the first place. For instance, when *Socio* opened the first time, sex was permissible anywhere. People had great fun [having sex] with each other in the streets or in the City Hall. Very soon, those same players came to me with complaints that they couldn't go anywhere without stepping in virtual body fluids and demanded that I implement some rules to prevent that. After a few review cycles, we reached the present system where robot guards patrol certain areas and kick butt should anybody have sex in public places. In turn, to bring up your exhibitionism urge [a statistic in the game], which in turn gives you certain advantages in fight, you have to have sex in public places thus taking a risk. Also, characters now have cameras to take pictures of other characters that have sex in public places in case no guard is present, and thus bring them to justice. This shows that the sexual behavior that one might expect in a virtual playground like *Socio* isn't necessarily what the people really want, even in a game. There are certainly interesting behavioral patterns to explore once the artificial restrictions of human society are gone.

What type of sexual content is found in Sociolotron?

Sociolotron offers very straightforward sexual depiction. Since we don't allow minors in our game, we don't have to cover up anything and can pretty much do anything as long as it's legal. Unfortunately, what we can show is restricted by technology. Since *Socio* is a small-scale game project, and I am no trained graphic artist, I had to use ready-made characters and cloths for *Poser 5* to create the animations. Since 3D multicharacter animations like embrace, insertion, and so on are hard to depict with 2D overlay graphics like the sprites used in *Socio*, the graphics don't always fit. Also, we have memory restrictions since every new position causes hundreds of kilobytes or several megabytes of new graphics for all the cloths, equipment, and so on that must be rendered for all animation steps for the new posture. Our sexual content is therefore restricted to a handful of different postures, something in the dimension of 10 or so, which can be combined in various ways to create a multitude of sexual interactions. In addition to the graphics, we have a lot of text output that describes what's going on just like in an automated story or a script. This text comes from a time when *Socio* was planned to be a pure text game where, of course, text was the only form of sexual activity. Therefore, these text descriptions are quite lavish now, more than you would expect from a graphical game. The style is debatable, though. I wanted to include sex in a more dirty form to give people a contrast to the vanilla sex most have at home, but many people don't like the style. Since I didn't have the time to add additional styles, I added a button that allows players to turn off the sexual descriptions altogether and rely completely on text-driven role play to describe their own actions. The graphical sex output is nice, but it's nothing to keep people hooked over a long period of time, just as a porn movie eventually gets old. That's why virtual sex will always have to rely on the fantasy and the writing abilities of the players involved. [Patric01]

INTERVIEW WITH RAY SCHWARTZ

Red Light Center is a virtual world where users meet regularly to chat, dance, and party within the environment. The world includes nightclubs, hotels, and even a brothel. Ray Schwartz is the president of Utherverse, Inc., the developer of the online world.

What can visitors do in Red Light Center?

Just like a real city, *RedLightCenter.com* offers users a wide range of virtual reality attractions such as live shows in theaters, live bands in concert halls, erotic story readings, movies, shopping, art galleries, and a host of other events that can be enjoyed with other users in the world.

RedLightCenter.com is a 3D virtual overlay to the Internet. A free software package provides users with free access to our adult-oriented world. Once there, a user can customize their character "avatar," interact with other users/avatars all in real time, and explore our commercial free universe.

Inspired by the famous Red Light District in Amsterdam, *RedLightCenter.com* is a community of open-minded adults who are real people from across the globe. Although we operate the software, all the businesses that populate the city are independently owned and operated.

What would you say is particularly innovative about your world?

This is the Internet's most incredible social experience for adults. Women and men can live out any of their fantasies in a completely safe and empowering environment. After all, who wouldn't want to be able to socialize with beautiful real people who are there to have fun, without having to put themselves together, or fight traffic?

Within the *RedLightCenter* universe, women—and men—have the opportunity to "meet" within an erotic community and can then either text each other, or speak to each other using our Voice Over Internet Protocol (VoIP) chat features. Couples can have an exciting date at a club or at one of the art galleries or simply by taking a long walk around the romantic city. If they wish to engage in sexual activity, they have a variety of locations and opportunities to do so, providing both agree.

Game industry players say this is porn . . .

While *RedLightCenter* has adult movies and images for our VIP members, the majority of our users come to *RedLightCenter* to be part of our social community. Porn sites are created for an isolated, single user to watch adult material, and generally porn sites target to males.

RedLightCenter has created a site that's appealing for females. We've found out what women want and have been providing it. We rely on our community a lot, for feedback. We have a very active forum on the site and we've paid very close attention to what people have to say, especially women. We want them to feel comfortable and safe. We have many areas that are nonsexual, like our new Lagoon. It's a total underwater playground . . . women can become mermaids if they wish [Schwartz02].

REFERENCES

[Aero01] "Aerowolf," interview with Brenda Brathwaite, May 16, 2006.

[Aero02] "Aerowolf," interview with Brenda Brathwaite, May 16, 2006.

[Bartle01] Bartle, Richard, interview with Brenda Brathwaite, May 16, 2006.

[Bartle02] Bartle, Richard, interview with Brenda Brathwaite, May 16, 2006.

[Bartle03] Bartle, Richard, interview with Brenda Brathwaite, May 16, 2006.

[BBC01] BBC Online Network, "'Nude Raiders' Face Legal Action'," Available online at *http://news.bbc.co.uk/2/hi/science/nature/299040.stm.* Accessed July 1, 2006.

[Compton01] Compton, Jason, interview with Brenda Brathwaite, May 15, 2006.

[Compute01] Reeder, Sara, "Computer Game Ethics," *Compute!*, issue 137, p. 100, January 1992. Available online at *http://www.atarimagazines.com/compute/issue137/100_Computer_game_ethics.php.* Accessed June 12, 2006.

[ESA01] The Entertainment Software Association, "Essential Facts About the Computer and Video Game Industry," p. 2, 2006 edition. Available online at *http://www.theesa.com/archives/files/Essential%20Facts%202006.pdf.* Accessed July 2, 2006.

[GRay01] Graner Ray, Sheri, instant message to Brenda Brathwaite, July 3, 2006.

[Joystiq01] Cole, Vladimir, Joystiq.com, "Verizon, Cingular Whitewash Mobile content [update 1]," April 27, 2006. Available online at *http://www.joystiq .com/2006/04/27/verizons-rules-whitewash-mobile-content/*. Accessed June 15, 2006.

[Joystiq02] Quilty-Harper, Conrad, Joystiq.com, "Fox ""investigates"" PSP Porn [update 1]," June 1, 2006. Available online at *http://www.joystiq.com/2006/ 06/01/fox-investigates-psp-porn/*. Accessed June 16, 2006.

[Lula01] Lula 3D site, "Story." Available online at *http://www.lula.de/usa/index1 .htm*. Accessed June 1, 2006.

[Meretzky01] Meretzky, Steve, interview with Brenda Brathwaite, August 2, 2005.

[Meretzky02] Ibid.

[Meretzky03] Ibid.

[Meretzky04] Ibid.

[Newell01] Newell, Neil, interview with Brenda Brathwaite, May 18, 2006.

[Newell02] Ibid.

[Newell03] Ibid.

[Newell04] Ibid.

[Patric01] Lagny, Patric, interview with Brenda Brathwaite, June 24, 2005.

[Schwartz02] Schwartz, Ray, interview with Brenda Brathwaite, July 1, 2006.

[Scott01] Scott, Jason, interview with Brenda Brathwaite, May 16, 2006.

3 Emergent Sex

In This Chapter

- What Is Emergent Sex?
- Why Emergent Sex Appeals to Players
- Emergent Sex & Fetishes
- What Emergent Sex Can Teach Developers of Adult Content
- Emergent Sex Game Hardware
- Emergent Sex Economies
- Emergent Family Structures
- Jealousy in Virtual Worlds

WHAT IS EMERGENT SEX?

Emergent sex happens when two people have "cybersex" in a game not specifically created to allow or facilitate such behaviors. As with sex in our lives, emergent sex in a video game spans the full range of human behavior. Emergent sex can be as innocent as flirting between players of two avatars in an MMORPG, or may involve hardware that allows for pain actuation among players interested in virtual BDSM (bondage and sadomasochism). Emergent sex has spawned virtual pregnancies and births, entire economies, and even prostitution. Bear in mind that none of these systems or abilities was a part of the released game's design. They were created by the players and emerged from the desires, the systems, and the tools available to them.

Consider, for example, the game *World of Warcraft*. In *World of Warcraft*, players create avatars to play an online role-playing game. They solve quests, slay monsters, develop their avatars as they gain experience, and join guilds to partake in the social community that has developed around the game. The sexiest thing in all its design is the dance animation for the Night Elf character that sways her hips seductively back and forth. Despite this virtual lack of sexual content, however, *World of Warcraft* contains emergent sex. Using a personal instant messaging program built into the game, players type to one another. The content of their talk can get as steamy as their imaginations. One such conversation was inadvertently broadcast on the open chat channel—one that anyone can see—and its subsequent "video capture" made the rounds on various Internet sites. Another *real* video capture also made the rounds on the Internet, and featured a man caught masturbating to the same Night Elf animation mentioned earlier. Machinima porn—pornographic game movies—using *World of Warcraft* as its setting have also been developed. The game has even spawned an erotic site, World of Porncraft.

When emergent sex first appeared is difficult to pinpoint. There are several likely suspects:

MUD, 1978: Created by Richard Bartle and Roy Trubshaw at the University of Essex in 1978, *MUD* created the virtual gaming world. Within that world, however, there was no privacy, so what one member did, all could see. This lack of privacy likely kept the sexual appetites of many potential cyberers in check. Surely, some may have found the exhibitionist nature of *MUD* more of a turn on than a turn off. In an interview with this author, Bartle noted that to the best of his knowledge, no emergent sex occurred in *MUD*, at least early on [Bartle01]. It was only when *MUD* reached America that emergent sex appeared. Rather than his own game, however, Bartle thought another game might hold the honor.

Shades, 1984: Created by Neil Newell, a player of Bartle's and Trubshaw's *MUD*, *Shades* was also a multiuser environment, but featured one key thing *MUD* did not—private rooms. That private area, according to the game's author, is the reason why emergent sex likely first occurred in his world. "Back then, all other games gave high-level players unlimited power to see everything another player did," says Newell. "*Shades*, by comparison, had 'safe areas' where fighting was disallowed and snooping was impossible (even for programmers/admins)." *Shades* safe areas included a church, pub, and even a hotel with bedrooms and a bridal suite, and players could choose who came into those rooms with them. According to Newell, "people took to locking themselves in the bedrooms for private conversations and, as became apparent after a while, rather more than that!" [Newell01].

BBS Door Games, 1981: BBS door games allowed users to interact with one another in a virtual world of sorts. In effect, the BBS served as a "door" to an external application. The popularity of modems soared in 1984 with the release of the movie *Wargames*, and with that popularity came a flood of new people into these worlds. While it's possible that the first emergent sex occurred in a door game in the very early 1980s—1980, 1981, or 1982—so far, there is no *direct* evidence that it did, although this author certainly welcomes the possibility. From the early 1980s, however, there were sexually themed door games and BBSes. Clearly, in these worlds, sex was the theme. However, since it was welcomed, encouraged, and the primary topic of conversation, it doesn't qualify as emergent.

Today, emergent sex is common in all MMORPGs and many multiuser spaces such as MUDs, MUCKs, MOOs, and MUSHes.

When it comes to sheer volume of emergent sex within a single game, however, *Second Life* is the undisputed king. Players start the game with an average, off-the-shelf avatar that they can customize in literally hundreds of different ways, from the size and color of the lips to the width of the torso. Players can—and do—spend lots of time or lots of Lindens (the in-game currency) to make their avatars beautiful, whatever their definition of beauty might be. As in any game where hundreds of people play, emergent sex is present. Unlike other games, however, *Second Life*'s support of user-created content, including animations and attachments to characters, has allowed its emergent sexual content to go further than any game before.

How far have the players taken it and what can they do? The options seem virtually as endless as the imaginations and desires of its players. When *Second Life* avatars start the game, they are the virtual equivalent of dolls without any sex organs. However, since players can attach things to their characters, in-game stores have sprung up that sell virtual penises, breasts, and vaginas that may be "worn" by the characters. Unlike real-world strap-on penises, these meshes fit rather seamlessly over the avatar's body. In many cases, these objects have various states—flaccid and erect. They also come in many sizes, shapes, and colors. When the avatars of two players have sex, the penis and the vagina fit together as they would in the real world. Same sex pairings are also supported in the world, as is sex between non-human avatars. While people who have not played *Second Life* may visualize the world as a completely erotic one based on this information, it's not the case. In fact, unless they're in a location where it's encouraged and expected, players will not likely see people walking around with erections any more than they would in the real world. In fact, the *Second Life* community is very respectful of others.

Whether or not characters are equipped with virtual genitalia, they may have sex in hundreds of different ways (the genitalia merely adds something to the game's aesthetic). In a traditional MMO, avatars having sex are limited by the animations provided by the system. Often, they lay themselves down next to one another in the game, and all the "action" occurs in their imaginations and through a private chat channel. In *Second Life*, however, players use objects that contain "pose balls" that animate their avatars. Therefore, clicking on an object designed for sex, and there are many, the players can actually see their avatars having sex with another avatar.

The range of possibilities within *Second Life* is often boggling to those unfamiliar with the range of human sexual desire. *Second Life* is home to many communities—from BDSM to furries to fetishes not even possible in the real world. Rising to meet this demand, objects have been created that facilitate erotic encounters for a variety of tastes, whatever the taste may be. These objects can be purchased in *Second Life* at various stores and online at such places as SLBoutique.com. There are even locations within the world that are known for a specific type of content. Some advertise their services and admission to others is for members only. To cover all this emergent sexual content, in-game magazines such as "Sluster" and "Play Pony" have been created. The more mainstream "Second Life Herald" covers all manner of *Second Life* news in addition to stories relating to sexual content and regularly features a "Post Six Grrrl," a beautiful avatar from the game.

WHY EMERGENT SEX APPEALS TO PLAYERS

Emergent sex appeals to us for the same reason real sex appeals to us: humans are designed to react emotionally and physically to sexual stimuli. It's no different in game worlds where one human (or one thing) attracts another. But why emergent sex? Why seek romantic or sexual relationships and sex play in games not designed to promote or facilitate it? If players have easy access to online sex games and even massively multiplayer online erotic games, why would they return again and again to online worlds where no sexual content purposefully exists?

The reasons are varied.

Mimicry

Emergent sex mimics real life behavior. Consider for a moment a typical Friday night in Anytown, USA. A group of female friends is preparing to head out for the evening. They plan to go to the local dance club to have a good time. It's quite possible that one or more of them will meet a man at the club, and it's possible they may flirt with men and even develop relationships with them. Such behavior in the bar is emergent and rises from the community of people, the setting, and, in more than a few cases, the drinks available.

In MMOs, which are likewise a community of individuals with similar interests, the possibilities are the same. Players meet one another in dozens of different ways—through guilds, by teaming up to solve quests, or by just striking up a conversation when they happen to be online together. By mimicking the social communities and interactions of real life, players feel a degree of comfort when relationships develop. Such behavior is natural and normal whenever groups of humans interact.

Therefore, in many cases, emergent sex isn't the primary aim of players, but arises naturally, as it does in any social context where groups of human beings gather.

Social Acceptability

Although mainstream America largely eschews pornography and sexuality for more conservative media content, the vernacular America nonetheless is a heavy erotica consumer. However, despite people's inner desires, the outer social acceptability of their behavior still weighs upon people's buying and social decisions. This is particularly true in MMOs where communities form and continue to grow through real-world connections. When a woman plays, she may invite her husband and her friends to join her in the online world. Inviting someone with whom you are not intimate to a massively multiplayer online erotic game (MMOEG) is quite another matter, however.

Consider that same group of female friends mentioned earlier. Now, imagine that one of these women suggests to the group, "Hey, let's go to a swingers club tonight!" The reactions are likely to be quite varied. While open relationships are not uncommon, an average group of women is unlikely to a respond with a "Yeah, let's do that!" Singles bars likewise carry a social stigma, particularly to less liberal people.

The parallel between singles clubs and dance clubs and MMOEGs and MMORPGs is an important one. Some of the reasons—social stigmas, conservatism, and embarrassment—that keep people from a singles club may keep them from an MMOEG as well. At the same time, some of the barriers that keep people from exploring singles or swingers clubs in the real world don't apply in the online space where anonymity is a key factor. Playing under her avatar name, no one will ever know that the receptionist in the front office went onto *Second Life* last night and had an exceptionally wild time with multiple men, or that a quiet and soft-spoken man spent his time in *Second Life* playing as a for-hire female dominatrix named Cheri Horton (*www.apogeevr.com*).

Aside from these factors, the sheer number of people in nonsexually themed MMOs when taken in conjunction with basic human instinct and behavior is likely to produce the same results any gathering spot of human beings produces—friends, relationships, and even real-life weddings. Meeting someone on an MMO is unique but still, for the most part, socially acceptable. Meeting someone on an erotic online game tends to carry a certain degree of baggage.

Griefing and High-Speed Sex

In many online games, "griefing" is an issue. Griefing occurs when one player or a group of players hassles or kills another player's avatar or treats them in an inappropriate way. In MMOEGs and other online sex chat spaces, griefing most often comes in the form of unwanted advances or "high speed" sexual interactions.

To understand the nature of this issue, Yahoo® chat serves as a good laboratory. As a service, Yahoo chat has literally hundreds of different groups discussing a huge array of topics. Among these are groups where people go to meet others for relationships from the mild to the wild. Within seconds of arriving in one of these adult-themed groups, without fail, this author received a private message asking if she were interested in sex. Message after message after message followed, making it impossible to have any preliminary discussion with any of the other individuals online. "What did you expect?" is a fair and oft-asked question. In the course of researching this book, what this author expected is precisely what she found. However, for the average user, say a person interested in meeting others in an online space, such a deluge of messages may be overwhelming and off-putting. That many of the introductory messages were profoundly graphic was also disturbing. As in real life, foreplay is a part of the overall sexual experience. Many of the individuals interviewed on this topic and for this book noted that this was a key component of good cyber sex, too.

So how does this relate to emergent sex? Emergent sex provides a safer environment where sexual interaction is not expected. Therefore, players are far less likely to receive sexually themed griefing messages in these worlds, and the development of intimacy can take place in a "normal" environment instead of a sexually charged one in which sexual activity is presumed to be an end goal. Whether griefing regularly happens in online MMOEGs is a matter of debate. In some online worlds that are designed for erotic play, particularly those with small numbers of players, the players have established standards that all members of the community tend to abide by else they be booted from the world. As these online erotic worlds become bigger and more popular, however, they have the potential to develop problems similar to those of online chat groups. Nonerotic MMOs, by contrast, have few such issues, particularly when compared to the bulk of the communication and interaction in the game. Therefore, to minimize griefing and high-speed sex, many players seek emergent interactions in nonerotic MMOs instead.

Mystery and Surprise

Andrea is a frequent player of MMOs and enjoys emergent sex in these worlds. For her, the lure of MMOs versus MMOEGs is in the surprise and mystery she finds within the MMOs. "If I enter a sex-based game, I know what I am 'ordering' and what will be delivered, which waters it all down," she said. "Sex will be just a carton of milk from the local store instead of a gift wrapped bottle of champagne. In an MMORPG you never know what will happen and when, since sex is something that happens spontaneously" [Andrea01].

For Andrea, a sex-based game ruins the sense of mystery, of wondering what will happen, and that sense of mystery and wondering can be a turn on in itself, a form of cyber foreplay.

"When the game is sex-based, everyone knows why we are all there—for one thing only: to get sexual kicks. Now whilst this is kind of kinky and exciting to know that everyone you see there is 'on the prowl,' and you can literally smell the hormones in the air, at the same time, the sexual encounters lose some value because you are not special. You are just a sexual outlet for someone who crosses your path. Someone who has 'done' dozens before you and will 'do' dozens after. If you'll be remembered, it's only because you had a neat way of giving virtual [sex]. It's kind of degrading and hollow" [Andrea02].

In addition to the strong sense of mystery and surprise, MMOs also excel at the proverbial thrill of the chase. As Andrea says, "Although I am not one to enjoy relationship-based cat and mouse games, I do enjoy them for building up sexual tension. Cat and mouse games are just that—games. And like any game, they give you a sense of achievement when you are successful in luring the other on to the next level of intimacy. Those little triumphs make you feel sexually competent. How can you have that in a sex-based game when everyone knows what you are there for?" [Andrea03]. In an MMO, interaction between avatars and between players rarely starts with anything sexual. Rather, it builds up over time if the other party is receptive to such behavior. This give and take, this "cat and mouse" style and the excitement in the uncertainty within a game where sex is not a given, is more likely to produce the necessary sexual tension for many who enjoy cybersex.

Genuine Bonding

The development of sexual intimacy is often one of the last links in a long chain. A couple meets, they flirt, and they may date. They develop a friendship and an emotional trust that may then lead to emotional intimacy. Finally, their emotional involvement may lead to sexual intimacy. This entire process is one of genuine bonding. A "one night stand" or casual sex, while it may result in bonding of some sort, does not necessarily have the same impact. While such a description is clearly a simplified one, it nonetheless illustrates what may happen in MMOs versus MMOEGs.

Andrea described it this way, "Sex is wonderful, but when you are genuinely infatuated with someone you have gotten to know, any sexual chemistry is a zillion times more intense." Andrea believes that bonding is a normal part of MMORPGs, and indeed, it is. People bond for missions, as friends and in guilds. When that bonding happens on a romantic level, however, it can lead to a traditional and real-world style of courting that heightens the sexual chemistry between two individuals.

Andrea relates an experience that happened to her in *World of Warcraft*. "Why just last night I was standing on the docks of Booty Bay in *WoW*, fishing peacefully and watching the sea glitter as the sun was setting. It was beautiful and peaceful. Then along came a handsome fisherman who decided to join me. So, there we fished, side by side for about four hours, finding it hard to break away because of the great chemistry we had going. We talked and talked about a multitude of things and sure enough, it advanced to small flirtation. I added him secretly to my friends list because I felt that we bonded, even in that short time, and will look out for him from now on. Now if all that happened in one evening, just imagine what many more nights of romantic and relaxed fishing scenarios will do, and where it might lead in say a month's time? All the time it takes us to bond up to a possible sexual scenario is tantalizing and exciting. It's like mental foreplay building up to one huge explosion." [Andrea04].

By removing the presumption of cybersex, MMOs have an edge over MMOEGs in the development of bonding between individuals.

Spontaneity

Among lovers, spontaneity is sexy. Making love at 3 P.M. every single day, while still pleasurable, loses some of its heat when it's so planned. In existing relationships within MMOs, the effect of spontaneity is no different. Where sexual content is expected as in an MMOEG, some players believe a degree of spontaneity is lost.

"Let's say I have a lover in an MMORPG, and we've already taken it all the way, but since we like to spend time together in general, we go out hunting and questing, sit in taverns enjoying an ale and go out adventuring," said Andrea. "The sexual scenarios don't have a set time or place—nor are they regular. They happen spontaneously due to events in the game leading up to that certain moment." Andrea went on to describe an instance in *World of Warcraft* in which her character and that character's boyfriend went on a quest but had to travel through an Orc village to get to their destination. After the quest was done, they had to come back through that same village and decided to attack the Orcs on their way through. When the last of the Orcs had died, the couple felt like winners, like champions, with their pockets full of riches. They felt a certain happiness in rejoicing their success with one another. In this state of high, they then noticed a tilted stretched-out hide. "My character decided to lay down on it and noticed that she could look up at the starry night sky. She also exclaimed how comfy it was to lay there after the sweaty battle. Her boyfriend promptly joined her, and so there they lay, looking up at the stars together. They haven't known each other very long, so they are still a bit shy about touching, but that night had magic in it, and eventually they ended up in each others arms for the first time ever and ended up spending many hours just talking and enjoying the closeness." [Andrea05].

The Limits of Computer Graphics

When it first began, emergent sex in online worlds was completely text based. However, this never proved a limitation for anyone. In fact, many text-based worlds still exist. After all, steamy text can be as tantalizing, as stimulating as anything visual, and in many cases, it could be even more stimulating. Although chat exists in both MMOs and MMOEGs, MMOs might have the advantage.

At first, such a presumption seems odd. How could a game with sexual animations and graphics *not* be superior as a vehicle for sex? Simply put, baring a few exceptionally deep pockets within the video game space or games that rely on user-generated content like *Second Life*, few companies could afford to create enough animations and enough avatars to truly allow for a player's full freedom of choice. The art cannot keep up with the imagination, and if players are staring at avatars in a missionary position on the screen, they're more likely to discuss what they see *instead* of letting their imagination wander. Graphics are not the key thing here. As a case in point, consider how many couples turn out the light when they make love.

Ultimately, online worlds like *Second Life* are best positioned to satisfy players. By allowing users to create their own content, the game facilitates imagination through chat and animations.

Size of the Community

In standard MMOs, the user base is many hundreds of times larger than the average MMOEG. Such a huge amount of players provides people with more variety. Within these larger MMOs, communities that share like experiences tend to develop, and out of those communities and the larger community as a whole, relationships are formed. Through their sheer size and marketing power, they draw people by the thousands. It's only logical that more emergent behavior would take place in such worlds.

By comparison, consider a site like Match.com® with its millions of members. If you were looking for a place to meet people, would you select it or a community that had 100 members, at best?

While most people would choose the former, there are cases where people would choose a smaller community. Many of the existing MMOEGs are small by desire. They tend to cater to people with specific interests, and new members are often referred by existing members to protect the culture of the community.

EMERGENT SEX & FETISHES

People with various fetishes find outlets for them within video games, both single player and multiplayer. For instance, voraphiles—individuals who find being eaten sexually stimulating—can satisfy their fetish virtually in many video games. One game on which this author was a designer featured a monster that swallowed a character in the player's party. When the monster was killed, the character was retrieved, complete with acid damage. This game later turned up on a list of games at a voraphile site. In another example, games also allow "furries"—individuals who find others dressed and role playing as animals sexually stimulating—to actually play games as a furry creature.

Games can easily facilitate numerous fetishes, particularly in online worlds that allow user-created, highly customized avatars:

- **Andromimetophila:** Being turned on by women impersonating a man.
- **Necrophilia:** Being turned on by having sex with the dead (or undead).
- **Spectrophilia:** Being turned on by sex with spirits.
- **Morphophilia:** Being turned on by peculiar body shapes and sizes.

This list is but a small sample of the possibilities. In fact, online worlds are actually giving rise to new fetishes not possible in reality. If someone desires to have sexual encounters with an invisible being or while on fire or while a dragon, it'll be a challenge in the real world.

Where games facilitate fetishes, none of this facilitation was the direct intent of the game's designers. At best, it is indirect in worlds where user-created content is the norm and promoted by the MMO's host.

WHAT EMERGENT SEX CAN TEACH DEVELOPERS OF ADULT CONTENT

It happens every day in MMOs—two avatars lay next to each other in a virtual world chatting it up over an instant messaging program. While it may seem that an event like that wouldn't have much to teach developers of actual adult content, few things could be further from the truth. If players are going so far as to create complete sex economies, families, and a means of engaging in cybersex, clearly, there's something to be learned. It may be as simple as human nature applied: where there's a will, there's a way. For developers of adult content, however, the "way" needs to harness the existing "will" that's being displayed in spades in nonsexual online worlds. Beyond human nature, though, why are they doing this? What makes them comfortable? Why are women far more attracted to these types of scenarios than other online sex games? What are these nonsexual communities like *Second Life* doing right?

Setting Realistic Player Expectations

All game design factors in player expectation. What are they hoping to get when they buy a game? What options do they expect? Who do they want to be? What do they want to do? Each of these questions must be addressed by the game designer.

To the extent that designers meet or fail to meet these expectations, their products will succeed or fail. Sometimes, marketing or sales push player expectations too high, particularly when it comes to sexual content development. Trumpeting games as the "most life-like" and "guaranteed to satisfy" sets the bar unnecessarily high and, in effect, sets the game up to stumble before it's even left the proverbial gates. While it may seem like a logical "win" to many—games with some sexual content would be better than games with no sexual content—it's not necessarily true. When you set no bar at all, you can only go up. When you bill yourself as the "greatest in the world," you can only go down. When it comes to *emergent* sex in virtual worlds, players generally have no expectations. They're in the world to get gain levels, explore, and solve missions. They're not expecting to find a wife or form a relationship or have cybersex by the side of an in-game lake. They can only be surprised.

Realistic marketing and sales efforts coupled with a design that's not too ambitious can go a long way toward meeting player expectation. Surprise the player by being what you say you are.

Allow Players to Create Content in MMOEGs

No matter the number of artists and programmers thrown at a project, their work will never keep pace with the ability of the imagination's sexual desire. Worlds like *Second Life* recognize this and allow users to create their own content, from the animations to sexy clothing to genitals. What's not created now, provided there is a desire, is sure to be created in the future. In worlds like *World of Warcraft* where the sexual content is virtually nil and players cannot create animations, body parts, and clothing, players are able to chat about what they feel and would like to do to one another. In effect, the sexual landscape of these games is open-ended and unlimited. In *World of Warcraft*, if you can think it, you can type it. In *Second Life*, you can actually make it.

Games with sexual content, however, often don't think to give their players the same liberty. They create whole libraries of animations—man on top, woman on top, oral sex, and making out. This, then, is their closed "feature" set. When players wish for positions not provided, they don't view these positions as *opportunities* for creation. Rather, they view them as *limitations* and faults in the design. It's all a matter of player perception.

By enabling and allowing players to create their own content or to mod the product, their perception of the game is enhanced. In the end, the game is likely to enjoy a longer shelf life and the developer saves money on the most expensive part of game development—content creation.

Of course, it goes without saying that a tragic game cannot be saved by adding the ability for users to create content. If the core mechanics are not solid and the game doesn't have visual appeal, no amount of user created content will help it.

Marketing to Both Genders

Women like sex, too, but judging from the games online, few are trying to market to that segment of the market. Although some games could be of interest to women, the advertising or Web splash pages for them are so lopsided that in some cases, women may actually be repelled. Consider, for example, an online world that advertises "eager babes waiting to" do something with the player. While this may appeal to some women, in all likelihood, it will send a "this is for men" message to far more. Other games that feature virtual couples having sex could also appeal to women or couples who enjoy pornography. However, when the game refers to the women as "sluts" or "whores," its appeal goes down for many.

The video game market, while still plagued by its own issues of gender bias in advertising, is at least making inroads and discussing the issue. Sheri Graner Ray, author of *Gender Inclusive Game Design*, regularly appears at industry events to discuss barriers that keep women from playing games, including the Sex in Video Games Conference in the summer of 2006. Panels address marketing to women and whole conferences have been put together to tackle the very issue of women in games and marketing games to women.

Sex games, however, are a long way out.

How does this relate to emergent sex? Games in which emergent sex is the most prevalent also enjoy an audience composed of many female players. *Second Life*, for example, boasts that nearly half of its players are female. In June 2006, 57% of players were male compared with 43% female [Linden01]. By targeting and not repelling the female market, sex games stand to become more profitable.

Some adult game developers are catching on, though. By marketing their games to women, designing with them in mind, using respectful language, and incorporating safeguards into the design that prevent griefing, developers are hoping women will show up. The principle here has been applied a thousand times, from "ladies nights" at bars where women drink for free to 900 phone lines that allow women to call for free but charge the men who want to talk with them. If the women show up, so will the men.

The Range of Human Sexuality

Game developers are not sexologists, and the speed at which emergent sex in online worlds morphs and evolves is nothing short of astounding. New fetishes are created. Communities unite for and against issues. Communities emerge, communities grow, and communities that support particular fetishes sometimes go underground. When articles are written that address the behavior of a community, particularly if those articles are incorrect or incomplete in their analysis, the communities become quite vocal. All of these various activities are played out on an emergent stage and provide excellent research material for makers of adult content. In the preparation of this book, this author found these communities were more than willing to share information, secrets, and stories, provided they were treated with respect.

Online emergent sexual communities are only one such source for information, of course. Adult content developers would do well to tear a page from the book of standard software developers—hire experts. In the case of adult games, sexologists have much information to offer. The field of sexology in the online space is only beginning to be understood, however.

EMERGENT SEX GAME HARDWARE

When Sega released *Rez*™, their quirky music shooter on November 21, 2001, sex was nowhere to be found on its feature list. However, it has become one of the most well-known aspects of the game.

The premise of the *Rez* is simple enough. The player is a hacker who enters a computer system hoping to save Eden, the computer's AI and controller of its music. This is done by progressing through various levels and shooting anything that gets in the way. Each level starts with a basic musical score that grows in complexity the further players go, effectively allowing them to create their own music. Players even attack in rhythm with the game. The Japanese version of the game shipped with a unique hardware peripheral whose purpose, evidently, was to allow players to fully experience the pounding trance-like music they create as the game progresses. The peripheral, The Trance Vibrator, is approximately 5 inches long and 3 inches wide and plugs into the PS2's controller port. It has no buttons of any kind. In effect, it's a rectangle that vibrates, and its vibration is reportedly four times stronger than a PS2 controller's vibration [Wired01]. Not surprisingly, players have used it for purposes other than those intended by the developers.

The Web site *www.gamegirladvance.com* features a somewhat tongue-in-cheek commentary about a couple's experience with the game and its peripheral. In a nutshell, the woman's partner plays the game while she puts the peripheral between her legs to achieve sexual pleasure [GGA01].

In an article in the May 2003 issue of *Wired* magazine, the creator of *Rez*, Tetsuya Mizuguchi, notes that players are free to put the peripheral anywhere they like. Their choices, he notes, are limited only by their imagination [Wired02].

Although it's arguably the most famous, *Rez* was not the first emergent sexual hardware in games. In fact, the first perceived sexual hardware appeared nearly 18 years earlier. In 1973, Atari released the arcade game *Gotcha*. Its controls consisted of two pink rubber mounds. The game quickly became known as "the boob game" although the content of the game itself was not at all overtly sexual.

Engineers have also created sexual hardware mods. Since both the Xbox® and the PS®2 controllers support vibration, engineers can modify the controllers to provide sexual tactile feedback. Typically, developers use this feature to provide players feedback on an event in the game. For instance, it may signal a particularly devastating hit, a massive spell, or a jump from a great height. Controller modders remove the vibration devices from inside the controller and insert them into dildos. The site *www.slashdong.org* calls their version the SeXBox [SD01] (Figure 3.1) and offers their modded controllers for sale. Although it may go without saying, use of homemade electronics, particularly those inserted into the human body, is not recommended and could be harmful or fatal.

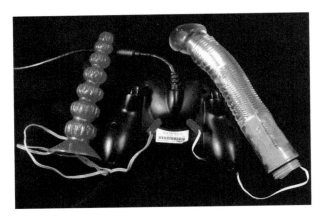

FIGURE 3.1 Slashdong.org's SeXBox. Image © 2005 Kyle Machulis. Reprinted with permission.

How did the SeXBox come to be? "To be honest, the initial SeXBox was just made out of boredom and silliness, and it had as much 'emergent meaning' as games have had 'emergent sex,'" says Kyle Machulis, creator of the SeXBox. "I've passed it off as a teledildonics device as a way to make games into sexual environments, as a teaching tool for electronics and engineering. As an idea, it's gained a life of its own, and I'm happy to let it grow that way" [Machulis02]. In the future, whether teledildonics and games will move beyond the emergent sexual sphere in any serious way is hard to say. Machulis believes that the merger is years away. While acknowledging that games already integrate vibration, Machulis says that "making it so that the games have context for the sexual version of feedback is going to be very difficult, and I think we'll see a lot of misses before we have any hits. We might see sex games that have hardware interaction inside of 2006. However, for mainstream use, people will have to get used to the idea of toys before they get used to the idea of games *with* toys, and that could takes years. All depends on the social climate of the times, and that's rather unpredictable these days" [Machulis03].

EMERGENT SEX ECONOMIES

As the first MMOs launched, no one thought, "How will we handle prostitution?" However, according to a game designer Richard Garriott, virtual prostitution was one of the early issues for *Ultima Online*. According to Garriott, virtual prostitution was "one of the first 'emergent behaviors'" and happened "within a few minutes of turning on the service."

"Two people had logged into the game and one person was 'pimping' for the other, who would then lead people into a storeroom along the docks where they hung out and 'ooh and ah' at the 'John.' The game supported no depictions of sex, but the player 'demand' was clearly present, and they engineered their own solution." [Garriott01].

Ultima Online was merely one of the first in a long chain of major MMOs to face the issue of virtual prostitution and escorts. From *World of Warcraft* to *Second Life*, prostitution is one of the online world's oldest professions. It's even made its way to eBay® where a seller once offered a date with a Night Elf, and is prevalent enough in some worlds that Web sites devoted to in-game escorts were born. The blog "Second Life Escort Ratings," for instance, ranks escorts in *Second Life*.

In early 2006, magazine *Computer Games World (CGW)* wrote an entire feature on a prostitution district within *Second Life*. *CGW* spoke with an escort, Taboo Heart, who worked in one of *Second Life*'s adult districts, Amster-Dame. According to the escort, customers generally approached her by sending an instant message requesting prices or other information. While some escorts approach customers with offers, this particular escort did not. Rather, she waited for johns to come to her. Tricks last 30 minutes, according to the article. The trick may include all kinds of sexual stimuli, from visual representations of the avatars having sex to custom-created sound and video clips that show the person behind the avatar masturbating [PCM01].

Some online games have tried to prevent prostitution, but ultimately, it's an uphill battle. As Garriott suggested, if player demand is present, they will engineer a solution. But what about games where there is no currency? If you can't pay for sex in a game, is virtual prostitution even possible? Experience suggests that it is. With no currency and prohibited from using sexual terms, players in a game called *Habbo Hotel* created an emergent sex economy and language—they "babboed" for furniture. Chairs actually became a commodity through which people paid for emergent sex. Some games in development as this book goes to press have suggested that by removing all economy from a game—nothing to trade and no money at all—they can get around the issue of emergent sex trade. As Kyle Machulis of the site MMOrgy.com put it, "That's when they'll go to *Paypal®*" [Machulis01].

EMERGENT FAMILY STRUCTURES

Sex may lead to pregnancy, and pregnancy leads to families. This process is now mirrored in some virtual worlds.

The following article, *A Bundle of Polys*, by Kyle Machulis appeared on the site MMOrgy.com and is reprinted here with permission.

For all of our coverage of virtual world sex, it would logically follow that at some point, someone would want to simulate full reproduction. Virtual conception and pregnancy are by no means a new idea. From the BBS days when couples could have children in LORD, games have evolved in terms of what players could do with conceiving children, with games like *Sociolotron* having built-in rule systems for pregnancy (including menstrual cycles), and virtual worlds like *Second Life* have emergent conception and pregnancy markets.

In this article, we start our series on in-world pregnancy by covering something that is general to all of the virtual worlds, reasons for wanting to engage in virtual conception and pregnancy. Though each world offers a different setting and rule structure, many of the reasons users would want to experience childbirth and raising [children] in a simulated environment stay the same.

The first question that comes to the non-user's mind is probably "What's available?" Though we'll be covering this for specific worlds in later articles, we'll discuss pregnancy in some of the MMOrgy covered worlds briefly. *Second Life* has a rather large pregnancy market. From ultrasound units and delivery rooms to scripted babies and nursery sets, the amount of baby related user-built content is massive. *Sociolotron* not only has breeding schedules built into female characters, conception and abortion are available (and sometimes required to have certain events happen in game). *Heavenly Bodies* (not yet released) will allow users to alter the genetic sequence of their children, with children being NPCs until they reach 18 years of age in game, at which point they can be taken over by a user. Child bearing also affects the stats of the player.

The next question is . . . why? In a world where you can do anything, be anything, why procreate in the same way we do in the real world? The answer mirrors the same reasons behind the act of conception or sex in general in virtual worlds. We do what we know how to do, we do what we want to do, [and] we do what we sometimes can't do.

Therapy

Probably the most talked about reasoning on the *Second Life* Forums is therapy. Many couples have expressed that they use *Second Life* to get over a miscarriage or infertility issues in real life. Whether or not this is safe is not something any of us here at MMOrgy are licensed to judge. The fact, that material/virtual things can make people feel better or worse is something that has kept therapists paid well for many a year. [Post from the *Second Life* forums is omitted, but may be found online at *http://secondlife.com/ss/?u=df31fad33033584e5be5f9c37bada267.*]

Practice

Virtual world babies are absolutely no replacement for real babies, but in terms of the "take care of an egg/sack of flour for a week" assignments of secondary school students, online environments can certainly teach as much, if not more. New couples can use virtual babies to get into the habit of child raising schedules and chores and talk to other couples about their experiences. The AI right now is such that the realism of a virtual environment isn't going to be a boon to real life experience, but it could certainly supplement topics learned from other mediums (books, TV, etc . . .).

Can't/Roleplay

Obviously, this can't happen in real life [the article shows a photo of a baby furry]. No matter how much you wish and dream and squeeze kittens and put your real baby in a fursuit (MMOrgy takes no responsibility for squozen kittens or for you putting your real baby in a fursuit), it won't be the same as a furry baby. As virtual worlds provide a way for people to act out fetishes that are not physically possible, it also allows them to live situations that can never be realized. Furry babies are a rather extreme example of this. A couple/group in a long distance relationship may be interested in having a family, and scripted babies may be as close as they can get. In situations such as that (where both parties are mentally stable enough to deal with the gap between reality and the virtual world), anything is better than nothing.

Fun

No one usually references the "Fun" reasons, because there's just not much to say. Virtual worlds are built for fun as much as anything else, and playing house is popular among children not only because it's mimicking actions of adults, but because it's also entertaining. If you can have a no-strings-attached baby, why not? There's no excuse not to have the experience if all it's going to cost is some virtual money. You may get bored with it in five minutes, or it may deepen your role play. But, it's something you can say you did, at least.

We don't claim this to be anywhere near a full list of the reasons users would want to have virtual children. As with all things in MMOs, experience and personal context are what drive the humans behind the [avatars] to do things, and the number of combinations of those is infinite.

[MMOrgy01]

JEALOUSY IN VIRTUAL WORLDS

As people develop online lovers, the specter of jealousy often rears its head. In this article, *Jealousy: An Emotion That Creeps Into Cyberspace*, Noche Kandora (who plays dominatrix Cheri Horton in *Second Life*) explores the topic. The article originally appeared on Apogeevr.com and is reprinted here with permission.

Let's say I have a crush on Avatar X. And one day, your oversexed avatar flirts with my love interest, gives the digital goods a few once-overs, and then the two of you ultimately go and do the wild thang behind my back. I find out. Would I get [upset]? Honestly, I'd say, . . . yes! I would in fact get [upset]. But to a degree.

Try as you may, it seems you can't totally inoculate yourself against jealousy when you're interacting in a virtual space like *Second Life*. It's a pretty resilient emotion, and one whose sting can easily penetrate the online world's virtual bubble.

The question is, "Where to draw the boundaries?" How much do you permit yourself to be haunted by such feelings while maintaining avatar-to-avatar relationships—and in a place where there is such wonderful leeway to explore fantasy and let go of the inhibitions, prejudices, and other types of hang-ups that plague us in real life?

Blixa Shirakawa, one of several *Second Life* residents whom I solicited thoughts from on this topic, suggests a pretty measured approach when dealing with this type of dilemma. "I believe you must separate your feelings when you're in game to an extent. You can express a part of yourself and bring emotion into your avatar, but you've got to know where the line is drawn once things get physical," Blixa says. "The whole purpose of the game is to explore and meet interesting people. What you choose to do with those people is solely at the discretion of the parties involved. Therefore, if you choose to become intimately involved with avatars and don't feel like playing house with just one, you must make your intentions known up front and make sure the potential partner is OK with it. If not, do not pursue anything other than friendship."

Blixa's philosophy was echoed by fellow SL'er [*Second Life* player] Allaria Campbell, who says she lays everything out bluntly in writing inside *Second Life*. All residents have to do is right click on her digital likeness and access a menu to find out how she feels about playing the field. "I think that like RL [real life], being clear what the terms of your relationship are from early on, and negotiating any changes to those terms, are the key things," she says. "For example: sitting in my SL profile are two things: (1) don't expect me to be faithful and (2) don't ask me questions about RL. Clear limits, expressed early."

Still, she admits being human is unavoidable. "Of course, it's all too easy for your emotions to get involved and to start breaking limits that you set yourself. And if you do get too involved, then jealousy, anger, and vengeance are just around the corner. I guess the key is to remember that it's not real, and to let it go," she says. "Having said all that, I don't doubt that I'll find it difficult when and if it happens to me."

darkchyld Maeterlynck, who seems pretty wise in the ways of Web-based love and lust, says she is no stranger to feeling jealousy's sting. "It rears its head all the time for me. I get those pangs at my heart, especially with those I have opened myself to, those that I love dearly," she says. "That being said, I can separate sex from love. I can accept a partner having sex with the random person in *SL*, but it's a partner's TIME that I get jealous of. It's the connection, the closeness that causes those strings of my heart to pluck."

Personally speaking, I admit that this emotion has stirred inside of me from time to time as I have engaged with the digital characterizations in SL, although I was initially unsure whether it had been completely justified or even rational of me to do so. I almost felt ashamed of having experienced such feelings, like I shouldn't be taking a virtual world so seriously. I mean, theoretically speaking, why should I even [care] about the indiscreet behavior of an avatar whom I have established a romantic connection with?

Well, I happen to think that there's a very real degree of legitimacy to online relationships, and they give rise to genuine human emotions in the people behind the avatars. Sure, you've got to maintain a reasonable perspective. But I think that online romance and cybersex are only going to get more commonplace as platforms like *Second Life* grow increasingly sophisticated and immersive and become more culturally diffused and omnipresent. And that means that human emotions will be proportionately in tow.

I really like darkchyld's thoughts on this phenomenon as it relates to *Second Life*: "We all bring our real selves into this dream world, and you can't totally divorce yourself from your avatar," darkchyld says. "Actually, I have a hard time with the people who do nothing but role-play their avatar. My avatar is me. Not visually, but when you talk to me, you aren't talking to some invented character —you're talking to the person on the other side of the keyboard."

I feel the same way. [Noche01]

REFERENCES

[Andrea01] Andrea, interview with Brenda Brathwaite, July 6, 2005.
[Andrea02] Ibid.

[Andrea03] Ibid.

[Andrea04] Ibid.

[Andrea05] Ibid.

[Bartle01] Bartle, Richard, interview with Brenda Brathwaite, May 16, 2006.

[Garriott01] Garriott, Richard, interview with Brenda Brathwaite, May 27, 2005.

[GGA01] jane, "Sex in Games=Rez+Vibrator,", Game+Girl=Advance, October 26, 2002. Available online at *http://www.gamegirladvance.com/archives/2002/10/26/sex_in_games_rezvibrator.html*. Accessed August 7, 2005.

[Linden01] Hursthouse, James, IGDA.org, "MMOG Demographics: Perspectives from Industry Insiders," *The Demographics Issue*, Volume 1, Issue 2, Spring 2005. Available online at *http://www.igda.org/online/quarterly/1_2/mmogdemographics.php*. Accessed April 22, 2006.

[Linden01] Smith, Catherine, Linden Labs, email to Brenda Brathwaite, June 26, 2006.

[Machulis01] Machulis, Kyle, conversation with Brenda Brathwaite, March 18, 2006.

[Machulis02] Machulis, Kyle, conversation with Brenda Brathwaite, April 20, 2006.

[Machulis03] Ibid.

[MMOrgy01] Machulis, Kyle, MMOrgy.com, "Bundle of Polys." Available online at *http://www.mmorgy.com/2005/12/bundle_of_polys.php*. Accessed April 16, 2006.

[Newell01] Newell, Neil, interview with Brenda Brathwaite, May 18, 2006.

[Noche01] Kandora, Noche, Apogeevr.com, "Jealousy: An Emotion That Creeps into Cyberspace," March 1, 2006. Available online at *http://www.apogeevr.com/2006/03/01/an-emotional-virus-that-easily-seeps-into-cyberspace/#more-67*. Accessed June 27, 2006.

[PCM01] Elliott, Shaun, "Escort Mission," PC Magazine online, May 16, 2006. Available online at *http://www.pcmag.com/article2/0,1895,1962547,00.asp*.

[SD01] qDot, "SeXBox version 2, or How to Create Your Own Army," *www.slashdong.org*.

Available online at *http://www.slashdong.org/content/projects/diy_sex_toys_and_teledildonics/sexboxSeXBox_version_2_or_how_to_create_your_own_army-000229.php*. Accessed August 7, 2005.

[Wired01] Kohler, Chris, "Better than a Joystick," *Wired*, November 5, 2003. Available online at *http://www.wired.com/wired/archive/11.05/play.html?pg=6*. Accessed August 7, 2005.

[Wired02] Kohler, Chris, "Better than a Joystick," *Wired*, November 5, 2003. Available online at *http://www.wired.com/wired/archive/11.05/play.html?pg=6*. Accessed August 7, 2005.

4 The Sexual Backlash–Hot Coffee

In This Chapter

- *Grand Theft Auto: San Andreas*
- Unfinished Code Discovered
- Going Forward
- Interview with Henry Jenkins
- Interview with Patrick Wildenborg

GRAND THEFT AUTO: SAN ANDREAS

Few games are as universally loved and hated as the *Grand Theft Auto* (*GTA*) series of games. Lauded by gamers, awarded by critics and industry, and derided by politicians, parents, and concerned groups, the *GTA* series and its maker Rockstar Games have long courted controversy. However, nothing in the company or the series' past could compare to the scandal that would rock the industry in 2005 when an interactive sex mini-game was discovered in the latest game in the series, *Grand Theft Auto: San Andreas (GTA:SA)*. The "Hot Coffee" mod, so named because the character in the game goes to his girlfriend's for a cup of hot coffee followed by sexual intercourse, was the topic of industry, national, and international news.

Before it was all over, the scandal would result in new legislation, retail recalls, international bans, and millions of dollars in lost revenue. It would shake the credibility and foundation of the ESRB and change the way games are rated forever.

Coffee as Served–PS2® Release Day–October 26, 2004

It's a surprise to many, but "coffee" had always been an accessible part of *GTA:SA*, even in the release version. Carl "CJ" Johnson, the main character in the game, was a lover of sorts who could court several women. When he had successfully wined and dined a woman enough, she invited him back to her house for coffee . . . and a little something more. The game's camera remained outside. What the player heard, however, was unmistakable—the sounds of a couple making love. In the United States, the game shipped rated "M" for "Mature" with the "Strong Sexual Content" descriptor on the box, among others.

UNFINISHED CODE DISCOVERED

Within hours of the game's release, modders were pouring over the files. *Modders*, a term for those who modify a game's source code or assets after release, are dedicated game designers, programmers, and artists in their own right with online communities and fan followings. While modifying a PS2 title isn't possible (PS2 game DVDs are not writeable), examining the files is possible for those with specialized knowledge and tools. One such person was modder "Barton Waterduck." By exploring the PS2 game files, he discovered unused code that placed the camera *inside* the woman's house. Until the release of the PC version, however, there was little modders could do with that knowledge except wonder [GTA02].

Release Day–Xbox & PC Version–June 7, 2005

By the dozens, boxes of *GTA:SA* were placed on store shelves in the United States. Wal-Mart, Target, Best Buy, GameStop, and EB Games prepared for the inevitable onslaught as hundreds of die-hard fans who had been with the award-winning series for years scrambled to get their copies. Patrick Wildenborg, a *GTA* fan and modder in the Netherlands, was among them, but he would have to wait until June 10, 2005, the official Dutch release date, to get his copy.

Since Barton's discovery, Patrick had been studying the *GTA* code. "After analyzing the parts of the code surrounding those references [to the animations Barton had discovered], I found out that they contained what looked like working code of a mini-game that was not in the game." The examination took Patrick several weeks. "They used a lot of new opcodes in the *San Andreas* SCM file of which the meaning was still to be figured out" [PatrickW]. By the time his study was finished, Patrick thought he knew what the code would do, and further knew what he had to do to activate it.

Now that the game had been released, at long last Patrick could test his theory out. Although it would be three days before he could pick up a copy of the PC version himself, a fellow modder in the United States sent him the PC's SCM file (a binary script file). Based on his previous examinations of the PS2 files, Patrick modified the PC file and sent it back to his contacts in the United States to test.

Within a short while, on a private forum and before Patrick had even played the game himself, "Hot Coffee" was seen for the very first time.

On June 10, 2005 (Netherlands' time), after the game had been released in the Netherlands, Patrick uploaded the mod to *www.gtagararage.com* under his username, PatrickW.

Hot Coffee Surfaces—June 9, 2005

The biggest scandal to hit video games in 20 years had begun. PatrickW's mod allowed CJ, the player's character, to go inside his girlfriend's house for "hot coffee" and, ultimately, a sex mini-game [GTA01]. PatrickW's posting was quickly picked up by *GTA:SA* mod and fan site *www.gtasanandreas.net.* In his posting, site member illspirit cited the work done by member Barton Waterduck and further credited PatrickW with unlocking and enabling the same code on the recently released PC version [GTA02]. The post provided a link to the mod file on the *www.gtagarage .com* site.

illspirit's post included several screenshots of the alleged sex mini-game and showed two clothed characters having sex. The HUD featured an excitement meter and directions that told the player to "push UP and DOWN in rhythm" or "JOY4 to change position" among other things [GTA03].

Word Travels—June 10, 2005

Within hours, news of the mod traveled through the hard core and *GTA* gaming community, and within a day, it was mentioned on at least one mainstream gaming site. Gamespot included news of the mod in its regular Rumor Control column on June 10. Rumor #5 stated that *GTA:SA*, at some point, had X-rated mini-games [GS01]. Gamespot had been tipped off to the then rumor by the site UK Resistance, which mocked the same images posted by illspirit on *www.gtasanandreas.net* [UK01]. Gamespot's Tor Thorsen was less than convinced, however, particularly given UK Resistance's comments on the quality of the images. The UK site felt the images were, in a nutshell, terrible and done by amateurs. Calling the rumor one of the funniest to date, Thorsen thought that it was unlikely that code left in the PS2 version was also left in the PC and Xbox versions of the game. Gamespot's Rumor Control decided the rumor was likely untrue [GS02]. Competing mainstream sites failed to comment on the emerging issue at all.

Popular gaming blog Kotaku was also early to break the story, but it was also on the fence and noted the images displayed in the *www.gtasanandreas.net* post were probably faked [KO01]. Nonetheless, it still asked the question—was there a sex mini-game in *GTA:SA*?

The Video & the Updated Mod—June 12, 2005

Gamespot and Kotaku weren't alone in their reservations. Many gamers thought the images were doctored, and some suggested the mod itself was a fake. The mod community was quick to respond, however. On June 12, 2005, *www.gtasanandreas .net* member DigitalD posted the link that was sent around the world: *http:// files.gtanet.com/gtasa/videos/hotcoffee.wmv*.

The link sent people to a video of the "Hot Coffee" sex mini-game in action. The 90-second video footage was incredibly compelling. In the footage, CJ gets out of his car and runs toward his girlfriend's house. She answers the door, and he goes in. The two characters begin with oral sex and eventually have simulated sexual intercourse. During intercourse, they change positions numerous times until the woman achieves orgasm, and the game resumes. CJ remains clothed, however, and no genitalia are seen. The animations in the video do not appear to be final production quality (the man's hands frequently clip through the female character's body, and some textures appear to be missing), but overall, the video was hard to dismiss and raised many eyebrows. Could it have been faked? Perhaps, but it would have taken much more than a few modders and two days to complete. The possibility that modders had somehow done this all ahead of time in an effort to orchestrate an enormous hoax upon gamers and the industry itself seemed far more unlikely, particularly given that the modders in question were huge fans of the *GTA* franchise.

In his post, DigitalD also included a link to an updated mod from PatrickW that let players get to the sex mini-game more easily to see for themselves [GTA04]. According to PatrickW's site, the "Hot Coffee v2" mod included fully nude models, modder Craig Kostelecky's "Opened up" mod, and modder Hammer83's "sacensor" tool [PatrickW01]. Taken together, these mods allowed players to get to Hot Coffee more quickly.

On its site, Kotaku reported the appearance of the video the following day and acknowledged that the purported rumor might be true [KO02].

Inside the Industry—June 12, 2005

Among video game developers and publishers, production ground to a halt. Emails flew fast and furious, and mailing lists and discussion boards frequented by developers were jammed with *GTA:SA* discussion. Although people would be arguing for weeks to come over who created the content and gameplay seen in the "Hot Coffee" mod, in the development community, for the most part, people knew. "There's no way that content is *not* on the disc," a developer told this author when shown the video of the sex mini-game. "In two days a modder put together animations, audio, an interior, everything for that mini-game? I'm not buying it. And look at the size of the mod," he said, referring to the mod's file size. "At that size, it doesn't contain art or audio of any kind." He was emphatic. "Hot Coffee shipped on that disc" [Anon02].

While some accepted that as a foregone conclusion, other developers were still in disbelief. Granted, Rockstar Games was no stranger to controversy, but this seemed extreme, even by Rockstar standards. Some speculated that Rockstar Games had left the content on the disc on purpose, knowing that a modder would certainly uncover it once the PC version was released. Others speculated that the sex mini-game had been cut at some point during production, possibly to avoid an AO rating, but the code had not been removed. Such practice is common in game development where removing code can often create a flurry of "bugs" or errors in the software. Instead of removing code, developers simply disable it and leave it on the disc. Still others speculated that the whole scandal was a means to generate sales for a product in a waning sales curve.

Whatever the reason, Rockstar Games remained silent through it all.

Industry news source GameDAILY BIZ later reported that an informed industry source told them that Rockstar cut the sex mini-game to avoid the "AO" rating [GDB01]. Rockstar did not confirm or deny this report.

GamePolitics Raises Possibly of Legislation—June 17, 2005

As members of the development community argued among themselves, some wondered what fallout there was going to be. GamePolitics, a popular blog written by Dennis McCauley that covers political, legal, and legislative matters involving games, first raised the specter of legislation.

Referencing Kotaku's coverage of the brewing controversy, McCauley wondered if the industry had just inadvertently handed politicians the ammunition they needed to make permanent legislation regulating video games. Up until Hot Coffee's discovery, all legislation that had passed throughout the United States had ultimately been overturned, largely on First Amendment grounds. However, if legislators could show that a game was obscene, protection under the First Amendment would no longer apply. If the content—the sex mini-game—was present on the discs, McCauley noted, a court could declare *GTA:SA* obscene, not for its violent content, but for the sexual content. If the courts declared the game obscene, sales to minors could be legally prohibited, the same way minors cannot buy pornography [GP01]. In effect, it would be the proverbial smoking gun that legislators needed to pass legislation and make it stick through the certain appeals.

ESRB Signals Investigation Is Underway—June 20, 2005

Realizing that Hot Coffee had the potential to tip *GTA:SA's* rating from "M" to "AO," GamePolitics contacted the ESRB to get its take on the situation. Patricia Vance, president of the ESRB, responded to GamePolitics in an email on June 20, 2005 that signaled an investigation of some sort was underway.

"We are currently looking into this situation," Vance told GamePolitics. "We do not know the source of the content nor the code that was created to access it. As always, we will ensure that all ESRB rules and regulations were properly followed by those participating in the rating process" [GP05].

The Modder Surfaces—June 22, 2005

As it does with all its articles, GamePolitics posted the June 17 piece on Hot Coffee and the possibility of legislation on Live Journal (*www.livejournal.com*) where its readers could comment. Much like the developer boards, discussion went back and forth on whether Hot Coffee was created by modders or shipped on the disc. In addition, and in response to the article, readers debated whether *GTA:SA* could itself be considered obscene when one had to do intentional work to uncover the allegedly obscene content.

In the midst of this debate came a post from Patrick Wildenborg:

"Hi everyone, my name is PatrickW from the Netherlands, and I created the HOT COFFEE mod for *San Andreas*. I can confirm (and prove if needed), that all the code, models, textures, and animations for the XXX interactive scenes are present on R*'s release DVD. The only thing that is needed to unlock it is toggling a single bit. Also, the fully nude models that are featured in a separate version of the HOT COFFEE mod are present on the R* DVD. In addition to the scenes that are featured in the movie that is circulating the Internet, there is also an S&M type game that has been unlocked. A screen of that game can be found on the site below." Patrick provided a link to the gtagarage.com site.

Patrick was on the brink of becoming, arguably, the most famous modder of all time and had publicly addressed the growing controversy for the first time [GP02].

GamePolitics Interviews Patrick—June 30, 2005

Although it had been more than two weeks since Hot Coffee surfaced, the matter of who created the content—Rockstar or the mod community—had yet to be settled. Seeking more information and hoping to determine who was to blame, GamePolitics contacted Patrick and asked him to prove that the content shipped on the disc as he had claimed. "Well how do you prove such a thing?" Patrick responded. "It depends on how skeptic your editor is. For a 100% proof I would recommend the following scenario:

1. Do a clean install of *San Andreas*.
2. Get hold of a savefile, where you have a high-relation level with one or more of your girlfriends (use your own savefile or gtagarage.com has some savefiles available for download).

3. On a different PC, patch the savefile with the sacensor.exe tool (giving the name of the savefile as only command-line parameter to the sacensor tool).
4. If needed, confirm with a binary editor that only 1 or two bytes have changed in the savefile.
5. Move the savefile to the PC with *San Andreas* on it, and load the savefile.
6. Go on a date with one of your girlfriends, and you when she invites you for coffee, the animations will be shown" [GP03].

If GamePolitics doubted him any further, Patrick welcomed an invite and the chance to prove its existence in person. He suggested they put him, an unaltered, PC version of *GTA:SA*, and a hex editor in a room. Doing so, he could produce the same results.

In an effort to get its side of the story, GamePolitics contacted Rockstar, but its calls were not returned. Not dissuaded, GamePolitics also contacted Rockstar's publisher, Take-Two Interactive. Take-Two said only that they did not comment on the work of the mod community [GP04]. Of course, whether it was the work of the mod community had yet to be established.

ESRB Comes Under Fire—July 6, 2005

Three weeks into the controversy, major media in the industry and in general had failed to pick up on the developing story. GamePolitics, however, was still on the proverbial beat. In a July 6, 2005, editorial, the site criticized the ESRB's response to Hot Coffee. Under the headline, "Fatally Flawed Video Game Rating System Must Change," GamePolitics chastised the organization's silence on the matter and questioned their accountability. "[T]he *GTA: San Andreas* fiasco points out an intrinsic flaw in the ESRB system," the story said. "The organization is simply not accountable—not to the media, not to the government, and certainly not to parents" [GP06].

"While the ESRB has a purported role as a watchdog agency," the story continued, "the companies it is 'watching' are paying its bills—and its payroll." The ESRB is funded through the fees it charges to companies for rating its games. Funding is also provided by the Entertainment Software Association, the trade group that represents publishers of video games. Referring to the Hot Coffee scandal and the ESRB's silence on it, GamePolitics asked, "Is it any wonder why we can't get answers to the tough questions" [GP07]?

GamePolitics, a regular defender of the ESRB, demanded the ESRB be held accountable and called on the public, the media, or Congress to ensure that it was. As the "foundation of the game industry's defense" against critics who seek to pass legislation upon the sale and distribution of video games, it was critical that people could trust the ESRB. However, GamePolitics felt the "foundation was cracked" [GP07A].

GamePolitics found itself unlikely allies with Assembly Speaker pro Tem Leland Yee (D-San Francisco/Daly City). Late on July 6, 2005, Yee's office issued a press release blasting the ESRB for what he termed its failure to appropriately rate *GTA:SA*. Yee, a child psychologist and member of the California Assembly, had introduced numerous bills with the aim of restricting children's access to violent video games. "Once again, ESRB has failed our parents," said the press release. "This particular game has been known to include extremely heinous acts of violence, and now it has been uncovered that the game also includes explicit sexual scenes that are inappropriate for our children. I have urged the ESRB on numerous occasions to rate this game AO based on its blatantly graphic nature."

Yee's press release also cited the same conflict of interest that GamePolitics had. "While ESRB claims to be a nonbiased ratings board that gives parents a valuable tool in deciding appropriateness of games for their children, they are funded by the makers of video games who have a financial interest in making sure their games are not rated AO." The press release further quoted Yee as saying, "Clearly the ESRB has a conflict of interest in rating these games. Plain and simple, parents cannot trust the ESRB to rate games appropriately or the industry to look out for our children's best interests" [Yee01].

The ESRB was quick to fire back. "Assemblyman Yee has been on a crusade for years to undermine the integrity of the ESRB, and in so doing, generate support for his legislative agenda. His latest attempt to win political points is to claim, without any legitimate basis, that a game rated for ages 17 and older with explicit content descriptors prominently displayed on every box has been inappropriately rated," a prepared statement read [CNet01]. The ESRB maintained that no one took its ratings more seriously than they, themselves, did, and that they would do whatever was necessary to maintain their integrity.

Meanwhile, the servers that hosted Patrick's "Hot Coffee" mod went into overdrive. "Before NIMF and Yee 'warned' everybody about Hot Coffee, we only had a couple of thousand downloads on the mod," illspirit told this author. "After the media panic, over a million! In late summer of last year, our server was pushing like 7TB of data a month" [illspirit01].

ESRB Launches Investigation—July 8, 2005

On July 8, 2005, the ESRB officially opened its Hot Coffee investigation. In a statement issued to the press, ESRB president Patricia Vance said that the organization had begun an investigation to determine if ESRB rules and regulations had been violated. The rules, according to Vance, called for full disclosure of all content pertinent to a rating decision. Although the ESRB had come into critics' crosshairs due to the hidden content in the game, its release made clear that the failure was not theirs, but instead rested with those who failed to disclose the content.

"The integrity of the ESRB rating system is founded on the trust of consumers who increasingly depend on it to provide complete and accurate information about what's in a game," the statement continued. "If after a thorough and objective investigation of all the relevant facts surrounding this modification, we determine a violation of our rules has occurred, we will take appropriate action" [ESRB01]. In response to the ESRB investigation, the National Institute on Media and the Family, a media watchdog group, issued a national parental warning later the same day. Citing its previous warnings about the sexual and violent content found in *GTA:SA*, its latest warning alerted parents to the hidden content under investigation, and cautioned them that a patch, readily available on the Internet, made this content visible. The association further called for Rockstar to admit its part in the controversy [NMF01].

Hot Coffee Goes Mainstream—July 8, 2005

When the National Institute on Media and the Family's warning crossed AP writer Ron Harris' desk, he picked up on the emerging story. In an effort to get both sides, Harris contacted Rockstar Games and Patrick Wildenborg, the creator of the "Hot Coffee" mod. According to Harris' story, Rodney Walker, a spokesperson for Rockstar Games, would not discuss the developer's role in the creation of the sexual content seen in the "Hot Coffee" mod. Wildenborg, however, was more than willing to discuss it. In an email to Harris, Wildenborg reiterated what he had told GamePolitics a week earlier—he had not created any of the Hot Coffee content. His mod merely unlocked content that was already there. Again, Wildenborg welcomed a chance to prove himself. An unedited copy of the game, a computer, a hex editor, and a few moments of time were all he needed [AP01].

When the AP story broke, Hot Coffee was in the mainstream. Within a matter of hours, the story was picked up by newspapers, news sites, and television stations around the world.

When asked why it took so long for the mainstream media to pick up on the story, GamePolitics' Dennis McCauley said, "I don't think the mainstream media really understood the issues involved. Hidden code, a somewhat confusing rating system, and general unfamiliarity with games made this a complex issue for nongamers. The industry itself was keeping a low profile on the issue. It really didn't break out until the National Institute for Media and Family and Leland Yee made an issue of it" [DM01].

CNNMoney.com's Director of Content Development Chris Morris also had some ideas. "The timing was bad enough, as the country was still getting over the whole Janet Jackson Super Bowl half-time fiasco. Sexual content was already at the forefront of a lot of people's minds. But given that this was in a '*Grand Theft Auto*' game, it escalated things. The series has been under fire for a long, long time, but people weren't listening to arguments that it was too violent. This presented a new 'hook' for industry critics—and they took full advantage of it. The fact of the matter is: the video game industry's opponents are much more competent than its defenders. This quickly became their rallying point." Sexual content and violence aside, Morris also notes the strength of the story and gives that credit for its widespread appeal. "[T]he removal of the most popular game from store shelves is a major story. It wasn't too long before national and prominent politicians began to weigh in on the matter, which kept it in the spotlight" [Morris01].

Rockstar Games Breaks Its Silence—July 8, 2005

One month to the day after Hot Coffee surfaced, Rockstar Games finally broke its silence. In a press release issued in response to the ESRB investigation, Rockstar confirmed that its game *GTA:SA* was under investigation. "We thoroughly support the work of the ESRB, and believe that it has an exemplary record of rating games and promoting understanding of video game content," the statement read. "We also feel confident that the investigation will uphold the original rating of the game, as the work of the mod community is beyond the scope of either publishers or the ESRB" [GS03].

Of course, whether the work was actually the work of the mod community was still up for debate. Clearly, the content could not be accessed by normal means. However, developers, press, politicians, and raters wanted to know if the content—the animations, the mini-game, the audio—was on the discs as shipped, locked away or not.

Upon receiving the press release, Gamespot's Curt Feldman contacted Rockstar for more details. Asking if the code for Hot Coffee was included on the DVDs as the modder claimed, Feldman reported that a Rockstar spokesperson said it was not [GS04].

Rockstar Blames Hackers—July 11, 2005

As the ESRB investigation continued, news reports from all over the world broadcast the story, and reporters from *The New York Times* to *The Boston Globe* were on its trail. Seemingly, figuring out who was telling the truth—Rockstar or the modder—should been an easy matter, but for Hot Coffee, it was anything but.

On July 11, 2005, Rockstar Games issued another statement about the progress of the investigation. "So far we have learned that the 'hot coffee' modification is the work of a determined group of hackers who have gone to significant trouble to alter scenes in the official version of the game. In violation of the software user agreement, hackers created the 'hot coffee' modification by combining, reconstituting, and altering the game's source code." The statement continued, "Since the 'hot coffee' scenes cannot be created without intentional and significant technical modifications to the game's source code, we are currently investigating ways that we can increase the security protection of the source code and prevent the game from being altered by the 'hot coffee' modification" [GDB02].

The statement was an odd one for the mod community who felt, in many respects, betrayed. With the finger pointed squarely in their direction, modders nonetheless understood Rockstar's need to protect the company. However, they also felt like quite the scapegoats. Many games, the *GTA* series among them, are popular with the mod community. By making new levels, new items, and new missions for games, modders regularly extend the shelf life and sales of games. In fact, game developers, with publisher's permission, commonly leave open portions of the game's assets or code to facilitate modding. This sudden shift in attitude— from welcoming and encouraging the mod community to calling them a "determined group of hackers" in "violation of the software user agreement"—was difficult to take.

To others, the Rockstar statement was equally mystifying. Carefully worded and not denying the presence of the content on the discs, Rockstar's statement nonetheless seemed to distance the company from any blame. While Patrick claimed that a single bit flag was all that separated a gamer and Hot Coffee, Rockstar's release indicated otherwise. It only deepened the controversy.

Later that same day, GameDAILY BIZ, an online industry newsletter and news site, reported that an informed industry source claimed Rockstar had created but later removed the Hot Coffee content from *GTA:SA* during development to avoid an AO rating [GDB03].

GamePolitics, now a month into its investigation, begged for the truth. "Pardon us for being confused, but can't some disinterested party (put your hand down, Rockstar) with game programming skills peer into Wildenborg's mod and tell the world the truth?" Patrick, himself, contacted GamePolitics shortly thereafter to say that with the right tools, such as a hex editor, and the right knowledge, it was certainly possible. As he had all along, Patrick maintained his position, and felt confident that the investigators would discover the Hot Coffee content on the shipped disc, just as he had claimed. As the controversy became ever more heated, Patrick told GamePolitics that he was "hanging in here, waiting for my 15 minutes of fame to end" [GP08].

That wasn't going to happen anytime soon. By July 16, the story would be on the front page of CNN.com.

PS2 Codes Posted—July 12, 2005

Although it would go largely unnoticed for several days, user FNG posted a series of codes in the forums of the Web site TheGFCC.com. Using the codes provided by FNG and an Action Replay Max, a device that allows players to enter cheat codes into games to alter the gameplay experience, a player could access the Hot Coffee content on the PS2 [GFCC01].

Hillary Clinton Enters the Fray—July 14, 2005

Senator Hillary Rodham Clinton (D-NY) was outraged by the latest allegations of hidden pornographic content in a video game. Never a fan of the *GTA* series, she had previously criticized the game and its makers for allowing gamers to have virtual sex with hookers before killing them to get their money back [KO03].

On July 14, 2005, and in response to the Hot Coffee controversy, Clinton announced her intent to pursue legislation barring the sale of such games to minors and further called upon the Federal Trade Commission (FTC) to investigate the source of the Hot Coffee content. "The disturbing material in *Grand Theft Auto* and other games like it is stealing the innocence of our children and it's making the difficult job of being a parent even harder," said Senator Clinton. "I am announcing these measures today because I believe that the ability of our children to access pornographic and outrageously violent material on video games rated for adults is spiraling out of control" [HRC01].

GTA:SA's M rating also drew Clinton's ire. According to the release, "Senator Clinton urged the FTC to determine whether an Adults Only (AO) rating is more appropriate than the current Mature (M) rating for the *Grand Theft Auto: San Andreas* video game given this new, alarming content" [HRC02].

In her letter to Deborah Platt Majoras, Chairwoman of the Federal Trade Commission, Senator Clinton implored the agency to investigate the content and determine its source, something the industry had yet to do. "We should all be deeply disturbed that a game which now permits the simulation of lewd sexual acts in an interactive format with highly realistic graphics has fallen into the hands of young people across the country," said Clinton. "I therefore urge you to take immediate action to determine the source of this content and the appropriateness of the M rating in light of its vast accessibility, and to make your findings public" [HRC03].

"Alarmingly, it seems that no one yet knows the source of this content," Clinton said [HRC04].

The ESRB and the Entertainment Software Association (ESA) were quick to respond to Clinton's announcement.

Noting that an investigation was already underway, the ESRB urged Clinton and other concerned parties "not to rush to judgment until all of the relevant facts, some of which are highly technical and complicated, have been established." Vance added that, "Any second-guessing at this point would be premature and inappropriate as this investigation continues" [ESRB02]. Noting that the game was never meant for or rated for children—it carried an M rating and descriptors including "Strong Sexual Content" upon release—Vance reiterated her group's and Clinton's shared interest in protecting children and providing parents the information they needed to make informed choices in purchasing video games.

ESA President Douglas Lowenstein also expressed his agency's and the Senator's shared concerns. In his statement, he noted that he agreed with Senator Clinton and other concerned individuals that video games meant for adults should not be sold to minors. At the same time, Lowenstein made no bones about the futility of such legislation.

"The legislation proposed by Senator Clinton is unconstitutional on its face as it amounts to government enacted restrictions on creative and artistic expression protected by the First Amendment," Lowenstein said. "This is not just our view, but the view of every Federal Court which has rendered final judgment on similar laws enacted by states in recent years, including appellate courts in the Seventh and Eighth Circuits, and the Western District United States District Court. So while we understand Senator Clinton's motivation, in the end her solution will never pass constitutional muster and thus will do nothing to help parents raise their kids" [ESA01].

Lowenstein further noted his concerns that even if it were to pass and stick, legislation would not solve the problem. "[A]ccording to the Federal Trade Commission (FTC), parents are involved in the purchase and rental of games more than 80% of the time, which means that in the vast majority of cases when kids get games that may not be appropriate, they get them from Mom and Dad. You can introduce all the bills in the world but none of them will ensure that parents exercise the necessary control over the games they buy for their kids" [ESA02].

Lowenstein expressed the hope that upon further investigation, Clinton would abandon her legislative efforts and work with the industry to achieve the common goal of helping parents to make informed choices. However, on December 16, 2005, Senators Hillary Rodham Clinton, Joe Lieberman, and Evan Bayh introduced the promised legislation [HRC05].

Kotaku Posts the Codes—July 15, 2005

Now a month and a half into the controversy, the source of the Hot Coffee content, as Senator Clinton and others were quick to point out, had not yet been officially established by anyone other than modder Patrick Wildenborg who, as he had all along, insisted that everything one needed to see and play the "Hot Coffee" mini-game had shipped on the disc.

At long last, Patrick was about to get the ally and the proof he needed.

On July 15, 2005, Kotaku posted the codes found on the Web site TheGFCC. Kotaku made the obvious connection—if the content was accessible on the PS2, then Rockstar's last defense was gone. PS2 DVDs are not writable, and therefore, cannot be altered by anyone. If these codes and their poster were telling the truth, then the code had shipped on the discs, just as Patrick had claimed. Kotaku asked readers with access to both an Action Replay Max device at *GTA:SA* to try it out and confirm the post's accuracy [KO04]. A fellow gaming site rose to the challenge.

Gamespot.com Confirms Content on Disc—July 15, 2005

Acquiring the codes from Kotaku, Gamespot's writers set about to prove or disprove the existence of the Hot Coffee content on the PS2. Acquiring all the necessary components—a list of the codes, an Action Replay Max device, and a PS2 version *GTA:SA*—the writers entered the codes into the game and used two cheats, "Enable all Girlfriends" and another to give CJ, the main character in the game, maximum sex appeal. The two cheats, while having no effect on the Hot Coffee content itself, made it much easier to get to the content in question.

Gamespot's writer then developed a relationship between CJ and a woman in the game. After the fourth date, the woman invited CJ back to her place for coffee. The next moment would be crucial. Would the player's character be invited inside and would he and his girlfriend take part in a sex mini-game, or would the camera stay outside only hinting at the possibilities within?

According to Gamespot, the next screen showed the inside of girlfriend's bedroom. The girlfriend was performing oral sex on CJ. The oral sex was followed by the sex mini-game, almost identical to footage DigitalD had posted on June 12, over a month earlier, and proving beyond a shadow of a doubt that the Hot Coffee content shipped on the disc [GS05].

Inside the Industry—July 15, 2005

The link to the Gamespot confirmation was forwarded through email again and again and again. A collective "wow" rang out from inside the video game industry. Those with access to an Action Replay Max and a PS2 version of *GTA:SA* tried out the codes for themselves. Others had already experimented with the PC version.

Still, there was an eerie silence from developers, particularly in the media. The development community is a fairly closed and tight knit group and unlikely to bash itself, particularly given the numerous and regular bashes it receives from politicians and other concerned groups and individuals.

Many wondered what would happen now. Some speculated that the game would be re-rated, but even then, there was no precedent. What happens if a game's rating goes from M to AO?

They were about to find out.

ESRB Rates *GTA:SA* "AO"—July 20, 2005

On July 20, 2005, the ESRB issued a landmark press release declaring that it had concluded its investigation into the *GTA:SA* Hot Coffee modification and, as a result of that investigation, would be revoking the game's M rating and assigning it an AO rating instead. The release further noted that Take-Two Interactive, the game's publisher, would be advising retailers to halt sales of the game until ESRB-mandated corrective actions could be taken.

"After a thorough investigation, we have concluded that sexually explicit material exists in a fully rendered, unmodified form on the final discs of all three platform versions of the game (i.e., PC CD-ROM, Xbox, and PS2)," said Patricia Vance, president of the ESRB. "However, the material was programmed by Rockstar to be inaccessible to the player, and they have stated that it was never intended to be made accessible. The material can only be accessed by downloading a software patch, created by an independent third party without Rockstar's permission, which is now freely available on the Internet and through console accessories. Considering the existence of the undisclosed and highly pertinent content on the final discs, compounded by the broad distribution of the third-party modification, the credibility and utility of the initial ESRB rating has been seriously undermined" [ESRB03A]. The ESRB also required that the existing inventory in stores be relabeled with AO stickers or exchanged for updated versions of *GTA:SA* with the offending content removed. Furthermore, Rockstar was ordered to make available a patch that would render the material and the "Hot Coffee" mod inoperable on the PC version.

In a more far-reaching sense, the ESRB also called on developers and publishers to proactively protect their games from modders. "Going forward, the ESRB will now require all game publishers to submit any pertinent content shipped in final product even if is not intended to ever be accessed during gameplay, or remove it from the final disc. Furthermore, the ESRB calls on the computer and video game industry to proactively protect their games from illegal modifications by third parties, particularly when they serve to undermine the accuracy of the rating" [ESRB03].

The news shot 'round the industry. The ESA was quick to issue a statement in support of the ESRB. "The action announced by ESRB today should be seen as a clear reflection of the effectiveness of video game industry self regulation," said Doug Lowenstein, President of the ESA. Targeting the politicians who had previously targeted the ESRB, Lowenstein noted, "We hope that in the future, industry critics will avoid jumping to conclusions before the ESRB has time to complete its investigations, and will instead choose to use their resources to focus on greater cooperative efforts to ensure that parents make use of ESRB ratings so they can make the right game choices for their unique families" [ESA03].

Shortly thereafter, the Interactive Entertainment Merchants Association (IEMA), the association that represents the majority of entertainment software retailers, issued a statement in reaction to the re-rating. "Our members intend to immediately cease all sales of the game until existing inventory can either be re-stickered with an AO (Adults Only) rating, or exchanged for new versions of the game that has the hidden content removed and the original M (Mature 17+) rating intact," the statement read. "Though not a policy, IEMA members generally do not carry AO-rated games any differently than we do not carry X-rated videos or DVDs, thus it is likely that our members will be removing all copies of the current version and re-stocking with the updated version." [IEMA01]. At Wal-Mart, Best Buy, Target—one by one, the industry's retail giants pulled the now infamous game from their shelves while opportunists put copies of the M labeled but now AO rated game up for sale on auction sites. Although the shelves of IEMA members would remain *GTA:SA* free for a while, other stores such as the author's local EB Games would continue to sell the game, now with its AO rating and sticker. Some independent game stores also continued to sell the game. One storeowner shared that he wished he had 10 times his current inventory noting that since they re-rated the game, he couldn't keep them in stock.

For politicians, the re-rating of the game was a welcome gesture. Senator Hillary Rodham Clinton's office issued a statement in which the Senator noted she was pleased that the ESRB had resolved the troubling issue and taken action against the game. However, at the same time, Clinton also expressed her concerns. "[T]he fact remains that the company gamed the ratings system and enabled pornographic material to get into the hands of children." Clinton urged the ESRB to do what was necessary to make sure something like the Hot Coffee scandal didn't happen again [HRC06].

Take-Two Reacts to Re-Rating—July 20, 2005

No other party was as affected by the ESRB's announcement as Take-Two Interactive, the publisher of *GTA:SA*. In a release issued that same day, Take-Two notified the public that Rockstar Games would stop manufacture of the current version of *GTA:SA* and, in response to ESRB mandates, would make available a patch that prevented modification of the game. The company also noted that it would be lowering its third quarter and fiscal year predictions to "reflect the expected negative impact on the title's retail performance" [TTWO01].

"As a result of the re-rating of the game," the statement read, "Take-Two is lowering guidance for the third fiscal quarter ending July 31, 2005 to $160 to $170 million in net sales and a net loss per share of $(0.40) to $(0.45) to provide reserves for the value of the title's current North American retail inventory" [TTWO02]. Although a costly move to be sure, the lowered guidance reflected a worst-case scenario where all existing games in the retail space were recalled, and not re-stickered and sold or exchanged for an M-rated version when one was made available.

In the same statement, Paul Eibeler, the president and chief executive officer of Take-Two, expressed his support for the ESRB system and noted that his company would continue to work closely with the organization to make sure consumers had the information they needed. At the same time, Eibeler expressed concern over the possible precedent the re-rating set. "The ESRB's decision to re-rate a game based on an unauthorized third-party modification presents a new challenge for parents, the interactive entertainment industry. and anyone who distributes or consumes digital content" [TTWO03]. Eibeler's concern was valid. Many games are modded after release, and if these mods could cause a re-rating, then developers and publishers of video games were in for a challenging ride. What a modder decides to create is out of the hands of the developer. The best it can do is to prevent access to the source code and assets so modifications cannot take place. Key to this issue and to the re-rating, although missing from the release, was that the "Hot Coffee" mod merely activated pre-existing content found on the disc, and that content was not a creation of the mod community. The "key" to access it, however, was.

Distancing itself from the cause of the controversy, the statement noted that, "The scenes depicted in the 'hot coffee' modification are not playable in the retail version of the game unless the user downloads and/or installs unauthorized software that alters the content of the original retail version of the title, representing a violation of Take-Two and Rockstar's end user license agreement (EULA) and intellectual property rights" [TTWO04].

Eibeler added, "We are deeply concerned that the publicity surrounding these unauthorized modifications has caused the game to be misrepresented to the public and has detracted from the creative merits of this award winning product." The release also hinted at further legal action noting that Take-Two was "exploring its legal options as it relates to companies that profited from creating and distributing tools for altering the content of *Grand Theft Auto: San Andreas*" [TTWO05].

In the eyes of many, the finger was still clearly pointed at the mod community.

In the days that followed, some questioned whether Take-Two and Rockstar Games got off too easy. Although the game was re-rated and would certainly cost Take-Two a substantial sum of money to recall, re-sticker, fix, and remanufacture the product, for some, that seemed like little more than a slap on the wrist, particularly considering all the press it brought the company in the meantime.

In an article on CNNMoney.com, Chris Morris noted that there were some in the industry who were not happy with the decision. Reporting from the IEMA Executive Summit in California, Morris noted that both retailers and publishers were privately upset about the ESRB's decision. Some wondered why Take-Two was not fined or forced to offer rebates [CNN01].

Morris interviewed numerous individuals, asking what the ESRB could have done instead. According to Morris, people were of varied opinions. Although some suggested fines and rebates, the idea that most intrigued Morris came from game designer Greg Costikyan. Costikyan suggested that Take-Two be prohibited from receiving a rating from the ESRB for two years [CNN02].

As Morris noted, such a move could seriously impact Take-Two's business. Major retailers require that games be rated, and without a rating, the publisher's titles could not be sold in such stores as Wal-Mart, Target, or Best Buy. Morris felt that such a move would strengthen the ESRB and send a message to developers and publishers that failure to tell the truth brings significant consequences [CNN03].

Mod Community Defends Itself—July 25, 2005

Throughout the controversy, the role of the mod community had constantly been called into question. First, it was accused of creating the content "by combining, re-constituting, and altering the game's source code" [GDB04]. Rockstar had even gone so far as to tell a Gamespot journalist that the content was not on the disc [GS06]. Later, once it was determined that the content did exist on the disc, al-though inaccessible straight off the shelf, the mod community was still lambasted for creating a means to access it. The ESRB encouraged developers to "proactively protect their games from illegal modifications by third parties particularly when they serve to undermine the accuracy of the rating" [ESRB04], and politicians called on the industry to make sure something similar didn't happen again. Take-Two even threatened legal action noting that it was exploring its options "as it re-lates to companies that profited from creating and distributing tools for altering the content of *Grand Theft Auto: San Andreas*" [TTWO06].

None of this sat well with the mod community, which had begun to feel like a pin cushion and a scapegoat. The administration of GTAgarage.com, the same site where Patrick uploaded the original "Hot Coffee" mod, had had enough and sent a letter to Senator Clinton, Assemblymember Yee, and Jack Thompson, a lawyer who had been particularly vocal in the media and often spoke out against the *GTA* series. The letter was also sent to the ESRB with a preface. It read as follows:

To whom it may concern,

We just fired this message off to Senator Clinton, Assemblymember Yee, and the rather excitable Jack Thompson. Your attacks on the customers you are supposed to protect are reprehensible to say the least. The gaming public knows very well you have rated more explicit games as "M" than what is con-tained in the allegedly obscene content (hot coffee) which you have admon-ished us over. Granted, your demonizing of the mod community may be only PR and politics, but we do not appreciate being a tertiary scapegoat for you to pass the already misplaced blame of irresponsible parents along to. So, please, find another patsy. Just thought it would be fair to give you the heads up we never got. Cheers, the administration of gtagarage.com [GP09]

The letter sent to Senator Clinton, Assemblymember Leland Yee, and Jack Thompson read as follows:

Dear Mrs. Clinton, Mr. Yee, and Mr. Thompson,

In recent statements by the ESRB, they have accused the mod community of undermining their ratings by putting sexually explicit material into PC games, namely San Andreas, which was already rated "M." However, if you look into a game by the name of "Singles—Flirt up your Life," it becomes quite clear they are doing a good job of that all by themselves. This "M" rated game features full frontal nudity (and not androgynous "barbies" like The Sims) and characters engaging in interactive sexual scenes. Screenshots of this game can be seen over at IGN: *http://media.pc.ign.com/media/667/667197/imgs_1.html*. And for that matter, what of the game "Playboy: The Mansion," which is based on the skin magazine, and is also rated "M"?! Seeing as these game contains *far* more graphic depictions of sex than anything found in San Andreas, including the scenes involving nudity which we modded into the game (by default, "Hot Coffee" did contain fully clothed actors . . .), how exactly have we undermined their rating? If anything, what was left on the disc by Rockstar and modded into the game by us doesn't even come close to what the ESRB itself considers "M" material, let alone rising to their very own standards of "AO." To blame the mod community for this is not only hypocritical, but quite deceptive as well. Not to mention the fact that they've essentially had one title banned for containing "pornography," while they let more explicit games get by them.

For the record, we feel that "M" is an appropriate rating for these games, as their contents are no worse than R-rated films which have long been considered "okay" for ages 17 and up. However, we do agree with you all that the ESRB is a big joke. Especially now that they're attacking their own customers for content which they obviously don't seem to have a problem with. Why should we the consumers be persecuted for adding something to a game which the ESRB has already demonstrated as perfectly acceptable for titles in the "M" range? San Andreas originally carried a warning for "strong sexual content," and judging by their previous ratings, we would insist that we released the "Hot Coffee" mod well within the ESRB's (apparently broken) guidelines.

Best Regards,

the administration of gtagarage.com [GP10]

Politicians Call for FTC Investigation—July 25, 2005

On July 25, 2005, Senator Sam Brownback of Kansas introduced a resolution on the floor of the Senate calling for an FTC investigation of Rockstar Games. In a statement issued by his office on July 27, 2005, Brownback noted that Rockstar Games may have intentionally deceived the ESRB. "It would be inexcusable for any maker of video games to intentionally deceive the ratings board," Brownback said. "Inserting pornographic content into any video game used by teenagers or even younger children is unacceptable, and pretending it got there by mistake is even more egregious" [SSB01]. The resolution passed 355 to 21 [GS07].

Take-Two confirmed they were under investigation the next day. In a statement issued to the press and shareholders, Take-Two noted that the FTC's Division of Advertising Practices had begun an investigation into the claims made in advertisements for *GTA:SA* and that the company was cooperating fully with the inquiry. They further expressed their confidence that no wrongdoing would be found [TTWO07].

The FTC investigation was the largest iceberg in the waters for Take-Two, but it had also drawn the ire of other groups and individuals. In New York City, for instance, Florence Cohen, an 85-year-old grandmother, filed a lawsuit against Rockstar Games and Take-Two arguing that advertising for *GTA:SA* was false and deceptive. Cohen had purchased the game for her grandson. In the lawsuit, unspecified damages were sought [MSNBC01].

In August, a group calling themselves the Peaceoholics held a protest outside Take-Two's offices in New York. Incensed by both the Hot Coffee and Rockstar's then upcoming game *Bully*, the group carried signs calling for the prosecution of Rockstar, among other things, and presented the company with a list of demands. Among its demands, the Peaceoholics wanted Take-Two to sell its games containing violent or sexual content exclusively in adult video stores, allow parents to return *GTA:SA* for a full refund until such time that Take-Two had completed a national campaign to educate parents about the game's contents and the effects such content could have, and issue a national apology [GP11].

High-profile anti–video game violence activist and lawyer Jack Thompson also regularly criticized the game in the national media and on his own site. Others made light of the controversy that had, by now, reached virtually epic proportions. Among them was ThinkGeek.com, a Web site and online retailer devoted to geek culture. ThinkGeek.com offered a "Hot Coffee" shirt that poked fun at the now infamous game and its sex scene [TG01].

No More Hot Coffee Patch Issued—August 8, 2005

On August 8, 2005, and in keeping with the ESRB's re-rating mandate, Rockstar Games issued the "No More Hot Coffee" patch. Available for the PC at the Web site *http://nomorehotcoffee.com/*, the patch prevented alteration of existing copies of *GTA:SA* and repaired copies that had been previously modified.

In keeping with previous statements, a question and answer section on the Web site was careful to note the original Hot Coffee modifications were third-party, unauthorized modifications to the existing game and that without code supplied by a third party or significant effort on the part of the player, the Hot Coffee content was inaccessible.

ESRB Launches Industry-Wide Investigation—September 9, 2005

By September, the industry and the media that followed it had moved on from the controversy. The holiday release season was in full swing and the media carried almost hourly headlines noting upcoming release dates, new reviews and previews, and, unfortunately for gamers, more than a few postponements. Although the controversy was no longer on the radar of most, it was very much on the minds of those at the ESRB. In particular, they wanted to make sure that nothing like Hot Coffee ever happened again.

On September 9, 2005, the organization contacted publishers notifying them that all games made since September 2004 had to be checked for hidden content. Should such content be found, publishers had until January 2006 to notify the ESRB. Failure to disclose the content, they warned, could result in punitive and corrective damages [BW01].

When asked what effect Hot Coffee had on the public perception of the ESRB overall, Patricia Vance, president of the ESRB, was optimistic. "I think there are two positives that emerged for ESRB from the 'Hot Coffee' controversy," she said. "First, and most important, awareness of ESRB ratings has been increased through the exposure of this story, and that's certainly welcome. The story permeated through national and worldwide media, and the message to check the ratings and take them seriously got through to lots of parents. The second positive was that ESRB demonstrated its ability and willingness to take action to protect the integrity of its ratings and ensure that parents, who rely on our ratings, can trust that they are accurate and representative of game content." She added that the organization had received many letters from parents thanking them for taking action [PV01].

Take-Two and FTC Settle Charges—June 8, 2006

One day short of its year anniversary, the FTC issued a release noting that Take-Two and the FTC had reached a settlement. The statement read:

Makers of Grand Theft Auto: San Andreas Settle FTC Charges
FTC Alleged Companies' Game Content Claims Deceptive

The companies behind the popular Grand Theft Auto: San Andreas video game have agreed to settle Federal Trade Commission charges that they failed to disclose important information about the game's content to consumers. According to the FTC, the companies, in advertising the Entertainment Software Rating Board ("ESRB") rating for the game, did not tell consumers that the game discs contained potentially viewable nude female characters and a potentially playable sex mini-game. Although San Andreas players could not access or view this sexual content during normal game play, sophisticated players posted a program on the Internet, dubbed "Hot Coffee," that revealed this content on the PC version of the game. PlayStation 2 and Xbox players eventually were able to access the Hot Coffee content by modifying or adding an accessory to their game consoles, installing special software, and inputting "cheat codes" developed by third parties. These developments led to a more restrictive rating by the ESRB.

"Parents have the right to rely on the accuracy of the entertainment rating system," said Lydia Parnes, Director of the FTC's Bureau of Consumer Protection. "We allege that Take-Two and Rockstar's actions undermined the industry's own rating system and deceived consumers. This is a matter of serious concern to the Commission, and if they violate this order, they can be heavily fined."

The ESRB originally rated the game's three versions, for PlayStation 2, PC, and Xbox, as "M" for Mature, with the accompanying content descriptors of Blood and Gore, Intense Violence, Strong Language, Strong Sexual Content, and Use of Drugs. According to the ESRB, video games rated "M" contain content that may be appropriate for those aged 17 and older. The rating information, including the rating symbol and content descriptors, appeared in print, television, and retailer ads for the game, and on game packaging for all three versions, including the claims "MATURE 17+" and "CONTENT RATED BY ESRB."

The ESRB re-rated San Andreas as AO ("Adults Only"). Games rated AO, according to the ESRB, have content that should only be played by persons 18 and older. As a result of the re-rating, many national retailers pulled the game from their shelves.

Under the terms of an agreement with the ESRB, the companies released a patch that, if downloaded and installed on the game, disables the "Hot Coffee" program; the patch is available for download at www.nomorehotcoffee.com.

The companies also agreed to re-label or recall all existing inventory. According to the game's publisher, Take-Two Interactive Software, Inc., the company incurred $24.5 million in costs associated with returns of San Andreas stemming from the re-rating. The companies subsequently published a second, M-rated edition of San Andreas without the nude images and mini-game content.

The companies that developed and marketed San Andreas, Take-Two and Rockstar Games, Inc., are both headquartered in New York City. The FTC's complaint charges that the companies violated the FTC Act by representing that San Andreas had been rated "Mature" and assigned certain content descriptors by the ESRB, but failing to disclose to consumers that the game discs contained unused, but potentially viewable, nude female images and disabled, but potentially playable, software code for a sexually explicit mini-game that the ESRB had not rated.

The proposed consent agreement with the FTC requires Take-Two and Rockstar Games to clearly and prominently disclose on product packaging and in any promotion or advertisement for electronic games, content relevant to the rating, unless that content had been disclosed sufficiently in prior submissions to the rating authority. In addition, the companies cannot misrepresent the rating or content descriptors for an electronic game. Finally, the companies must establish, implement, and maintain a comprehensive system reasonably designed to ensure that all content in an electronic game is considered and reviewed in preparing submissions to a rating authority. Once the order becomes final, the companies will be subject to civil penalties of up to $11,000 per violation if they violate the order. The companies will be subject to compliance reporting requirements to ensure that they meet the terms of the order.

The Commission vote to accept the proposed consent agreement was 5–0. The FTC will publish an announcement regarding the agreement in the Federal Register shortly. The agreement will be subject to public comment for 30 days, beginning today and continuing through July 10, after which the Commission will decide whether to make it final" [FTC01].

GOING FORWARD

It's hard to say what the ultimate fallout of the Hot Coffee controversy will be. Clearly, its effects will be felt politically and within the video game industry for some time to come, and it continues to raise its head in new legislation, lawsuits, and calls for action. In February 2006, for example, SWOP-USA, the Sex Workers Outreach Program, called for a boycott due to the treatment of prostitutes in the game.

Among developers, some fear a conservative crackdown. One developer who spoke on the condition of anonymity said, "I'd hate to be the first company submitting a game to the ESRB after Hot Coffee. My fear is that all sexual content will be rated much more harshly than it was ever rated before—and it was already pretty strict, particularly when you consider how they rated the violence" [Anon01].

Others thought the most likely to suffer were the modders. Should the industry lock down content to prevent any modification at all, the mod community would obviously have difficulty creating mods. In reality, however, a mod backlash is highly unlikely. Developers and publishers understand the difference between a mod—something like a user-created nude skin for the *Sims 2*, for instance—and developer-supplied content that's already supplied on a disc. The former is largely unpreventable. The latter is Hot Coffee. By creating additional content for the game, modders often extend the shelf life and sales curve of the products they modify, sometimes substantially. Developers and publishers know this and often leave game assets exposed to facilitate modding. The likelihood of developers and publishers doing something that would hurt their own bottom line is unlikely.

Politically, however, the stakes are higher. Henry Jenkins, a Professor of Literature and Comparative Media Studies at the Massachusetts Institute of Technology was quick to point out what he perceived to be Hot Coffee's long-term effects. "We are already seeing setbacks on almost every policy front—new state laws, new proposed federal regulation, new court cases, many of which can be directly traced back to outrage over the handling of Hot Coffee. In the past, many of these laws have simply sought to enforce the industry's own ratings—this is still the case with currently proposed federal legislation being backed by the dynamic duo of Lieberman and Clinton—but the Hot Coffee incident has raised skepticism about the ability of the industry to regulate itself or to accurately report the content of games to consumers. As I go out and speak with parents groups about games and education, I am seeing more and more parents who feel they cannot trust the labels on the boxes and this is going to have a prolonged effect on the public perception of the medium. The release of *Bully* will simply add more kerosene to the blazes" [HJ01].

Ultimately, of course, time will tell. Hot Coffee may become the combined *Night Trap* and *Mortal Kombat* of 2005, it may become a turning point in games, or it may end up living in an infamy of sorts, never to be forgotten.

INTERVIEW WITH HENRY JENKINS

Henry Jenkins is Professor of Literature and Comparative Media Studies at the Massachusetts Institute of Technology. He is the Director of their Comparative Media Studies Program and Co-Director of Media in Transition. Henry is a frequent speaker at video game industry events and is noted for his frequent defenses of the *Grand Theft Auto* series and support of a developer's First Amendment rights to create video games, including violent video games.

When news of the mod first reached you, what was your initial reaction?

I think I must have been slow on the uptake because I learned of the whole affair in one chunk—the Hot Coffee content, its discovery as a "mod," and the news that it almost certainly was put there by someone(s) inside the company. I wish I could say that I was surprised or shocked. I was certainly outraged—not by the content per se but by the way Rockstar handled this. I would have respected Rockstar if they had been up front about the content and presented it as one more controversial feature of a game that was targeted for mature consumers. I do think that the current ratings structure punishes sex and nudity while accepting violence as a "natural" aspect of game content. There is also something odd about standards that see sexual representation that would get PG in a movie as unacceptable for anyone under 18 [in a game]. So, if Rockstar had taken on this question directly, I could have respected the choice. But sneaking the content past the industry's own regulatory body and past the eyes of parents seemed to me to be a cowardly way of dealing with the issue. Kurt Squire and I wrote a three-part series for *Computer Games* magazine that makes the case that Rockstar has done more to undermine free expression in the game industry than many of the industry's most hostile critics. What they have done is none the less deadly just because it amounts to friendly fire.

How did that evolve from the first reaction to the announcement that yes, the content was on the disc? What were your feelings/thoughts through the process?

As I said above, I got the whole package more or less at once, and then went out to see the Hot Coffee content for myself, talk to folks around the game industry, talk with students, and get some sense of its long-term impact. For me, it was the last straw in terms of my attitudes toward Rockstar. I had gone on the *Donahue* show and taken a lot of heat to defend *Grand Theft Auto* when it first came out. I wrote about the experience for *Salon* further providing some support to the company against would-be censors. And I felt personally betrayed by their cynical exploitation of this situation. I was angry that they had undercut the industry's efforts at self-regulation and made those of us who have defended them in the past look absurd. They have once again exploited controversy to sell more titles with little or no regard of the degree to which they are fanning the flames of moral panic about games content. I might accept all of this if they were trying to say something through their games, but so often it seems to me that they are out for shock value for its own sake.

Long term, what do you think the fallout's going to be?

We are already seeing setbacks on almost every policy front—new state laws, new proposed federal regulation, new court cases, many of which can be directly traced back to outrage over the handling of Hot Coffee. In the past, many of these laws have simply sought to enforce the industry's own ratings—this is still the case with currently proposed federal legislation being backed by the dynamic duo of Lieberman and Clinton—but the Hot Coffee incident has raised skepticism about the ability of the industry to regulate itself or to accurately report the content of games to consumers. As I go out and speak with parents groups about games and education, I am seeing more and more parents who feel they cannot trust the labels on the boxes and this is going to have a prolonged effect on the public perception of the medium. The release of *Bully* will simply add more kerosene to the blazes.

To you, what was the most surprising thing about the whole debacle?

That so many gamers and game designers are silently fuming but are publicly unwilling to take a stand on what Rockstar is doing to the industry. I respect what they have accomplished as innovative game designers, technically, but I am more and more disappointed in the ways they are wasting the potential of their medium and by their refusal to take responsibility for the long-term impact of their choices. The challenge, of course, is how to be critical of their ethical and artistic choices without seeming to give support to the media effects argument, which, in this case, is beside the point. I am not worried about the impact of this material on kids. And I would still defend their constitutional rights to produce such games. I simply think that they show poor taste and bad judgment in the current cultural context. They are waving a red flag in front of a bull. And I personally feel some obligation to speak out about the choices they are making. [HJ02]

INTERVIEW WITH PATRICK WILDENBORG

Patrick Wildenborg is, arguably, the most famous modder in the world and the creator of the Hot Coffee mod for *Grand Theft Auto: San Andreas*. For weeks in the summer of 2005, he was at the center of the controversy. Patrick is a software engineer and system designer of embedded real-time systems.

Can you take me through the process of "day one"—you get the game home, look at it, and then what?

Well, at the time I got the game home, all of the work for the initial version of the mod was already done. Since the game was released in the States three days earlier, one of the guys had already sent me the SCM-file (binary script-file) of the PC version. I modified that one based on the knowledge I had from studying the PS2 version (which was very similar to the PC version of that file). After that, I sent it back for the guys in the USA to test. A short while after that, they posted the first movies of the "Hot Coffee" mod in action. This was on a private forum, between the release in the USA and the release in Europe. I released the mod to the public on the day of the release of the game in Europe (June 10). At that point, I still didn't have the game myself, and I had only seen the action of the mod in some movie clips.

To answer your question, when I got home with the game, I first started it up to see if it would run on my system. After that, I installed the mod that I had already released at that time, and checked out the Hot Coffee scenes myself.

"Barton Waterduck" had discovered some unused code in the PS2 version. When the PC version came out, was finding/hooking up that code one of the things you wanted to do?

Barton did discover the animation files and found some references to them in the script-file. After analyzing the parts of the code surrounding those references, I found out that they contained what looked like working code of a mini-game that was not in the game. This process took several weeks, as they used a lot of new opcodes in the *San Andreas* SCM file of which the meaning was still to be figured out. After spitting through the code for some weeks, I had a pretty good idea of what the code was suppose to do, and what had to be done to activate it. However, we were not able to make those changes on the PS2 version. So yeah, we have waited anxiously for a couple of months between these discoveries and the release of *San Andreas* for the PC.

When you had it working and realized that there was in fact a functional mini-game in there, what did you think? Were you surprised? Did you have any idea what you'd find in the code?

Just from analyzing the code, and that was the only thing that we could do at that time, we had a pretty good idea what that code would do. And, of course, we were surprised. Even people who knew about the discovery didn't believe that it would be actually working code. And yes, we all were surprised when it turned out to be working (although the code/models are clearly not fully developed).

When Rockstar finally spoke on the matter, they effectively challenged you, saying that the mod was the work of a "determined group of hackers," and noting that it involved "significant technical modifications" and "reconstituting the source code." What was your reaction knowing that it was a single flag?

My personal opinion was that a couple of lawyers without proper technical knowledge at Take-Two had made up that statement. In my eyes, it was just their way of damage control, and I was personally very proud of being called a "hacker." As you should know, in the software engineering scene, "hacker" is a term for a very talented programmer. Sadly, the general public has a much more negative image with the word "hacker."

Why did it take so long for someone to verify that you were, in fact, telling the truth and that Hot Coffee was on the disc? On June 22, 2005, you tell GamePolitics.com that it's on the disc, but it wasn't confirmed in the eyes of many until Gamespot.com confirmed its existence on the PS2 on July 15, 2005.

Your guess is as good as mine. It would have been very easy to prove just by having a look at the original SCM-file and the modified SCM-file with a hex file compare tool. The minimal changes would have been obvious.

Do you think Hot Coffee will change the way games are developed?

I assume that developers will double check what excess code they've left in the game before shipping it.

Do you think Hot Coffee will affect the ability of the mod community to mod games?

Concerning *GTA:SA*, it already did. The second edition of *SA* (with Hot Coffee stuff removed) has a lot of extra checks to prevent certain types of modding, but even beyond that, the ESRB discourages developers to make games easy moddable. I think that would be a very negative thing for gaming on the PC. In my opinion, mod-ability is one of the key selling points of PC games (months after the release of the same games on consoles). Modding also keeps fans interested in the games between the releases of different versions.

Many developers purposely leave their code modder-friendly. It can lead to a longer sales curve and more popularity for the game. Was the same thing true of GTA:SA?

Sure, although only up to a certain degree. They have a lot of settings for the game in plain ASCII files. Some of them even have extensive comments about the meaning of all the fields. But, on the other side, they are using a lot of proprietary formats for models, scripting, textures, and animations, and they don't supply any info or tools for those formats. The *GTA*-modding scene has analyzed all those file-formats themselves and made their own tools to edit them.

Did you have any idea of how big this story was going to be?

Of course not. This was far beyond our wildest dreams.

At its peak, what was it like?

Some days, I had over 50 emails a day about Hot Coffee, and those were mainly journalists requesting interviews and stuff. In addition to that, Dutch journalists even called on the phone. At a certain point, we had the phone disconnected for a couple of days to get some rest.

Do you feel that GTA:SA deserved the AO rating?

No, the AO rating was absurd. Even if the Hot Coffee scenes had been part of the actual gameplay, it didn't justify an AO rating. "Dry humping" with your clothes on? Another game that you might have heard of comes to mind: *Playboy: The Mansion*.

I think the action was at about the same level, based on reviews I've seen. Sadly, I have no copy of the game to check it myself. But besides that, I think it is absurd to give a game a rating based on stuff that isn't playable in any way, without making alterations to the game.

When did you finally feel vindicated, knowing that the rest of the world knew you were telling the truth?

I guess that point came after Gamespot made those cheat codes for the PS2 version public. From that point on, the general media finally accepted that the content was made by Rockstar.

If there is a lasting lesson to be learned from Hot Coffee, what is it?

The biggest eye opener for me personally with my European background was the twisted morals in the USA toward anything that has to do with SEX. It's okay if, in a game, you can beat your girlfriend with a baseball bat or shoot her. But when you share some intimate moments with her after having dated her for quite a while? Oh no. . . .

I hope that the lasting lesson learned by the general public will be that computer games are no longer just aimed at children. A large part of the gaming community consists of adults, and this ever-growing group demands adult themes in games [PatrickW02].

On June 21, 2006, MTV named PatrickW one of the top 10 most influential gamers of all time.

REFERENCES

[Anon01] Anonymous, discussion with Brenda Brathwaite, June 13, 2005.

[Anon02] Anonymous, interview with Brenda Brathwaite, July 14, 2005.

[AP01] Harris, Ron,. Associated Press,. "Investigation, Denials and Outcry over Video Game's Sex Scenes," July 8, 2005. Available online at *http://www .sfgate.com/cgi-bin/article.cgi?file=/news/archive/2005/07/08/ state/n164946D01.DTL*. Accessed December 30, 2005.

[BW01] ESRB Launches Industry Wide Investigation, *BusinessWeek* Online, September 14, 2005. Available online at *http://www.businessweek.com/innovate/ content/sep2005/id20050914_195800.htm?chan=tc*. Accessed February 14, 2006.

[CNet01] Feldman, Curt, "ESRB to Investigate 'San Andreas' Sex Content," CNet.com, July 8, 2005. Available online at *http://marketwatch-cnet.com .com/ESRB+to+investigate+San+Andreas+sex+content/2100-1043_3- 5780374.html*. Accessed July 13, 2006.

[CNN01] Morris, Chris, CNN.com, "Did 'Grand Theft Auto' Get Off Too Easy?" July 21, 2005. Available online at *http://money.cnn.com/2005/07/21/commentary/game_over/column_gaming/index.htm*. Accessed January 8, 2006.

[CNN02] Ibid.

[CNN03] Ibid.

[DM01] McCauley, Dennis, interview with Brenda Brathwaite, December 29, 2005.

[ESA01] Kotaku.com, "The ESA Strikes Back," July 14, 2005. Available online at *http://www.kotaku.com/gaming//the-esa-strikes-back-112665.php*. Accessed January 1, 2006.

[ESA02] Ibid.

[ESA03] Lowenstein, Doug, The Entertainment Software Association. Statement issued on July 20, 2005, in response to re-rating of *Grand Theft Auto: San Andreas.* July 20, 2005.

[ESRB01] Vance, Patricia, "Statement by ESRB President Patricia Vance Regarding Grand Theft Auto: San Andreas Modification," July 8, 2005. Available online at *http://www.esrb.org/about_updates.asp#7-8-05*. Accessed December 30, 2005.

[ESRB02] Vance, Patricia, "Statement by by ESRB President Patricia Vance Regarding Announcement by Senator Hillary Clinton," July 14, 2005. Available online at *http://www.esrb.org/about_updates.asp#7-20-05*. Accessed January 1, 2006.

[ESRB03] Ibid.

[ESRB03A] Vance, Patricia, "ESRB Concludes Investigation into Grand Theft Auto: San Andreas; Revokes M (Mature) Rating," July 20, 2005. Available online at *http://www.esrb.org/about_updates.asp#7-20-05*. Accessed January 1, 2006.

[ESRB04] Vance, Patricia, "ESRB concludes investigation into Grand Theft Auto: San Andreas; Revokes M (Mature) Rating," July 20, 2005. Available online at *http://www.esrb.org/about_updates.asp#7-20-05*. Accessed January 1, 2006.

[FTC01] Federal Trade Commission, "Makers of *Grand Theft Auto: San Andreas* Settle FTC Charges," June 8, 2006. Available online at *http://www.ftc.gov/opa/2006/06/grandtheftauto.htm*. Accessed June 22, 2006.

[GDB01] "NIMF Stirs GTA Hot Coffee Debate to Next Level," GameDAILY BIZ, July 11, 2005. Available online at *http://biz.gamedaily.com/features.asp?article_id=10037&section=feature&email*. Accessed December 11, 2005.

[GDB02] "NIMF Stirs GTA Hot Coffee Debate to Next Level," GameDAILY BIZ, July 11, 2005, Available online at *http://biz.gamedaily.com/features.asp?article_id=10037&section=feature&email*. Accessed December 30, 2005.

[GDB03] Ibid.

[GDB04] "NIMF Stirs GTA Hot Coffee Debate to Next Level," GameDAILY BIZ, July 11, 2005. Available online at *http://biz.gamedaily.com/features.asp?article_id=10037&section=feature&email*. Accessed December 30, 2005.

[GFCC01] User FNC, TheGFCC.com, "Hot Coffee Mod Will Be Available Today," July 12, 2005. Available online at *http://boards.thegfcc.com/viewtopic.php?p=79951*. Accessed January 1, 2006.

[GP01] "GTA: San Andreas: Do Hidden Sex Scenes Cross the Obscenity Threshold?" GamePolitics, June 17, 2005. Available online at *http://www.gamepolitics.com/GTASpecial-617.htm*. Accessed December 28, 2005.

[GP02] Wildenborg, Patrick, response to GamePolitics post "GTA: San Andreas: Do Hidden Sex Scenes Cross the Obscenity Threshold?", June 22, 2005. Available online at *http://www.livejournal.com/users/gamepolitics/30665.html*. Accessed December 28, 2005. Quote edited to correct spelling and grammatical errors.

[GP03] Wildenborg, Patrick, "Did Rockstar Circumvent the ESRB Rating System?", email to GamePolitics, June 30, 2005. Available online at *http://www.gamepolitics.com/GTASpecial-630.htm*. Accessed December 28, 2005.

[GP04] "Did Rockstar Circumvent the ESRB Rating System?", GamePolitics, June 30, 2005. Available online at *http://www.gamepolitics.com/GTASpecial-630.htm*. Accessed December 28, 2005.

[GP05] Vance, Patricia, "Did Rockstar Circumvent the ESRB Rating System?" email to GamePolitics, June 30, 2005. Available online at *http://www.gamepolitics.com/GTASpecial-630.htm*. Accessed December 28, 2005.

[GP06] GamePolitics, "Fatally Flawed Video Rating System Must Change," July 6, 2005. Available online at *http://www.gamepolitics.com/GTASpecial-706.htm*. Accessed December 29, 2005.

[GP07] GamePolitics, "Fatally Flawed Video Rating System Must Change," July 6, 2005. Available online at *http://www.gamepolitics.com/GTASpecial-706.htm*. Accessed December 29, 2005.

[GP07A] Ibid.

[GP08] GamePolitics, "Hot Coffee: Someone is Lying," July 12, 2005. Available online at *http://www.gamepolitics.com/GTASpecial-712-a.htm*. Accessed December 29, 2005.

[GP09] Administration of GTAgarage.com. Letter to the ESRB. GamePolitics.com, "GTA Mod Community Fires Back at ESRB in Hot Coffee Flap." Available online at *http://www.livejournal.com/users/gamepolitics/2005/07/26/*. Accessed January 8, 2006.

[GP10] Ibid.

[GP11] GamePolitics.com, "Anti-Violence Group Pickets Take-Two, Has Demands." Available online at *http://gamepolitics.livejournal.com/58015.html*. Accessed February 7, 2006.

[GS01] Thorsen, Tor, Gamespot.com, "Rumor Control: GTA PSP Screens and (More) Real-Time PS3 Demos," June 10, 2005. Available online at *http://www*

.gamespot.com/pc/action/gta4/news.html?page=1&sid=6127362. Accessed November 29, 2005.

[GS02] Thorsen, Tor,. Gamespot.com, "Rumor Control: GTA PSP Screens and (More) Real-Time PS3 Demos," June 10, 2005. Available online at *http://www.gamespot.com/pc/action/gta4/news.html?page=1&sid=6127362.* Accessed November 29, 2005.

[GS03] Feldman, Curt, "ESRB Investigating San Andreas Sex Minigames," Gamespot.com, July 8, 2005. Available online at *http://www.gamespot.com/news/2005/07/08/news_6128759.html.* Accessed December 31, 2005.

[GS04] Ibid.

[GS05] Thorsen, Tor, Gamespot.com, "Confirmed: Sex Minigame in PS2 San Andreas,", July 15, 2005. Available online at *http://www.gamespot.com/news/2005/07/15/news_6129301.html.* Accessed January 2, 2006.

[GS06] Feldman, Curt, "ESRB Investigating San Andreas Sex Minigames," Gamespot.com, July 8, 2005. Available online at *http://www.gamespot.com/news/2005/07/08/news_6128759.html.* Accessed December 31, 2005.

[GS07] Feldman, Curt, Gamespot.com. "House Backs Federal Investigation of Rockstar Games," July 25, 2005. Available online at *http://www.gamespot.com/xbox/action/gta4/news.html?page=1&sid=6129723.* Accessed January 8, 2006.

[GTA01] Wildenborg, Patrick, Hot Coffee mod, GTAGarage.com, June 9, 2005. Available online at *http://www.gtagarage.com/mods/show.php?id=28.* Accessed November 29, 2005. The mod itself has been removed as a sign of support toward Rockstar.

[GTA02] illspirit, gtasanandreas.net, "San Andreas: Uncensored," June 9, 2005. Available online at *http://www.gtasanandreas.net/news/single.php?id=1436.* Accessed November 29, 2005.

[GTA03] Grand Theft Auto "Hot Coffee" image. gtasanandreas.net image gallery. Available online at *http://www.gtasanandreas.net/screenshots/gallery.php?image=1913.* Accessed November 29, 2005.

[GTA04] DigitalD, gtasanandreas.net, "Hot Coffee Bogus? No Way!" June 12, 2005. Available online at *http://www.gtasanandreas.net/news/single.php?id=1469.* Accessed November 29, 2005.

[HJ01] Jenkins, Henry, interview with Brenda Brathwaite, December 5, 2005.

[HJ02] Ibid.

[HRC01] Rodham-Clinton, Sen. Hillary, "Senator Clinton Announces Legislation to Keep Inappropriate Video Games Out of the Hands of Children," July 14, 2005. Available online at *http://clinton.senate.gov/news/statements/details.cfm?id=240603&&.* Accessed December 30, 2005.

[HRC02] Ibid.

[HRC03] Ibid.

[HRC04] Ibid.

[HRC05] Office of Senator Hillary Rodham Clinton, press release, "Senators Clinton, Lieberman and Bayh Introduce Federal Legislation to Protect Children from Inappropriate Video Games," December 15, 2005. Available online at *http://clinton.senate.gov/news/statements/details.cfm?id=249860*. Accessed January 1, 2006.

[HRC06] Clinton, Senator Hillary Rodham, "Statement by Senator Hillary Rodham Clinton in Reaction to Entertainment Software Rating Board Investigation of Grand Theft Auto: San Andreas," July 20, 2005. Available online at *http://clinton.senate.gov/news/statements/details.cfm?id=241138&&*. Accessed January 8, 2005.

[IEMA01] Halpin, Hal. Interactive Entertainment Merchants Association, "Retail Reaction Statement to Violent Video Game Recall Leading Retailers Respond to Rating Revocation of Latest GTA Game" July 20, 2005. Available online at *http://www.iema.org/news/2005/07-20-05.htm*. Accessed January 5, 2006.

[illspirit01] illspirit, email to Brenda Brathwaite, February 21, 2006.

[KO01] Kotaku.com, "San Andreas Has Built-in Sex Game?" June 10, 2005. Available online at *http://kotaku.com/gaming/playstation-2/gta-san-andreas/san-andreas-has-builtin-sex-game-107361.php*. Accessed November 29, 2005.

[KO02] Kotaku.com, "GTA Sex Authentic and Unlocked?" June 13, 2005, Available online at *http://www.kotaku.com/gaming/pc/gta-sex-authentic-and-unlocked-107620.php*. Accessed November 29, 2005.

[KO03] Kotaku.com, "Hillary Clinton Attacks Grand Theft Auto, March 29, 2005. Available online at *http://kotaku.com/gaming/crime/hillary-clinton-attacks-grand-theft-auto-037463.php*. Accessed December 31, 2005.

[KO04] Kotaku.com, "Hot Coffee on the PS2!", July 15, 2005. Available online at *http://www.kotaku.com/gaming/top/hot-coffee-on-ps2-112800.php*. Accessed January 1, 2006.

[Morris01] Morris, Chris, CNNMoney.com, interview with Brenda Brathwaite, February 20, 2006.

[MSNBC01] Associated Press, "Grandmother Sues Maker of 'Grand Theft Auto,'" MSNBC.com, Available online at *http://www.msnbc.msn.com/id/8728577/*. Accessed February 7, 2006.

[NMF01] Press release,. "National Institute on Media and the Family Warns Parents of Secret *Grand Theft Auto: San Andreas* Content," National Institute on Media and the Family, July 8, 2005. Available online at *http://www.mediafamily.org/press/20050708.shtml*. Accessed February 14, 2006.

[PatrickW] Wildenborg, Patrick, interview with Brenda Brathwaite, February 22, 2006.

[PatrickW01] Wildenborg, Patrick, PatrickW GTA Modding. Available online at *http://patrickw.gtagames.nl/mods.html*. Accessed December 11, 2005.

[PatrickW02] Wildenborg, Patrick, interview with Brenda Brathwaite. February 22, 2006.

[PV01] Vance, Pat, interview with Brenda Brathwaite. June 30, 2005.

[SSB01] Brownback, Senator Sam, press release, "Brownback Asks FTC to Investigate Maker of Grand Theft Auto," July 27, 2005. Available online at *http://brownback.senate.gov/pressapp/record.cfm?id=241864&&days=365&*. Accessed January 8, 2006.

[TG01] Hot Coffee Tee Shirt, ThinkGeek.com. Available online at *http://www.thinkgeek.com/tshirts/gaming/7925/*. Accessed February 7, 2006.

[TTWO01] Take-Two Interactive, Inc., press statement, "Take-Two Interactive Software, Inc. Announces Conclusion of ESRB Investigation," July 20, 2005. Available online at *http://ir.take2games.com/print_release.cfm?releaseid=169278*. Accessed January 8, 2006.

[TTWO02] Ibid.

[TTWO03] Ibid.

[TTWO04] Ibid.

[TTWO05] Ibid.

[TTWO06] Take-Two Interactive, Inc. press statement, "Take-Two Interactive Software, Inc. Announces Conclusion of ESRB Investigation," July 20, 2005. Available online at *http://ir.take2games.com/print_release.cfm?releaseid=169278*. Accessed January 8, 2006.

[TTWO07] Press release, "Take-Two Interactive Software, Inc. Announces Federal Trade Commission Inquiry," July 26, 2005. Available online at *http://ir.take2games.com/ReleaseDetail.cfm?ReleaseID=169679*. Accessed January 8, 2006.

[UK01] Cmdr Zorg, UK Resistance, "GTA SAN ANDREAS — PORN SHAME!" June 10, 2005. Available online at *http://www.ukresistance.co.uk/2005/06/gta-san-andreas-porn-shame.html*. Accessed November 29, 2005.

[Yee01] Yee, Assembly Speaker pro Tem Leland Yee, "Speaker pro Tem Yee Blasts ESRB for Failing to Appropriately Rate *Grand Theft Auto: San Andreas*," press release, July 6, 2005. Available online at *http://democrats.assembly.ca.gov/members/a12/press/p122005060.htm*. Accessed December 29, 2005.

5 Positive Inclusion

In This Chapter

WHAT IS POSITIVE INCLUSION?

When one thinks of sexual content in games, he or she is more likely to think of "Hot Coffee" than the Swiss government or the Public Service Broadcasting Corporation (PBS). However, all three have developed games with sexual content. "Hot Coffee" is, of course, the now notorious sex mini-game uncovered in *Grand Theft Auto: San Andreas*. The latter two entities created educational games with sexual themes and are good examples of positive inclusion.

By and large, however, "positive inclusion" is an enigmatic thing—a grouping that reflects the mainstream culture's attitude toward sexual content in media. Generally, games with what one would consider positive inclusion of sexual content educate and inform through the medium of a game without presenting visually graphic content. However, outside the mainstream, the vernacular culture has a different definition of "positive inclusion"—a grouping that reflects the consumption of sexually themed entertainment and the enjoyment of sex for sex's sake. This chapter reflects both of these groups. Absent from this discussion, but acknowledged, is a third group—one that holds that any sexual content, including sexual education, is unacceptable in games or in any form of media at all.

More than anything, positive inclusion is one framework through which to view sexual content in games, a framework that views such games as, more or less, acceptable in mainstream society.

EDUCATIONAL GAMES

AIDS and STD prevention, safe sex practices, and birth control methods are all matters about which people desire to be educated, and games are being used to do just that. Although traditional methods such as television, print, and Web advertising do carry the necessary message and achieve the same ultimate end, few mediums have the ability to reach people as effectively and cheaply as Internet games.

One of the most popular sexually themed educational games to date is the Unicef®-sponsored 2001 release *Catch the Sperm*. The game is now a part of the Swiss Federal Office of Public Health and the Swiss AIDS Association "Love Life, Stop AIDS" campaign. Developed by Blackpencil Entertainment AG, *Catch the Sperm* promotes safe sex. As the title suggests, the aim of the game is to catch sperm, viruses, and other infectious agents in condoms as they pass through what one can safely assume is a body cavity of some type. The game is so successful that it has spawned five sequels to date, including carnival, Christmas, and soccer editions. The campaign's Web site is located at *www.stopaids.ch/stopaids.php*.

The UK Department of Health (NHS) also uses games to teach about STDs and safe sex practices. Its Web site, *www.playingsafely.co.uk*, features three different games: *Iffy Stiffy*, *Scratch My Box*, and the *Sex Lottery Game*. *Iffy Stiffy* features four apparently nude men with boxes obscuring their genitals. Players click one of the boxes and find out if they've picked up a sexually transmitted disease. If they have, the site provides information on that disease and links to further information about it. Even winners—those who didn't pick up a disease—are presented with information on what they *could* have caught. *Scratch My Box* and the *Sex Lottery Game* use similar mechanics, but feature female models and a slot machine, respectively. In addition to the games, the site also provides information on clinic locations and numbers for several 24-hour, free, confidential hotlines.

Planned Parenthood has also incorporated educational games with sexually themed content into its Teenwire.com site at *www.teenwire.com/interactive/do-archive-games.php*. Similar to the UK and Swiss sites, Teenwire.com features games that promote safe sex and provides information on sexually transmitted diseases.

Their game, *That Would Suck* mimics a television show where contestants must answer questions about HIV, condoms, and high-risk sexual behavior. The game presents players with questions about safe sex and sexual behavior. Answering correctly, they receive further information on the topic. If they get it wrong, they're allowed to try again. Another game, *The Sexually Transmitted Infection Petting Zoo*, takes players through an introductory, humorous, yet serious discussion of sexually transmitted diseases before providing players a quiz to test their knowledge of the same.

In addition, the site also features games that deal with abstinence, birth control, coming out, and sexual self-esteem. For instance, *Our Super Duper Planet: Nature Is Groovy* answers questions about breast and penis size and tries to impress acceptance upon those who might feel uncomfortable about themselves, while *Jim Dandy and His Very Gay Day* provides a gay-positive message for kids who might be questioning their sexuality. Teenwire's games can be found online at *www.teenwire .com/interactive/do-archive-games.php*.

Far removed from games that educate about sexually transmitted diseases is PBS's *The Mating Game*. A take on the old television series *The Dating Game,* this game teaches players about the mating habits and rituals of wildlife. As with the previous games, however, *The Mating Game* uses humor to get its educational message across. The game is available online at *www.pbs.org/wgbh/evolution/sex/ mating/*.

Other sexually themed educational games are provided on commercial sites. While these games seek to educate and entertain, they also carry the marketing message of their brand. One such game, *Sex Championships*, was created by UK condom retailer eCondoms.co.uk. Set in Casanova Stadium, if players lose their "self control," they lose the match. If they do well, they climb through 12 different ranks from "virgin" to "sexual superhero" to "sex champion." In its press release announcing the game, eCondoms.co.uk noted the increase in sexually transmitted diseases and safe sex practices as a prime motivator in its creation. Other condom makers also provide games to promote safe sex and brand awareness. Cool Condoms has released the *Cool Condoms Game*. In the game, the player sees a character on the screen in a sexual pose. The player must choose the matching sexual pose of the partner. The game can be found on the Cool Condoms site at *www.cool-condoms.com/eng/index.html*. Condom makers Durex and Trojan also feature games on their site. *Sue Jo's Fetish Flip n' Match Game* is another commercially sponsored game designed to educate players about fetishes while simultaneously promoting a brand—the "Sex Talk with Sue Johanson" radio and television show. The game is carried on *http://games.oxygen.com/*. Players flip cards over and attempt to match a fetish name with its description.

By incorporating games into their educational or marketing campaigns, these agencies and companies harness the Internet community to carry their message. Such games are inherently entertaining and silly all at the same time, and as such are likely to be discussed, forwarded, and forwarded again. The author of this book first became aware of *Catch the Sperm* through an email that had been forwarded from one person to the next purely due to its amusing and simultaneously serious message.

Why do these agencies use games to promote their sexually themed message? Because it works.

THERAPEUTIC GAMES

Games have long been used in therapy. Even back in the early 1980s, the *Wizardry®* series of role-playing games was used by a doctor to help children with social disorders learn about cooperation and compassion. Games also offer possibilities in the field of sexual therapy, although to date, no such games have been released commercially.

In the privacy of their own home, couples follow a prescribed course as outlined by their therapist. By using principles adapted from game design, software could be designed to be entertaining, easy-to-use, educational, therapeutic, and surprising all at the same time. Such games could be tailored to allow players to create individual avatars with detailed preferences and prohibitions they need not share with their partner until they choose to do so, if they choose to do so. During gameplay, such games could take these things into account, and the therapist's assessment to create courses for players to follow. Examples of this course would be shown on screen using the players' avatars. Outside of gameplay, such games could feature educational modes where players could learn about techniques, passions, phobias, fears, and other issues inherent in the formation of one's sexual identity. The games could also provide information on things that may improve their sexual performance, including diet, mood, and setting. By showing the hows and whys of a variety of situations in the safe and secure privacy of one's own home, such games have the potential to educate and entertain. Game mechanics can even be used to further facilitate and moderate conversations about sex. Consider the myriad conversations spawned on dozens of topics following the release of the breakaway trivia game *You Don't Know Jack*.

Despite the prevalence of sexual therapists and "self-help" books, as of the date of this book's publication, this author is unaware of any facilitated sex games on the market or in development.

COUPLE & GROUP GAMES

Outside of a therapist's facilitated sex game, the market for games that encourage sex play between couples is growing. The appropriately named *Bliss* is one such game. It was developed by a software engineer who was seeking something less "frat-like" and lewd for his own sex play with his wife. Unable to find anything on the Internet, he created his own product and, ultimately, a business.

In *Bliss*, players purchase and develop property similar to the game *Monopoly®*. The similarity ends there, however. The properties include such spaces as strip clubs and other potentially erotic venues. When a player lands on a space, he or she is given a particular task. What will *Bliss* have players do? Although the game assigns a task—everything from a simple kiss to oral sex to the use of whatever sex toys the players have on hand—what happens is completely up to the players, actually, and based on their predetermined preferences and passion levels. Before the game starts, each player customizes the game to his or her liking, assigning passion values to each action and his or her individual starting passion level (how "turned on" he or she feels currently at the beginning of a game session). These values, in turn, determine when, if at all, these actions show up in gameplay. For instance, one player may be embarrassed to do a strip dance in front of his partner. So, he'll set the value to 10 (never). Likewise, his wife may enjoy oral sex, but needs to be incredibly turned on before she's willing to receive it. So, she'll set its value to 8. As the play progresses, players can easily change things if anything makes them uncomfortable. What if players start the game at different passion levels? The game is balanced to accommodate that, and through actions eventually evens the partners out.

In addition to customizing the various actions, the game also lets players detail what they're wearing so that their clothing, naturally, becomes a part of the game, too. *Bliss* also allows players to add their own music to better enhance the mood. Bliss is available at *www.gamesforloving.com/* and features expansion packs for continued, specialty play.

Other games allow for couple and group play. *Onyx*, a game by Sym Toys, is for two to six adult players. Similar to *Bliss*, *Onyx* is essentially a *Monopoly*-style board game on a computer. If players land on owned property, they can pay the rent requested by the owner or choose an action card instead. The game board also features other spaces such as the "random encounter" square, "fate" square, and "center stage" square. Each square brings about the potential for sex play. Like *Bliss* and other games of this genre, *Onyx* allows players to customize their level of wildness beforehand so players aren't presented with actions or encounters that would make them uncomfortable. *Onyx* is available online at *www.symtoys.com/onyx.html*.

ONLINE ROMANTIC WORLDS

When Match.com debuted back in the late 1990s, friends of this author revealed that they met their mate through the service or another online venue. Such information was provided with the condition that it never, ever be revealed to another. In fact, some friends had elaborate cover stories to detail how they'd come to know someone from California when they were working in a small town in northern New York and never traveled. Nowadays, of course, such meetings and unions are common. "We met on eHarmony" isn't an embarrassing admission but rather a sophisticated and smart move for those looking to cut through the chaff and find the person of their dreams. Online worlds that facilitate romantic developments between players or members may be the next logical extension of such matchmaking services. In fact, some multiuser games already have informal matchmaking "services." Players create a profile and other players can search profiles for shared interests, including sexual proclivities and romantic preferences. For instance, the game *Star Wars Galaxies®*, incorporated a matchmaking service for players (not their characters, mind you), and let them set search criteria including likes and dislikes. At present, however, mainstream matchmaking services and video games have yet to meet.

Such a union will likely occur in the future, particularly as such services take notice of the success of subscription-based MMOs. A tremendous financial, marketing, and public relations opportunity is being missed as users of the various matchmaking sites "meet" their potential mates via email, phone, online chat, and, ultimately, a coffee shop. A more satisfying, safe, fun, and immersive experience could be had if such services leveraged MMO technology to allow people to communicate and meet in virtual worlds, too. By providing their subscribers a virtual world in which to meet and interact, a matchmaking site adds substantial dimension to its offerings, allowing people to inhabit the same space often weeks or months before they otherwise could. Although the costs to create a new MMO space are substantial, the technology itself could be licensed.

Those familiar with the powerful sense of community and camaraderie that develops in virtual spaces already see the benefit of creating online worlds that facilitate such relationships. Numerous MMO erotic games are designed to allow players to engage in the full range of human sexual experience—from romantic chat, dates, and kissing, to intercourse, should the parties so choose to engage in the act. Among these games are *Naughty America: The Game*, *Red Light Center*, *Erotasy Island*, *Heavenly Bodies*, and *Rapture Online*. Some of these games were still in development as this book went to press.

Online worlds also allow people to cross all kinds of unnecessary and artificial boundaries and encourage socialization. At 11 P.M. tonight, someone may not feel like heading out to a club, but he or she may be more than willing to go online to meet friends there. By the millions, subscribers are meeting others and forming life-long friendships. Increasingly, players are getting married. Online worlds also provide opportunities for those who would not otherwise be able to enjoy them. Consider shy people who, under the guise of a 47th level Warlock avatar, are able to meet and talk to women confidently and comfortably. Likewise, those separated by geography and sometimes even language have the opportunity to share a physical space and to interact despite these limitations.

The field of mainstream multi-user environments is, of course, as old as the Internet itself. It has yet to be explored to its fullest potential in the realm of human relationships. What if eHarmony met *Second Life*?

FETISH & DESIRE REALIZATION

As artistic and engineering creations, video games have the ability to create interactive and virtual people, places, things, and situations that no other medium could possibly create or re-create. For instance, *Roboho*, an online robot sex sim game, allows the player to engage in acts of robotic sex while playing as a robot. *Second Life*, an online MMO, has an active "furry" community, as do numerous other multiuser online spaces. Video games allow players to engage in fetish and desire realization that simply would not be possible in real life.

Consider for a moment women and men who like men with large penises. On the Internet and in magazines, content can be found to somewhat satiate this desire. Without the aid of an artist and the appropriate software, however, such content is unlikely to be longer than 14 inches in length. While the mainstream would consider this more than sufficient, what about people who are aroused by the possibility of impossibly large penises? For them, such desires can be realized and made interactive through the medium of video games. Games like *DreamStripper* and even *Playboy: The Mansion* offer such possibilities to those attracted to impossibly large breasts as well. In 2006, *DreamStripper* upgraded its software to allow users to modify the dancer's breast size. *Playboy: The Mansion* featured several "cheats" that allowed the player to do the same thing. Not all desires and fetishes are as common as these, however.

For those with less mainstream desires, the Internet offers a welcome respite. There, communities form within virtual worlds—some created expressly for that purpose—where they can meet others who share similar desires. As was mentioned, *Second Life* supports an active furry community, but it is by no means the only adult-themed community in *Second Life*. Whatever the fetish, whatever the desire, it is bound to be in *Second Life*. While the fetish and desire communities that have formed in *Second Life* are emergent and user created, other online communities have been created expressly for this purpose. These communities allow their players to engage in mutually satisfactory fetish play. Out of respect for those communities whose memberships are frequently small and invite-only and whose servers are not built to handle an overwhelming amount of curious sightseers, their names will not be printed here.

By allowing players with similar fetishes and desires to gather, video games and online worlds facilitate the safe exploration of one's sexuality and the healthy acceptance and exploration of sexual desires and fetishes.

6 Self-Regulation

In This Chapter

- Rating Games
- The Game Content Guidelines
- The Videogame Rating Council
- The Ratings Battle
- The Recreational Software Advisory Council (RSAC)
- The Entertainment Software Rating Board (ESRB)
- Other Rating Initiatives
- Interview with Patricia Vance

RATING GAMES

From the beginning—or very close to it, anyway—there have been video game ratings. In the very early days, games like the Online System's *Softporn Adventure* billed themselves as "R-Rated" on the cover of the game sleeve. Other games like Mystique's *Custer's Revenge* noted that the game was for adults only and even carried the text prohibiting the sale of the game to minors in large type on the game box cover. Until 1985, however, such ratings were wholly voluntary efforts.

THE GAME CONTENT GUIDELINES

The first content restriction guidelines were created by Nintendo of America in 1985. The Game Content Guidelines were a set of standards that games had to meet to receive the official Nintendo "Seal of Quality."

The two previous years had been difficult for the video game market. Publishers were eager to make a buck from gamers' voracious appetites and so flooded the market with games of questionable quality. Other video game hardware makers such as Atari and Sega had seen their systems attracting games with increasingly sexual and violent content. By creating its "Seal of Quality" and adopting content standards, Nintendo hoped to reassure customers of both the playability and suitability of its games.

Howard Lincoln, then Nintendo of America's senior vice president, cited Nintendo's standards in his testimony before Congress on December 9, 1993:

- No sexually suggestive or explicit content
- No sexist language or depictions
- No random, gratuitous, or excessive violence
- No graphic illustration of death
- No domestic violence or abuse
- No excessive force in sports games
- No ethnic, racial, religious, or sexual stereotypes
- No profanity or obscenity
- No use of drugs, smoking materials, or alcohol
- No subliminal political messages or overt political statements

In the same testimony, Lincoln cited content that Nintendo deemed offensive and, if found in a game, would insist its licensees change. Among the sexual content Nintendo deemed inappropriate were women dressed as Playboy Bunnies, men whistling at women, a woman who "shakes her breasts," and a game in which a female's clothing did not "adequately cover her body" [Lincoln01].

In recent years, Nintendo has eased up considerably in its content standards. According to the ESRB's site, and as of this writing, 83 M-rated titles have been released for the Game Boy®, Game Boy® Advance, GameCube™, Nintendo Entertainment System®, and Nintendo DS™. Of those, only 13 titles were assigned content descriptors for sexual content [ESRB01].

THE VIDEOGAME RATING COUNCIL

Cited as the first rating system in the industry, Sega of America created the Videogame Rating Council (VRC) in 1993. The previous year had been an interesting one for Sega. It had released the game *Night Trap*™, which featured full motion video of co-eds in lingerie, and was planning to release its most violent video game to date, a Sega Genesis™ version of Midway's *Mortal Kombat*®.

The original arcade version of the *Mortal Kombat* had hit a new high for violent entertainment. It featured finishing fatality moves that, among other things, allowed players to rip out their opponent's spine. Both Sega and Nintendo were planning to release a home version of the game, but Sega's would be the only one to contain the original game's gruesome moves. Although they would be accessible only if the player entered a secret code, the code's secret would travel gamer-to-gamer fast.

Unlike Nintendo's pass or fail system, the VRC assigned three different ratings: GA for general audiences, MA-13 for mature audiences 13 and up, and MA-17 for mature audiences 17 and up. However, the ratings system was plagued by problems and inconsistencies. Its GA rating was too broad to provide parents the necessary level of differentiation they required. A game that was all right for a 12-year-old to play may be too scary for a younger child. Furthermore, games were rated inconsistently. *Mortal Kombat* received an MA-13 rating on the Sega Genesis and an MA-17 rating on the Sega CD. The two contained the same content, although the Genesis version's most gruesome moves needed to be unlocked.

Ultimately, Sega abandoned the VRC system.

THE RATINGS BATTLE

Following the Congressional hearings of 1993, and under great political pressure to do so, industry leaders got together to hammer out a voluntary ratings system that could be applied to video games. Two groups rose to the challenge: the Software Publishers Association (SPA) and the Interactive Digital Software Association (IDSA), now known as the Entertainment Software Association (ESA). The two groups presented their ratings systems for the first time before Congress on July 29, 1994.

Robert Sirotek, then co-owner and vice president of Sir-tech Software, Inc., was an active member of the SPA's ratings committee. "Lieberman was looking for legislation that would protect the innocence of children. I don't think there was any concern by industry trades people about the positive results that that could have on society," Sirotek remembers. "It was a matter of understanding how to best implement it, and how to cater best to Joe Lieberman so that it wouldn't ultimately be slammed down the industry's throats. It was either do it voluntarily or the Senate will legislate it to be done" [Sirotek01]. At the time, of course, some developers and publishers, like Sega, were labeling their software, and others placed warnings on packages that they felt contained mature content. However, there was no universal rating system that was used by all. So, for all the seeming saber rattling of the politicians, the industry had already shown a desire to inform consumers about the content present in video games. For the industry, it was a matter of responding to Congress while providing consumers as much information as possible.

The SPA formed the Recreational Software Advisory Council (RSAC) and the IDSA formed the Entertainment Software Rating Board (ESRB) to handle the job. Both ratings systems are covered in detail later in this chapter. However, in brief, the RSAC system and the ESRB system were quite different in numerous ways.

Rating metric: The ESRB system rates by age group (i.e., E for everybody, T for Teen, and so on), and RSAC rated by volume content (i.e., a 2 out of 4 for Violence). Both systems provided content descriptors to supplement their ratings.

Rating method: The ESRB uses anonymous panels to review a game's content and select a rating, and RSAC asked developers to review their own content and RSAC assigned a rating accordingly.

Rating criteria: The ESRB provides its raters general guidelines to follow, and RSAC provided a specific checklist to developers and publishers.

The divide between the two groups was deeper than their rating system, however. The SPA was supported by a majority of computer game publishers, while the IDSA represented mostly video game publishers. This led to some political struggles between the two organizations. Computer game publishers did not feel comfortable having their games rated by an organization set up by video game manufacturers, and the distrust was mutual. Meanwhile, some game publishers—both video and computer—that were members of the SPA felt marginalized by the same organization. At the time, game publishers did not command the same respect as publishers of serious software. As such, they felt that the SPA would not do an adequate job of representing them before Congress or creating a rating system that was truly tailored to their needs.

Speaking about the SPA and video game publishers, Sirotek remembers the divide between the video game market and the SPA. "The SPA's focus was on other industry segments," Sirotek said, "and the entertainment sector felt very neglected by the SPA. Ultimately, that led to the departure of the whole entertainment business from the SPA" [Sirotek02].

Even within the IDSA group, there were bitter rivalries. In a hearing before Congress, the very hearing that would ultimately prove the catalyst for the creation of the IDSA, Sega and Nintendo announced their intent to support the development of a ratings system along with other future members of the IDSA. Shortly after the announcement, the two attacked each other on the floor of Congress. In a widely publicized incident, Nintendo decried Sega's use of violence in its games prompting Sega's spokesperson to retaliate by displaying a prop gun featured in some Nintendo titles. Ultimately, however, the two saw eye to eye.

International politics were also involved. According to a member of the original committee who requested anonymity, "The political side of it was that the Software Publishers Association was primarily backed by American software corporations and the other association was backed by the Japanese corporations with the exception of Electronic Arts, which had a huge stake in this thing. Naturally, being an American corporation, I was trying to get a rating system that would become the standard backed by corporations in America, but that didn't come to be and that was that" [Anon01].

Ultimately, Senator Lieberman selected the ESRB system. "We presented [the RSAC system] to Senator Lieberman, and his office reviewed it," said Sirotek. "Ultimately, another rating system by the IDSA [now the ESA] was chosen. This was a rating system that is currently in use today" [Sirotek03].

Theoretically, that could have been the end of the ratings battle. However, some computer game developers and publishers continued to use the RSAC system until 1999 when RSAC exited the game rating business.

"The RSAC rating system just faded out," said Sirotek. "We were frankly concerned about this. If the other rating system became the standard, its name would be in the limelight, and indeed, that's what happened." Sirotek also felt that the SPA's inability to gain the support of the entertainment segment of the industry was a major factor in RSAC's failure [Sirotek04].

Following the death of the RSAC ratings, virtually all games sold in the United States used the ESRB system and still do today. Large retailers such as Wal-Mart, Best Buy, and others opted to carry only games that were rated. When the Interactive Entertainment Merchants Association (IEMA) was founded in 1997, it ratified this unspoken policy. Going unrated was not an option for games hoping to be marketed in the traditional channel.

"They're doing a good job," said Sirotek speaking about the ESRB. "[Sir-tech Software, Inc.] worked with them after the RSAC system failed. We submitted products for ratings, and they were very impartial with everything. They were extensive, they were quick in their decision making, and they were quite thorough and got it right on the money most of the time. So, I can't fault them. However, at the time the two rating systems were being evaluated by Senator Lieberman, I tell you, there was a fierce battle going on between RSAC and the IDSA" [Sirotek05].

A committee member who preferred anonymity added, "It was all about who would be the mouthpiece for the entertainment sector. The last thing we wanted to see was to hand over control of the video game business to the Japanese, as is the case in electronics. But, fortunately, that hasn't happened" [Anon02].

THE RECREATIONAL SOFTWARE ADVISORY COUNCIL (RSAC)

The RSAC rating system had three components: "violence," "nudity/sex," and "language." Each of these three components had five levels, ranging from "0," reserved for a minimum amount of content, to a high of "4" (Figure 6.1).

Category	Level 0	Level 1	Level 2	Level 3	Level 4
Violence	Harmless conflict; some damage to objects	Creatures injured or killed; damage to objects; fighting	Humans injured or killed; with small amount of blood	Humans injured or killed; blood and gore	Wanton and gratuitous violence; torture; rape
Nudity/Sex	No nudity or revealing attire / Romance, no sex	Revealing attire / Passionate kissing	Partial nudity / Clothed sexual touching	Non-sexual frontal nudity / Non-explicit sexual activity	Provocative frontal nudity / Explicit sexual activity; sex crimes
Language	Inoffensive slang; no profanity	Mild expletives	Expletives; non-sexual anatomical references	Strong, vulgar language; obscene gestures	Crude or explicit sexual references

FIGURE 6.1 RSAC rating information. Copyright © 2006, Internet Content Rating Association®. Reprinted with permission of the Internet Content Rating Association®.

These levels were represented on game boxes using a thermometer. Next to these iconic thermometers, descriptors notified buyers what the objectionable content was, whether it be blood, expletives, or nudity (Figure 6.2).

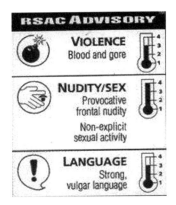

FIGURE 6.2 RSAC rating as it appears on game packaging.

Copyright © 2006, Internet Content Rating Association®. Reprinted with permission of the Internet Content Rating Association®.

Getting Rated

RSAC's rating method was voluntary and ran on the honor system. Publishers received a form that listed specific types of content in each of its three categories. After completing the form, publishers returned it to RSAC who then applied ratings from zero to four in each of its categories. To ensure compliance, RSAC randomly sampled games to verify the publisher's claims. Violators faced fines of up to $10,000 and possible recalls.

RSAC Today

RSAC's basic principles of protecting children from harmful content still exist today. In 1996, RSAC began to rate Internet content. In 1999, RSAC was folded into the Internet Content Rating Association (ICRA) and counts AOL, Microsoft, and Verizon among its many members. They can be found on the Web at *www.icra.org*.

THE ENTERTAINMENT SOFTWARE RATING BOARD (ESRB)

The ESRB rating system has two components: rating symbols and content descriptors. The symbols denote the appropriate age group for the game and the descriptors highlight the content that may have caused the rating or might be of interest or concern to a consumer. Ratings range from "EC" for Early Childhood to "AO" for Adults Only (Figure 6.3).

The ESRB uses 32 content descriptors. Those that cover sexual content range from "Comic Mischief" to "Strong Sexual Content" (Figure 6.4).

The assigned rating appears on the front and back of the game packaging. On the back, the necessary content descriptors are also listed along with the rating icon. ESRB ratings are also used in the game advertising, whether the ad appears in print, on the Internet, on television, or radio. Ratings are also used in game trailers and demos. Games that have not yet been rated carry the "RP" rating, but this only appears in advertising materials.

An arm of the ESRB, the Advertising Review Council (ARC) monitors all game advertising to ensure it is thorough in its display of rating information and is consistent, accurate, and targeting the appropriate audiences.

Getting Rated

The ESRB uses an anonymous, independent panel of three or more trained individuals to develop a rating and assign content descriptors for a game. Along with a detailed questionnaire, content creators supply the ESRB with gameplay footage and other material showing the most objectionable content found in the game, its context, and the part it plays in the product as a whole.

The raters, who have no connection whatsoever to the game industry or to each other, recommend ratings for the game on a scene-by-scene basis, and for the game overall after reviewing the material. Although ratings can and, on occasion, have varied widely—what someone might consider suitable for an E rating, another

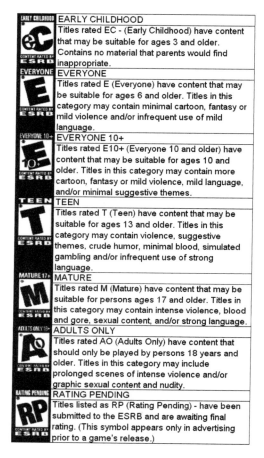

EARLY CHILDHOOD	Titles rated EC - (Early Childhood) have content that may be suitable for ages 3 and older. Contains no material that parents would find inappropriate.
EVERYONE	Titles rated E (Everyone) have content that may be suitable for ages 6 and older. Titles in this category may contain minimal cartoon, fantasy or mild violence and/or infrequent use of mild language.
EVERYONE 10+	Titles rated E10+ (Everyone 10 and older) have content that may be suitable for ages 10 and older. Titles in this category may contain more cartoon, fantasy or mild violence, mild language, and/or minimal suggestive themes.
TEEN	Titles rated T (Teen) have content that may be suitable for ages 13 and older. Titles in this category may contain violence, suggestive themes, crude humor, minimal blood, simulated gambling and/or infrequent use of strong language.
MATURE	Titles rated M (Mature) have content that may be suitable for persons ages 17 and older. Titles in this category may contain intense violence, blood and gore, sexual content, and/or strong language.
ADULTS ONLY	Titles rated AO (Adults Only) have content that should only be played by persons 18 years and older. Titles in this category may include prolonged scenes of intense violence and/or graphic sexual content and nudity.
RATING PENDING	Titles listed as RP (Rating Pending) - have been submitted to the ESRB and are awaiting final rating. (This symbol appears only in advertising prior to a game's release.)

FIGURE 6.3 ESRB rating icons and descriptions. Copyright © 2006 Entertainment Software Rating Board/Entertainment Software Association. Reprinted with permission of the Entertainment Software Association.

might rate T or even M—the ESRB will continue the rating process by calling in additional raters until it identifies a majority consensus. When a consensus is found, the ESRB sends the content provider a rating certificate noting the game's rating and content descriptors. Publishers are also required to provide final product to the ESRB to ensure they have met the necessary labeling requirements, and the ESRB randomly tests products for full content disclosure.

Of course, sometimes, content providers don't want the rating they've been assigned. Developers create games with a particular market and marketing plan in place, and as such, getting an "M" or an "AO" rating when you wanted a "T" or

Comic Mischief	Depictions or dialogue involving slapstick or suggestive humor
Crude Humor	Depictions or dialogue involving vulgar antics, including "bathroom" humor
Mature Humor	Depictions or dialogue involving "adult" humor, including sexual references
Nudity	Graphic or prolonged depictions of nudity
Partial Nudity	Brief and/or mild depictions of nudity
Sexual Themes	Mild to moderate sexual references and/or depictions. May include partial nudity
Sexual Violence	Depictions of rape or other violent sexual acts
Strong Sexual Content	Graphic references to and/or depictions of sexual behavior, possibly including nudity
Suggestive Themes	Mild provocative references or materials

FIGURE 6.4   ESRB sexual content descriptors and descriptions. Copyright © 2006 Entertainment Software Rating Board/Entertainment Software Association. Reprinted with permission of the Entertainment Software Association.

an "M" can and has forced some back into development. After the content has been altered, many resubmit hoping for a lower rating.

Using a panel of in-house experts, the ESRB randomly samples games to ensure that the game was released as rated and as submitted and that no content that would affect a game's rating was omitted from the ratings process or added afterward. The "Hot Coffee" scandal, of course, was a singular event that resulted in changes in submission policies at the ESRB. Those changes are covered later in this chapter.

Sex and Ratings

Since it began rating games and as of the date of this writing, 1306 titles have been released that contain some type of sexual content (from comic mischief to strong sexual content), of which 69 contain strong sexual content. AO games number 22. Nudity or partial nudity can be found in 43 titles, 11 of them T-rated [ESRB02].

OTHER RATING INITIATIVES

The ESRB system is the predominant system in both the United States and Canada. Outside of North America, however, other ratings systems and boards exist. The main systems are:

- The Pan European Game Information (PEGI) system is used in 16 European nations, including the UK, Italy, Ireland, France, and Denmark. PEGI is an age-based ratings system that also uses content descriptors to note such things as violence, bad language, fear, sex, drugs, and discrimination. It can be found on the Internet at *www.pegi.info*.

- The British Board of Film Classification (BBFC) rates games that contain specific types of sexual or violent content under the Video Recordings Act. The BBFC can be found on the Internet at *www.bbfc.co.uk/*.

- The Office of Film and Literature Classification (OFLC) rates games and other media in Australia. The rating for games caps at "MA 15+." Games deemed too graphic for a 15-year-old are refused classification and may not be sold or distributed in the country, even to or among adults. While the OFLC does provide R18+ and X18+ ratings for movies, they have yet to do so for video games. The OFLC can be found online at *www.oflc.gov.au*. A complete list of games that have been refused classification is available at *www.refused-classification.com/*.

- The Computer Entertainment Rating Organization (CERO) rates video games in Japan using an aged-based rating system that includes content descriptors. CERO can be found on the Internet at *www.cero.gr.jp/*.

- Unterhaltungssoftware SelbstKontrolle (USK) rates video games in Germany using an aged-based rating system. In addition to the USK ratings, Germany also has what's known as The Index. A list maintained by the Bundesprüfstelle für jugendgefährdende Medien (BPjM), The Index contains a list of games and other media that are unsuitable to anyone under the age of 18 or contain banned material such as Nazi symbols. The BPjM can be found online at *http://bundespruefstelle.de*. The USK can be found online at *www.usk.de*.

INTERVIEW WITH PATRICIA VANCE

Patricia Vance is president of the Entertainment Software Rating Board, the self-regulatory body for the computer and video game industry based in the United States.

Can you tell me about the early days of the ESRB?

The ESRB was created in the wake of Congressional hearings about marketing of violent and sexually explicit entertainment products to children. These hearings identified the need to have accurate labeling to inform consumers about the content in the game they're purchasing. So, in 1994, after conducting extensive nationwide research, particularly with parents, the industry went about creating a rating system specific to computer and video games. We brought in a whole host of childhood development experts and other professionals to help, and focused on trying to understand what would be most beneficial to consumers. Historically, entertainment ratings systems had focused on age appropriateness and less on specific content disclosure. For instance, a rating system like the Motion Picture Association of America's (MPAA's) was primarily based on age categories and the extent to which a parent needed to be cautioned, but didn't tell you very much about what you could expect to see in the movie. What we learned in our research was that it was very important to consumers to understand why a game got the rating that it did. This feedback was the genesis of our two-part system. The two-part ESRB system has been praised as the most informative and effective of all entertainment rating systems, and the fact that we have both age categories and content descriptors is the main reason. We know that parents ultimately want to make their own decisions about what's appropriate for their kids. Parents want to have the flexibility of making a decision not solely based on someone else's age recommendation, but even more importantly, what's in the game. They want to be able to answer two key questions, "What will I or will I not be exposing my child to?" and based on the answer to the first question, ultimately, "Is this game OK for my child to play?" The latter question is one that only a parent can answer, and the rating system is just one tool among several to help them do so.

Some people suggest that consumers aren't taking the ratings seriously. They say that mothers go out and pick up Grand Theft Auto *for their kids and say, "It's just a game," and . . .*

Actually, our research indicates that most parents don't allow their children to play M-rated games. But for those who do, that's their decision. The product is labeled with a Mature rating symbol, with age 17+ on it. You can flip the box over and look at the screen shots, read the publisher's description of the gameplay, and also see that there are five different ESRB content descriptors for *Grand Theft Auto*—Intense Violence, Blood and Gore, Use of Drugs, Strong Sexual Content, and Strong Language. You have to ask yourself, at what point does it shift from being ESRB's responsibility to the parent's? The product is very clearly labeled, and we've done an awful lot in the last several years to make sure that parents are aware of both parts of the system and know how to use them. And the vast majority of parents do. But we can't force every parent to do so.

What is the ESRB doing to improve parental awareness?

Well, we're doing a lot. We launched a new, multifaceted public service campaign in 2003 with the "Okay to Play?" slogan. A key component of the campaign is a print ad that was placed in numerous mass-consumer publications, particularly publications that reach moms (e.g., *Ladies Home Journal, Redbook, TV Guide, Oprah,* etc.). Along with the print ad, we launched an Internet advertising campaign with broad distribution on game enthusiast and retailer sites, among others. A critical component of the campaign was the creation of a retail partnership program. We realized that the in-store retail environment is one of the most effective environments for educating consumers about the ESRB ratings system. Our retail partnership program, in which virtually every major retailer in the U.S. and in Canada participates, includes a variety of ratings education materials that can be incorporated into existing displays and merchandising vehicles in the store. Prior to the launch of this program, we would send posters and brochures into the retail channel, and keep our fingers crossed that they'd be displayed or made available to consumers. But that's not how retail merchandising works. The in-store environment is well thought out and every square inch is planned. In fact, there's something called a "plan-o-gram," which many retail chains use and which dictates how local stores promote and display product. Everything that is supposed to be displayed on the floor is specified on that plan-o-gram. So, upon meeting with the retailers, we asked them what they needed from us to become part of that plan. They told us. Since that date, it has worked beautifully. Today, if you walk into any store that is part of a major chain that sells computer and video games, you will likely see one, if not several different components of our ratings education program displayed. We also provide training materials to help educate store associates about the rating system. We'll even create store policy signs regarding the sale of Mature-rated games if they want us to. Retailers now have a whole host of ESRB materials that they can use in their stores in a very customized way. In terms of the program's impact, it's very hard to measure, but in the first year alone, we calculated that this retail partnership program generated over a billion consumer impressions.

There has been a flurry of legislation recently. Some politicians say the industry's efforts at self-regulation aren't working. How do you respond to that?

Well, it depends on what you mean by "not working." When they say "not working," I assume they're referring to enforcement of the rating system at the retail level. Well, that was never the intention or mission of the rating system. The mission of the rating system is to inform consumers so they can make an educated purchase decision. In terms of fulfilling that mission, I think anyone would be hard-pressed to say that the system is not working. In fact, it works beautifully. The system has very high awareness now—83% among parents with children under the age of 17 that play video games, with regular use of the ratings at about 74%. Talk about success of the rating system! We're going gangbusters!

So, when legislators start talking about the ratings "not working," what are they really talking about? Is it sending a kid into a store with $50 to see whether they can purchase an M-rated game? That is not something that we set out to prevent with the rating system. That's someone else's goal and mission. Do we support store policies at the retail level? Absolutely. We encourage retailers not to sell M-rated games to children. But, ultimately, it's their own store policy to implement, and they're the only ones who can enforce it. And let's not forget that 90% of game purchases are made by adults, to which those policies would not even apply.

For now, we're extremely pleased with how far we've come with the ratings education program we launched with retailers, and we will continue to encourage them to implement and enforce responsible sales policies.

How does the ESRB handle rating emergent game content? For example, there have been virtual prostitution rings in many of the MMORPGs.

When online game communities started to evolve, the rating system established an online rating notice for any game that had an online component that allowed users to actually create content that might change the game experience for others playing the game. This could be anything from player-generated chat, to maps and skins, to other types of game modifications. The notice reads, "Game experience may change during online play," and it's displayed next to the rating icon on the front of the box. It's also required on the game's Web site and when the player launches the game. Frankly, when it comes to user-generated content, there's not a lot more we can do. If a parent doesn't want their child to be exposed to unrated content, including chatting with other players online, they should make the effort to monitor their child's use of the game when and if playing online.

Another example of emergent gameplay has also created a ratings stir. In GTA, you can kill people, and when you do, you get their money. You can also have sex with prostitutes. When the two systems come together, you can have sex with a prostitute, kill her, and get your money back. Some charge that this is an example of the ESRB rating too lightly.

I don't consider a Mature (M) rating for ages 17 and up with the descriptors "intense violence," "blood and gore," "use of drugs," "strong sexual content," and "strong language" as "light." I don't see a problem with the appearance of prostitutes as characters in games that carry an M rating. Except for the "Hot Coffee" mini-game, there are no explicit depictions of sex in *GTA* that would have warranted an Adults Only (AO) rating. Yes, you can kill prostitutes in *GTA*, but you can kill virtually anyone else in the game, as well. And that's one of the reasons why the game was assigned an "intense violence" descriptor. The fact that there is some kind of reward for committing violent acts is not uncommon in Mature-rated titles. However, it should also be noted that you can't win the game if all you do is go around killing everyone in sight. Bottom line, *GTA*'s an intensely violent game with a Mature rating for ages 17 and up and plenty of content descriptors to sufficiently inform anyone interested in purchasing it about its contents.

In popular culture today, rightly or wrongly, killing is not typically something that's rated in the most restrictive category. *Pulp Fiction*, *Kill Bill*, many horror movies with intense violence, they're all assigned an R rating by the MPAA, which is not that system's most restrictive category and is akin to our Mature rating. When I look at some of the intensely violent scenes in R-rated movies, such as those mentioned above, or even *Passion of the Christ*, I think it's fair to say that the content typically found in games carrying a Mature rating is well within culturally acceptable norms for a 17 and older age group in this country.

What is the process of getting a game rated?

First of all, publishers must fill out an extensive written submission form, detailing content across all the pertinent categories. Our content descriptors will provide a sense of what those categories are. Publishers have to be very specific, in writing, about not just general aspects of gameplay, but the most extreme depictions in each of those categories of content. Then, along with the written form, publishers must submit a videotape that captures the essence and context of game play as detailed on the written form. The video submission should basically walk our raters through the experience of playing the game—the setup, the storyline, the objectives, the missions, and a sense of typical gameplay—as well as the most extreme depictions and elements in the game. Publishers are also required to submit to the ESRB lyric sheets, scripts, and other pertinent materials.

In light of the GTA:SA Hot Coffee scandal, there has been some confusion over what a game maker must declare in its ESRB submission. Exactly what must a publisher declare?

The controversy over the Hot Coffee content brought to light a serious issue with regard to the accuracy and integrity of ESRB ratings. In the past, the ESRB only considered content that was intended for gameplay or would be accessible through the game engine (including cheat codes, player unlocked levels, "Easter eggs," etc.) for rating the game. The Hot Coffee scenes were fully rendered in an unmodified form on the game disc, and once made accessible through a third-party modification and broadly distributed, could no longer be considered "unplayable." Had the Hot Coffee scenes not been present on the game disc and pertinent enough to undermine the game's rating, then we would not have had to re-rate the game. However, this was not the case.

Today, the vast mod community has sophisticated means to identify and unlock content. What the "Hot Coffee" mod clearly illustrated to the ESRB and the game publishing industry at large is that it has become too great a risk to the accuracy of the rating to leave highly pertinent content on discs, even though programmed to be unplayable, only to be found and subsequently released by the mod community. It is in the best interests of the entire industry to have a rating system that is accurate and reliable, and so the ESRB has put the onus on publishers to be responsible for what they put on their discs. If it's on the disc, and if it's pertinent to a rating, the ESRB now requires that it be disclosed during the rating process. This is a positive step that helps preserve the integrity of the ESRB ratings.

Oblivion *was also re-rated by the ESRB. Can you comment on that?*

The more recent re-rating of *The Elder Scrolls IV: Oblivion* from Teen to Mature was due, in part, to a failure to disclose pertinent, locked-out content as required by the new policy, namely an art file that allowed users to play the game with topless versions of female characters. The more significant reason for the re-rating of the game, however, had to do with more extreme depictions of blood and gore that were not disclosed. The ESRB discovered depictions of blood and gore in the game that exceeded those disclosed by the publisher in terms of detail and intensity, and when we asked our raters to re-rate the game along with the newly found content, they assigned the game a Mature rating, indicating that the initial rating was inaccurate. Both of these instances, though rare and unfortunate, underscore just how agile and effective the ESRB's enforcement system is, and how willing and able the ESRB is to forcefully use it to ensure accurate and reliable ratings.

Most games aren't finished when they're submitted . . .

That's right. Oftentimes, when publishers submit a product for rating, the game is not finished. For example, oftentimes the voiceovers are not yet completed or integrated when a game is submitted. Therefore, publishers have to provide us with a script with all of the pertinent dialogue highlighted. It's the same thing with soundtracks. We typically review lyric sheets during the rating process. So, there are various other materials that the ESRB has to review to ensure that all potentially pertinent content is factored into a rating assignment. Bottom line, the game has to be close enough to completion for us to gauge the intensity of the graphic depictions and review all other potentially extreme content that will make its way into the final product.

Once the submission materials are complete and ready to be reviewed, we have a minimum of three raters independently look at them. For virtually every scene or action sequence, or whenever they see content that would warrant a rating assignment, they enter a rating category into our computer system. Then at the end of the rating session, ESRB reviews all of the data input from raters to determine the consensus. If there is no majority consensus, more raters will view the submission. We could have 6, 9, 12 raters for a game depending on how borderline or controversial the game is. Once we get that majority consensus, we'll issue a rating. If the publisher decides it doesn't want the rating we assigned for whatever reason, whether it's a content descriptor they have an issue with or the rating category itself, they can review the consensus report and see exactly which depictions warranted a particular rating or content descriptor. If a publisher wishes to obtain a different rating than the one assigned by the ESRB, it can make changes to the product and resubmit materials to the ESRB, at which point the process starts all over again.

What is the makeup of the rater pool?

We recruit from a diverse pool. We're located in New York City, so we benefit from having an extremely diverse population close by from which to recruit. All of our raters are adults, and work for us no more than a few hours a week. They have no ties to the industry, and their identities are kept anonymous to help ensure their independence. We look for adults who have had experience with children, whether that's through a profession, education, being a parent, or caring for young kids. Raters don't have to be expert gamers. In fact, they don't actually play games when they rate. Their job is view video content of gameplay and rate what they see purely for age appropriateness and full content disclosure, not for quality of game design, challenge, or fun. Obviously, we train them so that they can identify what's pertinent and what they need to be looking for, but it's really up to them, using their own judgment, to assign age ratings and content descriptors that they feel are appropriate. Additionally, considering that it can take 50 or more hours to play through a game, it's critical that raters are exposed to all of the content that is pertinent to a rating, including content they may not find on their own.

One question people often ask is, "Why aren't there more AO games?" I know that the "AO" rating is the kiss of death at retail, and as such, developers will cut objectionable content and resubmit. Is that the case?

When I'm asked that same question, I say that we do indeed assign that rating. However, we've assigned it more frequently than it has stuck. When we do assign it, the reaction we typically get from a publisher is, "Well, I can't release this product with an AO rating on it, because the retailers won't carry it. What do I have to do to get it to an M?" Then, they go back, and oftentimes with the help of a report that includes the raters' feedback, make changes to the game and resubmit it for rating. As I said, we do assign the AO rating when it is called for and when our raters feel that certain content just goes too far for the Mature category, be it sexual, violent, or otherwise. In fact, we have done so more frequently in the last 12 months than ever before. It just doesn't often stick. Publishers will always have the option of not accepting an ESRB rating and resubmitting their edited product.

What affect do you think Hot Coffee had on the public perception of the ESRB overall?

I think there are two positives that emerged for the ESRB from the Hot Coffee controversy. First, and most important, awareness of ESRB ratings has increased through the exposure of this story, and that's certainly welcome. The story permeated throughout national and worldwide media, and the message to check the ratings and take them seriously got through to lots of parents.

The second positive was that ESRB demonstrated its ability and willingness to take action to protect the integrity of its ratings and ensure that parents, who rely on our ratings, can trust that they are accurate and representative of game content. An effective and independent self-regulatory body is essential for the video game industry, and the ESRB has proven once again that it is capable of effectively regulating the industry. In fact, we've received many letters from parents across the country thanking us for taking the action that we did to protect the interests of parents and consumers [Vance01].

REFERENCES

[Anon01] Anonymous, interviewInterview with Brenda Brathwaite, June 17, 2005.

[Anon02] Anonymous, interview with Brenda Brathwaite, June 17, 2005.

[ESRB01] Entertainment Software Rating Board. Available online at *http://www .esrb.org*. Accessed June 28, 2006.

[ESRB02] Entertainment Software Rating Board. Available online at *http://www .esrb.org*. Accessed June 28, 2006.

[ESRB02] Ibid.

[Lincoln01] Lincoln, Howard C., *Testimony Before Senate Subcommittee on Regulation and Government Information and the Committee on the Judiciary's Subcommittee on Juvenile Justice,* December 9, 1993.

[Sirotek01] Sirotek, Robert F., interview with Brenda Brathwaite, June 16, 2005.

[Sirotek02] Ibid.

[Sirotek03] Sirotek, Robert F., interview with Brenda Brathwaite, June 16, 2005.

[Sirotek04] Ibid.

[Sirotek05] Ibid.

[Vance01] Vance, Patricia, interview with Brenda Brathwaite, June 28, 2006.

7 ▪ Censorship

In This Chapter

- ▪ Legislation or Censorship?
- ▪ Government Regulation
- ▪ The "Wal-Mart M"-Pseudo Censorship
- ▪ Industry Response
- ▪ Interview with Jason Della Rocca
- ▪ Interview with Hal Halpin

LEGISLATION OR CENSORSHIP?

In the short history of video games, the medium has been a target of much federal, state, and local legislation seeking to regulate sales and distribution. In some countries other than the United States, video games have been outright banned. While politicians, when called on the issue, are reluctant to admit that this legislation amounts to censorship, many game developers don't agree, particularly since such things as books, movies, and the like are not given similar treatment.

While video games may seem like today's target of choice, they do, in fact, share a long history with other technologies, all considered dangerous at one point or another. The printing press, televisions, phones, VCRs, computers, comics, and movies—at one point, each was considered a threat to "family values." Even in recent times, the paper role-playing game *Dungeons & Dragons*® was regularly cited as a potentially contributing factor when teenagers got into trouble. In an interview on GameSpy.com, Gary Gygax, the co-creator of *Dungeons & Dragons*, discussed the parallel between video games' troubles today and his game's troubles in the

1980s. For Gygax, the idea that his game or that a video game is somehow something more than exactly what it is—just a game—is faulty logic. To illustrate his point, he uses the game of golf. If a golfer decides to play during bad weather and is struck by lightning, is that the fault of the game or the fault of a golfer who clearly did not make good decisions [Gygax01]?

Whether it's the fault of the game or the player is still being played out in the courts and on the floor of Congress. Meanwhile, every violent or reckless incident involving video games and teens no matter how tangentially—particularly the ones that get lots of media attention like 2005's Hot Coffee scandal, school shootings, or other incidents of violence—bring about more attempts at legislation, and in doing so, more attempts to censor video games as a creative medium.

How are video games censored?

GOVERNMENT REGULATION

Legislation targeting the games with sexual content has been exceptionally varied, from outright banning of all video games to prohibiting possession by minors. Penalties have ranged from $1,000 fines to suspension of a business license to actual jail time. While this book has been in production, over a dozen new pieces of legislation have been introduced, at least half a dozen have been declared unconstitutional, and still others have been promised as forthcoming by politicians.

Prohibiting the Sale or Rental of Adult Games to Minors

The most common form of regulation targeting sex in video games prohibits the sale, rental, or loan of M- and AO-rated games or games with specific content to minors. California, Maryland, Mississippi, Minnesota, Missouri, Alabama, Michigan, New Jersey, Florida, Georgia, Illinois, North Carolina, Pennsylvania, and Washington, DC among others have all put forth legislation aimed at some type of sales restriction, while politicians in other states hinted at such regulation in the future.

One of the (if not the) earliest attempts at this type of regulation predated traditional computer games and occurred in Mesquite, Texas, in 1976. The city council passed an ordinance that barred anyone under the age of 17 from operating an "amusement device" unless accompanied by a parent or guardian. The ordinance's purpose was only partly to preserve and protect the moral well being of the city's children, however. Council members were concerned about the spread of organized crime, and they believed that organized crime was in some way involved with Aladdin's Castle, Inc., a fast-growing chain of arcades. They were using this ordinance as a means to strike back. The case was appealed all the way to the U.S. Supreme Court, which overturned the age restriction on February 23, 1982, citing the Texas Constitution. As a note, Mesquite, Texas, would years later become home to id Software, makers of the critically acclaimed *Doom* and *Quake* series of games.

The most prominent of all modern day bills is The Family Entertainment Protection Act introduced by Senators Hillary Rodham Clinton, Joe Lieberman, and Evan Bayh in December 2005. A statement issued by Senator Clinton's office noted that she "was motivated to take action on this issue when it was revealed in July [2005] that Rockstar Games had embedded illicit sexual content in the video game *Grand Theft Auto: San Andreas*. This game had received a Mature rating from the Entertainment Software Ratings Board (ESRB), which was unaware of the embedded content." The statement goes on to note that when the now infamous "Hot Coffee" mod was released and the content discovered, Senator Clinton asked the FTC to investigate and promised legislation. In announcing The Family Entertainment Protection Act, the Senator was, in effect, delivering on that promise [Clinton01].

Senator Lieberman was careful to note that the bill did not amount to censorship. "We are not interested in censoring videos meant for adult entertainment, but we do want to ensure that these videos are not purchased by minors. Our bill will help accomplish this by imposing fines on those retailers that sell M-rated games to minors," Senator Lieberman said [Lieberman01].

According to the statement, "The centerpiece of this bill is a prohibition against any business for selling or renting a Mature, Adults-Only, or Ratings Pending game to a person who is younger than seventeen" [Clinton02].

The bill would subject "on-site store managers" to "a fine of $1,000 or 100 hours of community service for the first offense; $5,000 or 500 hours of community service for each subsequent offense" [Clinton03].

The bill also calls for an annual analysis of the ESRB ratings system, provides authority for the FTC to investigate misleading ratings, gives consumers a means to register complaints to the Bureau of Consumer Protection, and establishes an annual retailer audit to be conducted by the FTC [Clinton04].

A federal bill similar to the one proposed by Clinton, Lieberman, and Bayh's bill has certainly been proposed before. Congressman Joe Baca championed the federal bill HR669 IH, also known as the "Protect Children from Video Game Sex and Violence Act of 2003." The original bill, HR669, failed to make it out of committee in 2002 due to First Amendment concerns and pressure from the video game industry. The bill states, "Whoever sells at retail or rents, or attempts to sell at retail or rent, to a minor any video game that depicts nudity, sexual conduct, or other content harmful to minors, shall be fined under this chapter."

The bill has the following definitions that relate to sex in games:

- Sexual conduct is defined as "acts, actual or virtual, of masturbation, sexual intercourse, or physical contact with a person's clothed or unclothed genitals, pubic area, buttocks or, if such person be a female, a breast."

- Nudity is defined as "the visual depiction, actual or virtual, of the human male or female genitals, pubic area or buttocks with less than a fully opaque covering, of a female breast with less than a fully opaque covering of any part of the nipple or of any portion of the breast below the nipple, or the depiction of covered male genitals in a discernibly turgid state."
- Conduct harmful to minors is defined as "(A) graphic violence; (B) sexual violence; or (C) strong sexual content" which "lacks serious literary, artistic, political, or scientific value for minors."
- Sexual violence as "the visual depiction, actual or virtual, of rape or other sexual assault."
- Strong sexual content is defined as "the visual depiction, actual or virtual, of human nudity or explicit human sexual behavior, including acts of masturbation, deviate sexual conduct, sexual intercourse, or fondling of genitals" [HR669].

In his fact sheet on the game, Congressmen Baca specifically mentions the video game *BMX XXX*, noting that the title "lets players spend their money in strip clubs, showing live-action footage of naked strippers," and further that the "game allows players to create female characters, with full control over breast size and the option to have the character ride topless."

"The bill will create consequences for those who profit from selling these games to our kids," notes the same fact sheet. First-time offenders face a fine of up to $1,000. A second offense calls for a fine of $1,000 to $5,000. Repeat offenders face fines greater than $5,000 [Baca01].

Bills in Maryland (HB698), Michigan (SB249), and other states have added jail time to possible fines, making the sale of an adult video game a criminal offense. In Maryland, the bill called for a fine of as much as $1,000 and six months in jail. The Michigan bill pressed for a year imprisonment, a fine of $5,000, or both.

What effect are these bills likely to have on video game developers? In theory, if fewer retailers carry M- and AO-rated games due to concerns over fines or possible jail time, fewer M- and AO-rated games will be made, plain and simple. More ominous, however, is the effect such legislation has on parents attempting to understand a ratings system.

In his article "Regulation Is Everyone's Business" posted on the IGDA's Web site, IGDA executive director Jason Della Rocca confronts the apathy he sees within the industry. Commenting on the notion that such legislation is merely trying to enforce the industry's ratings, Della Rocca points out that each bill proposed as of the date of his writing did not use the ESRB ratings system as its basis. Rather, each bill defined its own standards for acceptable sexual and violent content within games. Attempting to keep track of and stay within each state's restrictions would be a challenge for developers, retailers, and parents who have become used to and educated about an existing system. In effect, it creates a separate rating system on a state-by-state basis. An M-rated game that's acceptable for sale in one state may not be acceptable in another [Rocca01].

Doug Lowenstein, head of the Entertainment Software Association, questioned the need for such a bill at all. In an interview carried on TechNewsWorld.com, Lowenstein noted that the FTC's own data shows that parents are involved in 83% of game purchases or rentals. Therefore, Lowenstein suggests, parents are already heavily involved in their children's game decisions. Lowenstein also noted that in every case where similar bills were passed, they were overturned and found unconstitutional [Lowenstein01].

In 2006, however, the Entertainment Software Association did not oppose two bills, one in Maryland (HB707) and another in Louisiana (SB340), that restricted the sale of M- and AO-rated games with sexual content to minors. The bills treated sexually explicit video games equally to other sexually explicit forms of media, like pornographic films or erotic magazines.

> *What would Lord British do? Richard Garriott on video games in Britannia.*
>
> *If video games with sexual content somehow made their way into Britannia and the citizens demanded an audience with Lord British to discuss their concerns, what would he say?*

If video games with sexual content made it into Britannia and the citizens demanded an Audience, Lord British would of course grant the audience. He would listen to their concerns and validate those concerns that were expressed as parenting issues, but take issue with those who might prefer to legislate morality. Thus, he would work with the citizens to insure that parents had the tools they needed to make individual parenting decisions, while preserving the rights of free expression and general adult access. Lord British would favor solutions that had minimal governmental entanglement, but would demand of content makers to provide community demanded tools or expect further involvement [Garriott01]!

Requiring Labeling of Games

Labeling video games with an appropriate ESRB or international rating is a de facto *volunteer* standard within the U.S. video game industry. Some politicians have taken this a step further, however, and proposed legislation that *requires* ESRB labeling. Other legislators such as those in Missouri, Texas, New York City, and Virginia have gone above and beyond the traditional rating requirements and proposed legislation that would require retailers to provide additional labeling on games that contain offensive content.

In Missouri, for example, HB390, sponsored by Representative Jeff Harris on January 27, 2005, requires all games be labeled using the ESRB rating system. In addition to appropriate labeling, retailers are also required to post signs describing the ESRB rating system and to provide informational brochures on site. By requiring labeling, they hope to ensure 100% compliance with the rating system and prevent retailers from selling independent, unrated products [Miss01].

By contrast, Texas Bill HB866 introduced by Rep. Tony Goolsby, requires warning labels on all violent and sexually explicit video games. The bill calls for labels to be placed on the front of game packages and further, for a sign to be posted that explains the rating system used. Failure to comply will result in a class B misdemeanor for first offenses and a class A misdemeanor for subsequent offenses [Texas01].

Similarly, while not binding or required, the New York City resolution suggests that the ESRB "mimic the parental advisory program currently employed by the music and recording industry, wherein sound recordings that contain strong language or expressions of violence, sexual activity, or substance abuse are identified with a plainly worded, highly visible, and permanent parental advisory label" [NYC01].

While standard labeling such as that called for in the Missouri bill is unlikely to affect the game industry in any direct financial way, efforts such as the one in Texas add overhead and process and therefore would make it more expensive for retailers to stock such titles. These additional expenses may affect their stocking decisions. Other bills targeting violent video games may actually undermine existing game ratings.

"The Violent Video Games Law," a companion law to "The Sexually Explicit Video Games Law" and an act with the Safe Games Illinois Act (HB4023), requires that all violent video games as defined within the bill display a 2" × 2", solid white "18" outlined in black on the front of the package. As defined in the bill, violent games include "depictions of or simulations of human-on-human violence in which the player kills, seriously injures, or otherwise causes serious physical harm to another human, including, but not limited to depictions of death, dismemberment, amputation, decapitation, maiming, disfigurement, mutilation of body parts, or rape" [HB4023A]. As written, the definition could conceivably include sports games that allow for player injury while leaving untouched games that featured exceptional nonhuman blood and gore. While games in the *Grand Theft Auto* series would most certainly warrant an "18" label, a simple and minor change would leave the game rated as it is—make the avatar an alien, a robot, or anything nonhuman and leave the rest of the game untouched. As such, parents who use the "18" label as a gauge to determine a product's level of violence may be disappointed or, worse, misled [HB4023B]. Such bills frequently fail to note who will be making these content judgments. What's labeled "18" at one store may be considered okay at the next.

Some in the industry have criticized lawmakers' attempts to increase the size of the label as an attack unfairly leveled at only a single type of media. Why, they ask, aren't politicians concerned with ratings on other packages? On IGDA Sex & Games blog run by the IGDA's Sexuality Special Interest Group, an image appeared that compared the ESRB rating for *Grand Theft Auto: San Andreas* to that of the

Shaun of the Dead DVD. The image of it is available at *www.igda.org/sex/archives/ 2006/04/more_on_the_har.html*. The two products were scanned side by side. In the image, the video game label is easily the more legible of the two. The video game rating system is also many font sizes larger than the small "R" that appears on the *Shaun of the Dead* box.

For the video game industry, however, such arguments—comparing video game sex and violence with the portrayal of sex and violence in other media—rarely gain any traction. Like comics years ago, the perception that video games are for children persists and colors the opinions of legislators.

Requiring an Electronic Prompt for Retailers

In addition to its labeling requirement, "The Sexually Explicit Video Games Law," an act with the Safe Games Illinois Act, requires that anyone who sells or rents sexually explicit video games and uses electronic scanning at the checkout must "program the electronic scanner to prompt salesclerks to check identification before the sale or rental transaction is completed." The condition also applies to games sold on any self-scanning checkouts [HB4023C].

While the idea is absolutely a good one, legislating compliance is extreme and confusing. In the Illinois bill, definitions of what video games would qualify as "sexually explicit" are vague and put retailers in a difficult spot. As defined in the bill, sexually explicit games are "those that the average person, applying contemporary community standards would find, with respect to minors, is designed to appeal or pander to the prurient interest and depicts or represents in a manner patently offensive with respect to minors, an actual or simulated sexual act or sexual contact, an actual or simulated normal or perverted sexual act, or a lewd exhibition of the genitals or post-pubescent female breast" [HB4023D]. Under such a definition, such games as T-rated *The Sims*™ by Electronic Arts could likely find themselves tagged. If such a piece of legislation were enacted, at best, retailers within a state would work together to determine what titles were "sexually explicit" under this definition and which were not. At worst, a game buyer could find a title tagged at one store, walk to the store next door and find it untagged, available for purchase. Such ambiguity has the potential to confuse retailers and game players, and parents trying to control the purchases of their children.

Requiring an "Entertainment Endorsement"

Likening violent and sexually explicit video games to poison, Washington, DC, Mayor Anthony Williams announced the "Youth Protection From Obscene Video Games Act of 2005." The bill calls for all businesses that sell, rent, or otherwise furnish video games within the city to obtain an entertainment endorsement in addition to a standard business license.

What is most striking about this bill is the severity of its punishment: businesses that fail to abide by the specified provisions of the bill may have their business license suspended or revoked by the Department of Consumer and Regulatory Affairs. Businesses also face fines ranging from $1,000 to $10,000 for repeat offenders.

The bill also calls for posting of the basic business license, the ESRB ratings, clear labeling on game packages, and a warning sign visible at all times that reinforces the age requirements necessary to purchase or otherwise procure video games [DC02].

Requiring the Posting or Availability of Ratings at the Retail Level

Another common feature of recent legislation calls for the posting of ESRB ratings within retail establishments that carry video games. As with other ideas, this one is a good one, but legislation is not necessary. The ESRB and the Interactive Entertainment Merchants Association (IEMA), the trade association that represents the majority of video game retailers, have worked toward this goal successfully, and virtually every chain store already displays video game rating information. In June 2006, the ESRB Retail Council reaffirmed its intent with its "Commitment to Parents" campaign. As a part of the campaign, ESRB Retail Council members pledged to provide in-store ratings signage, conduct twice yearly "mystery shopper" audits, train associates about the ratings system, and provide ESRB ratings in advertising materials such as circulars among other initiates. Nonetheless, Georgia, Mississippi, Pennsylvania, Texas, Washington, and Washington, DC, among others have all proposed such legislation.

Some take the posting of ratings a step further and insist that brochures or other information be available for customers, particularly parents, to take home. Georgia Senate Bill 106, for instance, requires video game retailers to "post a sign providing information to consumers about any video game rating system that appears on a video game offered by such a retailer." In addition, the establishment "must make available to consumers, upon request, written information explaining each such rating system." Violators face fines ranging from $250 to $500 per day for failing to comply with the Georgia bill [GA01]. House Bill 866 in Texas would make such an offense a class A or class B misdemeanor [Texas02].

Declaring Video Games a Harmful Substance

Citing verse from the 1973 *Miller v. California* U.S. Supreme Court Case, some bills have declared video games harmful matter to minors, similar to pornography, cigarettes, or alcohol.

One particular bill, the failed California State Bill 1792 introduced by Assemblymember Leland Yee, sought to amend the state's Penal Code and to reclassify video games as harmful matter if they fit the bill's definition of violence or sexual content. Anyone providing video games to minors would be held criminally liable for doing so.

As defined in the bill, "harmful matter" is "Matter that, taken as a whole, to the average person, applying contemporary statewide standards, appeals to the prurient interest, that, taken as a whole, depicts or describes in a patently offensive way sexual conduct and that, taken as a whole, lacks serious literary, artistic, political, or scientific value for minors." [Yee01]

The bill was amended on 4/12/2004 to remove the portions relevant to harmful matter, but failed to make it out of the Assembly Committee on Arts, Entertainment, Sports, Tourism, and Internet Media for a full vote. Citing pressure from special interests, Assemblymember Lee's office issued a press release titled "Multi-Billion Dollar Entertainment Industry Shoots Down Bills to Protect Children from Violent Video Games."

"I am deeply disturbed that money ruled the day here in Sacramento," read the press release quoting Assemblymember Yee. "Rather than protecting our children and giving our parents a tool to help raise healthy kids, the multibillion dollar entertainment industry was allowed to shoot down necessary legislation" [Yee02].

Classifying M- and AO-Rated Games as Contraband

While some legislation has attempted to classify video games as substances harmful to minors, other legislation has gone a step further and proposed that M- and AO-rated games be classified as items of contraband. Those guilty of possessing contraband in a penal institution or providing contraband to a prisoner may be found criminally liable.

One such bill, Illinois House Bill 2412, introduced by Rep. John E. Bradley on February 17, 2005, lists items of contraband as follows: alcoholic liquor, cannabis, controlled substances, a hypodermic syringe, a weapon or something that could be used as a weapon, a firearm, firearm ammunition, explosives, tools to defeat security mechanisms, a cutting tool, electronic contraband (cell phones, etc.), and M- and AO-rated video games [IL01].

Reclassifying Game Retailers as Adult Video Stores

In a bill introduced in the Alabama House of Representatives by Representative Brewbacker on March 3, 2005, the definition of an "adult video store" was expanded to include those retailers who sell, rent, or loan sexually explicit video games.

House Bill 573 amends the definition of adult video and bookstores as follows: "A commercial establishment in which is offered for sale or rent any book, video, film, video game, or other medium which in the aggregate constitute substantially all of its stock or inventory which depicts sexual conduct as defined herein."

Sexual conduct is further defined as: "a. Any act of sexual intercourse, masturbation, urination, defecation, lewd exhibition of the genitals, sado-masochistic abuse, bestiality, or the fondling of the sex organs of animals; or b. Any other physical contact with a person's unclothed genitals, pubic area, buttocks, or the breast or breasts of a female, whether alone or between members of the same or opposite sex or between a human and an animal, in an act of sexual stimulation, gratification or perversion" [AL01].

While one or two copies of an AO-rated game would not be enough to warrant a reclassification of the average video game retailer, the ambiguity of the bill leaves room for concern. The text of the bill includes definitions for everything from "sado-masochistic abuse" to "breast nudity," but fails to define one of its most critical points: "substantially all of its stock." In sufficient quantity, stocking such titles as *The Sims*, which features obscured urination (the bill makes no distinction between urination for sexual purposes or standard urination) or *God of War* could turn stores from game shops to porn places overnight [AL02].

What effect is this likely to have on businesses? Not much. Businesses that sell "substantially all" pornography already have taken measures to prohibit the rental or sale of their products to minors; such measures are required by law. Furthermore, game retailers would have to oddly modify their offerings to affect their classification. Currently, according to the Entertainment Software Association, M-rated titles account for only 16% of retailers' sales, and AO-rated titles accounted for less than 1% [ESA01]. Such titles taken together don't account for one quarter of games being sold.

Segregating M- and AO-Rated Video Games

Taking sale restrictions to minors a step further, some legislators have recommended segregating M- and AO-rated video games entirely.

One such bill, AB1793, introduced by Assemblymember Leland Yee in the California Assembly on January 5, 2004, requires retailers to place M-rated video games on shelves not less than 5 feet high and only with other M-rated titles. The bill also calls for retailers who sell or rent AO-rated games to create a unique area within their business to stock these video games, and any material that advertises these games, not unlike the "adults only" rooms found in video stores that carry pornographic titles. The term "advertising" was not defined in the bill. Its ambiguity may have required retailers to place game magazines that sometimes contain advertisements for AO-rated games out of sight, too. As proposed, the bill would most certainly keeps AO video games out of all standard retail shops that are not already equipped with an "adults only" area. There are simply not enough modern AO-rated titles to warrant a large shelf, let alone an area [Yee03].

After six amendments, four in the Assembly and two in the Senate, a substantially weakened bill was signed by Governor Schwarzenegger on September 21, 2004. Gone were all the hallmarks of the original bill—segregation of AO-rated titles, displaying M-rated titles in an exclusive grouping and on a shelf not less than five feet tall. The bill that passed called for posting of a video game rating system or merely telling customers of the rating system and providing them with information on the system upon request [Yee04].

Banning Specific Titles

One of the most extreme forms of censorship and regulation is the ban—when a government forbids a game from being sold, possessed, or played within its borders. Such actions are not uncommon in Germany, New Zealand, and Australia, which has banned numerous sexually themed titles—*Leisure Suit Larry: Magna Cum Laude* and *BMX XXX* among them.

Edward Kuehnel, formerly a game designer at High Voltage Software, creators of *Leisure Suit Larry: Magna Cum Laude*, noted that the company "received very little information as to why it was banned" [Kuehnel01]. A company press release on the ban stated that the game was rejected based on its sexual activity and nudity.

"I don't think management at High Voltage Software was pleased at the loss of potential sales," Kuehnel continued, "though I have to admit I found it rather amusing and at first was somewhat proud of the achievement. Not many people can say they've written something that's been banned from an entire country. I'll admit to still being a bit perplexed at the ban, however. Maybe it's all those *Crocodile Dundee* movies, but I'd always thought of Australia as this laid back, easy going country with a strong commitment to free speech and an independent streak as big and wide as the outback. At least they're not hypocrites; they ban games for being violent too" [Kuehnel02].

Games in Australia are rated by the Office of Film and Literature Classification (OFLC). Under their rating system, MA 15+ is the most restrictive rating a game can receive. Although R 18+ and X 18+ ratings are available for films, the OFLC has so far refused to place such ratings on games. As such, any software sold in Australia must be acceptable to 15- and 16-year-old children, not the traditional 17-year-old young adult as required by the ESRB. This can create substantial problems for makers of games who are trying to reach an adult software market. If games cannot be rated for adults, they cannot be sold at all. Most, if not all, sexually themed games would fall under the R 18+ or X 18+ movie rating.

Games the OFLC finds unacceptable are rated "RC" for "Refused Classification." A complete list of titles that have been refused classification can be found online at *www.refused-classification.com/Games_A-Z.htm*. In an effort to avoid a ban, some developers and publishers opt to create special versions for countries with sizeable markets, or edit their content and resubmit.

Banning All Games

The ultimate form of censorship is a complete ban of all games. Both Greece and Afghanistan have legislated such bans, although both were later modified.

The Greek ban, Law Number 3037, was originally enacted on July 30, 2002 as a means to control illegal gambling in Internet cafés. The wording of the ban was ambiguous, however, and as a result, it ended up outlawing *all* games played in public. Those found playing games on any machine that ran software—their hand-helds, cell phones, computers, or consoles—faced fines of 5,000 to 75,000 euros and a jail sentence. After pressure from the Internet café owners and the European Union, the Greek government amended the law allowing for games to be played anywhere except Internet cafés [Greece01].

In Afghanistan, restrictions were far more severe. Many forms of media including television, newspapers, and video games were banned by the Taliban government when they came to power in 1995. After the Taliban regime was removed in December 2001, Afghanistan's new central government made it legal to own televisions. However, according to a PBS article "Afghanistan's Growing Media," some of the country's provinces continue the ban on video games [Afghanistan01].

THE "WAL-MART M"—PSEUDO CENSORSHIP

Without any legislation, retailers significantly affect what material appears in video games today. At the "Sexuality in Games" roundtable at the 2005 Game Developers Conference, a moderator called this effect the "Wal-Mart M." It's the unseen, unstated rating more powerful than that imposed by the ESRB or legislators. It's the level developers cannot go beyond to get their product onto retailers' shelves, and that level is rarely as simple as securing an "M" rating from the ESRB, particularly when it comes to games with sexual themes or sexual content within the game.

For instance, retailers such as Best Buy, Wal-Mart, and Target refused to stock the M-rated *Playboy: The Mansion*. Best Buy did carry the M-rated version of *Leisure Suit Larry: Magnum Cum Laude* but did not stock the AO-rated version.

"Like X-rated movies, IEMA members do not sell AO-rated games," notes Hal Halpin, president of the IEMA, the trade association that represents retailers. Beyond that, though, Halpin admits that, "Purchasing decisions are an inexact science, and as such, require us to arm ourselves with as much knowledge as possible. The more we know about a game, the better we can determine if it is appropriately suited to our demographic as a whole. As I mentioned earlier, there are titles where the industry knows in advance that a game's publisher is being intentionally sensationalistic about its content, promoting it for exploitative purposes, and usually it's because the game lacks the all-important playability aspect. Those games are easier for us to filter out, because the information is so widely available" [Halpin01].

Since exclusion in retail can significantly affect a product's sales, some developers and publishers adjust their content to suit a chain's restrictions or develop with those restrictions in mind. One developer who was working on a project that was later canceled told this author that while the project was in development, his employer was "proceeding with more caution" and had "opened up a dialogue with some of the major retailers" it hoped would sell the game. The publisher provided major retailers with prototypes to get feedback. "Early on, we developed a prototype for a massage game in which you'd rub a girl's back, shoulders, etc. then make your way to her breasts and other naughty bits. Retailers objected to the game, so we toned it down so that you were just rubbing her back and shoulders—nothing else. Again retailers objected, with one buyer giving the reason that he found it unacceptable the player was allowed to directly manipulate (using the gamepad) a woman for the purposes of giving her physical pleasure" [Dev01].

Even with the prototypes and regular course corrections, however, the road to retail for M-rated games that contain sexual content is unclear. Few developers are in a position to make a game without regard for its profit potential. Fewer still are those who would want to. Developers and publishers are in the business of making games for a profit, and as such, the content in their games will be heavily affected if major retailers refuse to carry them.

A notable exception to this, however, was 2005's critically acclaimed hit, *God of War*. Wal-Mart and some other large retailers did not stock the game when it was released. According to a participant at the 2006 Game Developers Conference "Sexuality in Games: Hardcore" roundtable who was also a part of the development team, the retailers' decisions not to stock the game was directly related to the sexual content contained in the game. It seems, however, that capitalism eventually won out over morality. When the game started selling like hotcakes elsewhere, retailers began stocking the game. The sexual content found in *God of War*, of course, is minor when compared to games like *Playboy: The Mansion* or *Leisure Suit Larry: Magna Cum Laude*. Furthermore, the game itself and the marketing that supported it did not mention or sensationalize the content's inclusion.

INDUSTRY RESPONSE

The video game industry is represented by three main groups: the International Game Developers Association (IGDA), the Interactive Entertainment Merchants Association (IEMA), and the Entertainment Software Association (ESA). Each group has been active and assertive in voicing its concerns over any kind of legislation. The Video Software Dealers Association (VSDA) also plays a part in the industry, although to a lesser extent than the three groups noted previously.

International Game Developers Association (IGDA)

Founded in 1995, the IGDA is a nonprofit organization that speaks for the game development community. It was established after the Congressional hearings in 1994 to give a voice to those who had, up to that point in time, no one else to speak for them.

Today, the IGDA is an active participant in the anti-censorship movement. In the face of pending legislation, the IGDA frequently issues a "call to action" asking its members in a particular state to contact their legislators to speak out on pending bills. Furthermore, through its anti-censorship committee, the IGDA works to educate legislators and others interested in censorship on the side effects of legislation, chief among them a developer's right to creative freedom and parents' right to exercise judgment over the games their children play.

The IGDA also supports the IGDA Sex SIG, a special interest group that focuses on all facets of adult content development.

The IGDA is clear in its position on censorship: "The IGDA opposes any effort that would treat video games differently from other forms of media. Digital games are an expressive medium worthy of the same respect, and protections, as movies, literature, and other forms of art and entertainment. The IGDA fully stands behind voluntary, industry driven, content ratings that allow consumers to make informed purchasing/playing decisions for themselves and their families. Games are part of our cultural fabric and are enjoyed by diverse audiences" [IGDA01].

In response to the pending regulation and censorship, which has seen games derided as neither art nor a worthy form of entertainment, the IGDA has issued these 10 key points.

1. A Medium of Expression
Video games are emerging as the leading art form of the 21st century. Through video games, developers impart their vision of fantastical worlds, characters and adventure—and include commentary on the state of the human condition. Further, through their interactivity, games are in essence co-authored by the game player as they navigate the play space and experience the narrative arc of a game.

2. An Artful and Complex Endeavor
Game creation is a massively complex mix of science and art. From software engineers to script writers to animators to music composers, there is a great need for talented, creative, and educated individuals that must work in unison to see a game become a reality. In step with the growing need for talent, universities and colleges worldwide are implementing game development courses and degree programs.

3. A Diverse Audience

Unlike the stereotypical pimpled teen male, game players represent a diverse mix of age, gender, and cultural background. Like other forms of art and entertainment, there is content with themes targeted at those diverse audiences. From the cute cartoon game for the kiddies to seedy city streets, and everything in between, there is a game to appeal to everyone. Further, with such diversity comes the understanding that content does not need to be dumbed-down to suit any one particular audience (i.e., children).

4. Rated for Content

Games are rated for content in most countries/regions they are sold (e.g., ESRB in North America, PEGI in Europe, etc). These descriptive ratings are meant to aid consumers in making age-appropriate purchases. What's more, copious literature and notes are provided online and at the point-of-sale to aid in the decision making process. Further, many countries have advertising and marketing review councils to ensure that games are appropriately marketed.

5. Worthy of Academic Study

Games have become such a pervasive part of our culture, and speak deeply to so many players that academics have started to study them as cultural artifacts. Academics are studying such things as the aesthetics of design, the cultural impact of games relative to other media, the anthropology of play, and gender-role dynamics to name but a few areas of inquiry.

6. Significant Economic Impact

The game industry grosses over $10 billion in the USA, with worldwide estimates in the $25 billion range. In several countries—England being one example—exports from game sales represent one of the highest outputs of all export industries. Further, well over a hundred thousand people are employed worldwide, on the development side as well as the business end of games.

7. A Serious Side to Play

More and more, games and game-technologies are being used for "serious" applications such as corporate training, military simulation, scholastic learning, and public policy decision making. Further, games are being used in medical and therapeutic scenarios (e.g., aid in treating ADD or to train diabetic kids to take their medicine).

8. Media Effects Fact/Fiction

There are many reports claiming that games cause one thing or another. But, for every such report, there's another to either debunk its claims or to make new claims in the opposite direction. To date, research and debate on the effects of media have been inconclusive. Fundamentally, most research is conducted without an actual understanding of games and their players.

9. Crime Rates in Decline
In the USA, violent crime rates among youth have been declining steadily over the past decade. Conversely, the increase in media attention of any one crime leads to the public perception that such violent crimes are pervasive—when in fact they are not. Further, in other countries with high levels of game consumption (e.g., Japan, Canada), youth crime is almost nonexistent.

10. Distraction from Real Problems
As the US Surgeon General has pointed out, there are very serious woes in our society—poverty, education levels, substance abuse, and domestic violence to name but a few—that directly and tangibly contribute to violent behavior. These problems need to be addressed in a meaningful way. Pointing to games and other forms of art and entertainment as scapegoats will not solve anything, but rather serve as an ongoing distraction from addressing these hard-to-deal-with societal issues. [IGDA02]

The Entertainment Software Association (ESA)

Video game publishers are represented by the Entertainment Software Association (ESA). Its members' products account for over 90% of the video games sold in the United States in 2004 [ESA02]. The ESA also owns the Electronic Entertainment Expo (E3), the world's largest show devoted to video games.

The ESA is a vocal and active critic of regulation and censorship. Doug Lowenstein, president of the ESA, has testified before government committees investigating video games and video game ratings and regularly speaks out against legislation. The ESA also frequently files briefs with courts examining the constitutionality of passed legislation and regularly issues position statements or press releases to coincide with a politician's introduction of a bill.

In addition to its legislative activity, the ESA Web site provides information for those who wish to learn more about the issue at *www.TheESA.com.*

In 2006, the ESA established the Video Game Voters Network in an effort to get gamers active in the issues that are affecting their hobby. By turning their passion for games into votes, the ESA hopes to create a movement away from unnecessary legislation targeting video games. So far and by numerous accounts, the initiative has been successful, although its effect at the polls is still unknown.

Interactive Entertainment Merchants Association (IEMA)

The nonprofit Interactive Entertainment Merchants Association (IEMA) is the trade organization that represents the retailers of interactive entertainment. Among its members are 29 of the 30 largest retailers of interactive entertainment. It was founded in1997.

The IEMA takes an active role and a pro-active role, addressing parent and legislator concerns while campaigning against legislation. IEMA member retailers require that games be rated and further require all members to display signs explaining the rating system. Members also agreed to voluntarily carding people purchasing M-rated games. Most recently, the IEMA members agreed to a policy that would limit the amount of M-rated content shown on product previews within the store.

Politically, the IEMA speaks for retailers on issues before various governmental bodies issuing statements on legislation pending, passed, and appealed. On its site, *www.iema.org*, the IEMA maintains a legislative tracker that shows the status of all bills affecting video games in the United States on a month-by-month and yearly basis.

Video Software Dealers Association (VSDA)

The Video Software Dealers Association (VSDA) is a nonprofit trade association for the home rental market. Founded in 1981, its members own over 12,500 retail stores that rent, sell, or loan video games along with traditional video store offerings such as videos and DVDs [VSDA02].

The VSDA and its members take a pro-active role, encouraging members to work with parents to make sure they have access to the information they need to make purchase decisions, while putting in place practices that ensure minors do not have access to games unsuitable for them.

"VSDA recognizes that the home video industry has a critical role to play in educating parents about movie and video game ratings and ensuring that children do not gain access to movies and video games their parents deem inappropriate for them," its Web site notes. "We believe the best control is parental control, and there is no better place than in a home video store for parents to control the content of movies and video games to which their children have access" [VSDA03].

To assist members in fulfilling their role, the VSDA has created the following voluntary guidelines:

1. Post MPAA and/or ESRB ratings information where customers can view them.
2. Train employees in the ratings systems.
3. Not rent or sell videos rated R or video games rated M to persons under age 17.

4. Not rent or sell videos rated NC-17, video games rated Adults Only, or videos or video games that a reasonable person would consider to be legally "obscene for minors" to persons under age 18.

5. Include the rating icon, rating explanation, and the reason for the rating prominently on any Web page that offers a movie or video game for rental or sale.

6. Include links to *www.parentalguide.org* from Web sites where movies and/or video games can be rented or purchased.

7. Clearly and conspicuously display the ratings in all advertising for movies and video games, and to the extent feasible, the reason for the rating.

8. Not specifically target advertising for R-rated movies and M-rated video games to persons under age 17.

9. Not place advertising for R-rated movies and M-rated video games in media or venues with a substantial under-17 audience.

10. Designate an employee as the "ratings compliance officer" for the company and empower the designated individual to ensure adherence to the company's policies regarding motion picture and video game ratings education, enforcement, and advertising. [VSDA04]

In addition to these guidelines, the VSDA has a "Pledge to Parents" program whose goal is twofold: to educating parents about ratings and to make sure member stores enforce those ratings.

On April 11, 2006, the IEMA and the VSDA merged into a single trade association to represent retailers and distributors of both videos and video games. By doing so, the organizations hope to leverage their collective power to benefit their member companies.

INTERVIEW WITH JASON DELLA ROCCA

Jason Della Rocca is the IGDA's executive director and oversees the day-to-day operation of the association. He has been an active voice against legislation and censorship.

To what do you attribute the sudden flurry of legislative bills in various states?

Fear? Ignorance? Technophobia? It's hard to say. Overall, the U.S. is going through another phase of prohibitionist crusading against entertainment forms that offend adult sensibilities. From Elvis to comics to rap and the Three Stooges, it is a pretty reliable pattern of the older generation disapproving of the upcoming cohort's pop-culture. In many ways, video games are just the next cultural product in the chain. Of course, most fail to realize that they grew up on all those previous "bad" cultural forms to no ill effect. Even Shakespeare was regarded as frivolous and only appealing to the prurient interests of the unwashed masses. Look at the respect he gets today!

Can you tell me about the role the IGDA takes for/against such legislation?

The IGDA opposes any effort that would treat video games differently from other forms of media. Video games are an expressive medium worthy of the same respect, and protections, as movies, literature, and other forms of art and entertainment.

That said, the IGDA fully stands behind voluntary, industry driven, content ratings that allow consumers to make informed purchasing/playing decisions for themselves and their families.

I've heard developers say, "What's the big deal? They're just trying to enforce industry ratings." What are your thoughts on that?

Right, that's a common reaction, but one based on limited knowledge of the facts. The reality is that none of the proposed bills is based on the ESRB ratings system. In fact, it's unconstitutional for the U.S. government to regulate or enforce a private ratings system. As such, each bill aims to set its own moral barometer and establish often-vague metrics for what is acceptable for everyone to purchase and play. Dancing around a state-by-state patchwork of content restrictions and peculiarities would be prohibitive not only for developers, but also for time-deprived parents and retailers who are already working with the existing consistent/national ESRB rating system.

To add emphasis, most of these bills leave it up to each retailer to determine if a given game falls on the "good" or "bad" side of the law!

Why should developers who make games with nonviolent, nonsexual content care about these regulations?

Standing up for creative freedom isn't about fighting for the rights of any one specific game or developer. The industry needs to stand up for the medium as a whole. While I may not personally agree with some design choices, I strongly believe in developers' freedom of expression. Where will it end?

The government's current fascination with violence and sex in games may soon expand and put other games square in their viewfinder. Case in point, an Australian minister wanted to ban *Project Gotham Racing® 2* (rated E for everyone, containing no violence or sex) because he feared it would promote reckless driving in the streets of Sydney!

Similarly, a lot of large cities were not keen on *Jet Set Radio*™ because of the emphasis on the spray painting/tagging gameplay mechanic. Sega had a lot of pressure to alter the game and in the end inserted a "don't do this in real life" warning each time the game loaded up. Mark Ecko's *Getting Up: Contents Under Pressure*™ is receiving similar criticism. And, the list goes on. China will ban a game if they believe it to "conflict" with Chinese culture (which they did to a soccer game for depicting Tibet as having a "national" soccer team). So, it is really not just about violence and sex.

Again and again, one name is mentioned: Grand Theft Auto (GTA). *It seems to be the game that pushed legislators over the edge on so many grounds: prostitution, killing of a prostitute, killing of law enforcement officers, racial slurs. Can you talk separately about its effect on the industry, politicians, and retailers?*

The full answer to this question is a book unto itself! Ironically, *GTA* has done a lot of good for the industry: It was a wake-up call to all the parents and politicians that video games have grown up. And, just like movies, TV, books, and other forms of art/entertainment, there is a diverse range of games to appeal to a diverse range of gamers.

To this day, "it's just a game" is a common phrase uttered by parents buying *GTA* for their kids. That is, if a parent's understanding of games is "toys for children," why should they ever be concerned about potentially objectionable content? If you perceived every movie to be a Pixar cartoon or every TV show to be Barney™, would you ever be concerned with such things as ratings, or monitoring what your kids are playing/watching? No.

So, when a parent or politician is presented with a game like *GTA* it simply does not match their mental model of what a game is supposed to be (i.e., "toys for children").

Overall, this means that the industry has to continue to educate parents/consumers on the ratings system and the diversity of game content. It means retailers have to be ever more diligent of voluntarily limiting mature game sales to minors, etc.

Of all attempted legislation, there are a couple that stand out to me. In Alabama, HB573 attempted to add video games to the types of material used to determine if a store is an "adult video store," and in Washington, HB2718 advocates holding game makers accountable for player's actions. Can you please comment individually on how bills of this type would ultimately affect the industry and what the IGDA is doing about them?

These bills are mind boggling, really scary, and yet laughable at the same time.

Washington's HB2718 is simply absurd and blows the lid completely off personal accountability. Are they going to hold gun manufacturers accountable for murders? Or Wal-Mart for selling the bullets that got into the wrong hands? This style of legislation would result in an endless passing of blame and pointing of fingers.

Alabama's HB573 is more a question of impacting freedom of expression on the part of game developers, and the freedom of choice of consumers.

Let's just imagine that Wal-Mart were at risk of being reclassified as an "adult video store" because it stocked *GTA* and other mature games. All those games would quickly be pulled from the shelves. Ditto for all the other retailers.

Without a viable means to sell these games, publishers would divert production funding to other less "controversial" games. This would essentially limit the creative and expressive options of developers, and kill off entire game genres/themes. The risk of a chilling effect is very real. [Rocca02]

INTERVIEW WITH HAL HALPIN

Hal Halpin is the president and founder of the IEMA. As president, he runs the organization and is involved in all related issues, ranging from legislative and legal concerns to the standardization of the PC games box and its related trademark and everything in between.

Even before Hot Coffee, there has been a lot of recent legislation targeting video games. To what do you attribute the sudden flurry of legislative bills in various states?

I believe it's an unfortunate convergence of events mixed with political opportunism. The FTC (Federal Trade Commission) did several studies regarding the broader entertainment industry's marketing and sales practices to youth and found that we all had a lot of work to do. Over the ensuing years, our sectors of the business improved through voluntary efforts of our respective member companies. The trade associations involved include: Movies—MPAA, NATO, VSDA; Music—RIAA, NARM, and DiMA; Games—ESA, IEMA, and IGDA. In terms of self-regulatory efforts, it was only the National Association of Theatre Owners (NATO), the movie theatre owners, who had any comprehensive and fully compliant system in place, and as such, their group's success has been held up as the gold standard to which politicians and special interest groups would like to measure the rest of us. Needless to say, it's an unfair benchmark. Movie theatres essentially sell one product and do so using a 50-year-old ratings system that has become a part of the collective unconscious. Game retailers, with the notable exception of the two specialty stores, sell tens of thousands of products of which games often represent a very small fraction—and they do so using a 10-year-old ratings system. Couple negative results in old sting operations with a politically charged climate of "me-too politics" and both parties rushing to take the moral high ground, and you have a volatile climate for First Amendment issues.

Can you tell me about the role the IEMA takes in general for or against such legislation and what it does?

The IEMA is an active, and often leading, vocal opponent in fighting legislation that would be harmful to our member companies and counterintuitive in terms of providing a social good. We announced in December 2003 that by December 2004, all IEMA member companies would volunteer to self-regulate the sale of mature-rated games using the ESRB guidelines in an effort to stem the sale of inappropriate games to minors. We met that goal, and in the process changed the way that games are both merchandised and sold. ESRB ratings signage went up in every store—tens of thousands across the country—often in the place of revenue-generating vendor signage. Store-level staff were retrained, and new staff were instructed. Some members even installed cash register prompting technology at their own expense. It was a comprehensive and exhausting effort to which our members felt they had a social obligation and thus committed themselves. It was one of the prouder moments of my professional career.

Unfortunately, all of those efforts were unseen by politicians who were more interested in advancing their political careers, riding a wave of chest-thumping morality in the post-Janet Jackson era, and postulating about the evils of the interactive entertainment business.

Since that time—ironically one month after we had made all of these voluntary commitments—we have faced 17 pieces of legislation around the country, lobbying sensible legislators and defending the industry against the others.

In Illinois, the Safe Games Illinois Act calls for, among other things, retailers who use scanning machines to program them to prompt clerks to require ID for M- and AO-rated games. What are your thoughts on this bill?

Governor Blagojevich was misled when he began this crusade in December 2004. He was rightly outraged about a game he heard about involving the assignation of President Kennedy, but wholly incorrect about its distribution. It was an Internet game created by foreign developers and not distributed in the U.S. or sold by our members. What is was was an excuse to forge ahead with a win-win political issue that he believed no one could vote against—politically speaking.

The matter of turning retailers into the ethics police, charging them individually with attempting to decide what is inappropriate versus not, and even asking for a labeling system to augment the ESRB voluntary system is all lunacy. Substantially, all of this language has already played out in courts and been proven time and again untenable and moreover unconstitutional.

Many pieces of legislation prohibit retailers from selling M- and AO-rated games to minors. What is the IEMA's position on these pieces of legislation?

These pieces of legislation are quite simply wholly unnecessary. We are, and were, already committed to our self-regulatory efforts. For their bills to make any sense, they intend to view games more like alcohol, tobacco, and firearms than they do music, movies, and literature, and it is there that the courts have consistently found that games are protected free speech and enjoy the same level of protection as other forms of entertainment.

Retailers have been cautious of the controversial content they buy for their stores ever since the original *Mortal Kombat®* game came out. They recognize that their first obligation is to their customers and providing them with the type, style, and environment in which they want to purchase games. To that end, most IEMA members chose not to sell the highly controversial *BMX XXX™* game, as they believed, like many, that it was sensationalism for its own sake rather than an important element to gameplay.

Many bills also call for retailers to post the ESRB ratings and to provide brochures or informational handouts to customers . . .

We had already committed, voluntarily, to those measures, so we believe the laws to be unnecessary. We oppose them not because of what they stand for in principle, but because we don't want to be fined when a sign falls down, or in some cases, for civil suits to be enabled against our members. Again, we are being held up to the movie theatre owners as the gold standard for this issue, and ask nothing more than to be treated similarly, despite the disparity.

From a retail perspective, what is the cost of all this legislation?

The cost of legislation and subsequent litigation is very, very high to all parties concerned. It has proven out to be unduly burdensome to everyone and an utter waste of taxpayer resources. Clearly, working with the entertainment industry as opposed to against it is the most prudent, and ultimately effective, course of action. The political grand standing gains them short-term spotlight, but when the bills fail to meet muster, all of that positive press comes back to haunt them.

I was recently asked by a legislator who did not want to vote to pass a bill what he could do to aid the industry in our voluntary commitments. I responded by saying that he could join with us and bring his considerable clout, special interest groups, and communication venues with constituents to bear. He could explain to his voters—parents, educators, religious leaders, and the like—that we have a comprehensive ratings system, the major retailers have committed to partnering with them, and that it is up to them to get the word out and do the right thing. Parents are responsible for purchasing M-rated games over 90% of the time! We have given them informed tools and systems with which to make those decisions. The choice to buy their kid *Grand Theft Auto* or to bring them to see *Kill Bill* is theirs to make.

With all this legislation, is there a possibility that retailers will just stop stocking M- and AO-rated titles?

Honestly, that is a grave concern for the content community. We already do not stock AO-rated product. Should even some of the IEMA members choose not to sell M-rated games, it would have a chilling effect on the industry unlike anything we have seen since *Huckleberry Finn*. Imagine any major retailer suddenly deciding to no longer stock M-rated games and R-rated movies. It would have a devastating impact on the entertainment industry. It would curtail story-telling and the art forms themselves. The freedom of speech and freedom of expression would be put to the ultimate test. Consumers rights would be diminished and whole sectors would be financially ravished.

Some developers have expressed frustration at retailers who sell M- and AO-rated games to minors. They believe retailers don't take the ratings seriously. What is the retail channel doing to improve compliance with the ratings? Is there a general policy the IEMA or its members have?

We believe in these new policies, and we volunteered to implement them nationwide in tens of thousands of stores with hundreds of thousands of employees long before this wave of moralism came about. I would urge the development community to support our voluntary efforts in much the same way that we support their creative rights, because it's the right thing to do.

As for policies, they vary depending upon the chain but hold to a common underlying belief in carding for M-rated games. Some stores use cash register prompting, others lock the games behind glass or store them behind the counter. All means to the same end.

Anything else you'd like to add?

It's worth mentioning that sting operations that are done by the media—or worse, politicians—are often misleading and scientifically challenged to say the least. IEMA member stores are generally in stand-alone or strip-mall locations, requiring a parent or guardian to drive the at-risk 10-year-old to the merchant. Also important is the supposed $50 to $100 in disposable income that these stings assume that the 10-year-old has readily available without their parent's knowledge. Some stings are actually performed with the "observer" standing in close proximity to the child, perhaps implying consent to the unknowing clerk.

These are all important reasons why we, as an industry, take the FTC's studies so seriously. They do over 900 shops with people of varying ages, ethnicities, and both sexes, which—any researcher worth his weight in spreadsheets can tell you—is the most objective and accurate method to employ. I don't expect that the next FTC study will prove that we or our systems are perfect, far from it, but I do believe that in the course of a few short years we can reverse the 70/30 split, putting us on par with the theatre owners and hopefully silencing our critics in the process. [Halpin02]

REFERENCES

[Afghanistan01] Harper, Liz, Online NewsHour, PBS.org, "Afghanistan's Growing Media." Available online at *www.pbs.org/newshour/bb/asia/afghanistan/aug03/media.html*. Accessed April 28, 2006.

[AL01] Brewbacker, et al., House of Representatives Bill 573. Amendment to Section 13A-12-200.1 of the Code of Alabama 1975. Alabama House of Representatives.

[AL02] Ibid.

[Baca01] Baca, Congressmen Joe, "Fact Sheet on H.R. 669: Protect Children from Video Game Sex & Violence Act of 2003." Available online at *www.house.gov/baca/hotissues/video_factsheet.htm*. Accessed April 24, 2006.

[Clinton01] Office of Clinton, Senator Hillary Rodham, press statement, "Senators Clinton, Lieberman Announce Federal Legislation to Protect Children from Inappropriate Video Games," November 29, 2005. Available online at *www.senate.gov/~clinton/news/statements/details.cfm?id=249368*. Accessed April 26, 2006.

[Clinton02] Office of Clinton, Senator Hillary Rodham, press statement, "Senators Clinton, Lieberman Announce Federal Legislation to Protect Children from Inappropriate Video Games," November 29, 2005. Available online at *www.senate.gov/~clinton/news/statements/details.cfm?id=249368*. Accessed April 26, 2006.

[Clinton03] Office of Clinton, Senator Hillary Rodham, press statement, "Senators Clinton, Lieberman and Bayh Introduce Federal Legislation to Protect Children from Inappropriate Video Games," December 16, 2005. Available online at *http://clinton.senate.gov/news/statements/details.cfm?id= 249860&&*. Accessed April 26, 2006.

[Clinton04] Office of Clinton, Senator Hillary Rodham, press statement, "Senators Clinton, Lieberman Announce Federal Legislation to Protect Children from Inappropriate Video Games," November 29, 2005. Available online at *www.senate.gov/~clinton/news/statements/details.cfm?id=249368*. Accessed April 26, 2006.

[DC01] Weiss, Eric M. and Vargas, Jose Antonio (of *The Washington Post*), "Leaders Tie Video Game Violence to Problems in D.C's Streets." Post-Gazette.com. "Available online at *www.post-gazette.com/pg/05037/453010.stm*.

[DC02] Councilmember Fenty, Adrian M., Amendment to Title 47, Chapter 28 of the District of Columbia Code, "Youth Protection from Obscene Video Games Act of 2005." Available online at *www.dccouncil.washington.dc.us/lims/ getleg1.asp?legno=B16-0125*. Accessed April 27, 2006.

[Dev01] Anonymous, interview with Brenda Brathwaite, 2005.

[ESA01] The Entertainment Software Association, "2005 Essential Facts About the Computer and Video Game Industry." Available online at *(www.theesa .com/files/2005EssentialFacts.pdf*. Accessed April 28, 2006.

[ESA02] The Entertainment Software Association, "About the ESA." Available on-line at *www.theesa.com/about/index.php*. Accessed April 28, 2006.

[GA01] Stoner, et al., Senate Bill 106 Amendment to Code Section 16-12-103. Georgia General Assembly. Available online at *www.legis.state.ga.us/legis/ 2005_06/fulltext/sb106.htm* (2005). Accessed May 20, 2005.

[Garriott01] Garriott, Richard, interview with Brenda Brathwaite, May 27, 2005.

[Greece01] Staff report, "Greeks Fight Computer Game Ban," BBC News, September 5, 2002. Available online at *http://news.bbc.co.uk/1/hi/technology/ 2238242.stm*. Accessed April 28, 2006.

[Gygax01] Rausch, Allen, GameSpy.com, "The History of Dungeons & Dragons, Interview with Gary Gygax—Part 1," August 15, 2004. Available online at *http://pc.gamespy.com/articles/538/538817p4.html*. Accessed April 24, 2006.

[Halpin01] Halpin, Hal, interview with Brenda Brathwaite. May 23, 2005.

[Halpin02] Halpin, Hal, interview with Brenda Brathwaite. May 23, 2005.

[HB4023A] Chapa LaVia, Representative Linda, et al., Illinois General Assembly, HB4023, "Amendment to Section 5 of the Criminal Code." Available online at *www.ilga.gov/legislation/fulltext.asp?DocName=&SessionId=50&GA=94& DocTypeId=HB&DocNum=4023&GAID=8&LegID=20889&SpecSess=& Session=*. Accessed April 27, 2006.

[HB4023B] Ibid.

[HB4023C] Ibid.

[HB4023D] Ibid.

[HR669] Baca, Congressmen Joe, Amend title 18, United States Code, "H.R. 669 Protect Children from Video Game Sex and Violence Act of 2003," February 11, 2003. Available via search for "HR669" online at *http://thomas.loc.gov/ cgi-bin/query*. Accessed April 24, 2006.

[HR669] Baca, Congressmen Joe, H.R. 669 "Protect Children from Video Game Sex and Violence Act of 2003 (Introduced in House)," February 11, 2003. Available online at *http://thomas.loc.gov/cgi-bin/query* (search for HR 669).

[IGDA01] International Game Developers Association, Position Statement on Censorship. Available online at *www.igda.org/censorship/*. Accessed April 28, 2006.

[IGDA02] International Game Developers Association, "Anti-Censorship—Key Points." Available online at *www.igda.org/censorship/points.php*. Accessed April 28, 2006.

[IL01] Bradley, Representative John E., House Bill 2412. Amendment to Criminal Code of 1961. Illinois General Assembly. Available online at *www.ilga.gov/ legislation/fulltext.asp?DocName=09400HB2412ham001&GA=94& SessionId=50&DocTypeId=HB&DocNum=2412&GAID=8* (2005). Accessed May 21, 2005

[Kuehnel01] Kuehnel, Ed, interview with Brenda Brathwaite, August 4, 2005.

[Kuehnel02] Ibid.

[Lieberman01] Office of Clinton, Senator Hillary Rodham, press statement,. "Senators Clinton, Lieberman Announce Federal Legislation to Protect Children from Inappropriate Video Games," November 29, 2005. Available online at *www.senate.gov/~clinton/news/statements/details.cfm?id=249368*. Accessed April 26, 2006.

[Lowenstein01] Mello, John P. Jr., "Video Game Violence Leads to Florida Law," TechNewsWorld.com, January 20, 2004. Available online at *www.technews-world.com/story/32638.html*. Accessed April 27, 2006.

[Miss01] Harris, Representative Jeff, et al., General Assembly of the State of Missouri. HB390, "To Repeal Section 568.070, RSMo, and to Enact In Lieu Thereof One New Section Relating to Unlawful Transactions with a Child, with Penalty Provisions." Available online at *www.house.state.mo.us/bills051/ bills/HB390.HTM*. Accessed April 27, 2006.

[NYC01] Brewer, Councilmember Gale et al., Resolution 12. New York City Council. Available online at *http://webdocs.nyccouncil.info/textfiles/Res%200012-2004.htm?CFID=567608&CFTOKEN=93331726* (2005). Accessed May 20, 2005.

[Rocca01] Della Rocca, Jason, "Regulation Is Everyone's Business," International Game Developers Organization. Available online at *www.igda.org/articles/dellarocca_regulation.php*. Accessed April 27, 2006.

[Rocca02] Della Rocca, Jason, interview with Brenda Brathwaite.

[Texas01] Goolsby, Representative Tony, Texas House of Representatives. House Bill 866, "Amendment to Section 1, Chapter 35, Business & Commerce Code." Available online at *www.capitol.state.tx.us/tlo/79R/billtext/HB00866I.htmHTM* (2005). Accessed May 20, 2005.

[Texas02] Goolsby, Representative Tony, Texas House of Representatives .House Bill 866, "Amendment to Section 1, Chapter 35, Business & Commerce Code." Available online at *www.capitol.state.tx.us/tlo/79R/billtext/HB00866I. HTM* (2005). Accessed May 20, 2005.

[VSDA01] Video Software Dealers Association, "VSDA Position Statement on Video Segregation." Available online at *www.idealink.org/Resource.phx/vsda/government/positionstatements/videosegregation.htx*. Accessed April 28, 2006.

[VSDA02] Video Software Dealers Association, "What Is the Video Software Dealers Association (VSDA)?" Available online at *www.idealink.org/Resource.phx/public/aboutvsda.htx*. Accessed April 28, 2006.

[VSDA03] Video Software Dealers Association, "VSDA Position Statement on Video Segregation." Available online at *www.idealink.org/Resource.phx/vsda/government/positionstatements/videosegregation.htx*. Accessed April 28, 2006.

[VSDA04] Video Software Dealers Association, "Movie and Video Game Ratings Education, Enforcement, and Advertising Guidelines." Available online at *www.idealink.org/Resource.phx/vsda/government/ratingsempowermentindex.ht*. Accessed April 28, 2006.

[Yee01] Yee, Assemblymember Member Leland, et al., AB 1792. Amendment to Section 313 of the Penal Code. Available online at *www.leginfo.ca.gov/pub/03-04/bill/asm/ab_1751-1800/ab_1792_bill_20040105_introduced.html*. Accessed April 28, 2006.

[Yee02] Yee, Assemblymember Member Leland,. press release, "Multi-Billion Dollar Entertainment Industry Shoots Down Bills to Protect Children from Violent Video Games." Available online *at http://democrats.assembly.ca.gov/members/a12/press/p122004027.htm*. Accessed April 28, 2006.

[Yee03] Yee, Assemblymember Leland et al., Assembly Bill 1793. Amendment to Sections 313.1 and 313.4 of the Penal Code. California Assembly. Available online at *www.leginfo.ca.gov/pub/03-04/bill/asm/ab_1751-1800/ab_1793_bill_20040105_introduced.html* (2005). Accessed May 22, 2005.

[Yee04] Yee, Assemblymember Leland et al., Amended Assembly Bill 1793. Addition to Chapter 6.7 (commencing with Section 20650) to Division 8 of the Business and Professions Code. Available online at *www.leginfo.ca.gov/pub/03-04/bill/asm/ab_1751-1800/ab_1793_bill_20040921_chaptered.html* (2005). Accessed May 22, 2005.

8 Obscenity

by Deborah Solomon

In This Chapter

- Using U.S. Courts to Regulate Sexual Content in Games: Obscenity Versus Freedom of Speech
- Games as "Speech" Under the First Amendment
- The Dictionary Definition of Obscenity
- The Supreme Court Definition of Obscenity
- The Miller Test
- Does "Interactivity" Justify Increased Regulation for Video Games?
- Should Violent Content Receive More Constitutional Protection than Sexual Content?
- Right to Privacy Versus State's Right to Regulate Obscenity
- Indecency vs. Obscenity—Are Games "Broadcasting?"

USING U.S. COURTS TO REGULATE SEXUAL CONTENT IN GAMES: OBSCENITY VERSUS FREEDOM OF SPEECH

Can the legal system censor sex in games? Or does our right to "freedom of speech" prevent the government from restricting game content? Developers and publishers who want to include sexual content in their games, and concerned citizens who may be offended by sex in video games, should be aware of how the legal system has historically treated such content.

A variety of methods have been used to try to control sexual content in games, ranging from public pressure (petitions, boycotts, or simply not buying the game), corporate pressure (withdrawal of advertising, refusal to stock mature-rated games in retail outlets), legislation (direct bans on games and enforcement of rating systems[1], or indirect constraints such as zoning arcade locations, or preventing children from playing games during school hours), agency regulation (the FCC's monitoring of "indecent" broadcasts), and lawsuits (criminal or civil cases). This

175

section analyzes the criminal prosecution approach in the United States—specifically whether courts can enforce federal,[2] state, and local obscenity laws to censor sex in games—and explores the "free speech" defenses to such actions. Many of the other approaches are discussed elsewhere in this book.

This section focuses on court actions in the United States. Developers and publishers will, of course, want to be aware of laws in other jurisdictions where their games are sold or played; however, an entire book could be written about legal approaches in other countries, and they are beyond the scope of this section.[3]

In a nutshell, most U.S. judicial actions to censor sexual content in games are based on claims that the content offends public morality or harms children who are exposed to the games. The traditional game industry defense is that games are protected as "free speech" under the First Amendment of the U.S. Constitution and cannot be censored by the government.

The First Amendment argument almost always prevails in cases where specific types of content are under attack, whether in literature, film, or games. The First Amendment protects speech about hate, politically unpopular viewpoints, violence, and even depictions of cop killing. However, the First Amendment has been interpreted to have a rather large loophole: a category of speech called "obscenity" is accorded far less protection than other kinds of speech.

What is obscenity? Unfortunately, there is no easy answer. However, before we can start to define obscenity as applied to video games, we must first answer a preliminary question: are video games "speech" under the First Amendment?

GAMES AS "SPEECH" UNDER THE FIRST AMENDMENT

The First Amendment states, "Congress shall make no law respecting an establishment of religion, or prohibiting the free exercise thereof; or abridging the freedom of speech, or of the press; or the right of the people peaceably to assemble, and to petition the government for a redress of grievances."

The First Amendment's "freedom of speech" protection covers non-obscene sexual content, as discussed previously, but only when expressed as "speech." Expressive speech includes, for example, work that expresses "ideas, narratives, concepts, imagery, [or] opinions—scientific, political or aesthetic" where the speaker's goal is to "inform, edify, or entertain" an audience.[4] So, the first issue in determining whether games are even protected by the First Amendment—before getting into the obscenity test dilemma—is to determine if games are expressive speech. Books, film, and TV are considered forms of speech, as well as actual verbal utterances and other forms of media. Slogans on tee-shirts, black armbands worn to protest the Vietnam war, car license plates, paintings, music, dance, poetry, even the act of burning a draft card have all been treated as speech in some First Amendment contexts. But some legislators and courts have argued that games should not be considered "speech."

For example, St. Louis Judge Stephen Limbaugh ruled that video games do not express ideas and therefore should not be considered expressive speech. Limbaugh compared video games to games like basketball or bingo, and concluded that the First Amendment simply didn't apply.[5]

Judge Limbaugh's decision was resoundingly overturned by the 8th Circuit Court of Appeals, which explained, "If the First Amendment is versatile enough to 'shield [the] painting of Jackson Pollock, music of Arnold Schoenberg, or Jabberwocky verse of Lewis Carroll,' . . . we see no reason why the pictures, graphic design, concept art, sounds, music, stories and narrative present in video games are not entitled to similar protection. The mere fact that they appear in a novel medium is of no legal consequence."[6]

A number of other courts have also held that video games are protected speech, recognizing the significant storytelling features inherent in modern games.[7] However, there is a big difference between narrative-heavy games (*Final Fantasy*™, *Half-Life 2*™, *Zelda*™, etc.) and games where you'd really have to stretch to find a story (*Tetris*™, *Dance Dance Revolution*™, *Solitaire*™ etc.).

A Connecticut court decision cautions that not all video games are expressive: "In short, the label 'video game' is not talismanic, automatically making the object to which it is applied either speech or not speech."[8] The court explained further, "While video games that are merely digitized pinball machines are not protected speech, those that are analytically indistinguishable from other protected media, such as motion pictures or books, which convey information or evoke emotions by imagery, are protected under the First Amendment."[9]

A pinball machine is not considered speech, so neither are "video games that are merely digitized pinball machines." It is clear that games with narrative qualify as speech, but it is not clear whether games like *Solitaire* or *Tetris* would also get First Amendment protection.[10] This creates a possible strategy for game developers who think they may run into First Amendment issues. Include a storyline *somewhere* in the game, even if it is just backstory that sets up the gameplay.

For example, would a simple game like *Katamari Damacy*™ qualify as expressive speech? One could argue that the gameplay in *Katamari Damacy*™ is really just about rolling things up into big clumps. However, the game starts with an introductory backstory about the King of All Cosmos and his son, the Prince. The King has inadvertently lost all the stars in the Universe, so the Prince must collect items on Earth (by rolling them up into clumps called katamaris) to make new stars. The story continues with updates via cutscenes regarding the Prince's progress and his relationship with his father.[11] The inventive backstory and cutscenes provide a narrative to support the gameplay, making it expressive speech under the First Amendment.

Thus, games that include some sort of narrative, and are not just "digitized pinball machines," are highly likely to be deemed expressive speech. The next term to look at is "obscenity"; however, this is one of the most controversial and ill-defined terms in the history of the Supreme Court. Even now, after more than 100 years of jurisprudence on the subject, the Court has not been able to clearly define the term.

THE DICTIONARY DEFINITION OF OBSCENITY

A dictionary is a logical starting point for understanding the word "obscenity." However, *Webster*'s dictionary defines obscenity circularly as: "1: the quality or state of being obscene; 2: something (as an utterance or act) that is obscene."[12]

What does "obscene" mean? *Webster* further defines "obscene" as: "1: disgusting to the senses: REPULSIVE; 2: a: abhorrent to morality or virtue; *specifically*: designed to incite to lust or depravity, b: containing or being language regarded as taboo in polite usage <obscene lyrics>, c: repulsive by reason of crass disregard of moral or ethical principles <an obscene misuse of power>, d: so excessive as to be offensive."[13]

While *Webster*'s definition is interesting, it has little to do with the legal interpretation of "obscenity" by the U.S. Supreme Court, which has almost exclusively applied the term to sexual content. In other words, discussions about eating worms may be "disgusting to the senses" and CEO salaries "so excessive as to be offensive," but you won't see the Supreme Court applying the obscenity standard to such speech if there is no sex involved.

THE SUPREME COURT DEFINITION OF OBSCENITY

Some people, including several Supreme Court Justices, believe that obscenity simply is not definable. According to the Supreme Court, its own vague decisions on obscenity have had a "tortured history" and have been an "intractable problem."[14] Justice Potter Stewart, in a 1964 obscenity case, admitted that the court was "faced with the task of trying to define what may be indefinable"[15] and ultimately concluded with the famous phrase that, while he had difficulty defining obscenity, "I know it when I see it."[16]

THE MILLER TEST

In 1973, after years of confusing case law that swung from conservative to liberal and back again, the Supreme Court came up with a test for obscenity that is still in use today. In *Miller v. California,* the Court explained that "State statutes designed to regulate obscene materials must be carefully limited."[17] Specifically, the *Miller* test states that for a work to be obscene, it must meet all of the following tests:

"The average person applying contemporary community standards, would find that the work, taken as a whole, appeals to the prurient interest." And,

The work "depicts or describes, in a patently offensive way, sexual conduct specifically defined by applicable state law." And,

A reasonable person would find that "the work, taken as a whole, lacks serious literary, artistic, political, or scientific value" (the "SLAPS" test).[18]

With its focus on "contemporary community standards," the Supreme Court in *Miller* held that obscenity could be defined according to *local* tastes. This was a more conservative stance than prior, more liberal rulings that applied a national obscenity standard. Publishers can be sued in any locale where their media is sold, even when they have little control over where that material ends up. Therefore, the community standards approach makes them vulnerable to the most restrictive attitudes of local communities.

The Objectionable Content Must "Depict or Describe Sexual Conduct"

The *Miller* test limits obscenity to sexual conduct, specifically aiming at so-called "hard-core" pornography.[19] States have tried to argue that excessive *violence* in video games can be obscene,[20] but the Court has rejected this approach.

Obscenity is not limited to visual images; books, brochures, presentations, even stand-up comedy can be censored. Most obscenity cases these days involve visual images of sex—in photographs, TV, films, or games. However, in the past, obscenity law was used to prosecute comedians like Lenny Bruce and publishers of books by authors like Henry Miller, Vladimir Nabokov, and James Joyce. Even birth control information pamphlets were outlawed as illegally obscene until 1965.[21]

It's important to remember that not all sexual content can be labeled "obscene." The words "pornography" and "obscenity" are often interchanged, but they have very different meanings under the law. Pornography is not automatically obscene unless it fails the *Miller* test, especially if it is not "hard-core." Thus, many images and descriptions of sex *are* protected under the First Amendment.

The Prohibited Sexual Content Must Be "Described in the Law"

Laws must provide fair warning about what is to be considered a violation. Otherwise, a law would have little preventative purpose. After all, it is not fair to prosecute people if a law does not clearly explain what behavior is criminal and what is not. For these reasons, the *Miller* test requires obscenity laws to specifically describe the prohibited sexual content being regulated.

To give an easy example, doctors should not have to worry that medical posters depicting breast self-exams (to detect breast cancer) could run afoul of an obscenity statute that criminalizes depictions of "masturbation." Medical posters would be protected under the SLAPS prong of the Miller test as having "scientific value," discussed later. Nevertheless, laws should clearly describe what kinds of images are prohibited even before the SLAPS defense can be raised. We should keep in mind that not long ago, birth control pamphlets were considered obscene. What we consider today as being scientifically valuable was not always so.

A more difficult example is a pornographic magazine. Remember that, in the United States, pornography is not automatically considered "obscene" and is protected by the First Amendment. So how should the law delineate when pornographic content crosses the line into obscenity? By type of sexual act, orifice, or amount of penetration depicted? By the gender, sexual orientation, or number of participants? By the camera angle or degree of close-up? By the nature of the reaction or impact on viewers? Publishers of pornography, like any other business, have a right to know what content will get them in legal trouble; however, *Miller* has not resulted in clear definitions of what would be considered "obscene" under the law.

In *The Brethren*, reporter Bob Woodward describes the decision-making process underlying Supreme Court obscenity cases during the 1960s and 1970s. On "Movie Day," according to Woodward, many of the Justices and their law clerks would view the porn movies under review, and the law clerks took notes on how the Justices defined obscenity[22]: Justice Byron White believed that if no penises were erect and no penises were inserted into a body orifice, that no obscenity had occurred.[23] Brennan's definition of obscenity also included no erections. However, he allowed for penetration if there was no erection.[24]

Naturally, the justices were less direct in their official court opinion. Instead, they gave the following value-laden examples of how an obscenity statute might describe regulated material: 1) "Patently offensive representations or descriptions of ultimate sexual acts, normal or perverted, actual or simulated," and 2) "Patently offensive representations or descriptions of masturbation, excretory functions, and lewd exhibition of the genitals."[25]

The Court's examples do not provide clear warning to publishers. These examples rely on subjective evaluations like "patently offensive," "normal," "perverted," and "lewd." How can a game developer know what the community will find offensive and lewd, especially when community standards are constantly evolving? In *The Sims*, for example, urination by game characters is part of the gameplay because players control when their characters go to the bathroom. Some might consider this fairly mild game action a "patently offensive representation" of "excretory functions." Consider Michelangelo's masterpiece *David*, a famous statue of a nude man: how does one distinguish between a "lewd exhibition of the genitals" and a non-lewd display? The Court has been criticized for exactly what it sought to prevent: allowing subjectively worded obscenity laws that do not provide fair warning about what might be considered criminal.

Obscene Works Appeal to the "Prurient Interest," Are "Patently Offensive," and Have No "SLAPS" Value

The remaining elements of the *Miller* test are evaluations of worthiness versus offensiveness. Specifically, juries must decide if a work appeals to the "prurient interest," if it is "patently offensive," and if, *taken as a whole—not just the prurient, offensive parts*—it lacks "serious literary, artistic, political, or scientific value."

The Court explained that medical textbooks with graphic illustrations would have scientific value and thus could not be considered "obscene"; however, it gave little guidance for resolving more difficult determinations of merit. What is sufficiently "scientific?" Could a film or game depicting so-called "hard-core" sexual acts be allowable if it is used to teach doctors about sexual behavior? Could the same film or game be criminalized if displayed to the general public? When is a work sufficiently literary or artistic that "taken as a whole" it cannot be considered obscene? At one point, novels by James Joyce were banned as obscene; today they are considered part of the literary canon. These confusing and subjective questions are left for local juries to decide.

In addition, the prurient interest and patent offensiveness prongs of the *Miller* test may well be in conflict. Kathleen Sullivan, a former Dean of Stanford Law School, criticized these elements of the *Miller* test saying they were not easily understandable and asked one to be both aroused and repulsed.[26]

The Court attempted to clarify the obscenity test in 1985, explaining that obscenity predominantly appeals to a "shameful or morbid interest in nudity, sex, or excretions," whereas material provoking "normal sexual reactions" or "healthy sexual desires" would not be obscene.[27] The Court has tried to provide "concrete guidelines to isolate 'hardcore' pornography from expression protected by the First Amendment."[28] However, in *Miller* and later cases, it has just created new legal terms that lack real definition ("hard-core," "patently offensive," "prurient," "healthy," "normal," "shameful," "morbid," etc.). The Supreme Court's test merely throws the determination of obscenity back to juries expected to "know it when they see it."

Supreme Court Justice William Douglas, dissenting in *Miller*, pointed out that the majority's obscenity test was hopelessly flawed: "The Court has worked hard to define obscenity and concededly has failed."[29] He continued, "We deal with highly emotional, not rational questions. To many the Song of Solomon is obscene. I do not think we, the judges, were ever given the constitutional power to make definitions of obscenity. If it is to be defined, let the people debate and decide by a constitutional amendment what they want to ban as obscene and what standards they want the legislatures and the courts to apply. Perhaps the people will decide that the path toward a mature, integrated society requires that all ideas competing for acceptance must have no censor. Perhaps they will decide otherwise. Whatever the choice, the courts will have some guidelines. Now we have none except our own predilections."[30]

Justice Douglas believed that the *Miller* test would lead to "a regime of censorship"[31] where administrative agencies could generate criminal prosecutions against publishers without clear guidelines. Under this regime, he said, "the criminal law becomes a trap."[32] Vague laws give too much discretion to prosecutors, particularly when laws are on the books but rarely enforced. Obscenity laws enable inconsistent and politically driven prosecutions and fail to provide publishers with clear guidance on how to comply with the law and avoid criminal penalties.

Applying Contemporary Community Standards

So how are juries to decide these issues? According to the Court, juries should determine if a work appeals to the prurient interest and is patently offensive based on "the average person, applying contemporary community standards."[33] Different communities have different standards, and what may be offensive in Utah is not necessarily offensive in San Francisco. Therefore, the "community standards" test is local, not national or global. Juries are to apply the standards of their own local community, not the United States as a whole. (In contrast, the SLAPS prong of the test is based on a national, not local, standard.[34])

Furthermore, what may offend in Utah in 2006 differs from what was shocking in Utah in 1956. The community standards test is temporal and local—it changes as peoples' opinions and expectations evolve over time. While this builds a natural flexibility into the law, it also makes it much more difficult for publishers to stay abreast of evolving community mores.

The local standards approach leads to dilemmas for publishers of games, books, and films, because their products may end up in a variety of communities. Obscenity laws not only exist at the federal and state level; some cities and counties have their own versions of obscenity laws. Publishers are "forced to cope with the community standards of every hamlet into which their goods may wander. [Because] these variegated standards are impossible to discern, national distributors, fearful of risking the expense and difficulty of defending against prosecution in any of several remote communities, must inevitably [retreat] to debilitating self-censorship. [Consequently], the people of many communities will be 'protected' far beyond government's constitutional power to deny them access to sexually oriented materials."[35]

In other words, rather than expensively customizing materials to meet each community's differently evolving standards, publishers may be forced to protect themselves by using the most conservative community standards nationwide.

Of course, interesting questions arise when dealing with the Internet and games. If a game can be downloaded via the Internet to anywhere in the world, which community standards should apply? After all, an obscenity case can be prosecuted where the expression originated or where it was received. Should globally available Web sites and games be required to meet the most restrictive community standards, and how would this affect game content?

This situation was exemplified in a 1996 case where a California-based couple was convicted in Tennessee for distributing sexual material on the Internet. The couple was sent to jail for violating Tennessee community standards, even though the material probably would not have been obscene under California community standards.[36]

So far, we have just talked about the definition of obscenity in U.S. courts. However, many countries are more restrictive than the United States. Many Gulf states, for example, employ censors with magic markers who diligently scribble over images in magazines that expose female bellybuttons, couples kissing, or other "immodest" displays. Should game developers try to "modularize" sexual content in these countries, so that each nation is served permissible content? For example, games sold in Saudi Arabia might prevent players from removing clothing from their avatars. Offensive interactions and storylines, such as the notorious *Grand Theft Auto: San Andreas* Hot Coffee sex scenes, might be "unlockable" only in permissive countries.

Realistically, such modularization would be difficult to implement and could lead to more legal headaches. (For example, how to prevent the "wrong" copy of a game from being played in a restrictive nation? What if hackers find a way to "unlock" the offending scenes?) Modularization would also be time consuming and expensive for developers forced to make E-rated versions of risqué games. Furthermore, it is impossible to fully moderate game content in MMOGs where developers cede control to players who create their own characters, storylines, and in-game dialogue.

"We know it when we see it"—seems to be the rule in most countries, but the "we" is what differs. Community standards naturally depend on the community involved. Some nations, like the United States, focus on local community standards; some, like Canada, use national community standards when judging "obscenity"; and others, like many of the Gulf states, rely on religious edicts decreed by clerics. But some analysts propose instead that we should use *global* community standards when dealing with worldwide media like the Internet and online games. For example, rather than defining a community by its geographical borders, online works could be judged by a cybercommunity standard.[37] Thus far, however, the courts have rejected the cybercommunity standard approach. Instead, they continue to apply the *Miller* test, decided in 1973, long before the Internet became mainstream.

Further Limitations on First Amendment Protection

Even if a game survives the *Miller* test and is not "obscene," can it still be regulated? The answer is that access to non-obscene sexual material can still be limited, particularly for children or when the restriction just limits the "time, place, or manner" of access without directly censoring the content itself.

Let's say a developer creates a new video game that includes a story (so it will almost certainly be protected "speech"), and also includes sexual content but not "hard-core" pornography (so it is unlikely to be labeled "obscene" under the *Miller* Test). Does the First Amendment completely protect this non-obscene game from content regulation?

The First Amendment does not provide absolute protection for speech, even for speech that is not deemed "obscene." Instead, the court will look closely at the law to see if it reaches too broadly. In other words, content-based regulations on *protected* speech are not automatically unconstitutional. Instead, they are analyzed under a "strict scrutiny" test. Strict scrutiny means that a law will be upheld only if "necessary" and "narrowly tailored" to achieve a "compelling" state interest.[38]

Strict scrutiny is a difficult test to pass, and most regulations will be struck down. However, protecting children from sexually oriented material is considered a "compelling" state interest.[39] States cannot prevent *adults* from playing non-obscene, sexually graphic games, but they may be able to prevent *children* from playing such games (if the law is also "necessary" and "narrowly tailored").

For example, a New York law prevents dissemination of "indecent" sexual materials to minors, even when they are relatively mild. Mere depictions of "nudity" and "narrative accounts of sexual excitement"[40] are not permitted if New York deems them "harmful to minors." The "harmful to minors" definition uses language similar to the *Miller* test, but allows additional restrictions by referencing minors. For example, harmful material "is patently offensive to prevailing standards in the adult community as a whole *with respect to what is suitable material for minors*"[41] (emphasis added). In other words, it sounds like the "patently offensive" prong of the *Miller* test, but could actually include a wide range of material that is not obscene but merely what adults think is unsuitable for minors. Of course, while the law on the books is potentially quite restrictive, the reality is that it is rarely enforced. Most kids and adults in New York probably would be surprised to even know it exists.

There are limits to how much the courts can shield minors from sexually explicit material. In 2004, the Supreme Court rejected a federal law designed to protect children from online pornography.[42] The Child Online Protection Act (COPA) required Web sites to use credit cards or other access systems that would prevent minors from viewing the material. This was too broad a requirement, the Court held, and parent-installed filtering software would probably be a less restrictive alternative.[43]

States may also regulate non-obscene speech using "time, place, or manner" restrictions. These are allowable restrictions on the time, place, or manner of the speech at issue (e.g., zoning regulations applying to arcades or adult bookstores). Such regulations cannot outright censor the expressive content, but are allowable if they are narrowly tailored to serve a significant governmental interest and leave enough alternative channels for communicating the information.[44] Some commentators such as Lawrence G. Walters, Esq. and Clyde Dewitt of the law firm Weston, Garrou, DeWitt & Walters have suggested that "time, place, and manner" regulations are the way of the future: "Ultimately, lawmakers and the courts will need to move to some form of regulation of the time, place, and manner of distribution of hardcore erotic speech, as opposed to outright criminalization using obscenity laws based on the increasingly irrelevant concept of community standards. Restrictions that minimize the physical impact on the community, and the viewer's ability to shield himself or herself from accidental exposure to erotic speech, will take precedence over the limited modern utility of obscenity laws. Tomorrow's erotic content regulations will likely involve concepts such as labeling, filtering, warnings, and the like, instead of outright bans as have been used in the past."[45] This recommendation is reminiscent of conclusions drawn by the 1970 National Commission on Obscenity and Pornography (appointed by President Lyndon Johnson). The commission scandalized its conservative political supporters by suggesting that laws censoring obscenity for adults should be abolished and that future laws should concern themselves with regulating more realistic problems, like public displays, unsolicited mailings, and distribution to minors.

DOES "INTERACTIVITY" JUSTIFY INCREASED REGULATION FOR VIDEO GAMES?

If there is one thing we can learn from the history of obscenity law, it is that every *new* form of mass media generates alarm and attempts at predictably *old* forms of censorship. From the printing press to comic books, to TV, film, and home video, to the Internet and, of course, to video games, each media innovation has triggered public outcries about sexual and violent content. What is interesting is that the actual sexual content of so-called obscenity has not significantly changed over time; rather, it is the new means of expressing that content that is challenged in the courts. One would think that the government might set a single standard for content—whether in books, film, TV, or video games—but this is not always the case.

Innovators in the fields of media or games and simulations should be prepared for regular waves of attempted censorship whenever new technologies are invented. Even though the range of sexual behavior that tends to be labeled "obscene" does not change rapidly, any new form of expressing that sexual behavior (obscene or not) will doubtless trigger new attempts at regulation, particularly when the new technology begins to enter the mainstream consumer market. For example, movies were not considered worthy of First Amendment protection from censorship until 1952![46]

Some argue that games require different levels of regulation because they are interactive and because players can generate and distribute their own content within the game. However, this is true of the Internet in general. A blog or work of interactive fiction involves feedback from others, interaction, and publishing of new content by other users.[47] Theatre is an ancient interactive medium. Even a print newspaper can be said to be somewhat interactive (although not in real time) when readers' letters to the editor and opinion columns are published. As Judge Posner explained, "Maybe video games are different. They are, after all, interactive. But this point is superficial, in fact erroneous. All literature (here broadly defined to include movies, television, and the other photographic media, and popular as well as highbrow literature) is interactive; the better it is, the more interactive. Literature when it is successful draws the reader into the story, makes him identify with the characters, invites him to judge them and quarrel with them, to experience their joys and sufferings as the reader's own."[48]

Therefore, interactivity per se has not been grounds for new types of content regulation.[49]

Censorship attempts reveal the power of a medium. As author Jon Festinger aptly notes in his book *Video Game Law*, the more powerful the medium, the more fear it inspires. As video games grow in popularity, they set themselves squarely in censors' sights. Festinger notes that this signals the strength and success of games as a medium.[50] Demographic studies indicate that young people watch less TV and play more games than ever before. As gaming becomes more popular than TV, it is not surprising that social attention is focusing in on this powerful form of expression.

SHOULD VIOLENT CONTENT RECEIVE MORE CONSTITUTIONAL PROTECTION THAN SEXUAL CONTENT?

Is viewing sexual content more harmful than viewing violent content? The Supreme Court seems to think so. In the United States, violence in video games and other media is accorded much stronger protection than is sex. There is no "obscenity" type exception for violent content under the First Amendment. Attempts to censor violent games—for children or for adults—have failed to pass "strict scrutiny." According to Judge Posner, "To shield children right up to the age of 18 from exposure to violent descriptions and images would not only be quixotic, but deforming; it would leave them unequipped to cope with the world as we know it."[51]

As a result, video game legislation that conflates sex and violence is likely to be overturned as unconstitutional. While states may restrict children's access to sexual content, they have not been able to censor violence in games.

The United States approach is by no means universal. Some other countries are much more restrictive of violent than sexual content. In Germany, for example, games that graphically show humans being killed are put on *the index*—a list of media that cannot be advertised, publicly displayed, or sold to children. Sex in games is not necessarily considered as harmful to children as violence; games with sexual content also can be listed on *the index*, but generally only if the sexual acts are debasing, discriminatory, or sadistic.[52]

RIGHT TO PRIVACY VERSUS STATE'S RIGHT TO REGULATE OBSCENITY

Another quirk in U.S. First Amendment law is the right to be free from "unwanted governmental intrusions into one's privacy."[53] You cannot be prosecuted for viewing obscenity in your own home. In *Stanley vs. Georgia*, police, searching Mr. Stanley's home for unrelated items, happened to find obscene films in his bedroom. The Supreme Court held that Mr. Stanley was wrongly convicted of possessing obscene material because "mere private possession of obscene matter cannot constitutionally be made a crime."[54]

So *Miller* allows states to ban distribution and public exhibition of obscene works, even when they are only shown to consenting adults.[55] However, *Stanley* prevents states from banning private possession of those works. This dichotomy can be compared to banning drug distribution but allowing people to get high in the privacy of their own homes.

Not surprisingly, critics have assailed *Stanley* as incoherent and rationally absurd.[56] While still valid, *Stanley* has been construed narrowly; the government may still outlaw sending obscene material by mail, transporting such material across state lines, or importing such materials, even when intended only for private use.[57] Nor does *Stanley* protect any form of private possession of child pornography.[58]

What does *Stanley* mean for video games? It may mean that states cannot prosecute individuals playing "obscene" video games in the privacy of their own homes, even if they can regulate publishers and distributors of those games. In some cases, however, the players *are* the publishers. Players of modern online games are content publishers—they create new characters, dialogue, and storylines and publish them via the Internet to other players around the world. So are game masters and MMOG players potentially criminal actors under obscenity laws? What about mod makers who create new versions of existing games and make them freely available online for others to download—are they prosecutable if their mod contains "obscene" material?

Take as an example the "Hot Coffee" drama in *Grand Theft Auto: San Andreas*. If the *GTA:SA* sex scenes were deemed obscene, who would be the prosecutable publisher? The original game publisher or the player who modified the code?

INDECENCY VERSUS OBSCENITY—ARE GAMES "BROADCASTING?"

An interesting double standard exists in laws governing sex in the media. The FCC has jurisdiction over material that is "broadcast" like radio or TV. The FCC can censor broadcast material it considers "indecent" even if that material is not obscene under *Miller* (e.g., Janet Jackson's exposed breast at the 2004 Super Bowl show). The First Amendment prevents the government from regulating sexual content unless it is obscene (or fails the strict scrutiny test); however, the FCC can regulate non-obscene sexual content under the much more conservative "indecency" standard.

How is this possible? First, remember that the First Amendment uses the "strict scrutiny" test for non-obscene material, and the state's goal of protecting children is a "compelling interest" under that test. The Court decided that the pervasiveness of TV and radio means it is hard to prevent children from being exposed to broadcast media. Therefore, broadcast media has a special character that permits more restrictive regulation, similar to the "harmful to minors" laws. The Court allows the FCC to ban "language or material that, in context, depicts or describes, in terms patently offensive as measured by contemporary community standards in the broadcast medium, sexual or excretory activities or organs."[59] Unlike the *Miller* test, a single incidence can be considered "indecent," even if the program as a whole has serious value.

While the FCC tried to embrace the Internet as a "broadcast" medium under its regulatory jurisdiction, the Supreme Court disagreed. In *ACLU v. Reno*, the Court decreed that the Internet was not "broadcasting" and could not be subjected to the FCC's indecency rules.[60] Likewise, online games cannot be considered "broadcasting." However, traditional media and game technology are rapidly converging. It remains to be seen if some future combination of games and TV, for example, might be governed by the FCC. Or perhaps traditional broadcast media will be replaced by satellite and cable and the FCC will have nothing left to regulate.

Thus, four general categories of sexual content can be criminalized according to the U.S. Supreme Court: obscenity, material that is harmful to minors, indecency that is broadcast, and child pornography.[61] (The latter involves different criminal concerns about protecting children from abuse and is beyond the scope of this section.) None of these has clear definitions, and all have stirred passionate First Amendment debates.

In many cases, particularly with "obscenity" prosecutions, the definitions are left up to state juries applying local community standards. This leaves content creators—including game developers—in limbo. Since prosecution can be brought wherever games are produced or played, developers may be at the whim of the most conservative local communities.

Without being able to predict what a particular jury might find "prurient" or "patently offensive," it is difficult to stay within the bounds of the law. Even if developers could modularize game content so that explicit sexual content could be removed on a per-community basis, they would still need to know the standards applicable in each local community. The bright side for developers and downside for anti-obscenity advocates is that obscenity laws are rarely enforced. However, game developers should not become complacent because conservative organizations are advocating for more obscenity prosecutions and their requests are being heard at the highest levels.

A top priority of U.S. Attorney General Alberto Gonzales is to step up obscenity enforcement: "Another priority I have outlined is the aggressive and effective prosecution of those who create, sell, and distribute obscenity. I am strongly committed to ensuring the right of free speech. But the Supreme Court has ruled that the First Amendment does not protect obscene materials."[62] Gonzales also hopes to enforce a *mandatory* rating system for explicit sexual content on the Internet.[63] If this passes and is upheld by the courts, then mandatory ratings for games will not be far behind and could lead to new actions against game publishers.

As the law currently stands, it is vague, unpredictable, and sporadically enforced. Neither pro-censorship nor anti-censorship advocates have a solid foothold, and content creators are subject to the political whims of state and federal prosecutors. In this age of online games and global Internet availability, the idea of community can be redefined. While modern citizens may not even know their neighbors, they often share intimate details about their lives with communities of individuals from around the world who share their passions and interests. But our laws still reflect traditional notions of communities derived only from physical proximity.

ENDNOTES

1. So far, mandatory rating systems have been deemed unconstitutional. See, e.g., *Interstate Circuit v. Dallas*, 390 U.S. 676 (1968) (Dallas ordinance mandating movie ratings was unconstitutionally vague). However, the Bush administration has proposed a new mandatory rating system for sexually explicit Web sites; it remains to be seen how the courts will treat this system if it becomes law.
2. A list of federal obscenity laws can be found at *www.usdoj.gov/criminal/ceos/obscenity_stats.html*, last accessed 4/16/2006.
3. A partial list of "Video Game Legislation Around the World" can be found at *www.en.wikipedia.org/wiki/Video_game_controversy*, last accessed 2/20/2006.
4. *Swank v. Smart*, 898 F. 2d 1247 (7th Cir. 1990) at 1251.
5. *IDSA v. St. Louis County*, Missouri, 200 F. Supp. 2d 1126 (E.D. Mo. 2002).
6. *IDSA v. St. Louis County*, Missouri, 329 F.3d 954, 957 (8th Cir. 2003).

7. See, e.g., *Wilson v. Midway Games,* 198 F.Supp.2d 167 (Connecticut, 2002) and *Video Software Dealers Assn v. Norm Maleng,* 325 F. Supp. 2d 1180 (W.D. WA, Seattle Division, 2004).

8. *Midway Games,* supra at 181.

9. *Midway Games,* ibid.

10. But see IGDA's Brief of Amicus Curiae in *IDSA v. St. Louis,* pp. 10–11, at *www. igda.org/censorship/IGDA_StLouis_Brief_20020925.pdf,* last accessed 4/20/2006: "To be sure, not all video games contain complex narratives. That a particular video game lacks a strong narrative theme, however, does not diminish the appropriate First Amendment protection. The First Amendment does not require that expression be in narrative form; still less does it require that narratives, where present, be complex. The graphic design and sound elements of a puzzle game constitute a form of aesthetic expression akin to music or abstract art that clearly qualifies as protected expression within the First Amendment."

11. For more details about *Katamari Damacy,* see *www.gamespot.com/ps2/action/ katamaridamashii/review.html,* last accessed 2/20/2006.

12. *Merriam-Webster Online Dictionary, www.m-w.com/dictionary/obscenity,* last accessed 1/5/2006.

13. *Merriam-Webster Online Dictionary, www.m-w.com/dictionary/obscene,* last accessed 1/5/2006.

14. *Miller v. CA,* 413 U.S. 15 (1973). Also see *Fort Wayne Books v. Indiana,* 489 U.S. 46 (1989) (Stevens, J. dissenting), quoting Attorney General's Commission on Pornography, Final Report 260-261 (July 1986): "In 1970, . . . the President's Commission on Obscenity and Pornography advocated that laws regulating adults' access to sexually explicit materials be repealed. . . . The most recent federal pornography commission disagreed with this conclusion yet acknowledged that scholarly comment generally agrees with the dissenters: 'Numerous people . . . have urged upon us the view that the Supreme Court's approach is a mistaken interpretation of the First Amendment. They have argued that we should conclude that any criminal prosecution based on the distribution to consenting adults of sexually explicit material, no matter how offensive to some, and no matter how hard-core, and no matter how devoid of literary, artistic, political, or scientific value, is impermissible under the First Amendment. 'We have taken these arguments seriously. . . . Moreover, we recognize that the bulk of scholarly commentary is of the opinion that the Supreme Court's resolution of and basic approach . . . to the First Amendment issues is incorrect."

15. *Jacobellis v. Ohio,* (Stewart, J. concurring), 378 U.S. 184, 197 (1964): "I have reached the conclusion . . . that under the First and Fourteenth Amendments criminal laws in this area are constitutionally limited to hard-core pornography. I shall not today attempt further to define the kinds of material I understand to be embraced within that shorthand description; and perhaps I could never succeed in intelligibly doing so. But I know it when I see it, and the motion picture involved in this case is not that." The Jacobellis case concerned a French movie (Louis Malle's *The Lovers*) with a brief sex scene. Justice Stewart agreed with the majority that the film was *not* "hard-core pornography" (i.e., it was not "obscene") and should be protected by the First Amendment.

However, he wrote a concurring opinion because he did not think the majority opinion would be a coherent precedent for future obscenity cases.

16. Ibid.
17. *Miller v. California,* 413 U.S. 15 at 23-24 (1973). *Miller* concerned a mass mailing of advertising material for illustrated "adult" books. The brochures advertised four books entitled "Intercourse," "Man-Woman," "Sex Orgies Illustrated," and "An Illustrated History of Pornography," and a film called "Marital Intercourse." These brochures contained pictures "very explicitly depicting men and women in groups of two or more engaging in a variety of sexual activities, with genitals often prominently displayed." The brochures were opened by a restaurant manager and his mother, who had not requested the brochures, and who complained to the police. The Court concluded that this material could be considered obscene, hard-core pornography unprotected by the First Amendment.
18. Ibid, at 24.
19. Ibid, at 27.
20. *American Amusement Machine Ass'n, v. Kendrick,* 244 F.3d 572, 577, (7th Cir., 2001): "Violence and obscenity are distinct categories of objectionable depiction." However, the 7th Circuit did not rule that violence could never be considered legally obscene: "Maybe violent photographs of a person being drawn and quartered could be suppressed as disgusting, embarrassing, degrading, or disturbing without proof that they are likely to cause any of the viewers to commit a violent act. They might even be described as 'obscene,' in the same way that photographs of people defecating might be, and in many obscenity statutes are, included within the legal category of the obscene . . . even if they have nothing to do with sex. In common speech, indeed, 'obscene' is often just a synonym for repulsive, with no sexual overtones at all."
21. In 1873, Congress passed the notorious Comstock Law, which prohibited birth control information as obscene. It was not until 1965 that the Supreme Court gave married couples the right to use birth control in *Griswold v. Connecticut,* 381 US 479 (1965), and the right was not given to unmarried persons until 1972 in *Eisenstadt v. Baird,* 405 US 438 (1972).
22. *The Brethren,* Bob Woodward and Scott Armstrong (Simon & Schuster, 2005, originally published 1979).
23. Ibid, p. 232.
24. Ibid, p. 234.
25. In later cases, the Court made clear that these are not the only possible examples of conduct that might be obscene. See, e.g., *Ward v. Illinois,* 431 U.S. 767 (1977).
26. Children's Internet Protection Act (CIPA): Legal Definitions of Child Pornography, Obscenity and "Harmful to Minors," Mary Minow, 2003, at *www.llrx.com/features/updatecipa.htm,* last accessed 5/1/2005. (Also cited in *http://cites.boisestate.edu/civ3i12.pdf,* last accessed 5/1/2005 and other news sources.)
27. *Brockett v. Spokane Arcades,* 472 U.S. 491, 498 (1985).
28. *Miller,* supra at 27.
29. *Miller,* supra, Douglas dissenting, at 35 and 41.
30. *Miller,* supra, Douglas dissenting, at 47.

31. *Miller,* supra, Douglas dissenting, at 39.

32. *Miller,* supra, Douglas dissenting, at 41.

33. *Miller,* supra, at 24.

34. The SLAPS prong of the *Miller* test is usually interpreted as a "reasonable person"—not local community level—standard. See, e.g., *Pope v. Illinois,* 481 U.S. 497 (1987).

35. *Hamling v. US,* 418 U.S. 87, 144-145 (1974) (Brennan, J., dissenting). Also see *Ashcroft v. ACLU,* 535 U.S. 564, 603 (2002) (Stevens, J., dissenting) ("If a prurient appeal is offensive in a puritan village, it may be a crime to post it on the World Wide Web.")

36. *United States v. Thomas,* 74 F.3d 701 (6th Cir. 1996), cert. denied, 519 U.S. 820 (1996). ("If Defendants did not wish to subject themselves to liability in jurisdictions with less tolerant standards for determining obscenity, they could have refused to give passwords to members in those districts, thus precluding the risk of liability.") See also *United States v. Extreme Associates, Inc., et. al.,* 2005 W.L. 121749 (W.D. Pa. January 20, 2005), *Ashcroft v. ACLU,* 535 U.S. at 601-2 ("[P]rosecution may be proper 'in any district in which [an] offense was begun, continued, or completed.'"). Compare *Nitke v. Gonzales,* 253 F. Supp. 2d 587 (S.D.N.Y. 2003), and #01 CIV 11476 (RMB), aff'd without comment, 547 U.S. 05-526 (2006).

37. See "Cybercommunity Versus Geographical Community Standard for Online Pornography: A Technological Hierarchy in Judging Cyberspace Obscenity," Gyong Ho Kim, Anna R. Paddon, *Rutgers Computer & Technology Law Journal* (1999) and "Cybersmut and the First Amendment: A Call for a New Obscenity Standard," Debra Burke, *Harvard Journal of Law & Technology,* Vol. 9, No. 1 (Winter 1996). Also see Justice O'Connor's concurrence in *Ashcroft v. ACLU,* supra at 587-8, stating that Internet obscenity case should perhaps be subject to national, not community, standards.

38. *Turner Broad. Sys., Inc. v. FCC,* 512 U.S. 622, 664-65 (1994). *R.A.V. v. City of St. Paul,* 505 U.S. 377, 395 (1992)

39. *Ginsberg v. New York,* 390 U.S. 629 (1968) (non-obscene material could be sold to adults but the state could prevent distribution to children.) *U.S. v. American Library Association, Inc.,* 539 US 194 (2003). (Upholding Children's Internet Protection Act requiring libraries to use Web filtering software.) *FCC v. Pacifica Foundation,* 438 U.S. 726 (1978) (supporting FCC reprimand for broadcast of "dirty words" when children might be listing to the radio). See also "Can States Constitutionally Regulate Video Games, as California Is Considering Doing?" by Vikram David Amar & Alan Brownstein (May, 2004) *http://practice.findlaw.com/cyberlaw-0504.html,* last accessed July 2005.

40. P.L.§235.20-23. "Indecent material" includes, amongst other things, "any image of a person or portion of the human body which depicts nudity [or] sexual conduct" or "narrative accounts of sexual excitement" and is "harmful to minors." A "minor" is any person "less than seventeen years old."

   "'Harmful to minors' means that quality of any description or representation, in whatever form, of nudity, sexual conduct, sexual excitement, or sado-masochistic abuse, when it: (a) Considered as a whole, appeals to the prurient interest in sex of minors; and (b) Is patently offensive to prevailing standards in the adult community as a whole with respect to what is suitable material for minors; and (c) Considered as a whole, lacks serious literary, artistic, political and scientific value for minors."

41. Ibid.
42. *Ashcroft v. ACLU*, 535 US 564 (2002).
43. Additional cases reviewing federal laws on Internet porn include: *Reno v. ACLU*, 521 U.S. 844 (1997) (Supreme Court rejected language of the Communications Decency Act because it "place[d] and unacceptably heavy burden on protected speech"), *US v. American Library Ass'n*, supra, and *Nitke v. Gonzales*, supra.
44. See, e.g., *Ward v. Rock Against Racism*, 491 U.S. 781, 791 (1989), rev'g 848 F.2d 367 (2nd Cir. 1988).
45. "Obscenity in the Digital Age: The Re-Evaluation of Community Standards," Lawrence G. Walters and Clyde DeWitt, *www.firstamendment.com/digitalage.php*, last accessed 4/20/2006.
46. In 1915, the Court in *Mutual Film Corp. v. Industrial Commission of Ohio* held that movies were "a business pure and simple" and were not entitled to protections afforded to books and newspapers. This decision was reversed in 1952, when the Court in *Burstyn v. Wilson* held that that motion pictures were expressive speech under the First Amendment. See also "Rating & Labeling Entertainment" by Kyonzte Hughes, First Amendment Center at *www.firstamendmentcenter.org/Speech/arts/topic.aspx?topic= rating*.
47. *Reno v. ACLU*, 521 U.S. 844, 870 (1997): The Internet is a "dynamic, multifaceted category of communication [that] includes not only traditional print and news services, but also audio, video, and still images, as well as *interactive*, real-time dialogue."
48. *American Amusement Machine Ass'n v. Kendrick*, 244 F.3d 572, 577, (7th Cir., 2001).
49. But see "Freedom of Expression and Interactive Media: Video Games and the First Amendment," Carmen K. Hoyme, 2 *First Amend. L. Rev.* 377, 384 at 398 (2004): "The [Kendrick] opinion apparently equates the terms "engaging" and "interactive," which in fact are analytically distinguishable. An engaging narrative . . . may inspire rapt attention and enthusiasm, but it cannot involve the audience in the making of the story itself; the latter can be achieved only by a truly interactive medium."
50. Video Game Law, John Festinger (LexisNexis Butterworths; 2005), p. 115.
51. *American Amusement Machine Ass'n v. Kendrick*, 244 F.3d 572, 577, (7th Cir., 2001).
52. See "General information about the BPjM (Federal Department for Media Harmful to Young Persons)" at *www.bundespruefstelle.de/bpjm/information-in-english*.html, last accessed 4/16/2006. Further discussion of international attitudes toward sexual and violent content can be found in a recent article in *Game Developer* magazine, which explains, "For instance, the U.K. seems particularly concerned about bad language, more so than on the continent, but sexual content gets just a middling reaction, which is still more than in the Scandinavian countries which are extremely liberal in that regard. But when it comes to violence, the U.K. and other southern European countries are fairly accepting of it in their games, whereas Scandinavia is much more restrictive." "Rated and Willing: Where Game Rating Boards Differ," by Paul Hyman, *Game Developer,* December 2005, p.11.
53. *Stanley v. Georgia*, 394 U.S. 557 at 564-65 (1969).
54. *Stanley* at 559.
55. *Paris Adult Theatre I v. Slaton*, 413 US 49 (1973).

56. Katz, Privacy and Pornography: *Stanley v. Georgia*, 1969 Sup. Ct. Rev. 203, 213.

57. But see *US v. Extreme Associates, Inc.*, No. 03-0203, (W.D.Pa. Jan. 20. 2005) (finding federal obscenity statutes unconstitutional for banning distribution of material that is legal to possess).

58. *Osborne v. Ohio*, 110 S.Ct. 1691 (1990).

59. See, e.g., *Action For Children's Television v FCC*, 58 F. 3d 654 (D.C. Cir. 1995), cert. denied, 516 U.S. 1043 (1996) and *FCC v. Pacifica Foundation*, 438 U.S. 726 (1978).

60. *Reno V. ACLU*, 117 S. Ct. 2329, 138 L.Ed.2d 874 (1997).

61. But see *Ashcroft v. Free Speech Coalition*, 535 U.S. 234 (2002): In 1996, Congress passed the Child Pornography Prevention Act (CPPA), which forbade, among other things, the use of computer-generated, sexually explicit images of kids. Congress intended to make it harder for child pornographers to escape liability by arguing that they had not exploited "real" children but had only used images created on the computer. With CG images becoming almost indistinguishable from photographs, it would be impossible for the government to prove that the images used real children. In a ruling that shocked and upset many observers, the Supreme Court struck down CPPA, arguing that it violated the First Amendment. The Court said that actual child pornography is criminal and can be prosecuted, but 'virtual' images are protected by the First Amendment, unless they prove to be obscene. Looking deeper at the language of CPPA, it is less surprising that the law was overturned. For example, the law criminalized images of adults having sex if they looked under 18 years of age. The Court was concerned that the overbroad language of CPPA might censor artworks like *Romeo and Juliet* and the film *American Beauty* in which underage sexual relationships are portrayed, if not explicitly. This was one of the first Supreme Court cases involving realistic, modern computer-generated graphics, like those used in video games. Game developers may want to review the Court's treatment of CG content. However, be careful not to misinterpret the Court's ruling: The Court did not rule that any explicit CG content is always permissible. And dissenting Justices argued that the majority should not have struck the law outright because the Court could have preserved most of the law intact, by narrowing the overbroad provisions. Additionally, CG images may still be banned as obscene.

62. "Prepared Remarks of Attorney General Alberto R. Gonzales at the National Press Club," 5/20/2005, *www.usdoj.gov/ag/speeches/2005/052005agremarksnpr.htm*, last accessed 4/16/2006. See also, "U.S. Attorney's Porn Fight Gets Bad Reviews: Obscenity Prosecution Task Force will focus on Internet crimes and peer-to-peer distribution of pornography" by Julie Kay, Daily Business Review (August 30, 2005), *www.law.com/jsp/article.jsp?id=1125318960389*, last accessed 4/16/2006.

63. "Gonzales calls for mandatory Web labeling law," Declan McCullagh, CNET News, *http://news.com.com/2100-1028_3-6063554.html*, last accessed 4/23/2006: "Web site operators posting sexually explicit information must place official government warning labels on their pages or risk being imprisoned for up to five years, the Bush administration proposed Thursday."

9 What's Appropriate?

In This Chapter

- What's Appropriate?
- The Developer's Perspective
- What's Appropriate in an E-Rated Game?
- What's Appropriate in a T-Rated Game?
- What's Appropriate in an M-Rated Game?
- What's Appropriate in an AO-Rated Game?
- What's Never Appropriate
- Considerations & Consequences

WHAT'S APPROPRIATE?

"What rating are we shooting for?"

It's a question that's asked early in the development of every product. If it's not asked, it's because the answer is already known—the licensor or publisher already has a specific rating in mind or doesn't plan to get the product rated at all. Even unrated games have some kind of constraints or content restrictions, though. The no holds barred, anything goes sexual simulator needs to provide content that would appeal to—and not turn off—its target audience. Likewise, the unrated sexy game funded and commissioned by a beer manufacturer to pitch its products can't go beyond a certain level of sexual content or it risks alienating consumers, getting bad press, and upsetting stockholders.

Once a rating or target demographic is decided, the question then becomes, "What's appropriate within that rating or demographic?" and it's there, in that question, that the waters get murky. At the 2005 Game Developers Conference (GDC), a group of developers convened at the "Sexuality in Games: What's Appropriate?" roundtable to address and hopefully answer the question for themselves. However, the answers were elusive. The following year, at the "Sex in Games: Hardcore" roundtable at GDC, the answers were still not clear.

"What about the rating system? What do they say? Can you have nudity in M-rated games?" In fact, there is nudity in M-rated games, and some T-rated games feature brief partial nudity, too. However, due to the way games are rated by the ESRB and many other systems, there is no checklist, no convenient and conclusive way to say, "If you include nudity, you're going to get an M-rating." In fact, given historical precedent, games may get anywhere from a T to an AO rating in the United States. Like other rating systems, the ESRB system provides its raters with general guidelines, but ultimately, it's up to the raters to determine how the content rates. They take into account duration, context, and intensity of the content, and other things to arrive at a rating. For instance, although both *Grand Theft Auto: San Andreas* and *Playboy: The Mansion* feature characters having sexual intercourse, *Grand Theft Auto: San Andreas* was re-rated AO, while *Playboy: The Mansion* is rated M. Of the two games, the sexual content in *Grand Theft Auto: San Andreas* is interactive, allowing the player to control the thrusting of the male character. In *Playboy: The Mansion*, the player is only able to stop, but not control, the action when he or she decides to. *Grand Theft Auto: San Andreas* was later re-rated M when the interactive sex mini-game was removed. The M-rated *God of War* also features an interactive sexual component, but the player does not actually see the sex on screen. Rather, he sees a vase wobbling on a nearby table and tries to knock it off, presumably as a result of the active lovemaking on the bed.

THE DEVELOPER'S PERSPECTIVE

When asked what content they feel is appropriate at the various levels, developers were of varied opinions. Veteran game designer Richard Garriott, creator of the *Ultima*® series, admitted that the issue wasn't a simple one. "This is a complex societal question," said Garriott. "While there are some clear examples of things like keeping explicit sexual content away from youth, when you get to implied actions or 'bleeped' out words, it becomes far more complex" [Garriott01].

Some developers responded by suggesting new ways to rate content in video games. Rich Carlson, a game designer and musician with Digital Eel, tossed out the standard letter-ratings system altogether. In its place, Rich proposes a color- and age-based system:

Blue: Safe as milk, ages 1–5, sweetness and light, [Scholastic's] *The Magic School Bus*™ may even be too intense, characters can say "oopsie."

Green: Mostly harmless, ages 6–10, no "you know what," kissing is okay, no graphic dismemberment, ray guns are cool, characters can say "darn."

Yellow: Happy medium, ages 11–17, most movies, TV shows, and games fall here, just about everything goes, just don't show much of anything, characters can say "damn."

Orange: Hot stuff, ages 18+, everything goes except certain situations involving animal husbandry and sharing hats, characters can say "#@%$!&*!!!*."

Red: Toxic waste, nobody is old enough. [Carlson01]

Game developer Dave Taylor also supports a color-coded system to define what's appropriate. "I'm a big fan of empiricism," said Taylor. "The most sensational bits of a game should be distilled down to a video clip of tolerable length and go before large focus groups of at least 100 [people] who buy games on the platform you're distributing it for, and they should be polled for a rating from one ('Disney 1950s innocence') to five ('snuf porn dire wrongness')." Taylor would then compare the median score to other titles going through the process. "And instead of 'rating' it," Taylor added, "I'd re-brand the ratings to reflect the actual empirical measurements. Instead of 'Rated E,' I'd consider 'Tests E,' and indeed, instead of this 'Everyone/Teen/Mature/AO' nonsense, which ties age to maturity, I would go a bit symbolic and rate it 'Yellow/Green/Blue/Orange/Red' so that you get a vague sense of danger from the color associations without explicitly suggesting a title is only suitable for adults or really targeted for children. So for instance, 'Tests Blue' followed by its actual median score, the date it was tested, the measured deviations, and a tiny URL to a site that goes into detail on the tests, including individual comments from testers on their feedback forms, would be utterly fantabulous" [Taylor01].

Other developers used existing ratings symbols, but added their own descriptions. For instance, Matthew Ford, a programmer who worked on such titles as *Asheron's Call*™, split the ratings up this way:

E/E10: Kissing (but affectionate, not sexual), no signs of arousal or lengthy "snogging," just a quick kiss.

T: Passionate kissing, holding (but not sexual touching), implied (but not depicted) sexual activity (for example, entering/exiting a bedroom).

M: Pretty much what you'd see in a R-rated movie, depiction of any sexual activity including bare breasts/bum but no genitalia.

AO: Anything goes. [Ford01]

For some developers, the issue wasn't so much about what content was appropriate at a rating level, but rather, on what they perceived to be a disparity between the rating board's treatment of sexual content versus violent content.

"I'm not a fan of the ESRB rating system or any rating system," said veteran game designer Steve Meretzky. "For one thing, I think that just about every rating system, including the ESRB, gives too much weight to sexual content and language and too little attention to gore and physical violence" [Meretzky01].

Richard Garriott also commented on the issue. "As for me, I am more of a European thinker," said Garriott. "I think violence is far worse than sexuality" [Garriott02].

Developer Tom Forsyth of RAD Game Tools offered a suggestion. "I would at least attempt to remove the huge skew between sex/language and violence," said Forsyth. "It really is pretty lopsided in the U.S .compared to the rest of the world. In my opinion, the U.S. should move all the sex/language ratings down a notch, and all the violence ones up a notch. But obviously that will never happen, because it needs more than just a rating's change. It needs a readjustment of the entire country's attitudes toward [swearing], boobies, and decapitation" [Forsyth01]. Indeed, the ESRB ratings system is designed to reflect American attitudes toward specific types of content, and, as a country, the United States is more accepting of violent content than sexual content.

As an alternative to a ratings system, Meretzky thinks information would be more appropriate. "I prefer a description of what might be objectionable about a game, and it should be very game specific, not a 'one size fits all' checklist. In other words, 'Occasional humorous sexual foreplay, beneath bed sheets; frequent nudity from the waist up, but no full nudity' versus 'contains sex and nudity'" [Meretzky02].

Game designer and producer Linda Currie echoed Meretzky's sentiments. By itself, Currie felt, a game's rating didn't give the full picture, making it difficult for parents to determine what's appropriate. "What's often missing from a simple rating is the context, the intent, or theme of the subject matter that goes beyond the specific action. For instance, few people would question an E (or G) rating on a fairy tale. When the prince kisses the princess in *Sleeping Beauty* or *Snow White*, it's communicated in an innocent and happy fashion that is not draped in deep sexual overtones. A kiss in a different context, and it can be something else entirely" [Currie01].

Kelly Rued, game designer and president of Black Love Interactive, developers of *Rapture Online*™, a sexually themed MMORPG, thought the breakdown of sexual content within the various ratings levels was appropriate. "I also support the ESRB's system," she said, "and after reviewing the published guidelines, I have only the following suggestion: it would be enormously helpful to the adults-only game consumer if the 'sexual violence' descriptor were broken down to 'consensual sexual violence' and 'nonconsensual sexual violence' since there is a big difference for the players involved." In some video games, for instance, sexual violence can occur without the player's consent. However, as Rued pointed out, "in our games, people can role-play and invoke BDSM gameplay, which, while technically depicting sexually 'abusive' content, is consensual for everyone involved." To Rued, as a designer and as a player, the consent of the player makes a big difference in player purchasing decisions. "I wouldn't want to buy a game where I could just be randomly assaulted."

Rued also suggested that the ESRB alter their online play warnings to warn players and parents of potentially inappropriate content for the game's stated age rating. Currently, the warnings read, "Game Experience May Change During Online Play." According to Rued, however, "this in no way communicates to parents that the game contains content created by players that has not been rated by the ESRB." Such content, unrated as it is, could possibly be highly inappropriate for children. Rued offers the following suggestion in its place: "When played online, this game contains content created by players which is not rated by the ESRB." A similar warning could also be provided for games that allow online chat and downloadable mods. "Allowing or disallowing mods and online chat, etc. is an important decision for making a game child-safe and parents should be warned of the implications before they give kids games that include live chat and online mod capabilities, as many parents might not realize that could lead to M and AO content in the game" [Rued01].

Game designer Sheri Graner Ray agreed. "If a game is rated T, then it should be safe for kids, period. Although the current MMO boxes say 'game experience may change during online play,' I'm not sure that's enough for a T rating, and may in fact be a huge cop out. Think about it. How upset would you be if you sent your 12-year-old child to a movie that was rated G, but since its release, several very graphic sexual scenes had been added? And how much would you trust the rating system after that?" [Ray01].

Ultimately, when developers ask themselves, "What's appropriate?" they really face two distinct questions: "What do I personally feel is appropriate at the various rating levels?" and "What content can I put in my game and still stay at my desired rating level?" Developers of M-rated games want to know the limits of the rating—perhaps how far they can go—before they are rated AO. Likewise, developers of E- and T-rated games don't want to find themselves rated out of their target demographic. With every bump up in rating comes a smaller potential market. In asking "What's appropriate?" more than anything, developers seek answers, a set of general guidelines and rules to follow so they can get the desired rating the first time from ESRB. After all, resubmission takes time, and time—even a week—can cost developers hundreds of thousands of dollars. In the absence of such rules, historical game rating precedent serves as the only guide. By studying the ratings handed down by the ESRB in its 10-year history, patterns begin to emerge.

WHAT'S APPROPRIATE IN AN E-RATED GAME?

In the life of typical six-year-olds, the age at which the E game rating begins, they may see their mother and father hug. They may hear expressions of love or tell friends that they think the boy next door is cute. Of course, inevitably, there is also mention of cooties, boy germs, and other similarly gross things. The market for E-rated games parallels these experiences.

The ESRB breaks the E market into three segments: EC for early childhood, E for everyone aged 6 and up, and E10+ for everyone aged 10 and up. At the E level, no sexual content is appropriate. However, suggestive themes of the mildest sort have been allowed. The PC version of *Sid Meier's Pirates*, for instance, is rated E. Although it contains nothing one would normally think of as suggestive, the game does contain a mini-game where the player must impress the governor's daughter at a dance. The governor's daughter wears a dress typical of the period that reveals some of her cleavage.

While courting a governor's daughter in a period dress—particularly one reflective of the time in which the game is set—would not likely merit a mention at higher rating levels, at the E level, such content is not the norm and perhaps the reason for the "suggestive themes" descriptor on the *Pirates* box. Other E-rated games have also received the "suggestive themes" descriptor. *Dance Dance Revolution EXTREME*™ and *The Dukes of Hazzard*™: *Return of the General Lee* are among them. Such a descriptor is exceptionally uncommon, however. As of the date of this writing, fewer than 50 games in the E and E10 groups have been given the "suggestive themes" or "mild suggestive themes" descriptor. To date, over 7,000 titles have been rated in these categories [ESRB01]. Games with "suggestive themes" make up less than 1% of the total.

So, what sexual content is appropriate at the E level? Not surprisingly and with good reason, none.

WHAT'S APPROPRIATE IN A T-RATED GAME?

By the age of 13, the same girl who watched her parents hug and actively avoided boy germs has developed an acute awareness of her sexuality and all the pains that go with it. She is embarrassed by any parental display of affection and has started to flirt with boys or girls she likes. Her conversations are peppered with talk of who likes whom. Boys are likewise intrigued and have begun to master the art of crude humor.

Games designed for the teen market reflect the same level of sexuality. The ESRB's T rating is used for games it deems appropriate for those 13 and older. The T-rated *The Sims* series features relationship formation between characters that can lead to hugging and kissing. Characters in the *Sims 2* might also dive between the sheets, although it's impossible to see what's going on underneath the tussling covers. Such content undoubtedly contributes to *The Sims 2*'s "sexual themes" descriptor. *Tony Hawk's Underground* is also T rated. The game includes frequent uses of crude humor and a strip club. Access to the club is an "Easter egg," however, and requires the player to go in through the club's roof where he or she interrupts a stripper providing a private show for what appears to be a couple of businessmen. Such content is not typical of T-rated games, however.

In addition to suggestive themes and crude humor, some T-rated games have included partial nudity and sexual themes. Both *Atlantis Evolution* and *Monster Garage* earned the ESRB's "partial nudity" descriptor, and *DarkStalkers™ Chronicle: The Chaos Tower* was tagged for "sexual themes." However, as of this writing, 11 T-rated titles feature partial nudity and 36 titles feature sexual themes [ESRB02]. Both numbers represent less than 1% of all T-rated titles.

What sexual content is appropriate at the T level? While partial nudity and sexual themes have been included at this level, it's clear that they're profound exceptions. On the other hand, suggestive themes such as flirting and kissing, crude humor, and more revealing clothing like one might see on *Lara Croft* are more common. Titles featuring full nudity or strong sexual content have never been T rated.

WHAT'S APPROPRIATE IN AN M-RATED GAME?

At the age of 17, the same girl who flirted with boys has now become a young woman. She has been exposed to sexual themes in her books, magazines, movies, and television, and has, more than likely, been in at least one serious relationship. Young men of the same age are entering their sexual prime. Beyond these young men and women, of course, adults from 20 to twilight also enjoy video games.

Mature games that target this market reflect the "late-night television" version of sexuality. The ESRB's M rating is used for games considered appropriate for those 17 and older. The M-rated *Playboy: The Mansion* features many sexual situations, from simulated, but partially clothed intercourse to extended sessions of partial nudity during magazine photo shoots. As a *Playboy* game, some of the missions and "Easter eggs" in the game are also sexually themed. For instance, in mission one, the player, playing as Hef, meets a rock star and his twin girlfriends. If the player succeeds in seducing and sleeping with the twins, they'll send their friends the Brazilian triplets by in the next mission. The M-rated *Grand Theft Auto III* also features sexual content. Although the game is frequently criticized for its emergent sexual violence (that one can pay a hooker, have sex with her, and then kill her to get the money back), the actual sexual content in the game is tame by comparison to other games. When the character in the game has sex, the player sees the car bouncing up and down. No actual sex is shown.

At this rating level, games have nudity, partial nudity, and strong sexual themes of moderate duration and intensity. As of the date of this writing, 12 M-rated titles feature nudity, or less than 1% of all M-rated titles, and 50 titles, 5% of all M-rated titles, feature strong sexual content [ESRB03].

What sexual content is appropriate at the M level? Partial nudity, sexual themes, and strong sexual content are relatively common. Nudity is also generally accepted, if it is not prolonged. Interactive sexual content—where the player is allowed to directly control the action of a sexual nature—has received both M and AO ratings, possibly due to the degree of visual intensity. In *Grand Theft Auto: San Andreas*, the player controls and sees the sexual content. In *God of War*, the player controls but does not see the sexual act taking place. Since ratings take into account the context, intensity, and duration of any given action, it's also possible that graphic sexual activity could be rated higher in games that are also exceptionally violent, where it appears that relationship development is not a factor or where the sex is wholly gratuitous.

WHAT'S APPROPRIATE IN AN AO-RATED GAME?

At the age of 18, young men and women are full-fledged adults and allowed access to the extremes of entertainment, from violence to vice. He or she can rent pornographic videos, purchase sexual aids, and take advantage of the various forms of adult entertainment available online.

AO (adults only) games that target this market reflect the erotic or traditionally pornographic version of sexuality. The ESRB's AO rating is used for games considered appropriate for those 18 and older. While this rating targets an audience only one year removed from the ESRB's M rating, the single year isn't as important as what the AO rating calls out—the intensity and duration of the sexual content present in the game. Movies parallel this system. For instance, the R and NC-17 ratings are also separated by a year. However, the distinction between the ratings makes it clear to those considering the entertainment that the sexual content contained therein is a degree more significant in the NC-17 title. It has not so much to do with the age as it does with the intensity of content. For instance, the AO-rated versions of *Fahrenheit: Indigo Prophecy Director's Cut: PC CD ROM*, *Leisure Suit Larry: Magna Cum Laude*, and *The Singles: Flirt Up Your Life* contain more graphic and intense sexual content than their M-rated and for-sale-at-retail counterparts.

For the most part, however, few games are rated AO. In all likelihood, if a publisher received this rating from the ESRB, the publisher would remove the content that earned it that rating, seeking to get an M rating instead. Unless the game plans to sell outside of retail channels—at which point getting rated becomes less and less important—an AO rating is the proverbial kiss of death. AO games are not carried by big-box stores and drastically limit a game's ability to be profitable. Massively multiplayer online erotic games (MMOEGs) may embrace the AO rating as a positive thing and a means to form a community.

At the AO level, games have nudity, partial nudity, and strong sexual themes of substantial duration and intensity. As of the date of this writing, 22 titles have been rated AO by the ESRB [ESRB04]. They represent fewer than 1% of all the games ever rated by the ESRB.

WHAT'S NEVER APPROPRIATE

When developers were asked what type of sexual content was never appropriate in a game, their answers were the same again and again: nonconsensual sexual violence, particularly violence involving children or animals. Numerous developers also felt that other forms of sexual violence such as rape were inappropriate, whether consensual as in a rape fantasy or not.

Patric Lagny, developer of *Sociolotron*, one of earliest online MMOEGs, put it this way. "The question 'What is Appropriate' in a game when it comes to sexual content is quite easy to answer, actually. First, you have to rule out the legally forbidden stuff." Lagny also considers the people funding the game's development. Regardless of what the market or the players will allow, if the people funding the game have limits, they must be considered. "You check out your management, your owners, and your investors and see what they are comfortable with," he says. Often, publishers will alter sexual content in a game prior to release in certain territories. "For example, when Blue Byte did *Battle Isle® 3* in 1995, we had a picture of the main heroine where she was wearing some sort of leather or latex dress, and you could see the shape of nipples under the dress." For the American release, Lagny says, the pictures were retouched to remove those nipples completely [Lagny01]. Many other games have had sexual content similarly edited. Most recently, the game *Indigo Prophecy*, released in Europe as *Fahrenheit*, included numerous sexual scenes and nudity. In the United States release, however, some of the game's sexual content was cut.

Being an unrated, online game, Lagny's game, *Sociolotron,* has had no such edits. In creating a game with few limits, the appropriateness of the content is no longer just a question of appropriateness, but rather, how much risk a developer or publisher is willing to take on. In *Sociolotron*, for instance, rape is possible, and all players are aware of this possibility when they play the game.

Lagny does have his detractors. "I know that many people will now get out the big moralistic club and talk about the 'responsibility' game developers have, and I would say that is true when it comes to games for minors. Personally, I don't feel comfortable knowing that minors are allowed to play violent games or watch violent pictures on TV for that matter, but since we exclude minors explicitly from our audience, I don't think it is my responsibility to 'educate' adult players by determining what they can and what they can't do in a game. I just give them the tools, and what they make out of it is their issue" [Lagny03].

Lagny and those working on *Sociolotron* go to great lengths to protect the game's players from unwanted harassment, however. "Some people out there in the message boards can't believe that a game with few explicit restrictions has the concept of harassment, but it's true, even we have it. Sex and violence are parts of our game, but there are things that go beyond this. The borderline is if not the character but the player is involved." Lagny cited an example where a player was harassed online by her ex-fiancé. In this case, the issue had nothing to do with the characters in the game, but rather the people playing them in the real world. The ex-fiancé was ultimately banned from the game. "We are a very small game, and we have a very dedicated staff who is willing to investigate any case of possible harassment personally" [Lagny04].

When rape occurs in game worlds where the players are not aware of the possibility and that possibility is never intended by the game's designers, it's another matter entirely. In the *LambaMoo*, an early multiuser Internet environment, a player was virtually raped in the game. The incident was covered in a widely publicized 1993 article in the *Village Voice* titled "A Rape in Cyberspace." In the game, one character took control of other characters through use of a voodoo doll and forced these other characters to commit sexual acts within the game. The incident had a profound effect on the community who never expected anything like that to happen. Kelly Rued, developer of *Rapture Online*, an MMOEG, and a regular participant in the IGDA's Sex SIG forums, compared the *LambaMoo* rape with a rape in *Sociolotron*. Rued cited the following differences:

The rape in the *LambaMoo* incident:

- Players all consented to a virtual world with no good warning that something like the rape could happen to them.
- The rapist exploits something not normally used in that manner in the game to commit the rape (it's emergent behavior at best and flat-out game hacking/exploiting at worst).
- The nonconsensual nature of the rape was not intended by the game's designers and the game community was violated and upset.
- The raped parties were not consenting at that time in the game, regardless of prior or blanket consent to the open-ended role-playing parts.

The rape in *Sociolotron*:

- Players all consent to a virtual world with good warning of rape and sexual violence.
- The rapist uses features available to all players to commit the rape.
- The nonconsensual nature of the rape was intended by the game's designers and is appreciated and enjoyed by the game community.
- The raped party may or may not be consenting at the time of the rape, regardless of prior or blanket consent (having an exit strategy or "safe" word, any

means to quickly end a scene is what I would consider a reasonable sign you are in a "consensual rape fantasy experience" rather than a "nonconsensual rape fantasy experience" because even the most extreme consensual scenes involve a means for all parties to interrupt). [Rued02]

Furthermore, in *Sociolotron,* the game has a mechanism for dealing with a rapist if he is caught. He or she may be put on trial and spend time in the game's jail. Such mechanisms are not supported in games where sexual violence is emergent.

While the degree of appropriateness may vary with one's personal, moral, and ethical beliefs, what is clear is the need to inform players about the extremes of sexual content found in game, particularly the possibilities for consensual or non-consensual sexual content. In games like *Sociolotron* where the sexual content is one of the, if not the, major draws of the game, the extremes of its sexual content are well known in the community and are revealed to new players before they enter the game world. Developers and community managers of games where such content is not intended but develops as emergent sexual violence must take steps to protect and notify their player community and immediately address issues.

CONSIDERATIONS & CONSEQUENCES

At the 2005 Game Developers Conference "Sexuality in Games: What's Appropriate" roundtable, a developer of a sexually themed game raised an interesting question. What ethical responsibility do developers have when creating sexual content in video games? What ethical responsibility do developers have overall?

Designer Richard Garriott was presented with the same question. Garriott's *Ultima* games allow the player to play as "The Avatar" and are noted for the values, morals, and ethical challenges they present to the player.

"I am a devout believer that games of all types are fair and reasonable to create. I can even see how playing a game where the goal is to live out an unethical existence could be fun. And I have no problem with them being played by mature adults," said Garriott. "However, I am also a devout believer that 'role playing' is one of the most powerful teaching tools in the world. Think about young kids out on playgrounds playing imaginary games, be it pretend warfare, or tea parties in the clubhouse. In all these cases, kids are trying out interpersonal actions and honing their interpersonal skills. They find out that when you don't play well, others won't play with you. They find out that pulling someone's hair makes that person cry, and hopefully that makes the aggressor sad. To unleash a game that does not respond with the real world's countermeasures to player behavior, means that the game really does have a risk of 'teaching' bad behavior, or at least misses the opportunity to reinforce 'right and wrong.' So, while I don't think developers have a 'moral responsibility' to put ethical parables into their games (as I like to do), I do think content exposed to kids must be filtered. I also feel that great stories, interactive or linear, generally showcase the growth of the human spirit, in an individual or a society. And while there are great literary works that buck that trend, they are rare. Thus, I feel that while these morally ambiguous (or worse) games are popular right now, it's because the concept is fresh and relatively easy to create. It is much harder to craft, but ultimately much more valuable to include, moral dilemmas and temptations in an interactive experience that then rewards the player in a satisfying way, a better, more complex level of interaction. But, we as game developers will get there! At least I know I'm devoted to trying!" [Garriott03].

Designer Steve Meretzky agreed. "Of course we have an ethical responsibility, individually, collectively as companies, and collectively as an industry. We can't, on the one hand, crow about the power of software as a learning tool, and on the other hand say the immersion in realistic graphic violence has no impact on a player" [Meretzky03].

Bob Bates, with whom Meretzky worked on a number of titles, felt that all gamemakers and storytellers have ethical responsibilities. "We are the culture-makers. An author or designer is someone who has a particular (peculiar?) view of the way the world is, or the way it *should* be, and he/she uses a game or a story to impart that view. It may be that this view is a revolutionary one, where the author sees something wrong with the world that needs to be corrected—in that case, the author has an ethical responsibility to try to convert people to that point of view. On the other hand, it may be a conservative view, where the author sees a threat to the established order that must be challenged and defeated—in that case, too, the author has an ethical responsibility, even if the point of view is in direct conflict with that of the 'revolutionary' game maker." Said Bates, "Every living person has the responsibility to try to do what's right, but not necessarily to convert others to their point of view. Authors have the additional responsibility to try to convince others that their vision of the world is the correct one" [Bates01].

Ed Kuehnel, a writer for the *Leisure Suit Larry: Magna Cum Laude* game, agrees with the other designers when it comes to making content for children or even teens. "I would feel a responsibility not to send the wrong message, even in jest." When it comes to making content for adults, however, Kuehnel felt differently. "I like making adult content targeted to adults, specifically comedy or light-hearted fare. If I'm making content for adults, I feel I can safely assume they are not impressionable, and I feel I have a right to joke about anything I want to without an adult taking me seriously" [Kuehnel01].

While there is no clear answer or ethical line in the sand, developers interviewed by this author largely agree that developers do have some kind of ethical responsibility, particularly when it comes to younger audiences. The ESRB's rating system, designed to reflect the values of American citizens, attempts to mirror these ethics and morals. What's appropriate in sexual content, then, is an individual question with varied answers that reflect the game's audience, first and foremost, the developer's personal, ethical and moral beliefs, those of his or her publisher, and the country in which the game is to be sold.

REFERENCES

[Bates01] Bates, Bob, interview with Brenda Brathwaite, August 4, 2005.

[Carlson01] Carlson, Rich, interview with Brenda Brathwaite, August 5, 2005.

[Currie01] Currie, Linda, interview with Brenda Brathwaite, September 13, 2005.

[ESRB01] Entertainment Software Ratings Board, Titles with E and E10+ ratings with "suggestive themes" descriptor. Available online at *www.esrb.org*. Accessed June 25, 2006.

[ESRB02] Entertainment Software Ratings Board, Titles with T rating with "partial nudity" as a descriptor and "sexual themes" as a descriptor. Available online at *www.esrb.org*. Accessed June 26, 2006.

[ESRB03] Entertainment Software Ratings Board, Titles with M rating with "nudity" as a descriptor and "strong sexual content" as a descriptor. Available online at *www.esrb.org*. Accessed June 26, 2006.

[ESRB04] Entertainment Software Ratings Board, Titles with AO rating. Available online at *www.esrb.org*. Accessed June 26, 2006.

[Ford01] Ford, Matthew, interview with Brenda Brathwaite, September 13, 2005.

[Forsyth01] Forsyth, Tom, interview with Brenda Brathwaite, August 5, 2005.

[Garriott01] Garriott, Richard, interview with Brenda Brathwaite, May 27, 2005.

[Garriott02] Garriott, Richard, interview with Brenda Brathwaite, May 27, 2005.

[Garriott03] Garriott, Richard, interview with Brenda Brathwaite, May 27, 2005.

[Kuehnel01] Kuehnel, Ed, interview with Brenda Brathwaite, August 4, 2005.

[Lagny01] Lagny, Patric, interview with Brenda Brathwaite, May 25, 2005.

[Lagny02] Ibid.

[Lagny03] Ibid.

[Lagny04] Ibid.

[Meretzky01] Meretzky, Steve, interview with Brenda Brathwaite, August 2, 2005.

[Meretzky02] Meretzky, Steve, interview with Brenda Brathwaite, August 2, 2005.

[Meretzky03] Meretzky, Steve, interview with Brenda Brathwaite, August 2, 2005.

[Ray01] Graner-Ray, Sheri, interview with Brenda Brathwaite, March 7, 2006.

[Rued01] Rued, Kelly, interview with Brenda Brathwaite, September 12, 2005.

[Rued02] Rued, Kelly, post on the IGDA Sexuality Special Interest Group mailing list, September 12, 2005.

[Taylor01] Taylor, Dave, interview with Brenda Brathwaite, August 5, 2005.

10 Reaching the Market

In This Chapter

- The Retail Wall
- Selling AO Games
- The Adult Market
- Interview with Peter Payne, Peach Princess
- Resources

THE RETAIL WALL

Among the dozens of titles on retail shelves, there are two things you won't find together: the letters "A" and "O." In fact, until the re-rating of *Grand Theft Auto: San Andreas*, sales of AO-rated games at retail were virtually unheard of since the early days of the industry.

According to Hal Halpin, president of the IEMA, the organization that represents merchants of entertainment software, retailers have long been cautious when it comes to stocking controversial content. Such sensitivity, Halpin contends, goes back to 1993 when the original *Mortal Kombat* game was released [Halpin01].

"[Retailers] recognize that their first obligation is to their customers and providing them with the type, style, and environment [in] which they want to purchase games," Halpin said. "To that end, most IEMA members chose not to sell the highly controversial *BMX XXX* game, as they believed, like many, that it was sensationalism for its own sake rather than an important element to gameplay" [Halpin02].

Retailers do not have cut-and-dried policies regarding the content they stock, however. Some games that contain sexual content like *God of War*™, *Onimusha*™ *3: Demon Siege*, and *The Getaway* were carried in standard retail channels including Wal-Mart. In fact, *God of War* was among 2005's best sellers.

In describing how retailers determine whether to carry a game, Halpin said, "The more we know about a game, the better we can determine if it is appropriately suited to our demographic as a whole. As I mentioned earlier, there are titles where the industry knows in advance that a game's publisher is being intentionally sensationalistic about its content, promoting it for exploitative purposes, and usually it's because the game lacks the all-important playability aspect. Those games are easier for us to filter out, because the information is so widely available" [Halpin03].

Ultimately, Halpin notes, retail buyers are interested in the salability of products. "Many things factor into making a great-selling game. The most important is playability, then everything else—marketing, word of mouth, merchandising, reviews and previews, etc.—and there's no accounting for it in advance" [Halpin04]. Games like *God of War* that contain solid gameplay and whose marketing emphasis is on that gameplay rather than its brief sexual content stand a far better chance of being carried at retail despite their sexual content. Games whose gameplay is questionable or whose content is deliberately sensationalistic are not likely to be carried.

While retailers of video games show no signs of changing their policies to accept AO-rated games, there are some indications that the retail landscape is changing and becoming more liberal. In 2005, online retailer amazon.com entered the adult market in a big way by creating its "Sex & Sensuality" store. When it launched, the store carried thousands of sexual items, from condoms to sex swings to vibrators to edible underwear, something a storefront retailer would be hard pressed to duplicate [Amazon01]. Within amazon.com, and perhaps on purpose, the store itself is hard to find. Nothing trumpets its existence on the front page. In fact, according to many media outlets, amazon.com did no marketing of any kind to promote the store. The store itself is nestled under the Health & Personal Care section.

Amazon.com's "Sex & Sensuality" store does carry adult games. However, as of the date of this book's publication, no video games or computer games are listed among its offerings. Rather, amazon.com offers the traditional adult board, card- and book-based games. It seems, however, that such a possibility may not be far behind. In addition to its "Sex & Sensuality" store, amazon.com also stocks the AO-rated version of *Leisure Suit Larry: Uncut & Uncensored*. In addition, the store carries M-rated versions of *Playboy: The Mansion* and *The Singles: Flirt Up Your Life*.

Despite the changes made at amazon.com and a few smaller retailers, for the most part, a virtual "retail wall" remains between developers of sexually themed adult content and those who might buy it. It's unlikely Wal-Mart or other mass-market retailers will ever put any *Peach Princess* AO-rated bishoujo titles on their shelves. Until a major AO video game distribution system arises, AO game developers and publishers need to find another path to reach their audience. For some developers, that path is twofold—a retail and an online component. *Leisure Suit Larry: Magna Cum Laude*, for instance, released an M-rated version at retail and advertised the availability of their AO-rated game that was sold online. The AO-rated version evidently did quite well according to numerous sources who spoke with this author.

Online sales of AO-rated versions of M-rated retail games should be considered, according to Gabe Zichermann of Booty.com. "When building the narrative and storyboards for a game, most developers can tell if their idea should be executed as a truly 'AO' title; even if the ESRB's rating scheme is ambiguous. As a general rule, if your title is trending toward an AO—especially due to explicit sexual content—you should also make an M version for retail sale. Many retailers will stock only M and under rated titles. Be sure to promote the AO version of the title through specialist media as an uncut or special version. If your title could easily be M rated without a significant degradation in storyline, you're better off sticking to an M version alone, as it will sell better and reduce your development costs. Of course, you can always release an AO version later to get the fans to re-up, or as a form of pseudo-sequel" [Gabe01].

SELLING AO GAMES

When Peter Payne decided to bring English translations of successful Japanese bishoujo games to the United States, he quickly ran into the "retail wall." Convinced he had good products and equally convinced that there were customers waiting for what he had to offer, Payne founded his own distribution company.

"Basically, we realized two things early on when developing a market for bishoujo games in English. First, there is no distribution system in place for us as there is in Japan where several large dating-sim game distributors support the industry," says Payne. "So, we 'rolled our own,' creating PCR Distributing, a company in San Diego, to handle distribution for our games directly to shops and online stores" [Payne01].

The lack of an established distribution system was only a part of Payne's problem, however. Even if he were able to distribute the games, not everyone was going to carry them. "The second thing we realized was that 'family values' were going to keep our products out of [major chain stores], so we had to focus on the Internet, on anime, and comic retailers" [Payne02].

In the traditional video game market, developers hand off games to publishers, who sell them to distributors, who then sell them to retail outlets, who then get the products to the customer. At best, the system skips a channel, going from publisher to large chain retailer to the chain's individual stores. In Payne's case, however, no system existed. So, he did what many developers of sexual content do—he forged his own path to the customer by becoming developer, distributor, and retailer all rolled into one.

Hal Halpin, president of the IEMA, notes that those whose products won't be carried in the traditional channel need to expand their horizons, just as Payne did. "When developers come up to me at conferences to ask about alternative distribution, I advise them to think like independent film producers who have found a way to work outside of the traditional Hollywood system," says Halpin. "That does not mean that they didn't sell-in to theatres or release on DVD. It means that they approached the philosophy differently and leveraged the system. Re-imagining the entertainment industry is too unrealistic and unlikely a task. Work with the system in new and exciting ways. Make it work for you."

A Storefront on the Internet

In setting up his business, Payne created four separate Internet sites:

www.jastusa.com: The JAST USA site is the retail front end of Payne's game business. From this site, gamers can order games and other products. The site also provides links to Payne's distribution business and various game brands.

www.peachprincess.com: The *Peach Princess* site is a "brand" site for all of the *Peach Princess'* bishoujo products Payne carries. The various game brands Payne carries were added after JAST USA was created, allowing Payne to release games from various companies in Japan. The site allows for retail purchases and steers those interested in distributing or retailing the company's products to the company's distribution site.

www.pcrdist.com: The PCR Distribution site is the wholesale-only site that carries bishoujo games and other Japanese products, including hentai manga (erotic comic books), tee-shirts, and DVDs.

www.jlist.com: The J-List site offers a broad range of Japanese products at retail to the American English-speaking market including calendars, anime, and adult toys.

In creating his sites, Payne stuck to the standard business model—publisher, distributor, and retailer. The sites were designed to handle the variety of traffic that Payne's products would draw and to facilitate their distribution and his business's future growth. The sites are also cross-linked so that potential retailers visiting the *Peach Princess* brand site can easily find information on PCR Distributing should they choose to carry the products in their store.

Nowadays, all adult video game developers have, or plan to have if they are early in development, at least one site on the Internet where gamers can purchase their products. Hundreds, perhaps thousands, exist, from *Virtual Eve*, available at *www.virtualeve.com*, to *The Sex Ed Game*, available at *www.isergames.com*. While few are as structured as Payne's business, all are attempting to break through the retail wall to the consumer in one form or another.

Sales Models

Internet-based sexually themed games tend to use one of four different sales models in their attempt to reach consumers and to be profitable.

> **Download purchase model:** Users of this model charge players a flat fee to download or access their product for an unlimited period of time. One such game, *DreamStripper*, available at *www.dreamstripper.com*, charges users a flat fee to download the game.
>
> **Advertising model:** Games that use the advertising model are given away for free to players to drive sales of a particular product or brand. Such games as Gap Inc.'s humorous dressing room/strip game *Watch Me Change* available at *www.watchmechange.com* and Milwaukee's Best Light's game *Busted* available at *www.milbestlight.com* follow the advertising model. Both games are designed to highlight their sponsor's brand and image.
>
> **Subscription model:** Subscription-based games charge users a fee for a set period of time, usually 30 days. The sexually themed glam model simulator *Active Dolls*, available at *www.activedolls.com*, is one such game. Jenna Jameson's game *VirtuallyJenna*, available at *www.virtuallyjenna.com*, also charges users a flat monthly fee. In addition, *VirtuallyJenna* also features a "demo fee" that lets gamers play the game for a shorter time period.
>
> **Upgrade programs:** Developers of M-rated sexually themed video games occasionally offer AO-rated versions of their games for download only. *Leisure Suit Larry: Magna Cum Laude* and *The Singles: Flirt Up Your Life* both provided such upgrades. Some upgradeable games advertise the upgrade's availability in the M-rated game's packaging. A one-time cost is charged for the product.

In addition to these various sales models, thousands of free sexually themed games exist on the Internet. Dark Street Development's *Orgasm Girl* available at *www.2flashgames.com/f/f-738.htm* and Molleindustria's *Orgasm Simulator* available at *www.molleindustria.it/* are two such examples.

Driving Sales

With a virtual storefront established, developers need to drive traffic to their sites and maintain their current base of customers. While methods of marketing a product are similar regardless of the product's sexual content or lack thereof, titles with sexual content often find themselves restricted from advertisers and news outlets that normally welcome advertising or press releases. As such, developers of sexual content need to get creative, find new methods, or borrow methods from the adult industry to drive sales.

Getting Press

Traditional video game marketing travels a standard route. The PR or marketing team develops a marketing plan and Web site, announces plans for the game via a press campaign, and provides a playable demo or "teaser" screenshots. All of these efforts are generally supported by advertising in major gaming magazines and on gaming news sites.

David Potter, Director of Development for Ensign Games and developer of *DreamStripper*, found that such a route didn't exactly work for his game, however. Initially, Potter had difficulty getting news of his company's game out. "Yes, it is very hard," acknowledged Potter. "Most PC game sites won't touch us [since] we have adult content, even though we stayed away from any XXX stuff and [were] just 'R' rated" [Potter01].

Instead of limiting his advertising and press efforts to traditional gaming sites, Potter targeted another, larger market. "We started advertising on 'R' rated, picture-type sites, and then Fleshbot, AVN [Online] reported on us." Next, Potter says, they decided to issue a news release. "I first tried AddPR.com, but they rejected us due to adult content. We then started looking for other PR companies and found eReleases.com. They ended up sending out our press release with no problem" [Potter02]. Potter also tried to angle the product's press release to highlight the game's technical achievements instead of the adult aspects of the game.

After tackling the mainstream press, Potter also reached out to the "alternate press"—sex blogs and sex news sites. One of his early successes was unintentional, however. A *DreamStripper* forum request asked players what the next breast size of the game's model should be. The thread was picked up on a popular breast enlargement blog and resulted in a "ton of people" visiting Potter's site [Potter03]. According to Potter, when it comes to press, "the moral of the story is you need to get out to the sex sites and blogs" [Potter04].

Not every sexually themed game has difficulty getting press, however, particularly those that feature a celebrity or big name brand. Such a celebrity or brand can propel the game's PR and marketing well beyond traditional game channels.

That's precisely what happened to an XStream3D's *VirtuallyJenna* product. Brad Abram, president of XStream3D, and his team had been working on a sexually themed game. Brad realized that to make it big in North America, the game would need star power on its side. "We looked at mainstream entertainment stars like Pamela Anderson and Carmen Electra, and thought that if we had a cross-over celebrity, it would help mainstream our concept," says Abram. "Ultimately, however, it was easier to go on the adult side rather than the mainstream side of the market," he noted. In the end, Abram and his company teamed up with porn star Jenna Jameson.

"Jenna's the biggest in the business," notes Abram. "Jenna has fans in both the mainstream and adult worlds, and that would help attract more mainstream casual gamers as customers. I ended up going to Arizona and approached her directly through her production company CJI Digital and its president, Jay Grdina.

Abram's partnership with Jameson proved lucrative in the press. Major news outlets like CNN covered the game on its CNN/Money site, and *Wired* magazine also reviewed the game. Many of the major game sites also gave the game coverage. Another game that benefited from major name recognition was *Playboy: The Mansion*. Like *VirtuallyJenna*, the game received coverage on CNN, *Rolling Stone*, and *Maxim*.

Even without such name recognition, however, developers of sexual content can get and benefit from press attention to their game if the game's quality is superior. While mainstream coverage may be a challenge without a big name star or brand, it's still possible get the word out, as Potter's efforts show.

To get press for their game, developers must first be honest with themselves about the game's quality and newsworthiness. Depending on the game's size and quality, developers can then create a press plan. In developing and implementing that plan, developers should:

Get a name: Whether that name is a well-known star or a brand name, a popular name can open doors. Even games without a real-life name brand or personality should develop an in-game virtual celebrity and develop that character in their marketing. Characters like Duke Nukem, Lara Croft, BloodRayne, Luba Licious, and others have taken on a life of their own and have even appeared in *Playboy* magazine.

Develop a press list: Spend time researching the game and sex industry media, press, and blogs. Know whom to target.

Develop a press kit: Press kits should contain a press release in digital format, a feature list, sample screen shots or FTP access information, and a playable copy of the game if possible, or a means to download that game for free. Major media outlets expect to receive a free copy of the game for review with their press kit. If the game is not yet complete when you send out the press kit, follow up with a second product kit when the game is complete.

Focus on the positive, not the sensational: It's natural for editors and writers to brush off a sexually themed video game as something lacking in true gameplay and designed to make a quick buck. By *creating* and then focusing on *actual* gameplay mechanics in the game and in the press release, the product is likely to get more respect and more attention.

Affiliates Programs

Affiliates revenue-sharing programs are common in the sexual entertainment industry and are used to drive sales from one site to another. For instance, assume there are two sites, site A and site B. Site A offers an affiliate program. Site B signs up for that affiliate program and places a banner advertisement on site B that advertises site A. Site B is an affiliate of site A. Both *DreamStripper* and *VirtuallyJenna* offer such affiliate programs.

Under an affiliate program, developers provide the necessary assets and marketing tools to their affiliates. At minimum, the assets are a banner advertisement, HTML code, and link information. The affiliates then post the banner advertisements and marketing information on their site. When people click on an affiliate link, they're taken to the main site. Any sales that result are credited back to the affiliate. The developer is responsible for tracking sales through affiliates and paying a percentage of those sales to the affiliates. Under the *DreamStripper* program, for instance, affiliates receive 40% of the *DreamStripper* sales they initiate. Numerous companies provide affiliate tracking software.

Advertising

Similar to their editorial policies, some traditional gaming sites and magazines will not carry advertisements for sexually themed video games, particularly AO-rated video games. However, a quick survey of the target market for most sexually themed video games—men aged 18 to 35—reveals that gaming magazines aren't their only source of news and information.

When Potter advertised *DreamStripper*, advertisements appeared on *www .collegehumor.com*, *www.fleshbot.com*, and others. Likewise, Payne advertised his bishoujo offerings in nontraditional game places, too. "We do a bit of advertising here and there in major places like *Newtype*, *Play Magazine*, and so on," says Payne. "On the Web, we've been long-time advertisers on *The Onion*, which has helped us quite a lot, since people associate the good name of *The Onion* with J-List and hopefully vice versa" [Payne03]. The AVN Ads site features a sizeable database of places to advertise, hits, ratios, and charges for advertisers.

Games that use the advertising model also target nonstandard outlets for advertising. For instance, when Axe Unlimited introduced its new Axe Dry deodorant, it gave away sample product at EB Games. In addition, its game *Mojo Master* was advertised in banner ads on *Playboy.com*.

Conventions also provide outlets to advertise. Payne's company finds such conventions useful. "We do attend several of the major anime conventions, namely A-Kon in Dallas, Anime Expo in Anaheim, the San Diego Comic-Con International, and Otakon® in Baltimore, Maryland. Cons are great places since we can meet fans who wouldn't otherwise come across us" [Payne04]. Both the sex entertainment industry and the video game industry also have major conventions. The AVN® Adult Entertainment Expo held in January in Las Vegas and the Electronic Entertainment Expo held in May in Los Angeles are the largest.

Teasers

Teasers are often used to drive interest and sales when marketing any type of video game. Demos, trailers, and screenshots are commonplace. In the adult video game market, it's no different. *VirtuallyJenna.com*, for instance, features gameplay footage of *VirtuallyJenna*, screenshot galleries, and a downloadable demo. Similarly, *3D SexVilla* offers lots of screenshots and a downloadable demo on its site at *www.3dsexvilla.com*. Other games like *Red Light Center* welcomed gamers to try the game for free for a limited time at *www.redlightcenter.com*.

THE ADULT MARKET

"Why not sell the game in sex shops or at online sex sites?"

It's a common refrain when developers of sexual content talk about their distribution woes. At GDC 2005, many participants in the "Sexuality: What's Appropriate" roundtable asked exactly that question. No one had the answer, and if they did, they weren't talking. Why don't sexual content developers package their games like traditional video games and sell them to sex shops or the online sex product retailers?

Marlene, a product manager with one of the largest online sex toy sites in the world, unnamed by request, had a succinct answer: "As far as people selling adult video games, the problem they're going to run into is that nobody wants to deal with somebody who just manufactures one type of thing," she said. In the sex toy industry, large warehouses stock entire brand lines like Doc Johnson® and Pipedream® Products, each of which contains thousands of individual products. Distributors like Marlene's company buy from these warehouses. Since video game manufacturers might carry, at best, 100 products, Marlene noted that "it's very unlikely that they're going to be able to break into the mainstream" [Marlene01].

At the same time, Marlene didn't discount the value of footwork. "I mean they might do okay targeting specialty stores or privately owned adult stores directly. They would have to do the footwork and the networking, though, going to the stores to see if they could talk those people into carrying it" [Marlene02]. However, the "mainstream" adult audience sexual content developers seek would elude them.

A quick glance at almost any major sexual products site reveals a large variety of products, including board games. Although that at first may seem like a contradiction, Marlene was quick to explain. "The very few that we carry are because they're by the manufacturers that we use. For the large manufacturers, we will carry their whole line. The board games that you see are not from a bunch of different people or different companies who do board games. The games that we sell are a part of the existing lines that we already carry" [Marlene03].

Instead of approaching sex product sites, developers hoping for any degree of success would need to approach and get their product picked up by a sex product major manufacturer instead. Marlene was cautiously optimistic about such an approach. "Each manufacturer has their own Web page with a 'contact us' [link], but you rarely hear from them, particularly since there are so many people who think they've come up with the perfect sex toy. With video games, however, they might listen to you, because you're offering something that they don't have" [Marlene04].

And if a major manufacturer were to pick the line up? "That would get [the developer] into the mainstream," says Marlene. She also felt confident such a product would sell. "People are starved for things like that. It puts a creative spin to it. They would love to play a game" [Marlene05].

INTERVIEW WITH PETER PAYNE, PEACH PRINCESS

Peter Payne is the president of Peach Princess, a company that creates English-language versions of AO-rated bishoujo and anime-style games, and PCR Distributing, a distribution company that sells Peach Princess products and other products with similar themes through direct online sales and distribution at specialty stores.

How do you reach your market?

Basically, we realized two things early on when developing a market for bishoujo games in English. First, there is no distribution system in place for us as there is in Japan where several large dating-sim game distributors support the industry. So we "rolled our own," creating PCR Distributing, a company in San Diego, to handle distribution for our games directly to shops and online stores, and which can explain the many good points of our mature-audience games—the interesting cultural and dramatic elements in dating-sims, the breathtaking erotic art and stories—to retailers that might want to carry our products. The second thing we realized was that "family values" were going to keep our products out of major chain stores, and so we had to focus on the Internet, on anime, and comic retailers.

As far as advertising, we have a strong presence on the Web and reach out to customers directly as much as we can. People surfing the Web tend to know what the words "hentai" or "bishoujo game" mean and immediately recognize our products as interactive games they can play, rather than an anime DVD they can watch passively. Outside of the Web—say, at animation conventions—there's less knowledge of bishoujo games, and more explanation about our games is needed. All in all, we've managed to build a real business, helped partially by the nature of our products—the stories and characters are quite addictive, and once fans try one or two titles, they usually come back and pick up more.

PCR Distributing only distributes Japanese titles, correct? Would it be an outlet for creators of English AO titles that were not of the hentai/bishoujo mix?

Currently, we've positioned ourselves as a distributor of all kinds of Japan-related products, but if there were something that were well made, something which we felt we could work with, we'd be open to it.

Other than your distribution company, how do you reach out to and find the shops and online stores that carry your product, or do they find you?

We are well known in the anime community, and word of mouth helps us quite a bit. Also, many find us through J-List, our "everything from Japan" online shop. We also work with various shops, do mailings to comic shops, and so on. We do attend several of the major anime conventions, namely A-Kon in Dallas, Anime Expo in Anaheim, the San Diego Comic-Con, and Otakon. Cons are great places since we can meet fans who wouldn't otherwise come across us.

One thing that seems to be common to creators of successful AO content is a real emphasis on quality and customer service. Unlike traditional game publishers, they really need to keep customers coming back, because it's that much harder to reach new ones.

That's true, yes. Since the market for AO games is so tiny, we really do value each and every customer, since we've got a lot fewer of them than mainstream games. On the other hand, we're optimistic about the future. As the Internet spreads and more and more culture flows from it, it's easier for us to let people know about the various products we sell, the bishoujo games and so on. Also, while anime is a young movement in the U.S. today, with many fans in the 14–17 age bracket, we view this as a big opportunity, too, since when they turn 18 they'll want to express their interest in anime in "grown up" ways, which our games can serve very well. [Payne05]

RESOURCES

Otakon Convention: *www.otakon.com*
San Diego Comic-Con: *www.comic-con.org*
Electronic Entertainment Expo (E3): *www.e3expo.com*
The International Game Developers Association Sex Special Interest Group:
    www.igda.org/sex
Adult Video News Online: *www.avnonline.com*
AVN Ads: *www.avnads.com/index_avn.php*
SoftService, Ltd. (Affiliate Pro): *www.softservice.org*

REFERENCES

[Abram01] Abram, Brad, interview with Brenda Brathwaite, August 6, 2005.

[Amazon01] Search in "Products > Sex & Sexuality > Adult Toys & Games > Sex Toys > Vibrators," Amazon.com. Available online at *www.amazon.com/gp/ browse.html/ref=sc_bb_br_3777371_15/103-9616031-1732668?%5Fencoding= UTF8&node=3777831&no=3777371&me=ATVPDKIKX0DER*. Accessed September 3, 2005.

[Gabe01] Zichermann, Gabe, interview with Brenda Brathwaite, June 23, 2006.

[Halpin01] Halpin, Hal, interview with Brenda Brathwaite, May 23, 2005.

[Halpin02] Ibid.

[Halpin03] Ibid.

[Halpin04] Ibid.

[Marlene01] Marlene, last name withheld by request, interview with Brenda Brathwaite, September 3, 2005.

[Marlene02] Ibid.

[Marlene03] Ibid.

[Marlene04] Ibid.

[Marlene05] Ibid.

[Payne01] Payne, Peter, interview with Brenda Brathwaite, September 2, 2005.

[Payne02] Ibid.

[Payne03] Payne, Peter, interview with Brenda Brathwaite, September 2, 2005.

[Payne03] Payne, Peter, interview with Brenda Brathwaite, September 2, 2005.

[Payne04] Ibid.

[Potter01] Potter, David, interview with Brenda Brathwaite, August 7, 2005.

[Potter02] Ibid.

[Potter03] Potter, David, interview with Brenda Brathwaite, August 7, 2005.

[Potter04] Ibid.

11 Responsibility

In This Chapter

- Whose Problem Is This, Anyway?
- Parent Issues
- Retailer Issues
- Developer Issues
- Politician Issues
- A Proposed Solution

WHOSE PROBLEM IS THIS, ANYWAY?

When the dust settled on the *Grand Theft Auto: San Andreas* "Hot Coffee" scandal, people wanted answers. Politicians pointed their fingers at the ESRB and developers of violent and sexual content. Developers took parents and retailers to task. Parents demanded politicians do more and called on the ESRB to raise the game's rating. Although the various groups pointed their fingers angrily at one another, they seemed blind to the thing they had in common—the desire to keep mature and adult content out of children's hands.

Developers, retailers, parents, and politicians—each has a part to play, a shared responsibility to keep mature content away from children. Although assumptions and problems occasionally cause some groups to heap all the responsibility onto one party or another, it is only through a combined effort and a better understanding that the issue will see a positive resolution.

They want the same thing. Why can't they reach this common ground?

PARENT ISSUES

During the summer of 2005 while this author was writing this book, she stopped at a yard sale and found a pile of M-rated video games for sale, two *Grand Theft Auto* games among them. Enquiring about the cost of the various games, the seller said, "I have to get at least $10 each. My son just had to have them, but he only plays them for a little while." The seller gestured to her son, a boy no older than 10, sitting on the porch steps nearby.

Another parent who appeared in an ABC News' *Nightline* program titled "Grand Theft Auto: Just a Game?" admitted that she let her son play *Grand Theft Auto* and knew it was M-rated. However, she noted, it was "just a game," so she felt comfortable letting him play with his friends [ABC01].

In an interview with Springfield, Massachusetts, *Republican* reporter William Freebairn, Patricia Vance, president of the ESRB said such problems are not uncommon. Although surveys show that parents understand the ratings system, some let their kids play M-rated games anyway. Vance insisted, however, that parents have adequate information [Republican01]. A study commissioned by the Entertainment and Leisure Software Publishers Association (ESPLA) bears this out. Parents use the ratings as mere suggestion, the study finds, and are less concerned about *what* children play than how *long* they play [BBC01]. Furthermore, the Entertainment Software Association reports that when games are purchased, parents are present 92% of the time [ESA01].

"Games Are Just for Kids"

According to the most recent ESRB facts, 12% of video games are M- and AO-rated, and such games can feature, among other things, graphic violence and strong sexual content [ESRB01]. As with any other artistic medium, some games are made for children, some for teens, some late teens, and still others for adults only. Odds are the same parents would not let their young children into R-rated movies, provide them copies of *Hustler*, or books like *A Clockwork Orange*.

Parents must shake the assumption that games are just for kids. They're not. If parents decide to let their child play a game that is M- or AO-rated and whose descriptors plainly read "Blood and Gore, Intense Violence, Nudity, Strong Language, Strong Sexual Content, Use of Drugs," they have become a part of the problem they seek to solve [ESRB02]. They have, in effect, placed the very content they hope to keep out of children's hands *into* them. Games must be evaluated as any other form of media. It's a game, sure, but the rating tells you for whom it is appropriate—everyone, teens, those over 17, and adults only.

"I Just Don't Understand the Ratings."

When Internet messaging took off several years ago and in light of numerous disturbing reports of children having sexual conversations with adults online, parents armed themselves with information. They learned a complicated lingo—that "LOL" means "laugh out loud" and "POS" means "parent over shoulder." They learned how and where children came in contact with these predators. Major news outlets gave substantial coverage to the trend, its problems, and even offered numerous solutions. Similarly, the Web site MySpace.com received significant news coverage when it was revealed that children were posting inappropriate photos and revealing information such as their home address, schedules, and phone numbers online, making them easy prey for predators. In both cases, parents armed themselves with information. Parents learned about the lingo and MySpace.com because they perceived the danger to their children was imminent, substantial, and real.

However, when it comes to video game ratings, parents are less engaged. An article in *USA Today* sounds a familiar chord. Among other complaints, it notes that video game ratings are too confusing [USAToday01]. A universal rating system is necessary, critics say, to keep adult content out of children's hands. Such a system seems unlikely, however. Both the ESRB and MPAA ratings systems are registered trademarks and geared specifically toward the industries they serve. Neither is perfectly suited to rate another medium, nor likely to give up its registered trademarks for the other. In the absence of such a universal system, parents presently have two choices: remain uniformed or get educated. Even if such a universal system were developed, it would likely take a year or two for it to be implemented and to reach store shelves.

Are the ratings *that* complicated? No. They are certainly within the realm of easy comprehension. In fact, "M" for Mature is far more descriptive than the "R" for Restricted. Restricted to whom? Likewise, "AO" for Adults Only carries with it more information than the MPAA's NC-17 for "No Children Under 17 Admitted." In 1996, the MPAA changed the descriptor to "No One Under 17 Admitted," but kept the "NC-17" designation although it was no longer an accurate acronym of the name. In a random sampling of 10 individuals conducted by this author, none was able to identify what "NC-17" stood for. One thought it meant "Not Censored." Two had not heard of the rating category. The eight who had heard of it understood its meaning, but could not correctly expand on the acronym.

Why do people seem to understand and respect the recommendations of one system and not the other? The MPAA system has had nearly 50 years to become a part of the American collective conscience. By comparison, the ESRB system is a relative youngster having been established in 1993. It takes time and effort for something to become community knowledge. The ESRB has been proactive and worked with stores that now display descriptions of the ratings and the descriptors prominently. In June 2006, the ESRB launched a new initiative in conjunction with video game retailers it called a "commitment to parents." The initiative was announced on Capitol Hill on June 21, 2006, and backed by many of the power players in the industry, politics, and parenting, including Senators Rick Santorum, George Allen, and Mark Pryor, and National PTA deputy executive director Kimberly Barnes-O'Connor, and the Entertainment Software Association president Doug Lowenstein. Under the new program, which strengthened and enhanced existing policies, members of the ESRB Retail Council, including retailers like Best Buy, Wal-Mart, and Target agreed to participate in twice yearly "mystery shopper" audits, provide ratings in circulars and other promotional materials, train store employees about sales procedures and ratings, and share their successes and ideas with other ESRB Retail Council Members so that other stores—and ultimately parents—could benefit [ESRB05].

Oddly enough, despite all its problems, if there is something good to come of the *Grand Theft Auto: San Andreas* Hot Coffee scandal, it is the attention it brought to M- and AO-rated video games and the type of content they contain.

Parents must stay on top of emerging technologies and trends to protect their children from those things they find objectionable. Somehow, every parent has learned about the MPAA ratings. He or she knows the dangers of drugs. Parents are aware that the Internet itself is loaded with pornography and know that there are various software blockers, tools, and strategies that can protect their kids. Parents know not to let their children watch certain television shows—and often, it's not because of any explicit warning. Rather, they judge the appropriateness of a show by the time it's shown at night.

Brushing the ratings off as too complicated is no longer a valid argument. As with any other medium, parents need to learn about it. Nowadays, all major retailers post information on the ratings in their stores. Furthermore, every game features ratings information prominently on the front and back of the game package.

"He Plays It at His Friend's"

For many parents, the problem with mature content in video games doesn't come from within their home. Rather, their kids are exposed to violent and sexually themed video games when they go to friends' houses. While researching this book, this author talked with many parents who had this problem.

"I don't allow those games in my house," was the general sentiment. "He plays them when he goes over to his friend's house." Many parents were resigned to this as something beyond their control or something that "kids will just do."

When asked how they would react if they discovered their son had been allowed to watch *Scarface*, *Kill Bill*, or *Sin City* at the same friend's house, the response was much different. "I'd call their parents right away."

The content in today's video games can be as graphic as that found in movies, particularly as the processing power of consoles gets greater and greater. Parents need to be as disciplined with video games as they are with anything else their children use, regardless of where their kids may find access. Parents must call other parents to state their objections or prohibit their children from visiting the homes of children who play games not suitable for them.

"My Kid Tells Me It's No Big Deal"

To a child, a violent or sexually themed video game may not be a big deal. It may be exactly what he wants to play. However, as with anything, parents need to monitor the media their children consume. Children are not always the best judges of what's good for them, and parents should not treat such statements as fact. Would the parent react the same way if the child were talking about an R-rated movie or an adult magazine?

While it may be impossible for a parent to play through an entire to game to judge its appropriateness, a parent can judge the content by the game's ratings and its descriptors. A visit to a video game review site such as *www.gamespot.com* can also provide further information on a game. Game developers actively work to get lower ratings—the higher the rating, the smaller their potential audience. So, parents can rest assured that the rating on the package is indicative of its content.

"The great irony in the whole 'Hot Coffee' debacle," a developer said, "is how mad parents got when they found out there was sexual content in [*Grand Theft Auto: San Andreas*]. To me, the bigger story was how many parents had obviously allowed their children to play an incredibly violent video game. Why doesn't anyone take these parents to task for that?" [Anon01].

What Parents Can Do

What can parents do to keep their children's content age appropriate?

Learn about the ratings. Every ratings board has a Web site that provides thorough information on the rating system and descriptors. A list of these ratings boards appears at the end of this chapter. Information on ratings is also frequently available at the point of sale.

Respect the ratings. Ratings, like warning labels, are put there for children's protection. Parents should abide by these ratings.

Hold retailers accountable. If a child comes home with a game that's too advanced for his age, parents should take the game back to the retailer and ask to speak with the manager. It may not be enough to stop there. If possible, parents should call the corporate office of the company and complain. One parent in western Massachusetts even went so far as to contact a local television station, which, in turn, did a story on ratings. Pressure must be put on retailers to follow the industry ratings system. If a child were routinely being let in to see R- or X-rated films, what would parents do? The ESRB's new program calls for ESRB Retail Council member stores to accept video game returns from parents when the game was sold to someone for whom the rating was inappropriate.

Know the games. Parents should review the games their children play both on the console and on the computer. The ESRB's Web site provides a search feature that parents can use to get information on games rated by the ESRB. Another Web site, *www.mobygames.com*, has an excellent search feature and contains hundreds of games released worldwide. For full reviews on video games, visit *www.gamespot.com*.

RETAILER ISSUES

In a visit to the local game chain store to pick up a new game, this author asked the clerk if many parents came in to buy M-rated games for their children. "All the time," the clerk said. "Sometimes I even get grandparents coming in. The kids try to get them to buy *GTA* or something." Did he sell M-rated video games to those kids? "Not *San Andreas*," he offered. At the time of the interview, *Grand Theft Auto: San Andreas* was rated AO and had been re-stickered from its prior rating of M. The store was still carrying it. Why wouldn't he sell that one? "People are getting sued for that," he said.

If it's a young kid with a parent, the clerk noted that he'd educate them about what they were attempting to buy and suggest they pick up something different. "But if a kid's like 14 and he wants to buy something that's not so bad like *Halo 2*, I'll let him get it." When asked if it was a judgment call, the clerk admitted that "judgment" was only part of the story.

"We have quotas," he said. "52% of our sales need to come from pre-played games. So, if a kid comes up, and he has a pre-played game, and I think it's all right, I'm going to sell it to him." Pressure from district managers was strong, the clerk added, particularly since they could track sales individually by clerk. Such behavior was not isolated to that particular store. This author traveled to six stores in the same chain and received similar feedback.

IEMA member stores, whose members include the likes of Wal-Mart, Target, and Best Buy, have more consistent methods and policies. According to Hal Halpin, president of the IEMA, "We announced in December 2003 that by December 2004 all IEMA member companies would volunteer to self-regulate the sale of mature-rated games using the ESRB guidelines in an effort to stem the sale of inappropriate games to minors. We met that goal, and in the process changed the way that games are both merchandised and sold. ESRB ratings signage went up in every store—tens of thousands across the country—often in the place of revenue-generating vendor signage. Store-level staff were retrained, and new staff were instructed. Some members even installed cash register prompting technology at their own expense. It was a comprehensive and exhausting effort to which our members felt they had a social obligation and thus committed themselves" [Halpin01].

In announcing her intent to introduce legislation restricting the sale of violent and sexually explicit video games to minors, Senator Hillary Clinton noted that "the ability of our children to access pornographic and outrageously violent material on video games rated for adults is spiraling out of control" [Clinton01]. Clinton further cited research by the National Institute on Media and the Family, which showed that 50% of boys aged 7–14 were successfully able to purchase video games and that some of the retailers studied didn't understand, enforce, or train employees in the ratings [Media03].

"I Have a Quota to Meet"

When employees are faced with a quota—particularly one that tracks employees individually—the pressure to sell games is great, and the abstract nature of the consequences only compounds the problem. If a clerk is forced to choose between success in his job by meeting a quota or respecting the guidelines of an industry he or she is quite detached from, the choice will be an easy one to make. According to the clerks who spoke with this author, making the quota is a day-to-day challenge. District managers and store managers pressure employees to make sales, not to enforce ratings. When employees make choices on the basis of that quota, they undermine a system that was designed to protect consumers and the video game industry over all. Fortunately, most major retailers of games do not use such a quota system.

Inevitably, when video games are sold to minors, fingers are pointed toward the ratings board. People claim the ratings do not work. However, the ratings aren't the problem. They are clear, displayed prominently throughout stores and on the products. Flyers describing the ratings are available at the counter, and studies repeatedly show that parents understand the ratings. However, even lacking this information or knowledge, at the retail level, lack of buyer awareness is no excuse. If a 10-year-old child enters a store and tries to buy *Manhunt* without any awareness of the ratings, ultimately, it's the clerk's job to turn him down. Awareness is not the variable that determines success at the point of sale. If fingers are to be pointed, they should be aimed at the retailers who have put profits before people and failed to institute corporate policies, ethics, and consequences that deter such behavior.

"There's No Law That Says I Have To"

While it might be true in many places that no law requires compliance with the video game ratings system, such an argument doesn't really work. There's no law in any retail establishment that says clerks need to be nice to customers. There's no law that says employees must show up on time and stay a full eight hours. There's no law that says clerks must say "thank you" upon completing a purchase as opposed to "get out of my store." There's no law that says the words at the bottom of this page must continue on to the next.

However, in the absence of such laws, clerks are generally nice to customers. Employees show up for work, stay for their shift, and say "thank you" to their customers. They do these things because to do otherwise would result in consequences, mostly likely in lost sales or a lost job. Employers must dispel the notion that a law is required for enforcement of corporate policies. Arguments about the legality of video game sales, particularly when used to defend sales to minors, are ultimately self-defeating. One way or another, retailers *will* check identification, through voluntary means, through industry pressure, or, failing that, through legislation.

"It's a Judgment Call"

In the absence of clear policies and consequences for noncompliance, clerks at the retail level begin to use rationalizations to support their poor decisions. If the retailer in question uses quotas and other pressuring tactics, such rationalizations are easier and easier to swallow. Eventually, they become endemic within a store.

However, within a game's rating, there is no room for judgment. Working in conjunction with educators, psychologists, and scholars, the ratings system was developed. For a clerk to override this group's judgments with his or her own is not effective or in the best interests of the customer.

What Retailers Can Do

What should retailers do to keep adult content out of children's hands?

> **Create policies and procedures.** Management must create policies and procedures that respect video game ratings and train their managers and employees to use them. Furthermore, upper management must insure that these policies are being carried out on a store-to-store level by whatever means necessary.

> **Create consequence.** In the absence of any consequence, there is little incentive for clerks to follow the ratings system to the letter of the law. The employee may think it is genuinely okay to sell an M-rated game to a 14-year-old kid. However, it's not the employee's decision to make, but without consequence,

what causes him to reconsider? Employers must develop and communicate consequences to employees and be prepared to carry them out.

Create systems and standards. As a part of every sale, employees must be prompted to check the customer's identification, and systems must be put in place to facilitate this, whether it be through script training (a standard series of things employees say, most commonly used by telemarketers) or through point-of-sale prompts. In absence of systems that encourage patterns and accountability, employees may not abide by the ratings or company policy.

Eliminate quotas and high-pressure tactics. While quotas are a standard tool in the world of sales, their use in sales of video games is questionable. It may force employees into difficult positions where they are forced to choose between their own financial security, the interests of the customers they serve, and, ultimately, the industry at large.

DEVELOPER ISSUES

As news of "Hot Coffee" broke in the hard-core gaming media, primarily *GTA* fan sites at first and by mainstream gaming media later, the development community argued among itself and analyzed the controversy blow by blow. When Rockstar Games claimed that it was the fault of the modder, the community largely doubted it. Sure, people mod games, and sure, they create new animations and artwork, but that the modder created it all? Developers weren't buying it, particularly the ones who understood the technical ins-and-outs as described by the modder. When the issue came to a head, and it was revealed that the content had, in fact, been left on the disc, developers were of varied opinions. Some said Rockstar deserved whatever they had coming to them, while some called for voluntary restraint of violent and sexual content. Others suggested it was a marketing ploy to draw yet more attention to the product in its waning sales curve. All wondered what the ESRB would do, and many were certain the game's rating would be raised from M to AO.

Meanwhile, outside the development community, there was a virtual perfect storm forming. Parents, politicians, and media watchdogs all demanded action and promised legislation. Inside the development community, with some exceptions, the perfect storm raged unnoticed. Developers were less than interested in the potential fallout.

"I Don't Make M-Rated Games, So I Don't Care"

In the wake of promises to introduce legislation, developers of family friendly games sometimes feel safe, assured that their nonviolent and nonsexual games are off the radar and out of legislators' sites. If these hard-core games are the ones drawing the ire, they feel, they need not concern themselves with them. However, the central issue isn't M-rated games or even violent or sexually explicit games. Rather, it's something that affects all developers. It's about allowing others to define the limits of a game developer's creative freedom.

Developers of T- and even E-rated games need to be concerned. While legislators may be targeting M-rated games today, what's to say they won't legislate what's appropriate in T-rated games tomorrow? If nude women are considered obscene for adults, who's to say two women kissing in *The Sims* won't be ruled obscene for teens?

Legislation has even targeted games for content that is not violent or sexual. For instance, in Australia, State Labor Party member Paul Gibson announced his intent to ban the G-rated *Project Gotham Racing™ 2*. A level in the game takes place in Sydney, and this concerned Gibson who feared others would mimic the dangerous driving found in the game [Gamespot01]. In addition, New York City Council Member Peter F. Vallone called for a boycott of *Marc Ecko's Getting Up: Contents Under Pressure™* and branded the game a vandalism simulator [Yahoo01].

In his article "Regulation Is for Everyone," IGDA executive director Jason Della Rocca urges developers to see the effects of regulation in the broader context. "Standing up for creative freedom isn't about fighting for the rights of any one specific game or developer. We need to stand up for the medium as a whole. Who are we (or anyone else for that matter) to judge what is good or bad for others? While I may not personally agree with some design choices, I strongly believe in developers' freedom of expression."

Della Rocca asks, "Where will it end? The government's current fascination with violence may soon expand and put your nonviolent game square in their viewfinder" [IGDA01].

"As Developers, We Need to Practice More Self-Restraint"

When parents fail to monitor the games their children play and when retailers sell games to children who are not old enough to buy them, the suggestion inevitably arises: game developers should tone down the content they make and practice more self-restraint. The call for such measures even comes from within the industry. While gratuitous violence and sexual content may be unnecessary, it is nonetheless a developer's right to include such content in his or her games.

When applied to a medium outside this video game industry, the "self-restraint" argument looks odd. If a child were to sneak in to a screening of *Kill Bill*, would legislators ask Quentin Tarantino to tone it down, or would they demand theaters step up their efforts to keep kids out? If parents were purchasing copies of *Hustler®* for their children, would Larry Flynt be encouraged to print pictures appropriate for teenagers, or would parents be taken to task for buying the magazine in the first place?

Game developers have the right to express the full range of the human experience in their games. To limit developers to a family friendly palate stifles developers, and the medium overall. If any other medium were asked to remove sexual and violent content, its creators would be outraged. Consider, for a moment, no nudes in art or film, or extreme violence removed from the creative radar. What of Michelangelo's great statues? What about movies like *The Godfather* or *Scarface* or *Saving Private Ryan*? Operating under the restricted palate some suggest for video games, could movies like *Brokeback Mountain*, *Pulp Fiction*, *Silence of the Lambs*, or *Sideways* achieve critical or financial success? To limit game developers to a palate appropriate for consumption by one and all is nothing short of an absurd artistic restriction.

"They're Just Enforcing the Ratings"

In December 2004, Illinois Governor Rod Blagojevich proposed legislation to ban the sale and rental of games with violent and sexually explicit content to those under the age of 18, and the IGDA mobilized. They issued statements denouncing the action, sent "calls to action" to their substantial membership, lobbied politicians, and worked feverishly to get the word out to the development community and the community at large. In the eyes of the IGDA, this was a bill that didn't need to pass.

Many in the development community didn't understand all the commotion, however. On the face of it, Governor Blagojevich's plan sounded like a good one—one developers agreed with, in fact. After all, no one wanted kids playing games meant for adults. "What was the problem?" they wondered. "Isn't this exactly what we want anyway?"

In fact, it wasn't. Although the public face of the bill, HB4023, was a good one, the text of the actual bill reveals the confusion it creates. For starters, games that "include realistic depictions of human-on-human violence in which the player kills, seriously injures, or otherwise causes serious physical harm to another human" were to be labeled 18+ violent video games [HB402301]. Under such a rule, games like *Grand Theft Auto: San Andreas*, and *Manhunt* would certainly be affected. However, family friendly games like *The Oregon Trail®*, *The Sims*, and the *Madden* football series could be affected, too. In *The Oregon Trail*, a program used in many schools across the country at one time or another, players could equip their wagon train with no food on purpose and watch the train's children die along the way. In *The Sims*, players can easily orchestrate a fatal kitchen fire, and the *Madden* series of football games allows for and tracks injuries. Meanwhile, due to its stipulation that the violence be human-on-human, ultra-violent video games featuring human-like robots or animals would miss classification. What's worse, the text of the bill was not clear on who would actually administer these 18+ designations. So, what's 18+ at one store might not be at the next. All in all, the bill creates far more confusion—particularly for parents—than it solves. On the face of it, though, it looks good.

Developers can be uninformed, buying a political sales pitch and failing to look underneath to see what's really being sold. Although the text of the bills is online and easily accessible via links on the IGDA's Web site at *www.igda.org*, many developers don't look deeper. Some may not even feel the need to. Legislation doesn't make for interesting reading.

When this author spoke at Post Mortem, the Boston area's IGDA chapter meeting, on August 9, 2005, many developers in attendance were unaware of the ramifications of such legislation, particularly that based on obscenity statutes that vary community to community. What passes for acceptable in liberal Northampton, Massachusetts, might not hold true in a more conservative location like Salt Lake City, Utah. To abide by these various laws, developers would be required to make builds on a community-by-community basis that reflected the standards of each community. Since such an endeavor would be unrealistic if not impossible, developers would instead make a single build that was acceptable to the most stringent standards of all.

"Practice Safe Sex and Declare All Firearms"

In the production of almost any game, certain features inevitably need to be cut. Cuts happen for many reasons. Sometimes, there's not enough time in the schedule to finish the feature properly. Commonly, the feature just didn't work out as the developers hoped it would. Developers sometimes cut content to achieve a lower ESRB rating. For instance, they may have submitted the game and received an M rating in return. By cutting the elements that earned them that rating, they stand a better chance at getting a T rating on their next pass through the rating's process. Every game on every shelf at one point or another suffered such a cut whether in pre-production or shortly before it shipped.

Normally, when developers cut content, it's not a big deal. The code is sometimes cleaned up, and the assets—animations, art and voice, if necessary—may be removed to make room for more things on disc or in memory. Developers may also leave code in the game if they perceive that removing it could cause instability in the overall code base. In such cases, developers disable or bypass the code, but leave it largely intact.

While such practices are commonplace in software development, when the cut content is of a sexual nature, it takes on new and significant meaning just as it did with Hot Coffee. If enough assets and code are left on the disc that the feature could, with any effort, be put back into "play," such content must be declared to the ratings board. No longer is it a question of "if" it will be discovered, but "when." Modders who look for such things are among the cleverest "developers" out there.

In lieu of declaring such content to the ratings board for consideration, developers can go one step beyond disabling the code by removing the content from the disc. By removing the art, the animations, and the voice, and breaking or removing the functional code, modding a game becomes far more of an effort. Whoever chooses to expend that effort ends up being responsible for the mod. As the industry learned with Hot Coffee, just because a modder *enables* content, it doesn't absolve the developer of the responsibility for that content if it shipped on the disc. Games like *The Sims* have an active adult mod community. However, mod content for *The Sims* is created by mods developers and out of the publisher's hands.

What Developers Can Do

How can developers keep adult content out of children's hands?

Say what you ship. In addition to the content present in the game, if there's content left on the disc, it must be declared to the ratings board. As the recent *Oblivion* re-rating showed, accurate anatomical representations of breasts under clothing are an issue when that clothing can be removed through a mod and thus the breasts revealed.

Do not support legislation that treats games differently from other forms of media or art. Legislation that seeks to treat games differently from any other art form and imposes dissimilar ratings systems and community standards on video games only confuses the issue for parents and wastes thousands of taxpayer dollars. Legislation that treats video games the same as other forms of media, including magazines, film, and the like, has been supported recently by the Entertainment Software Association and the video game industry.

Reach out to politicians—kindly. Offer to work with politicians to help them understand the industry. Developers and gamers can be masters of hostile feedback. Flaming emails, angry posts on Web sites, and irate phone calls are all too common. Politicians are only responding to their constituent's needs and may lack an understanding of the industry. Reaching out in a spirit of cooperation is likely to be far more effective in reaching our mutual goals.

Demand retailer accountability. Talk with your local retailers and demand they abide by the industry ratings system. When they sell games to children, ultimately, it's the *developers* who are affected by increased parental and governmental pressure. Call the store. Call their head office. Talk to the press. Demand accountability.

Insist on parental responsibility. The most effective rating system in the world is a parent. Game developers must encourage parents to step up to the plate and take the game ratings system seriously. Not all games are for children.

Read the bills. Before expressing their support for a particular piece or type of legislation, developers need to read the text of the bill. Often, it's not what it seems to be. While reading bills isn't the most compelling, sites like *www.gamepolitics.com* offer a far more entertaining and provocative analysis.

Support all game developers. Creative freedom is not about choosing from a small, select, and safe middle ground. Rather, it includes the entire spectrum. While some developers may not choose to make violent or sexually themed content, nonetheless, it is important to support the right of other developers to do so.

Join the IGDA. The International Game Developers Association works for the betterment of game development and needs the support of game developers. Join at *www.igda.org/join*.

POLITICIAN ISSUES

The news had barely crossed the wires when the phones started to ring. Rockstar Games had done it again, and this time, it was serious (or at least more serious than the last time they'd offended politicians and parents alike). Politicians and media watchdogs demanded the ESRB take action, and some, including Senator Hillary Rodham Clinton, promised legislation and ultimately delivered on that promise.

Such actions were hardly surprising given the severity of the allegations and the political climate. In fact, the prior year, 2004, had been a banner year for video game legislation. States from California to New York to Texas to Illinois had seen some type of legislation put forth to curtail the sale of violent and sexually themed video games to children. Parents, outraged that their children's video games contained such mature content, pleaded with legislators to address the issue, and legislators, admirably doing their job, did just that.

"The Industry Is Out of Control"

In announcing her intent to introduce legislation restricting the sale of violent and sexually explicit video games to minors, Senator Hillary Rodham Clinton noted that "the ability of our children to access pornographic and outrageously violent material on video games rated for adults is spiraling out of control" [Clinton01]. Clinton further cited research by the National Institute on Media and the Family, which showed that 50% of boys aged 7–14 were successfully able to purchase video games and that some of the retailers studied didn't understand, enforce, or train employees in the ratings [Media01].

California Assemblymember Leland Yee also sternly criticized the industry in an editorial carried on his official state Web site. "Last session, we were successful in passing a bill that requires retailers to post a sign explaining the video game rating system," Yee wrote. "However, since that bill passed, many new games have been introduced, like *Manhunt* and *JFK Reloaded*, which are even more violent and realistic. Clearly, the video game industry is not concerned with the welfare of our children."

However, the industry itself—developers, publishers, and the ratings board—is, in fact, well in control and does care about the welfare of children. Nowadays, games simply don't make it to retail without an ESRB rating on the package, and the most offensive games like *Manhunt* are slapped with the harshest descriptors possible. *Manhunt*, for instance, was rated M and given the "blood and gore," "intense violence," and "strong language" descriptors [ESRB03]. To say that the video game industry does not care about children because it releases games like *Manhunt* is to say that the music industry doesn't care about children because it releases MP3s by Marilyn Manson. Furthermore, games like *JFK Reloaded* are anomalies. The game was not carried in any retail store, was not supported by any mainstream publisher or developer, and was available through download only. It is hardly reflective of the industry overall. To characterize an entire industry on the basis of one game is like characterizing mainstream Hollywood based on a single, independent snuff film, or all magazines based on *Penthouse*, or all books based on the wonderful but drug-filled *Trainspotting*, or all films based on Ron Jeremy's flicks. Games like *The Sims 2*, *Zoo Tycoon*, *Ratchet & Clank*™, and *World of Warcraft* are infinitely more representative of the industry overall. In fact, M-rated video games make up only 12% of video games sold [ESRB04].

Furthermore, the industry is far more *in* control than ever. "The Ninth Annual Mediawise® Video Game Report Card" released by the National Institute on Media and the Family praised the ESRB ratings, noting that they were the current benchmark for media ratings systems. The same report showed a 19% increase in retail enforcement policies among those who carry the industry's games, and a 20% decrease in the percentage of those under 17 who were able to buy an M-rated video game [Media02]. To claim the industry is out of control is no longer a valid argument.

"If Anything, Hot Coffee Proved the Ratings Don't Work"

On the contrary, Hot Coffee proved that the ratings *do* work. When the scandal broke, the ESRB mobilized a team to investigate the matter. Within a short amount of time, it had re-rated the game AO for Adults Only. Take-Two Interactive, the publishers of the Rockstar title, were required to re-label the game with the appropriate rating. Stores like Wal-Mart, Best Buy, and others quickly yanked the title from store shelves. Coupled with its ratings, the quick action of the ESRB warned retailers, parents, and kids alike exactly what content the game contained.

Even the FTC praised the industry and the ESRB, noting that the "electronic game industry continues to provide rating information prominently in most forms of advertising, which likely reflects its enforcement program. Although some areas still could be improved (e.g., including content descriptors in television advertising), there is much in the game industry's rating disclosure requirements that merits duplication by others" [FTC01].

"This Legislation Will Protect Our Children"

When legislators introduce and pass legislation, it is often, but not always, with the best intentions—to keep violent and sexually themed video games out of the hands of children. However, such legislation is far more likely to waste tens of thousands of taxpayer dollars, leaving kids no more "protected" than before. Citing First Amendment protections, video game legislation has been overturned coast to coast.

The drafters of Illinois bill HB4023, which contains both the "Sexually Explicit Video Games Law" and the "Violent Video Games Law," were well aware of the obstacles they faced when they crafted their bill. However, they felt certain that recent research by Harvard University would shield them from a First Amendment review [USA01]. One senator, Senator Deanna Demuzio, even went so far as to claim that video games couldn't be considered art or media. She likened video games to simulations similar to those used by the military for war games [Demuzio01].

Other legislators felt differently, however. Representative Bill Black disagreed with the legislation during the Assembly's debate. "We make some difficult decisions. That's what we're elected to do," he said. "I'm asking you today to stand up for the First Amendment. I'm asking you today to tell parents, 'That's your responsibility, not mine.'" [ILL01]. Noting that he was not prepared to "diminish the First Amendment," Black said he intended to vote no. "The Bill of Rights was given to us by remarkable people 225 years ago," Black said. "Our job is to see in a very, very changing world, I understand that, as to whether or not we can keep it" [ILL02].

Despite a near certainty that the bill would be overturned on First Amendment grounds, some senators felt pressured to vote "yes" anyway. In an Associated Press article, Senator Mike Jacobs admitted that he voted for the bill for purely political reasons. Jacobs feared that voting against the bill would ultimately be used against him in campaign advertising [Jacobs01].

"If any of us think the Bill is patently unconstitutional as written and then we vote for it anyway, ya know, that's the game we've played here for years," Representative Black said before the House. "We vote for some Bills so that we can go home and say, 'I'm tough on this or I did that.' And then hope that the Supreme Court will bail us out of an action that we took. Ladies and Gentlemen of the House, where do you stop? If you go down this road, where do you stop?"

Ultimately, legislation against video games wastes the very money of the taxpayers it seeks to serve.

What Politicians Can Do

What can politicians do to keep adult content out of children's hands?

Step up pressure on retailers. Legislation is a drastic solution. Demand that retailers adhere to the ratings system, and develop an annual retailer "report card." There are few things more effective than the possibility of negative public exposure, including legislation. A chain-by-chain report card issued yearly would have profound and immediate results. Best of all, its cost would be a fraction of the costs of legislation and the subsequent court fights to overturn it. A great many retailers adhere to the ESRB system, and should not be punished by the retailers that don't.

Demand parents step up to the plate. Legislation won't protect children—parents will. Parents are present 92% of the time when children purchase video games [ESA02]. Study after study has shown that parents know the ratings system. If parents understand the ratings, know what they mean and still choose to purchase M-rated games for their children, then it's the parents, not the ratings, who aren't working properly. Even with legislation barring stores from selling games to minors, without parents accepting their involvement in the problem and their responsibility to stop it, such legislation is ultimately doomed to failure.

Study the issue and the industry. Admittedly, being a politician is a challenging job. Every day, there are dozens and dozens of issues vying for their attention. However, politicians need to study the issue thoroughly to identify the real problems and possible solutions. Saying games are nothing more than "simulations" and are without any artistic value causes politicians to lose credibility among those they most need to impress. Video games are being studied—as artistic endeavors—at universities and colleges across the world.

Do not support legislation that is sure to be overturned. Wasting thousands of taxpayer dollars on legislation that's sure to be overturned on First Amendment grounds is not the best use of a government's limited resources. Vote "no." While the intent of such legislation is necessary and admirable—to keep violent video games out of the hands of kids—no matter what's done, a legislative solution won't fix the problem, because the problem is not within the industry itself.

A PROPOSED SOLUTION

Parents and politicians, developers and retailers all want the same thing—to keep adult content out of the hands of children. Instead of fighting against one another, the four groups must work together toward their common cause. The endless rounds of accusation, legislation, and court battles get the industry and those concerned with it nowhere.

Start Working Together

Developers, retailers, politicians, and parents must work together as they did to create the ESRB's new "Commitment to Parents" program. An interdisciplinary task force should be created to study the issue from all sides. By working together instead of against one another, such a group stands a real chance of keeping adult content out of children's hands. Developers and publishers must understand the games they make, and the pressure politicians have on them to restrict access to that content. Likewise, parents and retailers must understand the role they have to play in the issue. They need to know the consequences of the choices they make. They need to understand that selling to and buying games for children affects not just a child, but the creative freedom of thousands of game designers, programmers, artists, writers, musicians, and producers everywhere. Politicians need to accept the strength of the First Amendment and, in partnership with the industry, look for solutions that work.

Working together, such a task force could educate the individual groups and explore the issue in its entirety, taking into account the problems and possibilities on all sides. Furthermore, due to its interdisciplinary nature, its actions and recommendations have a real chance of being implemented throughout the entire industry.

Ultimately, however, the most important feature of such an interdisciplinary group will be its focus on what really matters—keeping adult content out of the hands of kids—instead of on the faults of the individual groups. The money, time, and energy used to defend the individual sides could be put toward a far greater purpose.

Demand Accountability

Within every software retailer there exists a public relations or marketing department. These departments exist to publicize and increase awareness of the company, and hence its sales, and to protect the company image.

When Nike Corporation faced accusations that it used child labor in the manufacture of its products, the international community was outraged and its image was suitably tarnished [CNN01]. Nike responded by creating a corporate responsibility statement that it completes yearly, and even devotes a whole section of its Web site, *www.nikebiz.com*, to the topic of corporate responsibility. Likewise, when critics of Wal-Mart accused it of negatively affecting areas into which it moved, providing its employees low wages and little chance for promotion, and importing millions of low-cost goods, the corporation responded with a PR blitz [CNN02]. Commercials featured employees talking about the company's benefits, the careers they had been given, and even what Wal-Mart has done for the community [Now01].

Bad publicity is an incredibly powerful force for corporations that spend millions of dollars to protect and promote their image. Naming names and providing public pressure where it is actually due is a far more effective agent of change than sweeping, but ultimately meaningless, claims that "an industry" is out of control, or legislation that, in most all cases, goes nowhere. It also discounts the work of organizations like the member companies of the IEMA and others that have committed themselves to the ESRB ratings.

Use the Ratings System with Full Disclosure

Nothing works unless you work it. When game developers don't disclose content or leave content on a disc that should have been removed, it creates problems for everyone. The ratings systems that vary from country to country must be used with full disclosure. What's in the game must be revealed to the ratings boards, regardless of how one accesses that content—be it a mod using shipped assets, an "Easter egg," or a part of standard gameplay.

The ratings boards could further insure compliance by playing the games they have rated, post release if necessary, instead of wholly relying on developer- or publisher-provided video footage of gameplay.

List of Industry Ratings Boards & Industry Contacts

Who rates video games? What associations are there? Who's who?

- Entertainment Software Rating Board (U.S.)—*www.esrb.org*
- Office of Film and Literature Classification (Australia)—*www.oflc.gov.au*
- British Board of Film Classification (UK)— *www.bbfc.co.uk*
- Pan European Game Information (Europe)—*www.pegi.info*
- Interactive Entertainment Merchants Association—*www.iema.org*
- International Association of Game Developers—*www.igda.org*
- Entertainment Software Association—*www.theesa.com*

REFERENCES

[ABC01] Koppel, Ted, "It's Just a Game," *Nightline*, ABC News, July 10, 2002.

[Anon01] Anonymous, interview with Brenda Brathwaite, August 15, 2005.

[BBC01] Hermida, Alfred, "Parents 'Ignore Game Age Ratings'," BBC News Online, June 24, 2005. Available online at *http://news.bbc.co.uk/2/hi/technology/4118270.stm*. Accessed August 15, 2005.

[Clinton01] Clinton, Senator Hillary Rodham, "Senator Clinton Announces Legislation to Keep Inappropriate Video Games Out of the Hands of Children," Press Release, July 14, 2005. Available online at *http://clinton.senate.gov/news/statements/details.cfm?id=240603*. Accessed August 17, 2005.

[CNN01] CNN.com, "Sports Giants Accused of Continued Labor Exploitation," March 7, 2002. Available online at *http://archives.cnn.com/2002/WORLD/asiapcf/southeast/03/07/indonesia.sportswear/index.html*. Accessed August 30, 2005.

[CNN02] CNN.com, "Wal-Mart Launches P.R. Blitz," January 13, 2005. Available online at *www.cnn.com/2005/US/01/13/walmart.pr/index.html*. Accessed August 30, 2005.

[CNN03] CNNMoney, "Wal-Mart Challenges Class-Action Ruling," August 8, 2005. Available online at *http://money.cnn.com/2005/08/08/news/fortune500/walmart_suit/*. Accessed August 30, 2005.

[Demuzio01] The Associated Press, "Illinois Senate OKs Limits on Sales of Violent Video Games," May 20, 2005. Available online at *www.firstamendmentcenter.org/news.aspx?id=15289*. Accessed August 29, 2005.

[ESA01] "2005 Essential Facts About the Computer and Video Game Industry: Sales, Demographics and Usage Data," The Entertainment Software Association. Available online at *www.theesa.com/files/2005EssentialFacts.pdf]*. Accessed August 14, 2005.

[ESA02] "2005 Essential Facts About the Computer and Video Game Industry: Sales, Demographics and Usage Data, The Entertainment Software Association. Available online at *www.theesa.com/files/2005EssentialFacts.pdf]*. Accessed August 14, 2005.

[ESRB01] Entertainment Software Rating Board, *Rating Category Breakdown: 2004*. "ESRB Newsletter: Summer 2005." Available online at *www.esrb.org/about_newsletters.asp#statistics*. Accessed August 29, 2005.

[ESRB02] Rating listing for *Grand Theft Auto: San Andreas*, "ESRB Game Ratings," Entertainment Software Rating Board. Available online at *www.esrb.org/search_results.asp?key=grand+theft+auto%3A+san+andreas&x=0&y=0&type=game&validateSearch=1*. Accessed August 14, 2005.

[ESRB03] Rating listing for *Manhunt*, "ESRB Game Ratings," Entertainment Software Rating Board. Available online at *www.esrb.org/search_results.asp?key= manhunt&x=43&y=7&type=game&validateSearch=1*. Accessed August 28, 2005.

[ESRB04] Entertainment Software Rating Board, *Rating Category Breakdown: 2004*. "ESRB Newsletter: Summer 2005." Available online at *www.esrb.org/ about_newsletters.asp#statistics*. Accessed August 29, 2005.

[ESRB05] Entertainment Software Rating Board, "ESRB Retail Council (ERC) Establishes Unprecedented 'Commitment to Parents' with National Video Game Retailers." Available online at *www.esrb.org/about/news/downloads/erc_ release_6_21_06.pdf*. Accessed June 22, 2006.

[FTC01] Muris, Chairman Timothy J., et al. Federal Trade Commission. "Marketing Violent Entertainment to Children: A Twenty-One Month Follow-Up Review of Industry Practices in the Motion Picture, Music Recording & Electronic Game Industries. A Report to Congress," June 2002, p. 7. Available online at *www.ftc.gov/reports/violence/mvecrpt0206.pdf*. Accessed August 27, 2005.

[Gamespot01] Feldman, Curt, "Gotham Racing 2 Hits Speed Bump Down Under," Gamespot, November 17, 2003. Available online at *www.gamespot.com/ xbox/driving/projectgothamracing2/news_6083742.html*. Accessed August 22, 2005.

[Halpin01] Halpin, Hal, interview with Brenda Brathwaite, May 23, 2005.

[HB402301] Chapa LaVia, Rep. Linda, et al., Bill HB4023. Amendment to Section 5, Articles 12A and 12B of the Illinois State Criminal Code. 94th General Assembly, State of Illinois, 2005 and 2006. Available online at *www.ilga.gov/ legislation/94/hb/09400hb4023.htm*. Accessed August 22, 2005.

[IGDA01] Della Rocca, Jason, "Regulation Is Everyone's Business," International Association of Game Developers. Available online at *www.igda.org/articles/d ellarocca_regulation.php*. Accessed August 22, 2005.

[ILL01] Black, Rep. Bill, Transcript Debate, State of Illinois, 94th General Assembly, House of Representatives, p. 36, March 16, 2005. Available online at *www.ilga .gov/house/transcripts/htrans94/09400031.pdf*. Accessed August 29, 2005.

[ILL02] Ibid.

[ILL03] Black, Rep. Bill, Transcript Debate, State of Illinois, 94th General Assembly, House of Representatives, p. 34, March 16, 2005. Available online at *www .ilga.gov/house/transcripts/htrans94/09400031.pdf*. Accessed August 29, 2005.

[Jacobs01] The Associated Press, "Illinois Senate OKs Limits on Sales of Violent Video Games," May 20, 2005. Available online at *www.firstamendmentcenter .org/news.aspx?id=15289*. Accessed August 29, 2005.

[Media01] Walsh, Dr. David, et al., National Institute on Media and the Family, "The Ninth Annual Mediawise Video Game Report Card," November 23, 2004. Available online at *www.mediafamily.org/research/report_vgrc_2004 .shtml*. Accessed August 28, 2005.

[Media02] Ibid.

[Media03] Walsh, Dr. David, et al., National Institute on Media and the Family, "The Ninth Annual Mediawise Video Game Report Card," November 23, 2004. Available online at *www.mediafamily.org/research/report_vgrc_2004. shtml*. Accessed August 28, 2005.

[Now01] Bennett, Lisa, "Wal-Mart Commercials Turn Workers' Frowns Upside Down Employees Told How to Get Public Assistance While Company Makes Billions," *National NOW Times*, Fall 2003. Available online at *www.now .org/nnt/fall-2003/walmart.html*. Accessed August 30, 2005.

[Republican01] Freebairn, William, "Parents Need to Step Up to the Plate," *Springfield Republican*, August 14, 2005. Available online at *www.masslive.com/ search/index.ssf?/base/business-0/1123919366107801.xml?bnae*. Accessed August 14, 2005.

[USA01] O'Connor, John, Associated Press, "Illinois House OK's Governor's Video-Game Ban," USATODAY.COM, March 17, 2005. Available online at *www.usatoday.com/tech/news/techpolicy/2005-03-17-illinois-game-ban_x.htm*. Accessed August 29, 2005.

[USAToday01] Oldenburg, Ann, "Ratings System Runs Adrift," *USA Today*, updated July 28, 2005. Available online at *www.usatoday.com/tech/products/ games/2005-07-27-parental-advisory-ratings_x.htm*. Accessed August 14, 2005.

[Yahoo01] Yahoo News, "Atari Gets Tagged: Vallone Calls for Boycott of Video Game Maker," July 21, 2005. Available online at *http://biz.yahoo.com/ prnews/050721/dcth003.html*. Accessed August 22, 2005.

[Yee01] Yee, Assembly Member Leland Y, Speaker pro Tempore, California State Assembly, "Violent Video Game Legislation Protects Children," undated. Available online at *http://democrats.assembly.ca.gov/members/a12/oped/ op122005002.htm*. Accessed August 28, 2005.

12 Corporate Concerns

In This Chapter

- Sex & The Corporate Image
- The Professional Office
- Get a Lawyer
- Interview with Kelly Rued, Black Love Interactive

SEX & THE CORPORATE IMAGE

Sooner or later, every developer or publisher considering the development of a game with significant sexual content asks themselves one particular question, "How will this affect my company?"

Will it tarnish their corporate image? Will they be seen as a shop that makes only sexually related material? Will people who want E-rated, T-rated, or even M-rated product come to them in the future? Will they be taken to court or be affected by a court ruling?

Working on a sexually themed game forces a company to stand on new ground and to consider various issues that may arise. In the United States in particular, violent video games are more readily accepted than games with sexual content, and as such, one can never make assumptions about how liberal potential employees, business partners, and vendors might be, not to mention the political climate.

Company Image

Companies spend millions of dollars crafting their corporate image. They advertise it, hire marketing departments to manicure it, sue others to protect it, and take on or reject particular products in keeping with the image they've created. It's reasonable and smart for companies to consider the effect a sexually themed game could have on their corporate image.

Prior to signing on as the developer of *Playboy: The Mansion*, Seth Spaulding, former president of Cyberlore Studios, Inc., considered the effect the game would have on his company. "There were a few people internally who expressed the worry that we would be seen within the industry as the 'porn-game' company. Would our next offers be from *Hustler* and *Maxim* instead of Sony and Microsoft? In fact, this clearly has not occurred. We did get approached by one publisher interested in another adult title, but far more continued to contact us regarding more conventional games" [Spaulding01].

In fact, working on *Playboy: The Mansion* provided Cyberlore with press and exposure it would have been hard pressed to receive in any other way. Major media outlets including CNN covered the game's announcement, development, and launch, and following its release, the game and company received major attention from print, broadcast, and online media. The game's publisher subsequently signed Cyberlore to do a follow-up expansion, *Playboy: The Mansion Party Pack*.

More difficult to gauge, however, is the negative effect it has on corporate image. It's impossible to account for publishers that decide not to work with companies because they work with sexual content. Furthermore, for all the positive or sensationalistic press sexually themed games receive, there is also a certain amount of negative press such games receive, too. Some developers find they are unable to get any press at all.

For companies with existing or strong corporate images, a move toward sexual content should be taken with exceptional caution, particularly if the company's current image, product line, or focus is in the education or children's markets. Imagine if Disney® published a *BMX XXX*? If such a suggestion sounds absurd, it should. It shows how strong both corporate images and the effect of sexual content on them can be.

Recruiting

Many companies add staff during a product's pre-production. While quality of life, pay, and location are all important factors for recruits, so is content. When it comes to sexually themed content, however, the benefits of the company can be trumped by a recruit's personal beliefs, family, and friends.

One employee who accepted a position with a developer working on a sexually themed game lost a friendship. "I'd known this guy for a few years, and we'd always gotten along real well. When I told him that I was leaving [the company] and going to work on [a sexually themed game], he was pretty frank with me," said the developer. "He told me that he wanted to be happy for me, but he couldn't, and he felt he couldn't continue a friendship. I was pretty surprised, but I got where the guy was coming from" [Anon01].

Another developer working on a sexually themed title told this author about two significant candidates they were considering for a lead position on the project. When the candidates learned of the nature of the product, they terminated the interview process. Other contractors working on art for a sexually themed project expressed concern about how their full-time employer would react if they found out about their contract job.

It's important to consider the effect a game could have on recruiting both now and in the future. While the games industry is noted for its liberal attitudes, the impact of sexual content on the recruitment pool, particularly among highly valued senior candidates, should not be underestimated.

Vendors

Middleware is a standard part of the development process. Compression technologies and prepackaged engines are things developers regularly use to save development time while keeping costs down. When working on a sexually themed game, however, one should never assume that vendors are on board.

"We had reached a point in development where we were ready for a [middleware application]," said one developer who spoke on the condition of anonymity. "We contacted the vendor only to be told that they would not allow us to use their product because they considered our game obscene. That was the end of that. We were baffled." As a result, the developer was forced to find another solution that required three additional weeks of development—time and money few development teams can afford. "It just never occurred to us that that was a possibility" [Anon02].

When the product is in the planning stages, developers should carefully research all middleware vendors they plan to use and verify their participation in the project up front.

THE PROFESSIONAL OFFICE

Developers working on games with sexual content must be aware of the unique needs and issues such content presents. In such an environment, artists may watch porn videos to get animations just right, and designers might study erotic magazines to get ideas for missions. Browser windows opened to porn sites can be commonplace.

To maintain a degree of professionalism and to insulate the company against potential problems, developers must institute professional standards and practices from day one. These standards should be discussed in depth with all team members and revisited regularly to ensure they are being followed. While it may be tempting to smirk and say, "C'mon, it's not *that* big of a deal," know that it is. Employees or their significant others may object to such content for personal, professional, or religious reasons.

"You need to balance the needs of the project with the culture of the project and the comfort of the individual employees," said Clarinda Merripen, former Director of Operations at Cyberlore Studios. "Not everyone will respond in the same way. The most extreme danger is an employee harassment suit. Yet, the more insidious danger is people not being able to concentrate, or those who are privately offended may start to look for another job. If our job as management is to clear away obstacles, why introduce new ones?" [Merripen01]

Any developer who has been through a project, sexually themed or not, knows that teams have enough issues—issues of communication, dynamics, burn out, and cohesion—without adding still more.

"Many teams are formed by throwing a bunch of people at a project based on their professional skills and saying 'voilà you're a team'," says Linda Currie, producer at Blue Fang Games and speaker on issues of team dynamics. "Yet team dynamics play a crucial role in the effectiveness and efficiency of team. Now, throw potential personal conflicts based on differing ideologies and levels of comfort with sexual themes into a team situation, and you have an added challenge to developing cohesive dynamics and a hot spot for team friction" [Currie01].

Employee Concerns

As soon as a company considers working on a game with sexual content, management should meet privately with individual employees to listen to them and to address their concerns. Employee concerns are particularly important in existing or smaller companies that are entering the sexual content space for the first time. Employees may suddenly find themselves working for a company that—given what they know now—they would have not previously considered.

Failure to address employee concerns can lead to low morale, employee loss, or even lawsuits. It's important that companies set aside time for each employee to make him or her feel comfortable working on a project or to accommodate them as much as possible, if possible.

Offer an Out

Some employees may not wish to be involved in a game with sexual content. The degree to which they wish to be removed from the project may vary, however. Employees should be offered the following options, if possible:

Credit list exclusion: Employees should be allowed to remain off the game's credits, if applicable. As a courtesy, however, employees should be polled again toward the end of development in case they've changed their minds (some employees who wanted to appear on the credits may no longer want to). Notify employees that you will be polling them a second time when you first poll them, however. Otherwise, it could be misinterpreted as a pressuring tactic. Offering such an option early on, while not necessary from a development point of view, nonetheless signals that a company is receptive to its employees' concerns.

Sexual content exclusion: Identify areas of the game that are entirely devoid of sexual content and offer these tasks to employees who prefer to work on sex-free content. Artists could build object models, create items, develop interface elements, or work on nonsexual animations. Programmers could develop any number of systems, from basic save/load functionality to pathing. Care should be taken not to expose such employees to sexual content inadvertently. For instance, a programmer who is assigned the work on the rewards screen could be exposed to a porn video when he tests the unlock functionality.

Team room exclusion: If the company is large enough to allow for such measures, employees with content concerns can be located away from the offending content. Since development is often an exceptionally vocal process, particularly in a "bull pen" setup where many employees are in a single room, moving such employees out of the room entirely is the best option. If such a measure is not possible, team members should be asked to be respectful of their fellow employees' concerns or to hold conversations about sexual material outside the main room.

Project exclusion: Employees who prefer to avoid work on a project with sexual content should be offered an alternate project, if possible.

Losing Employees

If a developer is unable to accommodate employees with sufficient work of a non-sexual nature and the employee refuses to work on content that is objectionable to him or her, parting ways may be the only option. Some employees may also leave the company on principle, regardless of any exclusionary measures offered.

When taking on projects of a sexual nature, particularly in existing companies with no previous history of such content, employers should gauge the possible effects it could have on employee turnover.

Addressing Harassment

Sexual harassment is a concern to all employers, but it is especially tricky for those who are making games with sexual content. When companies enter the sexual content space, they must immediately review, revise, and, if necessary, create a sexual harassment policy. Management should also review the policy with employees.

The United States Equal Employment Opportunity Commission identifies sexual harassment as: "Unwelcome sexual advances, requests for sexual favors, and other verbal or physical conduct of a sexual nature constitute sexual harassment when (1) submission to such conduct is made either explicitly or implicitly a term or condition of an individual's employment, (2) submission to or rejection of such conduct by an individual is used as the basis for employment decisions affecting such individual, or (3) such conduct has the purpose or effect of unreasonably interfering with an individual's work performance or creating an intimidating, hostile, or offensive working environment" [USEEOC01].

Sexual harassment is a major issue, and one beyond the scope of this book. All companies entering the sexual content space should contact a lawyer, review sexual harassment laws, and have systems in place to address employee concerns and complaints.

Clarinda Merripen, former Director of Operations at Cyberlore Studios, on Sexual Harassment.

In a purely legal sense, if the focus of your work incorporates sexual content, and, in the course of that work, you do research on sexual images or conversations or sounds, you're pretty much in the clear. However, it's a lot better if you begin your business with the expectation of sexual content rather than move a business and your employees from mundane to explicit content. The latter case is clearly the trickiest. You should read (and reread) your handbook and any employment contracts your employees signed to make sure you're in the clear. In fact, I would look at all your policies in conjunction with your employees to figure out the best way to bring the HR policies in line with the material.

By the way, forget free speech as it applies to an individual employee in the office. You don't "have the right" to post whatever you want, wherever you want it, in the office. Again, legally, an employer can dictate what goes up on the walls in a cubicle or by a desk as long as that policy applies universally.

Sexual harassment is about power, not sex. For sexual harassment to occur, legally, there needs to be some adverse effect: glass ceiling, skipped promotions, ostracizing, or some ill effect on the employee. The last two are social and are the hardest to prove, and yet they are the most often cited.

It's a disturbing fact that bullies often use the claim of harassment to further threaten their victims. Studies show about 1/3 of the time, the person who is doing the harassing brings claims to management.

> The whole reason to avoid even the appearance of harassment is to make sure that everyone is the most productive they can be so that the most work can get done. Framing issues in that light moves the issue from a "legal" framework back to a 'management' issue, making it far easier to deal with. [Merripen02]
>
> **Post on the IDGA's Sex Special Interest Group mailing list.** © Clarinda Merripen. Reprinted with permission.

Hiring

When adding new employees of any type, it is important to address the nature of the company's business or product as early in the interview process as possible, even if the product is still confidential.

Ask prospective employees if they are comfortable working on adult content, and explain the degree of sexual content involved. Some employees might be fine with nudity, but would draw the line at graphic sex.

Extend these measures to all employees, including interns, clerical staff, and support personnel. Although such employees are not directly connected to the development of sexual content, and in fact may be entirely isolated from it, they may nonetheless have issues working for a company that produces M- or AO-rated adult content. By bringing these matters to the table early in the interview process, time and money will be saved.

Keep It Contained

While working on *Playboy: The Mansion*, it was common to find magazines or *Playboy* reference books at the desks of artists and designers. Designers used the magazines to glean information for the game's missions, and artists used the magazines to develop clothing, models, and objects found within the game. When the necessary reference work was complete, the magazine or book was returned to its storage location behind the lead designer's or the lead artist's desk. Only the covers of a few magazines were visible, and no nudity was present on the covers. As the project's expansion pack entered development, the magazines were eventually moved into a large filing cabinet to secure them entirely. As an extra precaution, Cyberlore's team room for the *Playboy: The Mansion* project was entirely segregated from the rest of the company, and only those working on the project need ever enter the room.

When working on sexual content, and particularly when using actual models or pornographic material as reference, all sexual reference material should be contained when it is not in use. Furthermore, posters, calendars, or other material that may be objectionable to some employees should not be displayed in any public areas.

Development conversations should also respectfully be contained to "safe areas." If employees are talking about a motion capture session, and the conversation turns graphic, other employees could hear things they'd rather not hear. When talking about such things every day, the internal cues that normally give people a degree of discretion are simply not what they once were. Employees may need regular reminders to be considerate of others on the team and off the team who prefer not to be involved with adult content.

Create Structure

Develop a structure for development meetings beforehand, particularly those that involve larger groups. Meetings should have a moderator, or meeting leader, to keep things on track and to regularly reinforce the professional nature of the discussion. The project leads (programmer, designer, artist, and producer) also have a role to play in maintaining the tone and structure of the meetings.

"It's easy for it to turn into a frat party," said one designer speaking on the condition of anonymity. "We had one meeting where we were discussing the ways in which people in the game could have sex. It just got out of hand, and some people were clearly uncomfortable" [Anon03].

Developers need to guard against assumption in such situations as well. Some people assume that it's safe to discuss anything when they are in all-male or all-female company. Others assume that it's par for the course in sexual content development. They believe those on the team need to get used to the frank discussions or get off the team.

Of course, such assumptions are wrong, and dangerous. People have varying degrees of comfort in discussing sexual situations, and those who are least comfortable are least likely to speak up. By creating and maintaining structure within a development meeting, meetings can stick to the business at hand in a professional way, making the meeting acceptable to everyone and preventing the development of a frat-like atmosphere.

What if that frat-like atmosphere is critical to the creative process? Some development teams need to have such discussions to make their product the best it can be, particularly those who are trying to re-create the often funny synergy that happens when groups of people talk about sex. In such cases, everyone on the development team should know that "anything goes," so to speak, and be given the opportunity, if possible, to be transferred to another team or at least avoid the "anything goes" meetings. If such an option is not available, the employee may choose to leave the company.

Develop a Language

Before work begins on a project, take time to develop a language for discussion. Words that describe sexual actions or body parts are loaded with meaning and connotation. Without establishing a language, developers risk offending members of the team or others exposed to the team's documentation, including publishers.

Body parts: Refer to body parts by their anatomically correct name or use the industry generic term, "naughty bits." Use of slang terms—even terms that are perceived to be in regular use—run the risk of offending someone.

Sexual actions: Refer to sexual actions in a descriptive way. For instance, instead of using a slang term to describe a sexual encounter between two characters in a game, use descriptive text like "female to male oral sex" or "female on female prone sex."

Language in games extends beyond conversations. Design documentation, meeting notes, emails, and filenames should also follow a safe language convention.

Sometimes, offensive words are part of a game's dialogue, however. Such dialogue is, of course, perfectly acceptable within the context of an appropriately rated game. However, team members should not be exposed to it if they've expressed any concerns.

Frame Discussions

Among developers, it is common to speak in the first person when giving examples and exploring possible design decisions. "If I swing my sword at you, and succeed in hitting you," a developer might say, "then you'll react to the hit, take some damage, and lose hit points."

Although such conversations are virtually harmless, they take on a new, awkward, and possibly litigious meaning when the design decisions are for a sexually themed game. Consider the same example reframed for a sexually themed game. "If I try to have sex with you and succeed, then you'll open your legs, I'll get on top, and we'll both have an orgasm." Silly as such an example may seem, such a conversation could easily cause someone to feel uncomfortable.

"While working on [a sexually themed game], our development discussions were always crazy awkward. We'd be talking about the things that you could do in the game, and inevitably, our focus would be on the literal meaning of our words instead of on the example we were trying to convey," said a developer. "We're just used to talking about things you can do and substituting ourselves for the characters in the game. Eventually, we figured out a language to use, but it was awkward for a while" [Anon04].

Developers should be cautious to always frame discussions around the game's characters, actions, or mechanics. "If Character A tries to have sex with Character B, and Character B refuses, then they won't have sex." While this sounds obvious, overcoming years of habit can often be challenging. Reinforcing such standards regularly is a good practice. Some developers have substituted generic names such as "Cindy" and "Bob" for "Character A" and "Character B" in order to make the conversation more palatable.

Encourage Diversity

A diversified development team is important to all games, including those with sexual themes. For example, just because you're making a game that targets the adult male demographic, it's wrong to assume that a development team of all straight guys will deliver exactly what you're looking for. The more diverse the team, the better input they will provide.

In *Playboy: The Mansion*, for instance, characters can have sex on the couch. When two characters hit it off, the man walks ahead of the woman, and they then sit down together. To one female on the team, this didn't feel right. She checked her feelings with another a female on the team who agreed with her assessment. According to the team member, it was preferable to have the woman walk ahead of the man or to have the two walk hand in hand. Such distinctions are not trivial, even in a game like *Playboy: The Mansion*. According to Playboy Enterprises, Inc., 18% of *Playboy* magazine's readers are female [Playboy01]. In addition, the ESA's report "2005 Essential Facts About the Computer and Video Games Industry: Sales, Demographics and Usage Data" notes that 43% of game players are female [ESA01]. The men on *Playboy: The Mansion*'s development team were indifferent to the animation's order. Man or woman, it didn't matter who went first. By reversing the order, they stood to please both women and men. Without women on the development team, such an issue may have been overlooked.

According to Jeb Havens, a former designer at Cyberlore Studios, Inc. and the *Playboy: The Mansion* game and an active participant in the IGDA's diversity forums, the case for diversity among game developers is a strong one. "The first step to making sure that a group of individuals comes to the best solution to any problem is to make sure that the group is as diverse as possible. Although each member of the group must have some knowledge, diversity on its own often trumps expertise. With more diversity in decision making, any errors in judgment tend to cancel each other out rather than get compounded."

Havens points out that some developers don't encourage or actively seek out diversity, however. "Many development studios can be very resistant to diversity, since much of the bond and drive of their straight white male employees is dependent on the solidarity found in any 'boy's club' culture. Uniformity can help a team get things done that it already knows how to do, but diversity will help it innovate, make informed decisions, and change course when necessary."

Diversity means more than having just men and women on your staff, however. Havens believes that gay, lesbian, bisexual, and transgender employees can lend a unique and valuable perspective. "GLBT developers can add a great deal to any team by bringing along a culture that praises creativity and diversity and [offers] a unique perspective on many important issues," says Havens. "For example, more than any other group, GLBT people are confronted with issues of identity, especially its variability. Gender and sexuality roles are often the strongest and most well-defined identities in any culture. It's difficult to end up as an out-to-yourself GLBT individual without having confronted and seriously questioned the concept of a fixed identity. Increasingly, games are starting to realize the power of allowing players to explore issues of identity, and a large number of players (both gay and nongay) are drawn to the idea of trying out different identities. This can mean anything from switching the outfit on your snowboarder to playing an MMORPG with an avatar of the other gender" [Havens01].

The key success of a diversified team is, of course, its ability to mimic your potential market to provide a range of ideas that a narrow group would otherwise struggle to provide.

Public Speaking & Displays

Developers are frequently called upon to speak about their games at educational institutions or industry gatherings such as the local IGDA chapter meeting. When speaking in public, refrain from showing nudity or any clothed sexual contact unless all attendees will be aware of such content before the presentation begins. For adult content, attendees must be the age of majority.

Although it may be a safe assumption—or even an assurance—that all attendees will be adults, their acceptance of sexual matters cannot be guaranteed and could, in fact, cause great difficulty for the speaker and the institution where the discussion is taking place.

When speaking at universities about sexual content in video games, this author used screenshots edited with black bars to cover the breasts and pubic area, and in talking about the game, sexual actions were never referred to. When questions were asked about the sexual content in the game, if they required a descriptive and possibly offensive answer, they were deferred for individual discussion later. When speaking at the Women's Game Conference on sexual content in video games, the talk was advertised as "adults only" and made mention of the graphic nature of the content in the advertising of the conference. A disclaimer was also presented at the beginning of the lecture warning people about the graphic nature of the content.

Development Concerns in Online Games

While many of today's adult games use a player-to-computer stimulation model, MMORPGs involve an emergent player-to-player stimulation model. This level of interaction requires employers to put additional standards in place, particularly if the game is a Massively Multiplayer Online Erotic Game (MMOEG).

When acting on behalf of the company, or while on company time, property, or equipment, employees should never interact with the game or its players in any way that could be deemed sexual gameplay unless their job specifically requires them to do so. For instance, a helper in an online game may be asked to assist a player in understanding a particular component of gameplay. To do so, he or she might be required to execute several sexually themed commands or animations. However, if there is another way to show the player how to do the same thing without sexual content, that method should be employed first. The employee need not be a cold fish, of course. He or she can be friendly, kind, and courteous, provide the player the necessary information, and rebuff any possible player advances with subtle, kind language without detracting from the player's overall experience or removing him or her from the fiction of the game. The key is to be professional.

Sometimes, helpers in online games are there to show the player all the game can do or to provide interaction for paying members. It is important to work with the employee beforehand to establish any boundaries he or she may have in such a world, and to provide tools for protecting those limits. For instance, if a helper in an online world is asked to do something he personally feels uncomfortable about, he should have the necessary language, freedom, and knowledge to assess and adjust the situation to his liking.

Before beginning work, employee and employer should discuss:

Scope of sexual content: No one likes to be surprised by something that's uncomfortable, unfamiliar, or objectionable. Employees should be aware of the full range of sexual content ahead of time, particularly emergent sexual content.

Scope of player behavior: What's not acceptable player behavior? The employee should know the corporate line ahead of time and be provided with a range of responses to handle any issues that may arise.

Range of response: To please both customer and employee, responses to various situations should be provided by management to the employee before work begins. Such questions as, "What do I do if I encounter player harassment?" are best role-played ahead of time. The more employees are empowered and familiar with the corporate range of response, the more comfortable they'll be in doing their job.

Regardless of the game's theme, it is the responsibility of the employer to make all game players aware of rules concerning interaction with the company's employees and players online. By providing players guidelines to follow, issues will be fewer, and if they do arise, the company will have something to refer to the player should disciplinary measures be necessary.

Player-based issues and concerns such as harassment within MMORPGs are covered in Chapter 3.

GET A LAWYER

For companies considering sexual content development or those already working in the field, securing a qualified lawyer who understands First Amendment issues, censorship, and the unique legal challenges that adult content brings is critical.

In a speech at the 2006 Sex in Video Games Conference, lawyer Lawrence G. Walters, Esq., discussed the need for developers to retain an attorney, particularly as they enter the video game space. As a lawyer with the firm of Weston, Garrou, DeWitt & Walters (*www.GameAttorneys.com* and *www.FirstAmendment.com*), Walters specializes in censorship and free speech issues, has developed a reputation for taking on controversial topics, and has worked on many important cases, including seven before the U.S. Supreme Court. In the course of that work, Walters has naturally handled obscenity cases for clients ranging from Web sites to porn producers and performers.

Lawrence G. Walters, Esq., Weston, Garrou, DeWitt & Walters on why adult content developers need specialized legal council.

Why do developers of sexual content in video games need to work with First Amendment specialty lawyers? Initially, it is important to note that sexual expression is squarely in the sights of the "family values" groups and "morals voters" who helped put President George W. Bush in office in 2004. The conservative Congress has sought to appease these extremists ever since, with promises to crack down on sexually explicit media, in the name of protecting children. Thus, we have seen a wave of censorial legislation, at the state and federal levels, directed at all forms of erotic media, including video games. Many of these legislative proposals are unconstitutional, but they are considered, debated, and often passed into law nonetheless. It is then up to the various industry groups to challenge these laws, and hope that the courts do the right thing when confronted with unconstitutional legislation.

While the video games industry has enjoyed a string of Free Speech victories in the courts, which have unanimously struck down attempts to restrict the sale of violent video games, as a means of reducing adolescent aggression, the constitutional protection of sexually oriented speech is nowhere near 100%. In 1973, the United States Supreme Court decided the case of *Miller v. California,* which created the "Miller Test" for obscenity. This test separates criminal contraband from protected speech. If a particular book, magazine, film, or video game is determined to be "obscene," it is treated as illegal material, just like drugs or automatic weapons. Severe criminal penalties apply to the production, sale, or distribution of such material. Everyone along the chain of distribution can be charged, from the small time developer, to the nationwide distributor or retail outlet.

Some of what would ordinarily be considered logical defenses to obscenity charges do not exist. For example, you will not get far in defending an obscenity case with the argument that you did not know the material would be considered obscene. All the prosecution needs to prove is that you were aware of the general nature and character of the materials, not that you knew they may, or would be, found obscene. In other words, unlike many other criminal charges, the government does not need to prove that you possessed specific criminal intent to violate the obscenity laws. Claiming that you are unaware of the local community standards applicable to the materials at issue will also not operate as a defense, even if you are prosecuted in a community where you never set foot, or never intended your product to be distributed. The more money you make from the allegedly obscene material, the more time you'll spend in prison, given the way that sentencing often works in these cases.

There are infinite nuances in the law applicable to sexually oriented media that are beyond the ken of the average game developer or distributor. Many of these concepts are counter-intuitive and illogical. An experienced First Amendment attorney can help educate developers as to their rights and liabilities in creating content that comes with some risk.

Few lawyers practice in this field. Those who do are generally precluded from handling other types of work, once they get a reputation for representing adult clients. Our firm has, for example, specialized in representing the adult industry for over forty (40) years. Given the length of our involvement, we are in a position to understand and advise on historical prosecution trends and other matters, using a broad perspective. Many lawyers will jump at the chance to represent adult industry clients, even if it is outside their normal practice area, given the perceived "fun" factor associated with such representation. However, game developers should be wary of hiring inexperienced lawyers, or those who desire to learn the industry at their first client's expense. This type of legal work is not for the faint of heart, and you do not want to end up working with an attorney who decides that the heat in the kitchen is too much to handle—in the middle of your case.

We regularly deal with insults and threats from "militant" Christians and other conservative values groups, who view our defense of the First Amendment as immoral. We have become tremendously thick-skinned over the years, but such treatment may scare off novice practitioners. In sum, working with the right, experienced attorney in the field is critical to the success and protection of the sexually explicit video game developer. [Walters01]

INTERVIEW WITH KELLY RUED, BLACK LOVE INTERACTIVE

When working with a sexually themed product, what office standards do you have in place to keep things professional?

We have an open-door policy so that anyone at any level in the team understands they can approach a team lead or owner with concerns or complaints. We are all adults, and there is no reason for anyone to feel they are working in uncomfortable or demeaning conditions. Black Love Interactive only makes adult entertainment software, so there is no issue here with people coming on the team and not understanding what kind of work and dialogue is expected of them. We have not yet had a problem with offending team members, because I believe we communicate effectively the culture and sex-positive attitude of our company to every applicant even before they join our team. We include a "good sex-positive attitude" and "comfort with sexual content" as a list-item in our job ads, job descriptions, work evaluations, and minimum qualifications for every position on the team.

Have you developed a "language" structure when referring to specific things?

No. Due to the nature of the products we provide, we feel it's crucial that our developers are not squeamish about sex terminology, especially slang and off-color language. In creating sex entertainment, you will have a wide variety of interests and tastes to provide content for different markets (unless you deal with a very narrowly defined audience). Classy language is as important to our product's success and authenticity as racy, even crass, language. Because the language is in the context of the game development, there is no question about its appropriateness for the workplace. If, however, we had someone who took this kind of language and applied it interpersonally in an inappropriate and non-game-related context, we would deal with that as any other professional organization would through investigation, mediation, and, if necessary, disciplinary action. The sex-game content is not an excuse to be lewd or abusive to fellow developers, but luckily, we have a great team of good-humored people who know where these professional boundaries lie.

Did you have any problems with middleware vendors?

Not personally, because we've been able to find like-minded vendors who were interested in supporting our product or were indifferent to the sexual content. However, I have had casual encounters at industry after-parties and the like with other vendors where the owners or sales representatives were quite rude about the issue, even when we were not even considering their products. The "anti-sex-game" sentiment was basically expressed the moment we introduced ourselves. This is a very rare reaction, though, and there are more than enough middleware vendors around for adult games to choose from.

What unique issues do you face when working on sexually themed content?

I think there are numerous issues that only come up with sex content, and others that are shared problems for many game developers and publishers. A lack of respect for games as a medium and as an art form is a major issue for everyone, but it is particularly hard to resolve when you introduce erotic content. Eliciting arousal from your audience is typically a sign of successful communication in media or the arts (getting someone excited, motivated, and engaged or moved to action is usually an indicator of great accomplishment). For erotic works, the arousal is what people cite as the failure of the work. It's what discredits and stigmatizes the work. There is no easy solution to this cultural bias. However, if people strive to make intelligent, provocative, erotic works in interactive entertainment, over time, we will see a positive change in attitude. The false dichotomy between legitimate expression in media and erotic expression in media will become a quaint, archaic notion as culture adopts increasingly progressive and sex-positive views toward erotic experiences.

Have you or your company faced any discrimination due to your work on sexually themed games?

We've yet to face any significant, crippling discrimination like being denied access to suitable tools, not finding developers, or being shunned in development communities. However, when shipping AO product, one has to deal with the very real aftermath of "shock-and-awe" media stories and ridiculous characters all crusading against imaginary monsters so they can fancy themselves public heroes. There may be discrimination and misunderstandings, but we will not be intimidated by detractors. We're confident that we're doing good work and developing socially responsible, sex-positive entertainment experiences that adults can feel good about sharing.

From a corporate standpoint, what is the best and worst part of working on a sexually themed game?

For us, the best part of working on a sexually themed game is the enthusiasm we all share. This is an indie project financed cooperatively from our own resources, dedication, and passion. I created the original Rapture Online game design as a game that I would like to play, and one that could have a positive social impact and help combat sex-negativity in U.S. culture. It's seriously a labor of love (or lust maybe!) for all of us at Black Love Interactive.

The worst part of working on a sexually themed game is having to advocate constantly, to explain, and to defend the artistic and social merits of our work. We don't waste too much time trying to convert the naysayers, because I think the finished game and our continued support and innovation of the sex in games space will, in the end, vindicate our position, philosophy, and contributions to the game and adult entertainment industries. We are equally committed to serious games and to applying our work to therapy, research, and education in health and human sexuality. So, there are several ways we will achieve our mission in spite of some shortsighted critics we've endured so far. If we can help even a small group of people enjoy, explore, and expand their erotic and romantic experiences, then I'll consider any obstacles we've faced 100% worth the hassle. [Rued01]

REFERENCES

[Anon01] Anonymous, interview with Brenda Brathwaite, May 20, 2005.

[Anon02] Anonymous, interview with Brenda Brathwaite, May 10, 2005.

[Anon03] Anonymous, interview with Brenda Brathwaite, May 15, 2005.

[Anon04] Anonymous, interview with Brenda Brathwaite, May 14, 2005.

[Currie01] Currie, Linda, interview with Brenda Brathwaite, November 7, 2005.

[ESA01] "2005 Essential Facts About the Computer and Video Game Industry: Sales, Demographics and Usage Data," The Entertainment Software Association. Available online at *www.theesa.com/files/2005EssentialFacts.pdf]*. Accessed August 11, 2005.

[Havens01] Havens, Jeb, interview with Brenda Brathwaite, June 13, 2005.

[Merripen01] Merripen, Clarinda, interview with Brenda Brathwaite, June 13, 2005.

[Merripen02] Merripen, Clarinda, post on IGDA's Sexuality SIG mailing list, June 14, 2005.

[Playboy01] "Playboy Enterprises FAQ," Playboy Enterprises, Inc., Available online at *www.playboyenterprises.com/home/content.cfm?content=t_template&packet= 00017B97-9135-1C72-8FEA8304E50A010D&CFID=6803453& CFTOKEN=97443826.* Accessed August 11, 2005.

[Rued01] Rued, Kelly, interview with Brenda Brathwaite, November 8, 2005.

[Spaulding01] Spaulding, Seth, interview with Brenda Brathwaite, June 15, 2005.

[USEEOC01] *Code of Federal Regulations*, Guidelines on Discrimination Because of Sex, Title 29, Volume 4, Chapter XIV, Section Sec. 1604.11. United States Government Printing Office. Available online at *http://frwebgate.access.gpo.gov/ cgi-bin/get-cfr.cgi?TITLE=29&PART=1604&SECTION=11&YEAR=2001& TYPE=TEXT*. Accessed August 11, 2005.

[Walters01] Walters, Lawrence G., Esq., email to Brenda Brathwaite, June 16, 2006.

13 Sex Across Cultures

In This Chapter

- Sex Across Cultures
- Interview with Richard Cobbett, UK
- Interview with Anando Banerjee, India
- Interview with Peter Payne, Japan
- Interview with Guido Henkel, Germany
- Interview with "Jonathan," China
- Interview with Anonymous Female, India
- Interview with Matthew Ford, Australia

SEX ACROSS CULTURES

Different cultures. Different countries. Different attitudes toward sex. As Janet Jackson's wardrobe malfunction was making news in America, it was likewise making news in other countries where people asked themselves, "What are those Americans so bothered about?" Sexual attitudes are a means by which cultures compare and measure themselves against others. While some look at America as a bastion of liberalism, others see it as puritanical.

But how do those countries view sexual content in games? A single book could easily be written about each country's attitude toward sexual content in media and its consumption and regulation. Through interviews with gamers, game developers, and game journalists, the sexual attitudes in several countries were explored. Interviewees were asked the same questions so answers could be compared, but the interviews are published in one piece for ease of reading and continuity. Naturally, the opinions of one person are not necessarily reflective of everyone and the country from which he or she hails, nor are any of the interviewees experts in sexual content. Rather, their opinions are designed to give readers a broad view of the collective culture as these individuals see it.

261

What of the missing countries? If every country were represented, this book would easily be 500 pages longer. Instead, represented are those countries that have the largest game-playing populations as ranked by worldwide sales. India is also included. Much video game development is starting to spring up in that country, and therefore, its inclusion is relevant.

INTERVIEW WITH RICHARD COBBETT, UK

Richard Cobbett is an English-born-and-bred professional games journalist.

Overall, where would you place your country on a scale of 1-10, ten being the most liberal sexually?

Seven. It's a rather bizarre mix of good humour, prudishness, gossip, privacy, and fun—keeping the bedroom to the bedroom, but with a sense of perspective, and the ability to laugh. Not to mention that it's a country where mental images of judges in frilly stockings, and politicians in nappies are as established elements of satire as anything else in a comedian's notebook. That said, anyone "doing it" in doorways tends to get looked down on. There's a heavy moral majority willing to pounce on anything they determine "sick filth," and there's a reason why a million jokes start with the words "Why do Essex girls . . ."

Is your country less or more conservative than the U.S.?

[We have] quite a few of the same rules, in theory, but less strictly applied. Where the whole U.S. shut down over that infamous nipple-slip, we have whole TV out-takes programs. [We have] much less of a religious edge to morality, coupled with an understanding that you can get away with almost anything if you can make someone laugh.

Where can you buy sex magazines in your country?

It depends what you mean—and whether nudity/erotica is counted as part of the group. Magazines like *Playboy* or *Penthouse* are likely to be found in most major magazine outlets, along with "lads' mags" such as *Front, Maxim, FHM*, and the like. They may also carry other sex-related titles, such as magazines aimed at the gay community, although not usually pornography. Newsagents, typically corner stores, will often carry more hard-core content. In general, these are known as "top-shelf" magazines—often bagged up or placed as high as possible so that kids can't get to them. Motorway service stations and similar locations tend to land somewhere in the middle of the two.

Overall, how would you sum up your country's attitude about nudity? For instance, how would people react to a woman sunbathing nude?

On a British beach, they'd be hard-pushed to notice through all the goose pimples! England is typically a "keep your clothes on" country, although the reaction is likely to be tutting and politely waiting for the lifeguard to turn up with a towel, or gawking, rather than actually making a scene. Of course, it depends a lot on the situation—a pub or nightclub is a very different place to a family beach.

However, in a wider context, while you don't see people stripping off in the streets for a quick frolic, nudity has a firm place in modern culture, and often where you wouldn't expect—for instance, Lady Godiva's infamous ride is often reenacted in processions (albeit with the woman playing her usually wearing "fleshings" rather than actually riding naked through Coventry), or the nude calendar done by the Rylstone and District Women's Institute—better known as the inspiration for the movie *Calendar Girls*. And, of course, on the other side of the gender gap, *The Full Monty*, a comedy about steel-workers turned male strippers, was a smash-success with men and women alike.

Is nudity automatically associated with sex, or is it no big deal?

Often, but not exclusively. Artwork is the obvious exception, but comedy undoubtedly the most popular. A lot of British humour is based on embarrassment—toe-curling characters like Basil Fawlty or David Brent, or mortifying situations like Bridget Jones finally hooking up with her dashing boss, only to remember too late that she's wearing grandmothers' underpants.

Nudity is no different—either a main character getting a touch too exposed, or in an equally difficult situation, such as walking in on someone in the shower, or finding themselves trying to desperately make light conversation in a room of nudists. There's no shortage of those, from the old *Carry On* films to Mr. Bean, Father Ted, Coupling, Jonathan Creek . . . sometimes with an attractive person, often not, but almost always as comedy first, eye-candy second. Men are most likely to be the stooge in such scenes, one way or the other.

Are there any cultural contradictions regarding sex?

The country does tend to be fairly conservative, no doubt helped by the Victorians and their love of shame, misery, and knocking the genitals off statues with hammers, but there are a few bizarre exceptions to the restrained rule. One very obvious one is "Page 3 girls"—topless models in daily tabloid newspapers sold to the mass market, notably *The Sun*. These have even made it into computer game form—*The Daily Sport Football Strip*, which mixed nude photos with sporting trivia questions.

And of course, your usual contradictions of disapproving comments and tutters from people who drink in every last story and piece of gossip. I think that's pretty much universal, though.

How much sexual content/nudity is found in advertising in your country?

Actual nudity, very little. Bath-time products (shower gel, shampoo, etc.) often feature concealed semi-nudity—bare backs in the shower, concealed profile shots and so on, but nothing very revealing. A handful of adverts push this a bit further, but not by much. You do get a few male bottoms, although very rarely, and almost invariably in comic rather than sexual contexts.

How much sexual content/nudity is found on television in your country?

TV is basically split into two forms—terrestrial (five channels) and satellite (loads). Terrestrial TV is the most common, and apart from a few films late at night, is usually pretty tame—there may be programs with this content (either homegrown or imported) but very little outright pornography. Satellite has dedicated adult channels, as well as regular channels that show porn as part of their regular programming—the Sci-Fi channel, for instance, often devotes its midnight slot to a series of films it dubs *The Sex Files*.

A lot of programs are imported from the U.S., so whatever you see in *The Sopranos* over there, we see over here, usually unedited. One key difference is that nudity/sexual content in UK-based programs tends to be more casual—a couple in bed, a joke, or similar, and typically with average looking people, rather than long, loving camera pans over topless models brought in specially for the occasion. As a general rule, you won't find much of either before 9 P.M. on terrestrial, and 8 P.M on satellite—a point known as "the watershed."

Of late, there have been a few other types of programs—reality shows like *Big Brother* getting progressively raunchier, along with extreme makeover programs and advice shows with names like "The Sex Inspectors," again, usually late at night.

How is sexual content in video games treated in your country?

It's barely noticed, to be honest. Games like *Playboy: The Mansion*, *Private Dancer*, *Singles*, and the other sexually themed games that occasionally appear are filed on the shelf according to their name (and this has historically been the case, with games like *Voyeur*, *Phantasmagoria 2*, and *Tender Loving Care* receiving no special treatment—although a cynic might point out that there aren't really enough commercial games with such themes to make it worth sectioning them off.

The rating system in the UK has a lot to do with this. Unlike the USA, there's one organization that rates everything from movies to games—the British Board of Film Classification (BBFC). This is an independent organization, but the statutory authority for content in the UK—and unlike voluntary rating systems, like PEGI (Pan European Game Information), the restrictions that it assigns are legally binding. Any store selling, for instance, *Leisure Suit Larry: Magna Cum Laude* (rated 18) to anyone under that age can face all sorts of legal trouble.

As part of this, however, games are treated much like films, whether it's a full-scale sex scene like *Fahrenheit* (*Indigo Prophecy*), or just a revealing costume. There's no confusion between ratings like T, M, and AO on the shelves—just a straight 15 or 18, and that's if the game even needs to be rated at all. Only games with realistic or semi-realistic depictions of sex and violence, or the likelihood of encouraging it in the players, have to have ratings. Duke Nukem blowing away hordes of aliens counts; Mario knocking Bowser into a river of lava doesn't—even if he does get a kiss from the Princess afterwards.

Still, most games stick rigidly to what the developers can get away with in America. Very few games serve up a more adventurous Europe-only release, with only the sex scenes in *Fahrenheit* and the uncut *Leisure Suit Larry: Magna Cum Laude* springing to mind in recent years. The rest, such as *7 Sins*, may sport an 18 rating for context ("moderate sex and sexual voyeurism"), but the cast still comes with bras and underpants welded tight to their 3D torsos. In a similar vein, when Planet Moon found itself unable to get away with selling a half-naked siren/mermaid character in its action game *Giants*, it wasn't long before the first patch rushed an emergency bikini top across the ocean.

As an interesting aside, during the "Hot Coffee" scandal, with the whole world up in arms about the horrors of consensual sex in a game about murder, theft, drugs, destruction, prostitution, and every other sin under the sun, the BBFC's response was a shrug of "So? We already said it was only for adults," paraphrased, of course.

If your country has an "issue" with video games, something that tends to get press or is worrisome to people, what would it be?

The best phrase is probably "social damage." Games like *Carmageddon* and *Grand Theft Auto* take the brunt of it for glorifying being bad—although it tends to take a real-world event to push a game into the spotlight. *Carmageddon* is a particularly good example of a game that almost got banned in the UK, with arguments at the highest levels of politics, and a compromise release that switched the red blood for green goo (at least for the five seconds it took for everyone to patch it back in).

England in particular has tended to be somewhat bizarre in terms of what it considers a problem—not to mention, the solution. For instance, during the 1990s, ninja-themed weapons were considered to set a horrible example for children. As a result, we had the Teenage Mutant Hero Turtles, and 3D Realms' *Shadow Warrior* had to switch its shuriken weapon for darts, because apparently it's okay to get hit in the face with a dart, and they're much harder to come by than intricate metal death stars.

The most recent case involved Rockstar's *Manhunt*, blamed for the death of a 14-year-old in Leicester, dubbed "a manual for murder" by the victim's father and promptly pulled off shelves all over the country, despite the police not making any connection between the game and the killing, its 18 rating (neither the victim nor the killer should have been able to buy it in the first place), and the slight quibble that the killer didn't actually own a copy. Still, no matter.

Beyond that type of story, the biggest quarrels usually center on gaming itself—how much time players dedicate to their adventures, how it impacts schoolwork, and similar concerns. Specific games rarely get that much attention unless they're too big to ignore—a couple of the MMORPGs, for instance. [Cobbett]

INTERVIEW WITH ANANDO BANERJEE, INDIA

Anando has lived all his life in New Delhi, India, and is a project manager for a software company.

Overall, where would you place your country on a scale of 1 to 10 sexually, 10 being the most liberal?

There's a fair bit of an urban/ rural divide on this one. Urban would be a five, while rural would probably be a three. People's attitudes toward sex are pretty conservative. Public display of affection/intimacy is considered scandalous. In the big cities, though, this is changing. Consumption of pornographic material is considered downright depraved!

Is your country less or more conservative than the US?

More. Definitely!

Where can you buy sex magazines in your country?

There are only a couple of sex magazines that are probably published in India. The content of these magazines is usually quite "tame" compared to that of similar magazines published in the U.S. or Europe. These publications are usually available at select magazine stores. Laws may exist regarding the sale of such material, but such laws are hardly every enforced.

Importantly, though, there is social stigma associated with the purchase and consumption of pornographic material, and most sales of such material is done surreptitiously. Hence, seldom are such magazines put on public display at a newsstand.

Overall, how would you sum up your country's attitude about nudity? For instance, how would people react to a woman sunbathing nude?

Extremely conservative. A woman sunbathing topless would probably be arrested. And until the cops arrive, teeming multitudes would gather to get a glimpse. If she is unescorted, she may face some amount of harassment as well.

Models have, in the past, found themselves in a fair bit of hot water for posing nude or semi-nude in advertisements.

Is nudity automatically associated with sex, or is it no big deal?

Yes, nudity is automatically associated with sex.

Are there any cultural contradictions regarding sex?

Yes there are. However, this wasn't always so. Once, long ago, the Kamasutra and erotic carvings on temple walls were a part of people's everyday lives. Sex wasn't such a dirty word then, but then came 700 years of rule by kings who imposed their own puritan value system and attitudes. All traces of liberalism toward sex were stamped out.

How much sexual content/nudity is found in advertising in your country?

There is a little nudity in advertising, but none of it explicit. That is, a nude woman in an ad will probably face away from the camera, or have her body obscured in some other manner. Such advertisements often face the wrath of conservative religious organizations, or militant women's organizations.

How much sexual content/nudity is found on television in your country?

Television programs usually have little sexual content or nudity. Music videos can sometimes be raunchy. Sexual content on television is more suggestive than explicit. There is strict government regulation for the broadcast media, and private TV channels (there are probably close to 100 of them) have run into trouble for beaming content that the government deemed "pornographic." A French fashion channel got into a fair amount of trouble (with the government threatening to ban the channel) for showing semi-nude women. The channel has, since then, toned down its content.

How is sexual content in video games treated in your country?

There is a growing market for games with sexual content. Such games are not available legally. Typically, games with explicit animated sex do well.

If your country has an "issue" with video games, something that tends to get press or is worrisome to people, what would it be?

The country is still "waking" up to video games, and your average gamer is your stereotypical adolescent male. Video game inspired crimes are as yet unknown. Concerns about video games typically relate to violent content or how they adversely affect the academic performance of young people (school- and college-going Indians face immense parental and peer pressure for doing well). [Banerjee]

INTERVIEW WITH PETER PAYNE, JAPAN

Peter Payne is the founder of JAST USA, the primary company involved with licensing and translating Japanese bishoujo games (aka "hentai games") to the English-speaking market. Peter is also the founder of J-List better, an online store based in Japan that sells just about anything eccentric that's Japan-related.

Overall, where would you place your country on a scale of 1 to 10, 10 being the most liberal sexually?

I'd say Japan is quite liberal, all things considered, although you never know when conservative attitudes will show up. For example, during the early 1990s there was a lot of "naughty" TV on late at night, mainly a show called *Gilgamesh Night* that did things like mini-skirt sumo wrestling (two women had to pull each other's mini-skirts off in a sumo ring), basically Benny Hill-esque. But these shows have been taken off the air over the past 10 years or so, reflecting concerns about kids staying up to watch the shows. You do still have nudity and sex in many places you don't find it in the U.S., though, such as news magazines like "Friday," which always have one "nude girl of the week" sandwiched in between articles on *endaka* and *defure* (the high yen and deflation).

Sex is perceived as healthy, more so than in the U.S., where you have odd beliefs leftover from the Puritans still hanging around. For example, young people obviously need somewhere where they can go be alone for a few hours, since Japanese often live at home well into their twenties, and if they're the oldest son or daughter, never leave home at all. So, there are thousands of "love hotels" in Japan where you can pay $40 for a two-hour "rest" or stay overnight for about twice this amount.

Is your country less or more conservative than the U.S.?

In general, Japan is less hung up about sex than the U.S. (of course, that's like saying Canada is colder than Venus).

Where can you buy sex magazines in your country?

You can buy soft-core magazines in convenience stores, and harder core ones in normal bookstores. Most every bookstore open today has an "ero" section, although there are often limitations. For example, bookstores in Kanagawa Prefecture (where Yokohama is located) must devote 51% of their floor space to non-adult books, thus you often have adult bookstores with tons of used manga on display

Overall, how would you sum up your country's attitude about nudity? For instance, how would people react to a woman sunbathing nude?

In Japan, most everyone bathes in front of others in the nude at some point or another, in public baths (*sento*) or hot springs (*onsen*). I believe the "freak out" factor over simple nudity is much less here.

How much sexual content/nudity is found in advertising in your country?

Not that much. Showing extremely sexy ads might be offensive to the average Japanese consumer, especially women, who make most purchasing decisions. However, the use of extremely *kawaii* (cute) idols and actresses to catch people's eye is very common.

How much sexual content/nudity is found on television in your country?

It can differ. While most late-night sex shows have gone off the air, they do have some which introduce viewers to new trends in love hotels, pink salons (where a man can go to get a "handjob" or more), soaplands (where a beautiful girl will wash you), and so on.

How is sexual content in video games treated in your country?

Adult PC games have been around since the first color computers appeared, with interactive "bishoujo" ("pretty girl") games in which you have to figure out how to make a certain girl, or several girls, open up to you sexually. There have always been sexual PC video games, both for use in the home on PCs (and the Japanese predecessors, DOS/V, PC98, etc.) as well as in the arcade, in the form of mahjong games that show you a naked pretty girl when you beat her. As you might expect, it's frowned upon in some circles, but tolerated as harmless for the most part.

If your country has an "issue" with video games, something that tends to get press or is worrisome to people, what would it be?

Since, over the years, some of the bishoujo game titles released in Japan have caused concern about their negative influence on society, the industry is currently self-regulated, through an organization called the Software Morality Association (Sof-Rin) which sets standards for the games. No characters under 18, no themes such as incest or bestiality, and so on. For the most part, these efforts keep the bishoujo game industry out of trouble as far as the law is concerned.

Part of the reason why adult dating-sims get extra leeway is that they aren't live-action and aren't really viewed as porn in a real sense. Also, many of the current popular anime shows started out as dating-sim games for PCs with good old adult content, but after they attained major popularity with fans based on the quality of the stories and characters, they were remade into "PG" games for PlayStation, and later, as mainstream boy-meets-girl anime shows. One good example is a popular game-turned-anime called *Kimi ga Nozomu Eien* (The Eternity You Wish For), which you can read about here: *http://en.wikipedia.org/wiki/Kimi_Ga_Nozomu_Eien*. [Payne]

INTERVIEW WITH GUIDO HENKEL, GERMANY

Guido Henkel is veteran game developer and is currently the CEO of G3 Studios.

Overall, where would you place your country on a scale of 1 to 10, 10 being the most liberal sexually?

Eight. I do not rate it a 9, because I know of countries that are even more liberal sexually, and I do not rate it a 10 because of certain restrictions when it comes to actual pornography. Sexuality is a nonissue, in general. It is part of our everyday lives without too many taboos. Advertising frequently uses naked people to sell shampoo, soap, and other items, and frontal nudity is often part of these ads. The same goes for print media where you will find plenty of nudity in ads and editorial content, oftentimes. Teenage magazines, for example, have sex education columns, complete with nude images, illustrations, and images of the genitalia. You will also frequently find nude images on the front covers of magazines.

On TV, nudity is part of the programming as part of film productions. It is rarely used as an "effect," but simply part of the natural behavior of people. You see them take a shower realistically, without awkwardly grappling for a towel in their own home to make sure nothing is exposed. Nudity is, as I said, simply part of our social lives.

There are also TV shows on cable that contain sexual content, ranging from game shows where people will have to strip, to sex education in moving images, all the way to soft-core pornography.

Hard-core pornography on the other hand is handled a bit more restrictively and has limitations. There are certain guidelines in place as to where hard-core porn begins, as the creators/publishers need to make sure hard-core porn is not being made available to minors. Therefore hard-core pornography is usually not available over-the-counter, requires age verification, and is typically sold only in dedicated adult book stores, etc.

Then there is illegal pornography. Things like rape, bestiality, etc. is flat-out illegal in Germany. We also frown very much upon films that contain rape scenes, for example, that show rape for its own sake or even glorify it.

In addition to the above, Germany is also open to sex education. In school, starting around 5th grade, students are introduced to sex with illustrations, photos, and educational films. These materials are educational in nature, documentaries of sorts, but are very explicit in nature and feature full frontal nudity as well as sexual situations.

Is your country less or more conservative than the U.S.?

Significantly less conservative and prude. Sexuality and nakedness is part of our society, and we are not ashamed of it. There is nothing more unnatural in our understanding than people trying to behave as if sex and nudity do not exist or are something bad.

Where can you buy sex magazines in your country?

It depends whether it falls into the soft- or hard-core category. Soft-core content can be purchased in every grocery store and is, in fact, part of every grocery store's magazine offering.

Hard-core content is usually sold at gas stations, under-the-counter, or dedicated adult stores, video stores, etc. where the proprietors can ensure that no minors have access.

The kind of cover-blocking and cover-touch-ups we have in the U.S. is not known in Germany at all. As longs as it's not pornographic—and a nude image of a model is not considered pornographic, for example—as long as you cannot see "beyond the bush"—it can be displayed publicly anywhere. Magazines like *Penthouse*, *Playboy*, etc., usually use tasteful covers showing breasts but no more, and were available for sale at every kiosk or grocery store that decided to carry them.

Pornographic materials, on the other hand, are simply prohibited from display in areas where minors have access.

Overall, how would you sum up your country's attitude about nudity? For instance, how would people react to a woman sunbathing nude?

Healthy, without hypocrisy and bigotry. You see people sunbathing topless at every pool, any day of the week during the summer. It is absolutely common and without sexual connotations.

Saunas, for example, are fully nude as well. People "roast" themselves and swim in the nude there without inhibitions or sexual connotations. All saunas in the country also offer mixed days where men and women visit the sauna at the same time—all of them entirely in the nude and again, without sexual undertones.

Germans make a distinction between simply being naked and sexual acts, which is something Americans have never learned. Janet Jackson exposing her nipple on TV causes an uproar throughout the country, while there was nothing sexual about it. It was simply a piece of her skin. In Germany, people wouldn't even have paid attention to this and wouldn't even have realized that she did—or did not—show her nipple. I am sure everyone in Germany simply laughed when they heard what kind of uproar this brief little moment caused in the U.S. I know, I slapped my knees in laughter.

Is nudity automatically associated with sex, or is it no big deal?

No, nudity is not at all necessarily associated with sex. Nudity is simply what it is, people being naked. Sex is another act that is not directly related to nudity, and people make clear distinctions between these things.

Are there any cultural contradictions regarding sex?

No, I would not say so.

How much sexual content/nudity is found in advertising in your country?

It is permeating all media. You have nudity in print advertising, TV commercials, billboards, or anywhere else.

How much sexual content/nudity is found on television in your country?

Quite a bit, I would say, and it's separated in three categories. Nudity is part of the general TV programming. It is important to understand, however, that we do not look at nudity as implicitly sexual or pornographic, necessarily. Nudity is one thing.

Sex is an integral part of the late-night TV programming, including soft-core content and phone sex advertising, etc. Lastly, there is pornography, which cannot be found on regular television.

How is sexual content in video games treated in your country?

No one even cares. While it's being evaluated for ratings, unless it is a hard-core pornographic game, it is never even a remote factor.

If your country has an "issue" with video games, something that tends to get press or is worrisome to people, what would it be?

Violence is much more of an issue in Germany—and I think rightfully so. Violence has a negative impact on people—sexual content usually doesn't, unless it glorifies acts of violation. In fact, in Germany, we can only scratch our heads at the American mentality where it is okay to show someone's head being blown off during children's hour while it is not okay to show a woman taking off a shirt, showing her breasts. The paradox is that Americans are still wondering why people arbitrarily shoot each other in broad daylight at random in this country or why violence is erupting at every street corner, but that's a different discussion entirely.

The fact that 99% of all video games have violent premises is certainly worrisome for people, as it has become practically impossible to find any games that do not make rampant killing/shooting of people and destruction of things their core gameplay. But again, this is a different discussion entirely.

What do people think of pornographic movies in your country?

As mentioned above, pornography is handled very differently than general sexual content. It is very important to understand that Germans have different layers of sexuality, which would be sensuality, eroticism, sex, and pornography—in that order. While people do not object to the first three in any way, pornography is handled very differently.

Pornographic movies can be found in adult sections in every video store. Sex shops selling magazines and sex toys can be found in most major city shopping passages today, no longer relegated to the back alley status they once inhabited. While pornographic materials are not entirely mainstream, it is not a big deal to go out and rent a porn movie alongside with your copy of *Shrek* or whatnot. People are very open about their sexuality, as it is part of our lives, like it or not. [Henkel]

INTERVIEW WITH "JONATHAN," CHINA

Jonathan is a writer, game developer, and entrepreneur. He developed one of China's first generation PC games in the mid 1990s. He now lives in the United States.

Overall, where would you place your country on a scale of 1 to 10 sexually, 10 being the most liberal?

Seven. Traditional Chinese values were destroyed after Communists took power in 1949. They were replaced by Communist doctrines. During the period between 1949 and 1978, sex was a taboo topic in the society, and people were very conservative under the social and governmental pressure. However, once the Communism doctrines were abandoned in early 1980s, and China opened its door to the outside world, people's attitudes toward sex changed dramatically. Without a true value system to fill the vacuum and without any religion of their own, in the past 10 years we've seen a huge number of Chinese people becoming more liberal in sex than their Western counterparts (I believe religion still plays a big role in America in shaping people's attitudes toward sex). This happened to both young and older people. Chinese youngsters quickly adopted the "Western way" of living. I put quotes here because by "Western way," I meant the lifestyle depicted in Hollywood movies and other pop-culture products from the West. For older Chinese, throughout their lifetime, they've experienced the rise and collapse of Communist doctrines. They felt they were victimized. Now they don't want to believe in anything or respect any rules or principles. They too have become very liberal sexually.

Is your country less or more conservative than the U.S.?

Less conservative.

Where can you buy sex magazines in your country?

There are governmental regulations in China that ban sex magazines. So, you won't be able to go into a store and find sex magazines on the bookshelf. You have to turn to the underground market to find sex magazines, books, and DVDs. However, this doesn't necessarily mean Chinese society is conservative.

What do people think of pornographic movies in your country?

Again, although the Chinese government bans pornographic movies, they are easy to get in most Chinese cities through street vendors and Internet downloads.

Overall, how would you sum up your country's attitude about nudity? For instance, how would people react to a woman sunbathing nude?

Chinese people have two faces: one in private and the other in public. Chinese people tend to use a conservative face in public, but they behave more liberal in private. Knowing that Chinese have two faces is very important to understand their true attitudes toward sex and nudity, which are more open and liberal than they appear.

Is nudity automatically associated with sex, or is it no big deal?

Yes. It is automatically associated with sex.

Are there any cultural contradictions regarding sex?

Yes. China still has a very strong censorship system, and the government has a tight control over the media. As a result, you won't see a lot of sexual content openly in public. This may give you a wrong impression that Chinese society is still very conservative. However, that is just the tip of the iceberg. Underneath, you will find Chinese people are very liberal on sex.

How much sexual content/nudity is found in advertising in your country?

I would say there is little difference between Chinese TV commercials and American TV commercials. One interesting thing I do notice is that Chinese online portal sites have a lot of nudity and sexual content, whereas their U.S. counterparts such as Yahoo! and MSN have very little.

How much sexual content/nudity is found on television in your country?

There is some, but not many if compared to the U.S. television. China has a strong censorship system and it won't pass the government review if the TV program has too much sexual content.

How is sexual content in video games treated in your country?

Sex sells in China just like in the US In Chinese games, you will find sexy female characters just like those you find in American games. However, explicit or inexplicit depiction of sexual conduct is not allowed. Again, the strong censorship system works here.

If your country has an "issue" with video games, something that tends to get press or is worrisome to people, what would it be?

My country always has various issues with video games—violence, sex, addiction, nationalism, etc. Right now the biggest topic is online game addiction. Chinese government is working to impose a three-hour time limit on online gameplay. [Jonathan]

INTERVIEW WITH MICHAEL HENGST, GERMANY

Michael Hengst is a veteran of the video games industry, first as a reporter and editor and later as a developer. He is currently a freelance producer and consultant for various video game companies.

Overall, where would you place your country on a scale of 1 to 10, 10 being the most liberal sexually?

I'd say that Germany is pretty liberal if it comes down to sexuality—on a scale of 1 to 10, I'd give them an 8. We don't have a problem with sex. Sometimes, we think that the world around us is somewhat "oversexed," but other than that, we are pretty neutral toward sexuality. "So what!" would describe the attitude at its best. Small example: Berlin's Major Klaus Wowereit is gay and came out to a crowd in public, and about nobody was offended or made big fuss out of it. Of course, it was printed in magazines, and it was over the news, but in a very positive manner.

Is your country less or more conservative than the U.S.?

Depends on the area you live in. In general, the south, especially Bavaria, is supposed to be more conservative than the rest of Germany. The "eastern" part is supposed to be looser. However, overall, we are a lot less conservative than the U.S. Another example: If "Nipplegate" [the Janet Jackson wardrobe malfunction] would have happened here—let's say during a world league soccer match—nobody would have reacted the way the U.S. reacted. Actually, nobody would have cared. Heck, you even didn't see that much of Janet Jackson to get our attention at all. The only reason why we actually recognized it was the uproar that went on in the U.S. media. Or, maybe it was because we didn't see enough of Janet Jackson.

The way I see it, Americans are way beyond being conservative. During my last stay in Los Angeles, I saw a TV piece on some medical studies. They where showing X-Rays—and all the "dangerous" areas where blanked out. An X-Ray! Get a grip! Not that you see something really hot on an X-Ray anyway, but putting a pixilation area over the spots where genitalia or even breasts are supposed to be is way too much. And in a country which has the biggest chunk of the porn biz in the world? Sorry, but that is simply beyond me.

Where can you buy sex magazines in your country?

You can buy sex magazines basically everywhere—in a kiosk, at the gas station, at the grocery store, and so on. However, you have to understand that our sex magazines are not porn magazines. Our *Penthouse*, *Playboy*, or *Hustler* don't show genitalia and erect penises or explicit sexual actions in the way that they are shown in magazines in the U.S. Those would be regarded as porn.

And even though the society, in general, doesn't particularly care with a few exceptions, there are some limitations and laws, regarding porn. The biggest issue here is not the fact that shops carry porn, like 24/7 gas stations where you can buy hard-core magazines and even videos, but transport. By law, it is forbidden to send porn via mail or use a mail order service. However, you have porn shops where you can get everything if you are 18 or older. These shops are not in dark places or regarded as "filthy." In fact, some of these shops are in big shopping malls, at airports, or advertise their names on giant billboards right at the freeway. But that is for general porn.

The law is very strict if it comes down to child pornography, sex with animals, and violent porn (snuff movies, rape movies). The law is simple: do not show, do not sell, do not buy, and do not own those.

Overall, how would you sum up your country's attitude about nudity? For instance, how would people react to a woman sunbathing nude?

Nudity? Heck we practically invented it. In 1893, the "Naturheil-Verein Essen Ruhr" was founded, which was registered 12 years later as the first and therefore the eldest nudist club in the world. In 1900, the first nudist magazine was launched. So, that said, it is quite common that people sunbathe naked in public, namely in the English Garden in the centre of Munich. Big deal. Lying naked in a park or at a beach, sunbathing is not an issue. To a certain extent, being naked in public is, however. Walking totally naked in the middle of a town, or going to a mall without clothes on might be not such a good idea. Having sex in public is also not very bright. The latter is regarded as a public offence.

Is nudity automatically associated with sex, or is it no big deal?

Nudity doesn't equal automatically sex. Some men might think that, but it is not the case. A girl or a woman running around topless at a beach is very likely not looking for guys to hit on her. A man playing nudist volleyball with a bunch of friends is not looking for admiration from women, but simply enjoying a game of volleyball, period.

Are there any cultural contradictions regarding sex?

Nope. Well, not that I know of. Except that we invented the nudist movement, and there is still a nightclub in Hamburg where you won't see that boring table bar dancing, but real live action on stage.

How much sexual content/nudity is found in advertising in your country?

Some. That includes ads on billboards, in magazines, and on TV. Even a showering woman selling the newest shampoo is not uncommon during family hours. However, the sexuality aspects of ads have been cut back a lot during the last couple of years. The reason is simple: people are somewhat tired of seeing a chocolate bar being advertised by a mostly naked girl. These days, sex doesn't always sell anymore.

How much sexual content/nudity is found on television in your country?

Depends on the channel. We have our usual share of soft porn flicks after 11 P.M. Some smaller TV stations will show non-stop-striptease action after midnight, and the commercials in-between the strippers show phone sex ads. However, no hard core is allowed—no erect penises, no "spread eagle," no explicit sexual action with the genitals shown. Otherwise, it is fine. The problem here for the German government is the fact that we live in Europe and that we have satellite dishes. In Italy and in Spain, showing porn on television is not forbidden. If you get an Italian channel, just by accident, who is going to blame you, even if you won't understand a word of Italian?

How is sexual content in video games treated in your country?

We have sexual content in video games? Well, we have—some. But it is more than harmless. Reason again is simple: the age rating of games like *Lula* or *Singles: Flirt Up Your Life*, with sexual content are usually 16 to get listed by retailers. But the sexuality which is been shown in those games won't get you as much as your neck stiff—pardon my French.

If your country has an "issue" with video games, something that tends to get press or is worrisome to people, what would it be?

Violence! Violence! Violence! That has been and always will be a serious issue in this country. If something bad is happening, the media will blame violent games for that. Like back in 2002 when 19-year-old Robert Steinhäuser killed thirteen teachers, two schoolmates, one police officer, and finally himself in a high school in Erfurt. Steinhäuser played a lot of games, especially FPS titles, which fueled the discussion about getting a new law to protect the youth against violence in games. The media was all over that, and some of the coverage actually was pretty good. The majority of the press all joined in a witch hunt against violent games. [Hengst]

INTERVIEW WITH ANONYMOUS, INDIA

Anonymous is a female video game programmer from India who currently works in the North American video games industry.

Overall, where would you place your country on a scale of 1 to 10 sexually, 10 being the most liberal?

Four. The attitude has been evolving, but the topic is still taboo. The older generation still refuses to talk about it, but there are plenty of lewd jokes made by older men over drinks in the evening, for instance. The younger generation is more open.

Is your country less or more conservative than the U.S.?

More. Although it's difficult to exactly say, because the U.S. has some very conservative people, too. India's attitude toward issues related to sex has been evolving and becoming more open, but the topic is still not openly spoken about, except mainly by the new generation teen population. Conservative dress is still considered the norm, and shorts and tank tops only invite leery looks from men, and are usually the wrong kind of attention-grabbing attire. The chest must be covered at all times (people in some places frown on tee-shirts even). Short skirts are to be avoided, bare shoulders avoided, cleavage avoided. These days, women do dress in more western attire, but it is acceptable only to a certain extent, and that too mainly in the more cosmopolitan cities such as Mumbai. I can't think of shorts being acceptable in even Bangalore or Delhi, actually.

Other than dress issues, even holding hands in public is frowned upon. There are groups in Mumbai, Delhi, Chennai constantly trying to outlaw Valentine's Day or burning cards on that day or banning the sale of romantic cards, considering it to be alien to Indian tradition. Youngsters don't date, they "go around" with each other with the intent to marry. Live-in relationships are huge no-no's (although I've been told people are exploring this these days). Pre-marital sex is considered immoral.

Where can you buy sex magazines in your country?

I have no idea.

Overall, how would you sum up your country's attitude about nudity? For instance, how would people react to a woman sunbathing nude?

A woman sunbathing topless would invite disaster. At the very least, there would be a crowd of people ogling. She will almost certainly be subjected to catcalls and lewd comments, and may even be molested. Foreign tourists may go topless in the southwestern state of Goa, which is famous for its beaches, and was a Portuguese settlement in the yesteryears. Indians would not consider going topless in a public area at all, and even if they have a huge house with private grounds, there still are the servants around, and really, women would not do this. Except if they are prostitutes, I guess, and even then I do not think this happens.

Is nudity automatically associated with sex, or is it no big deal?

Yes. Nudity in films is still not ok.

Are there any cultural contradictions regarding sex?

Yes, there are many. For instance, Bollywood films center around love stories, and these days are trying to get more and more titillating. However, romance is not easily accepted. Young couples wanting to get married have to undergo serious emotional stress, with no guarantee that they will get married in the end, and some even elope or try to commit suicide because their families would not accept their union, for reasons such as being of different castes or classes or social standing or religion, etc.

Then, everyone expects married couples to produce children, and all kinds of "hints" are given to either one on how to go about this. But it's not ok to talk about it, abortion is a strict no-no, and I honestly do not know how society now feels about fertility methods like IVF or artificial insemination. Also, as far as I know, it is illegal to find out the sex of an unborn child. In many places, the woman is still held responsible for the sex of the child, and in some cases is mistreated and blamed if it is a girl.

The Kamasutra seems to be famous and talked-about only abroad, not in India. I had not spoken about it with anyone until I came to this country. Ancient temples have statues depicting sexual positions, and goddesses are shown wearing what could be considered an Indian version of a tube top and tights with layers (that's what they look like), but God help you if you walk around wearing a tube top and tights.

How much sexual content/nudity is found in advertising in your country?

I do not know of nudity being shown on television. Nudity on billboards is also not done. There are plenty of seductive ads and billboards, but naked men or women in ads are not acceptable. There was an ad a few years back, with naked models wrapped in a snake to cover their private parts, and quite a hue-and-cry was raised indeed. I don't know how it was settled, if it was even.

How much sexual content/nudity is found on television in your country?

Not much. There is a lot with sexual undertones, and lots of skin shows, but nothing direct, as far as I know.

How is sexual content in video games treated in your country?

Video games are not a big craze there. PCs and consoles are out of reach for a lot of the population, so game consoles are owned only by a privileged few. Mobile games seem to be growing in popularity there, from what I've been reading recently. There aren't many people playing video games. Playing games is considered a waste of time, so sexual content in a video game, while it may be exciting for young teens (mainly males), would definitely be greatly frowned upon.

If your country has an "issue" with video games, something that tends to get press or is worrisome to people, what would it be?

Playboy: The Mansion—a recent video game based on the life of Hugh Hefner—was playtested in Bangalore, a very cosmopolitan city and the IT hub of India. The game had some adult content, but it was not tested fully, maybe because the testers weren't comfortable testing the sex animations and having topless (pixellated!!) women walking around the mansion. This led to bugs not being found in the game—which was their job to find in the first place.

What do people think of pornographic movies in your country?

They are sold/rented in a similar way as in the U.S. Pornographic movies are watched, but very secretively, and played in sleazy theaters. When I was a little girl growing up, I used to go to this video rental place with a couple of girlfriends. The guy would look us up and down, and one day asked us if we wanted more interesting movies, and then led us to a back room where he had a huge collection of porn films. We never went back. [Anonymous]

INTERVIEW WITH MATTHEW FORD, AUSTRALIA

Matthew Ford is a Project Director at Auran Games and is an American transplant in Australia.

Overall, where would you place your country on a scale of 1 to 10, 10 being the most liberal sexually.

Six. Aussies are not very uptight about sex in that they frequently refer to it in a jokey way. Dirty jokes are told all the time at parties and in advertisements.

One of the things I love about Australians is that they are so much less uptight than the USA about sex. They use sex not in a creepy way or the blasé Euro way. Rather, it's fun and lusty and mischievous. Here are a few examples:

On the most popular nationwide breakfast news-lite show, they broadcast from a museum that had a whale penis on display. The onsite host and museum staffer played around with it, and the studio hosts, both male and female, made a number of naughty jokes about it.

The same show frequently has a "joke of the day," which is almost always some kind of dirty joke, read and submitted by both men and women.

A big billboard on the way out of the Brisbane airport touting a time-saving parking pass or the like has the tagline, "Slip in and out faster."

A TV commercial for "Titan" brand garage doors: A young man is talking with his dad in the yard standing in front of his garage. He says, "Hey da, you know how I was complaining that my last girlfriend didn't have a Titan?" Dad nods. "Well, this time I'm going to do interviews." The young guy talks with a number of sexy girls who are sitting up on his workbench right in front of him while his dad chats up the ones in line. The naughty part is that in the Australian accent, "Titan" sounds the same as "tight one." So the guy sounded like he was saying to his dad, "You know how I was complaining that my last girlfriend didn't have a tight one?"

Would any of this happen on USA broadcast TV? I think not.

Prostitution (in brothels) is legal and regulated in many parts of Australia, including major cities such as Sydney and Brisbane. Streetwalking is illegal in most or all places, though I think this is because of public health as much as perception. You can see open ads for brothels and escort services in the newspaper.

On the other hand, the actual depiction of sex can get people upset. When the reality TV show here, *Big Brother*, showed (in a blurred out fashion) footage of two people having sex under a bed sheet, it caused a lot of uproar of going too far. Most was on behalf of "the children"—though this segment broadcast after 10 P.M., it was popular with kids during its primetime slots, so the logic was that kids probably were watching the late slot as well. But it remained a very popular show.

Is your country less or more conservative than the U.S.?

Less conservative.

Where can you buy sex magazines in your country?

You can buy them in any corner shop. Maybe not the supermarket, but you can buy them anywhere that there are a substantial number of mags on sale. There does not seem to be a law about covering it up, or if there is, it's not universally followed. You see those boards sometimes, but it may just be a matter of courtesy.

Overall, how would you sum up your country's attitude about nudity? For instance, how would people react to a woman sunbathing nude?

It seems okay but not common to go topless, and nude beaches are easy to find. The main view seems to be that it's okay to show your breasts, but not okay to show off the bottom half unless you are far out of the way. I don't think there are indecency arrests, and if there are, they are few and far between. I sometimes see topless women on the beach but not often.

Is nudity automatically associated with sex, or is it no big deal?

[Australia] is pretty much like the USA in that nudity is largely equated with sex, not like perhaps parts of Europe where this link is not as strong. But you do hear from women who say just because I am topless on the beach does not mean I am looking for sex.

Are there any cultural contradictions regarding sex?

Not too much that way. However, the increase in immigration of sexually conservative countries and the general rise of theocratic thinking (thank you, America) is emboldening religious conservatives to call for crackdowns by law on sexual permissiveness.

How much sexual content/nudity is found in advertising in your country?

Naughty jokes are used often. Clothed "T&A" is used sometimes, but not as much as the USA; it is considered in poor taste if it is too crass, except in music videos. No nudity in billboards as I recall.

How much sexual content/nudity is found on television in your country?

You can see soft-core porn on broadcast TV late at night. No genitalia from what I hear, but there are depictions of sex and nudity.

How is sexual content in video games treated in your country?

Australia has no equivalent of an M rating; if something is supposed to be played only by 17 and up, it cannot be rated, and if it is not rated, *it legally cannot be sold*. Very bad! There is a big clamor by game devs to get that rating created, but there is resistance due to conservative grandstanding like you see in the USA.

> *If your country has an "issue" with video games, something that tends to get press or is worrisome to people, what would it be?*
>
> Australia is similar to the USA in that it has the fear of a corruptive influence of video games, but a lot milder. There is also a bit more concern than in the USA about the lazy nature of playing video games. Australia is a very active outdoorsy country, and the impression is that the streets are pretty safe, so there is pressure not to let kids sit around inside all day gaming. In my opinion, this is a good social pressure to have. [Ford]

REFERENCES

[Anonymous] Anonymous, female, interview with Brenda Brathwaite, October 13, 2005.

[Banerjee] Banerjee, Anando, interview with Brenda Brathwaite, October 17, 2005.

[Cobbett] Cobbett, Richard, interview with Brenda Brathwaite, October 11, 2005.

[Ford] Ford, Matthew, interview with Brenda Brathwaite, October 14, 2005.

[Hengst] Hengst, Michael, interview with Brenda Brathwaite, October 11, 2005.

[Henkel] Henkel, Guido, interview with Brenda Brathwaite, October 5, 2005.

[Payne] Payne, Peter, interview with Brenda Brathwaite, October 13, 2005.

[Jonathan] "Jonathan," interview with Brenda Brathwaite, November 23, 2005.

14 Interviews

In This Chapter

- Richard Garriott
- Bob Bates
- Steve Meretzky
- Edward Kuehnel
- Brad Abram
- Sheri Graner Ray

RICHARD GARRIOTT

Richard Garriott, also known as Lord British, is the founder of Origin and the *Ultima®* series of computer gamers, one of best-selling fantasy role-playing series of all time. Richard is now with NCsoft and is working on his first new world in many years, *Tabula Rasa*.

There's an old *Ultima* piece of trivia out there—after saving Joshua from the bandits in Moonglow, apparently you can find a book titled "Everything an Avatar Needs to Know About Sex." The same book is rumored to appear in *Ultima® VII*, too. Would the Avatar be alarmed or amused at the amount of sexual content in games today?

I think the Avatar would principally be amused. The Avatar would respect the diversity of games developed and the diversity of consumer demands. That being said, he would likely scoff at gratuitous uses of sex and violence and work to be sure content was only exposed to appropriate ages.

What sexual content is found in your games?

Not much! Although allusions to sex and occasional bawdy commentary can be found, there is no real depiction of sex. That being said, in *Ultima Online™*, one of the 1st "emergent" behaviors" in the game happened within a few minutes of turning on the service—virtual prostitution! Two people had logged into the game and one person was "pimping" for the other, who would then lead people into a storeroom along the docks where they hung out and "ooh and ah" at the "John." The game supported no depictions of sex, but the player "demand" was clearly present, and they engineered their own solution.

As an art form and a form of media, games have had an odd run of it. There's a perception games are for kids, even if they're rated "M." The average gamer is now a 30-year-old male. Can this perception be changed? How?

Absolutely! The perception is just lagging behind reality. As you have noted, the original group of gamers is aging, and so it is natural that the average age is increasing as is the spread between young gamers and older gamers. Still, over time, most games have been made for and marketed to youth. I believe this problem will naturally run its course.

It appears that there's a sudden growth in sexually themed games. Do you think more sexual games are being made, or are the ones being made now just getting more attention?

A little of both. Sexually oriented games have existed since the beginning. Even explicit "interactive" content was made very early on. I just think the fidelity of the experiences is "coming of age," and so it's getting more attention. Plus, most of the current examples of inclusion are based in either explicit and/or violent games where they are intended as shock value, nothing particularly "literary." I assume this "juvenile" phase will run its course.

Can sexual content be used in good way in a game? How?

Under the assumption someone thinks it can be used in a good way in movies or books, then of course—yes! That being said, I'd be hard pressed to think of an example today. In the future, just as intimacy can be used to show connections between movie and book characters, so it can be in games.

A producer of an M-rated game with sexual content raised this question at the "Sexuality in Games" roundtable at GDC. "Do we as developers have an ethical responsibility? Do we need to think about what we might be teaching people who play these games?" What do you think?

I am a devout believer that games of all types are fair and reasonable to create. I can even see how playing a game where the goal is to live out an unethical existence could be fun. And I have no problem with them being played by mature adults. However, I am also a devout believer that "role playing" is one of the most powerful teaching tools in the world. Think about young kids out on playgrounds playing imaginary games, be it pretend warfare, or tea parties in the clubhouse. In all these cases, kids are trying out interpersonal actions and honing their interpersonal skills. They find out that when you don't play well, others won't play with you. They find out that pulling someone's hair makes that person cry, and hopefully, that makes the aggressor sad. To unleash a game that does not respond with the real world's countermeasures to player behavior, means that the game really does have a risk of "teaching" bad behavior, or at least misses the opportunity to reinforce "right and wrong." So, while I don't think developers have a "moral responsibility" to put ethical parables into their games (as I like to do), I do think content exposed to kids must be filtered. I also feel that great stories, interactive or linear, generally showcase the growth of the human spirit, in an individual or a society. And while there are great literary works that buck that trend, they are rare. Thus, I feel that while these morally ambiguous (or worse) games are popular right now, it's because the concept is fresh and relatively easy to create. It is much harder to craft, but ultimately much more valuable to include, moral dilemmas and temptations in an interactive experience that then rewards the player in a satisfying way, a better, more complex level of interaction. But, we as game developers will get there! At least I know I'm devoted to trying!

What types of sexual content do you think are appropriate at the various rating levels?

This is a complex societal question. While there are some clear examples of things like keeping explicit sexual content away from youth, when you get to implied actions or "bleeped" out words, it becomes far more complex. As for me, I am more of a European thinker. I think violence is far worse than sexuality. Because there is so much debate as to what is bad and why, I believe what is appropriate is content labeling, with some general guidelines. Then let parents decide how to manage their family's exposure to certain kinds of content. To try to legislate a norm in the U.S. is implausible and wrong!

In recent months, many bills have made their way through state legislatures seeking to ban the sale of video games containing violent or sexual content to minors. How do you feel about such actions?

I should note that I don't agree with the current U.S. trend toward restricting public content across media like TV and radio. That being said, when there is a public backlash at games like you are seeing, it does imply that we as a game industry are failing to provide the tools that parents need to assist them in making decisions for their children. And while it might be easy to blame the parents for not using the tools we have, unfortunately that may not be enough. But we as an industry should solve this first!

Emergent sex is an alarming trend for some on-line games or PC/Xbox games that accept user created content. However, some players love it. What are your thoughts on this?

I have seen this in our games, too. Interesting issue. First, it should be noted that people will "find a way" to have "cyber sex" in online environments no matter what you do. As long as people can talk/chat, they will "talk dirty" if they want to. Once a game has even mildly sophisticated animations, they can be put to other uses.

I believe the reason this (and most potentially anti-social behavior) is more prevalent online than in reality on the streets is anonymity. In the real world, you don't strip, because people can see who you are, point, laugh, and throw you in jail. Online, you can always just log off and escape any of the normal societal backlashes for your behavior.

Thus, I believe eliminating anonymity and tracking player feedback is the answer to keep online behavior similar to real world behavior. Note how well eBay® works with a well-tracked personal history!

That being said, I'd love to play a well-crafted flirtatious interpersonal game. But the art form of designing such a game is far from ready!

When gauging the sexual or sexy content in your games, how do you make your decisions on what to include or not include?

In our case, most is excluded, principally, because we do not yet have the skills to make it compelling and meaningful.

Do you believe storytelling in games has evolved to the point that sexual content is necessary?

We are getting close, but no. But just as "relationships" are common in movies, they will be in games too, eventually.

If video games with sexual content somehow made their way into Britannia and the citizens demanded an audience with Lord British to discuss their concerns, what would he say?

If video games with sexual content made it into Britannia and the citizens demanded an audience, Lord British would of course grant the audience. He would listen to their concerns and validate those concerns that were expressed as parenting issues, but take issue with those who might prefer to legislate morality. Thus, he would work with the citizens to insure that parents had the tools they needed to make individual parenting decisions, while preserving the rights of free expression and general adult access. Lord British would favor solutions that had minimal governmental entanglement, but would demand of content makers to provide community demanded tools or expect further involvement. [Garriott01]

BOB BATES

Bob Bates began his game writing career at Infocom in 1986. Since then, he has written, co-designed, produced, or otherwise assisted in the development of more than 25 games that have won over 40 industry awards, including the 1993 Adventure Game of the Year, *Eric The Unready*™. The most recent titles he has produced are the best-selling *Unreal® II: The Awakening* (2003), and *Unreal® II: XMP* (2004).

In 1989, Bob co-founded Legend Entertainment and served as its president until the company's 1998 sale to GT Interactive (now Atari). He remained the Studio Head until Legend closed in January 2004. He is now an independent game designer, writer, and producer.

A frequent speaker at industry conferences and events, Bob is the chairman emeritus of the IGDA, and the co-founder and organizer of the Game Designer's Workshop, an annual invitation-only conference attended by many of the top storytelling game designers in the business.

Bob is the author of one of the industry's bestselling books on game development, *Game Design: The Art and Business of Creating Games,* which is currently being used as a textbook by several colleges and universities. He is also the editor of the *Game Developers Market Guide*.

What range sexual content is found in your games?

Sex is conspicuously absent from most of my games, with the exception of the comic *Eric the Unready*, a parser-driven game with a lot of sexual innuendo and semi-risqué answers to certain user inputs. In *John Saul's Blackstone Chronicles: An Adventure in Terror*, several of the ghost-inmates of the insane asylum were women, but their gender was relevant only as it pertained to their life circumstances, and sex didn't enter into it. In the science-fiction shooter *Unreal® 2: The Awakening*, the intelligence officer was a provocatively dressed woman, but no reference to her attire was made in the game, none of her crew-mates hit on her, and her character arc (growing from paranoid rebel to trusting friend) would have been just as suited to a man as a woman.

You've talked before about storytelling, mythmaking, and games. On television, we regularly see intimacy between characters. Has storytelling in games evolved to a point where sexual themes are necessary?

The only themes that are necessary are the ones you must have to tell your story. If your story is about a man's overcoming self-doubt to become courageous in battle, you probably won't need to introduce sex (although you could find a place for it if, for example, you wanted a woman to be the catalyst to his self-growth). If your story is about a teenage girl who routinely used sex to gain acceptance, but now wishes to have her own identity, then sexual issues will be at the heart of your game.

As developers will we arrive at a point where sexual content in games is necessary?

I don't know that we need to arrive at a point where mature sexual themes are *necessary*, so much as *possible*. Getting to the point where it *is* possible is part of a much larger problem, which is that we still haven't figured out how to do good, author-driven, storytelling in the context of a game. The conflicting demands of user freedom and author control still bedevil us, and despite the large number of people working on the problem, I don't think we've yet seen a game with a great story of *any* mature theme, much less a sexual one.

What are the challenges inherent in designing a game based on sexual content or which incorporates sexual content?

If you want the game to be commercially viable, the first problem would be getting it green-lit by publishers who are always looking over their shoulder at the politicians. In America, our culture is permissive toward violence and restrictive with regard to sex. In Europe, the opposite is true. So, the first step might be to approach a European publisher (although they, too, will have their eye on the U.S. market and may turn down the game for that reason).

If you're not concerned with commerciality, the design problems are the same as any other game. Your chief concern is to come up with interesting things for players to do, with an ascending level of difficulty that the player masters over time. If sex is your only activity, you won't hold their interest for long. With sex (and romance), the chase is more interesting than the act, and the chase is not something that naturally suggests gameplay activity with that rising level of difficulty.

Games that mix humor and sex like the old Leisure Suit Larry *series also did really well. Why does mixing humor and sex seem to work?*

Because sex is taboo. Anything that is forbidden is a good target for humor. Death, embarrassing bodily functions, defying authority, sex. Go to any second-grade class-room and you'll see all this at work.

Have you ever seen good use of sexual content in games?

I liked what Steve Meretzky did with *Leather Goddesses of Phobos* and the *Spellcasting* series.

As developers, do you believe we have an ethical responsibility? Do we need to think about what we might be teaching people who play these games?

All game-makers and storytellers have ethical responsibilities. We are the culture-makers. An author or designer is someone who has a particular (peculiar?) view of the way the world is, or the way it *should* be, and he/she uses a game or a story to impart that view. It may be that this view is a revolutionary one, where the author sees some-thing wrong with the world that needs to be corrected—in that case the author has an ethical responsibility to try to convert people to that point of view. On the other hand, it may be a conservative view, where the author sees a threat to the established order that must be challenged and defeated—in that case, too, the author has an ethical re-sponsibility, even if the point of view is in direct conflict with that of the "revolution-ary" game maker. Every living person has the responsibility to try to do what's right, but not necessarily to convert others to their point of view. Authors have the additional responsibility to try to convince others that their vision of the world is the correct one.

What's the future of sex in games?

I think it will be present in much the same way it is now—in bits and pieces, appro-priate and inappropriate, exploitative and sophomoric—until we as game designers figure out how to marry serious themes to our games. At that point, as we see with other forms of popular culture like books and movies, the silly stuff won't go away, but we will see a few games that actually move the player on a profound level, and change the way they lead their lives.

In an interview I did with Steve Meretzky many years ago, I posed a rhetorical question. I asked what type of game he'd make if he were stranded on an island with you, Sid Meier, and John Romero. I posed the same question to him again for this book, except I noted that John and Sid couldn't make it, but Hugh Hefner and Will Wright could. What type of game do you think you'd make this time?

So it's me, Steve, Hugh Hefner, and Will Wright? Will will create procedurally gener-ated algorithms that allow players to design and grow their own organisms. Hugh

Hefner will ensure those organisms have great bodies, and he will hire artists to create elegant and sophisticated clothes for them. Steve will create improbable and hilarious circumstances that require the characters to meet and shed those clothes. I will try (and fail) to write a story that ties it all together and explains that sex is grand and great fun, so long as everyone agrees to take care of the babies. [Bates01]

STEVE MERETZKY

Steve Meretzky has been designing games for over 20 years, starting at Infocom in the early 1980s. His first game, *Planetfall*™, was released in September 1983. These were followed by *Zork® Zero*, *The Hitchhiker's Guide to the Galaxy*™ (in collaboration with Douglas Adams), and *Leather Goddesses of Phobos*™.

Steve spent many years as a freelance designer, and was co-founder of a development studio called Boffo Games, which lasted from 1994 through 1997 and created *Hodj 'n' Podj®* and *The Space Bar*™.

Steve is currently a lead game designer at Floodgate Entertainment.

What range sexual content is found in your games?

My games that had any sexual content were *Leather Goddesses of Phobos*, and the games in the *Spellcasting* trilogy (*Spellcasting 101: Sorcerers Get All the Girls*™, *Spellcasting 201: The Sorcerer's Appliance*™, and *Spellcasting 301: Spring Break*™). Also, there was sexual content in *Leather Goddesses of Phobos 2*, which I designed for Activision a few years after the death of Infocom, but did not implement. In those games, the sexual content was always employed purely for humor. Lots of double entendres, such as in *Leather Goddess of Phobos*, when your new Tonto-like sidekick (Trent, if you're playing as a man, or Tiffany if you're playing as a woman) says, "We'll lick those Leather Goddesses together!" Lots of messing with players' expectations, such as in *Spellcasting 101*, where you find a spell of "bust enlargement"; you can try casting it on every woman in the game to no avail; it turns out to be useful if you cast it on a statuette sitting on a pedestal in the library.

There were literal sex scenes, but again they were always played for humor, such as the chapter in *Spellcasting 101* entitled "The Island of the Amazons." You land on this island of gorgeous Amazonian women, who have never seen a man and are all eyeing you hungrily. You are shown to your chambers, where the Amazon chief has her way with you. She's barely gone when another pops out from under your bed . . . then another comes out of the linen trunk . . . then another falls out of the air duct. If you don't escape, you'll never survive the onslaught!

The story of how Leather Goddesses of Phobos *came to be is a great one. Can you share it?*

It dates back to the very early days of Infocom, shortly after Infocom (having been a virtual company for the first two years of its existence) got its first office space at 55

Wheeler Street in Cambridge, Massachusetts. The space consisted of a handful of individual offices surrounding a large central space. That space doubled as a conference room and "micro room," where we kept one of each personal computer we supported (Apple II, Atari 800, TRS-80 Model III, etc.). One entire wall of that room was a chalkboard, wall-to-wall, floor-to-ceiling. We used it for a huge grid, dubbed "The Matrix," showing the release number of every SKU in release. So it had every micro[computer] across the top of the grid, and every Infocom game down the side of the grid. You could just look at the grid and see immediately that the version of *Zork II* in release for NEC PC-8000 was version 68.

Infocom was having its first party of any sort. It was just beer and pizza for a few dozen people—members of the press, local retailers, board members—to be held in this central conference room. Despite it being a small, low-key affair, Joel Berez, Infocom's president, and Marc Blank, my boss and Infocom's VP of Development, were pretty hyper about everything going perfectly.

A few hours before the party, I was in the conference room alone, and on a whim, and as a reaction to how hyper Joel and Marc were acting, I added a new line at the bottom of The Matrix, just below *Starcross*™, for a nonexistent game I entitled *Leather Goddesses of Phobos*. Joel noticed the addition just a few minutes before the first guests arrived and couldn't erase it fast enough.

But the name lived on, and for years after that, people would jokingly refer to it as one of our games in production. At some point, when it was time for me to start working on a new game, I thought about how much everyone loved the name, and that it made sense to write a game to go along with the name. I threw the idea out there, and Mike Dornbrook, Infocom's chief marketer, loved it and helped push it through. It was certainly the only time I've started with a name, and written a game to match it, rather than vice versa!

That game made you one of the pioneers of sexual content in games. When the game was in development, what types of concerns did you have?

My only concern was whether it would fly with Infocom's management. Our CEO, Al Vezza, was conservative (in the sense of "not daring") and humorless. Plus, at the time, Infocom was tottering at the verge of bankruptcy and shopping itself to several suitors. Chief among those suitors was Activision, and Activision's CEO, Jim Levy, was on site for a visit. As Vezza was showing Levy around, they came across some early mockups for the *Leather Goddesses* package. Al, flustered, said, "Of course, we haven't definitely decided to call it that," to which Jim immediately responded, "What? I wouldn't call it anything else!" Which, of course, made everyone feel a LOT better about the potential acquisition.

How was it received at retail and publicly? Were there any issues?

The publicity was favorable; reviewers "got the joke" and didn't take the sexual content seriously. I can't think of a single controversy, such as a store that wouldn't carry it, a magazine that wouldn't review it, a player who was offended and demanded a refund. By comparison, our fantasy/magic games (*Zork, Enchanter*™, etc.) generated a load of controversy from religious nut jobs, who thought that such games were in league with the devil, leading children toward the dark arts, an affront to God, and so forth. I remember one mailman who wrote us a letter saying that he was refusing to deliver any copies of *Boys' Life*® magazine, because it contained an ad depicting a wizard stirring a cauldron. I still have a thick file of such letters at home.

In fact, when I wrote *Spellcasting 201* for Legend, and Legend signed a distribution deal with Microprose in Hunt Valley, Maryland, two Microprose employees quit over it. They weren't at all bothered by the sexual content, but were appalled that Microprose was distributing a game where the main character used magic spells.

In the last few years, three major sexually themed games were released. Those that mixed humor with sex seemed to fare better critically. Why do you think that is?

I haven't played any of the three games, although I've read a lot about both *Leisure Suit Larry: Magna Cum Laude* and *Playboy: The Mansion. The Singles*, I know little about. I'm biased toward humor, so I think that anything with humor is better than an equivalent without humor. But I think it's a fact that people have a lot of hang-ups and insecurities when it comes to sexual content, and those hang-ups are probably more powerful when you are interacting/participating and not just watching as in more passive media. So, I think the humor helps people deal with the resulting tension.

What is the best use of sexual content that you've seen in a game so far?

I can't think of anything worthy of kudos. That might be because there isn't any. Or it might be because I just haven't run across it—there are a lot of games out there, and I've only played a fraction of them. Or, I might have seen something worthwhile, but I've just forgotten it because I'm going senile.

The ESRB, as you know, has several different rating levels. What amount of sexual content do you think is acceptable at the various levels—E, T, M and AO?

I'm not a fan of the ESRB rating system (or any rating system). For one thing, I think that just about every rating system, including the ESRB, gives too much weight to sexual content and language and too little attention to gore and physical violence. Also, it's a joke to think that any rating system will shield a minor from a given level of objectionable content. I won't allow first-person shooters to be played at home, but I know for sure that my kids played them at friend's houses, and at a pretty young age. Am I supposed to ask for a complete software inventory before allowing my kids to visit a friend's house?

As an alternative to a rating system, I prefer a description of what might be objectionable about a game, and it should be very game specific, not a one-size-fits-all checklist. In other words, "Occasional humorous sexual foreplay, beneath bed sheets; frequent nudity from the waist up, but no full nudity" versus "contains sex and nudity."

I'm also a fan of developers and publishers exhibiting self-restraint when it comes to objectionable content. Unfortunately, this has not been the case, and it becomes harder and harder to make the case against censorship laws.

Can sexual content be used in good way in a game?

As with all experiential media, I think games can be used to model positive and progressive attitudes toward sex and gender issues. For example, imagine a game where you play a prostitute and learn the pressures that lead someone to prostitution and the hardships of that life (compared to a game where you shoot whores and steal their money).

In recent months, more than a dozen separate bills have made their way through state legislatures seeking to ban the sale of video games containing violent or sexual content to minors. How do you feel about such actions?

I hate censorship even more than I hate ratings systems. I wish developers and publishers would show more voluntary restraint, so it was easier to make the case against such bills.

A producer of an M-rated sexually themed game raised this question at the GDC "Sexuality in Games" roundtable: "Do we as developers have an ethical responsibility? Do we need to think about what we might be teaching people who play these games?" What do you think?

Of course we have an ethical responsibility, individually, collectively as companies, and collectively as an industry. We can't, on the one hand, crow about the power of software as a learning tool, and on the other hand say the immersion in realistic graphic violence has no impact on a player.

In an interview I did with you many years ago, I posed a rhetorical question to you where I asked what type of game you'd make if you were stranded on an island with Bob Bates, Sid Meier, and John Romero. If John and Sid couldn't make it, but Hugh Hefner and Will Wright could, what type of game would you make this time?

Hmmm . . . I can't see what Hef would add to the mix, other than some publishing clout, which could be a consideration if we get rescued and decide to market the game. I suppose Will would want to create "SimCastaway" and I'd want to create "Mystery of the Pirate Wreck," or maybe some casual game involving bananas and coconut shells. Maybe Hef could also be in charge of testing . . .

What's the future of sex in games?

Near term, I think more of the same. Long term, as games mature as a story-telling medium, perhaps we'll see some games dealing with sexual themes in serious and interesting ways; sex is too central an element of the human condition for it not to be a significant part of any story-telling medium. Really long term, with new VR attachments, or even with hardware that can directly tap in to the experiential centers of brain activity, well, let's just say that when it comes to game addiction, we ain't seen nothin' yet. [Meretzky01]

EDWARD KUEHNEL

Edward Kuehnel was a game designer at High Voltage Software and wrote comedy for the company's *Leisure Suit Larry* series, over 12,000 lines of voice over for *Magna Cum Laude* alone. The titles stake their reputation on being titillating and funny, and have been nominated for various awards.

The new Leisure Suit Larry *titles are more hard-core than they were in the past. Can you talk a bit about the range of sexual content found your games?*

In *Magna Cum Laude*, we ran the gamut from brief nudity (toplessness) to soft-core sex. You see girls with their shirts off playing strip poker or making a hasty exit from our protagonist's dorm room, but you'd also see him lucky from time to time. We never tried to show actual penetration or make our soft-core scenes very titillating. The sex in our game was for comedic purposes. In one scene, our hero was wearing the school mascot costume when a fellow coed mauls him. In another, a girl goes down on him (implied, not shown) then reveals she's really a "he." At the end of the game, the player gets to pick one of three girls he'd like to have sex with, and with each, we show some pretty racy soft-core stuff, but again, it's mostly for comedic value. About the most sexual heat we put off is when two girls fondle each other's breasts and kiss for several seconds. It's possible by the end of the game to collect enough "secret tokens" to enable "fully nude mode" and see females in a complete state of undress, pubic hair and all, but that's entirely optional and not required to complete the game.

In our most recent endeavor, we anticipate toning things down a lot in order to gain more retail acceptance. The mature version of our game will likely feature no nudity whatsoever, and sex scenes will be few and far between and will likely be completely hidden by choice of camera cuts. You'll get the idea something's going down but won't see any of it.

Do you have any issues translating your games to different cultures?

Magna Cum Laude was translated into German, French, Spanish, Italian, and later on, Russian. There were no issues to speak of other than the discovery that European retailers and consumers had very little problem with the amount of sex and nudity in the game and, if anything, seemed to want more. Our publisher released a racier version rated AO for Adults Only that sold well in Europe and with gamers in the U.S. who bought it over their Web site.

As an interesting side note, early on in *Magna Cum Laude*, we decided to outsource some character models to a company that had artists based in Taiwan. We wanted them done fully nude, so they could be stripped down during poker or shown naked in cinemas. The artists sent us their "first pass" on the models without any pubic hair. Seems as if that's somewhat of a taboo in some Asian cultures.

You've also been affected by a ban. When Australia refused to allow Leisure Suit Larry: Magna Cum Laude *into the country, did they explain why? How did it affect the plans for the game?*

We received very little information as to why it was banned. The press release we received from the Australian Office of Film and Literature denied certification based on obscured or implied sexual activity and partial nudity. I don't think management at High Voltage Software was pleased at the loss of potential sales, though I have to admit I found it rather amusing and, at first, was somewhat proud of the achievement. Not many people can say they've written something that's been banned from an entire country. I'll admit to still being a bit perplexed at the ban, however. Maybe it's all those *Crocodile Dundee* movies, but I'd always thought of Australia as this laid back, easy-going country with a strong commitment to free speech and an independent streak as big and wide as the outback. At least they're not hypocrites; they ban games for being violent, too.

Did any retailers refuse to carry the game?

Wal-Mart banned it outright. Best Buy carried the PC version only, not the Xbox or PlayStation2. I believe it was banned in Target as well, though they may have sold the PC version in limited quantity as well. That's 60% of your retail chain; most games can't afford that kind of snubbing.

Our publisher, Vivendi/Universal Games, was in charge of the marketing and distribution for *Magna Cum Laude*. Due to the lack of major retailer participation, the marketing budget for the game was cut drastically. They did sign on EB Games™ to do some in-store promotional stuff, and managed to get some great PR for the game. In fact, one of our characters, Luba Licious, had an actual centerfold in *Playboy*. But for the most part, sales of *Magna Cum Laude* were from word of mouth. Though its gameplay was panned it garnered mostly stellar reviews for its humor and writing and broke new ground with some of the adult themes it encompassed.

What are you doing to get a broader distribution?

We are proceeding with more caution on our most recent title, and to that end, Vivendi has opened up a dialogue with some of the major retailers it wants to distribute the game to. Vivendi is going to be as proactive as they can with retailers to ensure we have more buy-in from the major ones. From what I understand, it is difficult, however, because no one wants to be the one to make any concrete decisions about what's okay and what's not. Understandably, no one wants to put their butt on the line only to find out later their CEO has a lower threshold for sexuality in games than they do.

For instance, early on, we developed a prototype for a massage game in which you'd rub a girl's back, shoulders, etc. then make your way to her breasts and other naughty bits. Retailers objected to the game, so we toned it down so that you were just rubbing her back and shoulders—nothing else. Again, retailers objected, with one buyer giving the reason that he found it unacceptable the player was allowed to directly manipulate (using the gamepad) a woman for the purposes of giving her physical pleasure.

Now, I'm not one to sit there and cry a river over "retailer hypocrisy" or rant about the average American's overt obsession with violence while they flagellate themselves for the dirty, dirty thoughts they have about hot man-on-man action when no one's looking. The way I see it, retailers own the shelves, and if they want to be hypocrites they can be, and Americans love violence and are ashamed of sex—weird but hey, that's just us. Life goes on. But this, this threw me for a bit of a loop. The same retailers who had no problem selling *Manhunt*, a game in which you could decapitate someone and carry their head in a sack, refused a game in which a woman asked you to work out a kink in her neck. Now that's messed up.

Did you work with the ESRB prior to release?

Prior to the release of *Magna Cum Laude*, we showed the ESRB scenes that represented the "worst" of what we had to offer. The ESRB was surprisingly okay with what we showed them, believing us to be well within the bounds of the M-rated category. We did need to re-edit a few cinemas that featured nudity and/or sex, however. We called it the "nine second rule." We could not have any nudity or sex in the same shot for more than nine seconds and still maintain an M rating. Not a big deal, we thought, and so we changed it.

Did you work with first party (Sony/Xbox) prior to release?

Sony and Microsoft were both a bit squeamish about *Magna Cum Laude*. Microsoft made a late decision not to include our game at their showroom at 2004's E3. The game was shown on Sony's floor, Vivendi's booth, and at the booth of graphic card manufacturer ATG. We made a PS2 demo of the game at Vivendi's request but *PlayStation Magazine* elected not to carry it. In the end, however, both console manufacturers were fine with the game as long as we kept to an M rating. The AO version, *Uncut and Uncensored* was only sold as a PC title.

What advice do you have for developers creating M- and AO-rated games?

Decide first how important sex, nudity, and/or sexual content are to your game. If it's vital to your game and promises to be prevalent, understand you will have limited retail support or distribution and plan accordingly. Your marketing effort should concentrate on finding your target market and connecting them to your much smaller, harder-to-find supply chain. If they're not vital, don't bother, no matter how much producer-types at your publisher may urge you on, when the time comes to market and distribute your product, marketing will be averse to giving you much support if retailers won't carry you. Make your bed, and then masturbate in it.

If you can't get distribution, it's tough to justify much of a development budget, particularly on a console where costs are often higher. Does sex in games pay?

In traditional console game development, sex does not pay. If it's too much the focus of what you're doing, it gets you banned from giant retail chains and even entire countries. Yes, you can set up a Web site with erotic video games like *VirtuallyJenna* where people pay to download content, but those games suck. There's nothing like two polygonal models with dead eyes lifelessly going through the motions of puppet-like intercourse. Real porn is cheaper and a lot more fun.

In the last few years, three major sexually themed games were released. Those that mixed humor with sex seemed to fare better. Why do you think that is?

3D polygonal sex isn't very hot. You can go to a million porn sites and watch free clips or buy cheap DVDs anonymously through the mail if you want to get off. Interactivity isn't proving to be much of a selling point here. It's mostly men who are into porn anyways, and we're a visual breed. I'd rather be passive when I watch porn and enjoy. Also, let's be honest, what good is watching porn if you don't have at least one hand free? Now, as for the humor part, it's an underserved niche that most developers don't do very well, but who doesn't like to laugh? Whether your comedy deals with sexual themes or not, if it's genuinely funny, it will get noticed and probably do well.

What is the best use of sexual content that you've seen in a game so far?

I loved having characters in *Magna Cum Laude* talk about topics that I'd never heard mentioned in a console game before. We joked about glory holes, snuff films, bukkake, bestiality—it was all in good fun. My writing partner, Matt Entin, and I are going to be watched a bit more carefully from now on, so I don't know how much we or anyone else will get away with for a while.

If Larry were a game developer instead of a game character, what type of game do you think he'd make?

It would be a bit like Peter Molyneux's *The Movies*, only you'd be a porn studio instead of a traditional movie studio. Also, Larry would both perform and direct in most of his productions. I'm sure he'd also find time to showcase some of his standup material, which is actually quite horrible.

As developers, do you think we have an ethical responsibility? Do we need to think about what we might be teaching people who play these games?

Mmmm . . . sorta perhaps. I like making adult content targeted to adults, specifically comedy or light-hearted fare. If I'm making content for adults, I feel I can safely assume they are not impressionable, and I feel I have a right to joke about anything I want to without an adult taking me seriously. If I were making content for children or even teens, it would be a different story. In that case, I would feel a responsibility not to send the wrong message, even in jest.

Some developers experienced discrimination because they were working on adult-themed material. Have you experienced anything like this?

I don't think so. I think, however, there is a higher percentage of people in the development community who are not receptive to adult-themed material than in the mainstream. Developers tend to be very smart (i.e., *nerds*, a term I use with the utmost respect and affection) and shy away from overtly sexual topics. They tend to be more uptight. It's my goal, then, not to get so typecast by *Leisure Suit Larry* that I can't find work doing anything else.

Why do you think we've seen more sexually themed games these last few years?

We're adults now, right? The average age of a gamer is 29, if you believe industry data. Games are starting to be taken more seriously as an entertainment medium, there's big money in them, and sex is the final frontier. Stories are becoming more important, and what's a good story without a little sex and romance? The screwball comedy is also something whose time has come in our industry. Movies like *American Pie* and *Old School* continue what *Animal House* began over 25 years ago and rack up impressive box office receipts along the way. What fun are those without a good shower scene or some scrambled porn or a girl taking her top off to a crazy sound effect? BOING! That's good stuff.

What's the future of sex in games?

More, more, more! Society has, by and large, become a bit more conservative as I write this, but it matters not. People want it, people need it, and people gotta have it. Games will continue to shed their image as "kids stuff," and eventually they'll at least catch up with film, which can get away with a lot more before their distribution is threatened. *Someday*, and this will take us well past the Xbox 360 or Sony's next console, game systems will be able to push enough polys, character models will have enough bones, and animators will find enough desperate out-of-work motion capture actors to make 3D sex hot, and whatever else anybody says, "It's not the polys, it's the psychological aspect, blah, blah, blah," that will make a huge difference. [Kuehnel01]

BRAD ABRAM

Brad Abram is the president of xStream3D Multimedia Inc, developers and publishers of *VirtuallyJenna*, the sex simulation game featuring porn star Jenna Jameson.

VirtuallyJenna was the first modern sex simulation to feature a big name porn star who crossed over into the mainstream market. Whose idea was VirtuallyJenna?

It was serendipitous timing. The original sex sim part was the idea of the developer of the core technology, "thriXXX." It started off as a joke, actually. They were discussing starting a company to develop a new 3D engine a few years ago when one of the founders suddenly blurted out, "We could even simulate sex in real-time 3D." Silence filled the room. The idea of developing a real-time 3D engine was born. And the slogan of the core technology/company basically encapsulates that idea: "thriXXX . . . simulates what stimulates!" The original simulation game was established over two years without personalized celebrity characters. We realized if we wanted to make it big in North America, it would be good to have a star to help promote the game.

We thought about who is the biggest in the business and researched that. We looked at mainstream entertainment stars like Pamela Anderson and Carmen Electra and thought that if we had a crossover celebrity, it would help mainstream our concept. It ultimately was easier to go on the adult side. Jenna's the biggest in the business. Her adult fan base is actually 50% women, and she has a growing mainstream fan base. We thought all the demographics would work. Jenna has fans in both the mainstream and adult worlds, and that would help attract more mainstream casual gamers as customers. I ended up going to Arizona and approached her directly through her production company CJI Digital and its president, Jay Grdina.

Unbeknownst to us, Club Jenna was looking for a way to get Jenna and her friends into the video game market. Jenna had appeared in games like *Grand Theft Auto*, but they wanted a vehicle for her to star in a game. CJI had been approached several times by game companies and others in the adult space, but none of them had the level of quality we had with a script where she was the main attraction. After a bit of negotiating, the decision was made to create *VirtuallyJenna* for Jenna and the rest of the Club Jenna contract women, Krystal Steal, Ashton Moore, Jesse Capelli, Mackenzie Lee, and Sophie Rossi. Additional women who are associated with Club Jenna Web sites are also slated to appear, including Tera Patrick, Brianna Banks, and others. We hope to have several hundred girls and guys in the game over the next few years.

What is the demographic of your players?

VirtuallyJenna has a breakdown of about 98% male and 2% female. We also have a gay version ready for launch where the breakdown will be similar, of course. Even hentai games get these rates. Our *VJ* game, however, is attracting more females since Jenna's hard-core fan base is 50% men and 50% women. We think once we have the IM-based head-to-head 3D chat systems in place, females will be more interested in playing. Play will be a mix of controlling the 3D avatars and using text to create your own fantasy stories in real time with another person. Our testing shows females will be more interested in this type of play.

Rather than just a pure sex simulation, you're hoping to make this a game as well. Can you talk about your ultimate vision for the game?

We want to develop a simulation system where our customers' needs are fulfilled 100%. Any sexual wish should come true. Of course, there are moral limits, but as far as we can go, we want provide an outstanding piece of software that makes every sexual dream possible.

How are your designers mixing sex and gameplay to make it fun? Can you give an example of a mission that includes elements of both?

The whole game is a complete erotic experience over a long period of time. The girls/guys will be kind of "virtual friends" with different needs and desires. The player has to build up a relationship over a few months and learn to treat her right. The better the relationship gets, the more possibilities the player gets and his girl will be willing to do more things. Additionally, adventure and role-playing elements will be added, like "Jenna's Secret Online Services." The player will have to seduce a girl in various scenes (e.g., small talk in a coffee shop, during a flight, on the beach, etc.). At first, these will be mini-game activities where a fantasy is presented, and you complete the mission, so to speak, interactively. These mini-games will be held together in the context of a story that involves more extensive gameplay where you are a bounty hunter, and you have to deal with the more sordid underside of society but in a hero role.

Keeping this in context, we don't want to create super elaborate sim games, but we do want to create highly re-playable fantasy situations with some kind of context. The game will also become a part of the community through 3D instant messaging (IM) where gamers get to interact in real time.

How do you keep sexual content entertaining without making it cheesy?

That is a challenge. People have strong opinions and expectations when it comes to sex. We are conquering the issues associated with motion capture and want to focus on quality graphics, sounds, and facial animation capabilities. We don't think we will ever be able to completely convince people that computer-generated characters are real, but people who play this type of game are already pre-disposed to wanting to buy into the fantasy and so are more forgiving.

Can you describe your photo personalization technology and what it will do for the player?

This kind of relates to the previous comment. Having your face in the game will help you buy into the fantasy. That said, we think the photo personalization will be attractive to the 3D IM systems users where they can create realistic avatars of themselves or even enhanced avatars to interact with like-minded individuals who are more into realistic fantasy imagery versus hentai or more cartoon-like imagery.

One of the questions the book asks is, "What's Appropriate" in sexual games. For hardcore on-line games, it might be easier to answer this question: what's not appropriate?

Child pornography, sex with animals, and extreme brutal sex are absolute NOs. We do have inquires, which is alarming, but we would never ever only think about adding any of these into our applications.

At a GDC roundtable discussing sex in games, distribution of titles was a serious issue for developers. Many big box retailers wouldn't stock the games. Do you have any alternate distribution suggestions?

Yes. Distribute them online like other role-playing games (monthly fee with monthly updates) and/or distribute them through the worldwide network of sex shops. Right now, we are using the traditional adult affiliate model which is based on revenue sharing with Webmasters who drive traffic to our site through various methods. We are pushing into mainstream portals in Europe like MSN's and AOL's and Yahoo's where there is a more liberal attitude toward a sex game.

Additionally we are looking at integrating SMS and MMS from cell phones to unlock game features by sending codes back and forth from the game to the real world and doing things with Sony PSP now that it has wireless connectivity. We can stream content to it without necessarily having to go through the publisher model.

We will have serialized monthly "sex packs" that get sent to subscribers that feature new girls, new rooms, new fantasy scenarios, kind of like 3D *Penthouse Forum* to keep customers engaged. The hope is that we will be able to tie this into the 3D IM systems and help stimulate the use of the content in head-to-head casual game interaction between subscribers.

What role has Jenna Jameson played in developing the game?

She was great. She gave us a lot of input and imagery to build our models from and let us participate in learning the industry ins and outs and do's and don'ts. She and her team have a great amount of experience in this kind of business. She also recorded hundreds of sounds to get *VirtuallyJenna* even more lifelike. She is truly the Queen in this business.

Due to distribution problems, some people ask if sex sells when it comes to games? Speaking specifically for your market, does it?

Does water sell in the desert? Yes, of course. We provide the experience that the community was waiting for in a sex simulation. We get ideas and great feedback every day from our growing online fan community, which encourages us to develop more and more.

Many sexually themed games—at least the ones the mass market knows about—are of the "sex in games marketed to gamers" variety. Yours appears to be "sex in games marketed to the adult market." Can you talk about that difference, how it affects your marketing and why it's critical?

Sex games for the adult market have to fulfill one simple quest: "Satisfy our customers within a few minutes." A sex game for players should be more like a RPG where you can meet other people and have sexual intercourse with each other.

How much did VirtuallyJenna *cost to develop?*

Four years of development with a team of 12 skilled developers. Now you can calculate on your own.

Many people are curious how you go about modeling the sex in such a game. Did you do motion capture for VirtuallyJenna?

We created everything from scratch and perfected it through trial and error. Getting 3D into a sex game is exceptionally challenging. Sex games take a huge amount of resources to pull off successfully. Otherwise, the characters look plastic. The human body by itself is challenging to model. It goes to the next level when you're trying to simulate sex between 3D rig characters. You have eyes that have to track you, jiggling breasts, hair, different looks and expressions, and it must all be incredibly detailed.

Is there a reason you didn't go with motion capture?

Motion capture doesn't work as well as you'd think for sex. Usually, mocap is done one character at a time. If you mocapped a fighting scene for a game, you would do one character at a time in different carefully choreographed sessions. Then, artists would tweak these into a fluid fighting scene. When mocap is done, sensors are placed on people's bodies, and those sensors must always be visible or occlusion occurs. With sex mocap, you end up getting so much occlusion that it's easier to create the animations from scratch than to clean up the data you get from a mocap session. We are working on it, however.

What do you see as the future of sexual hardware?

We do have inquires concerning devices like "Cyberpussies" or 3D glasses to bring this online sex simulation to a next level. Such toys must be easy to use and safe to install. However, this is secondary to our main initiatives into better casual gaming with the computer and 3D IMing.

How do you handle the negative feedback/criticism you receive?

We love negative feedback. It's the best way to improve our software and create a breathtaking experience. [Abram01]

SHERI GRANER RAY

Sheri Graner Ray is a game designer and developer and author of the book *Gender Inclusive Game Design: Expanding the Market*, which was nominated for a 2005 Game Developer's Choice award. A part of the games industry since 1990, Sheri has served in numerous capacities from game designer to studio head. Sheri is also a recipient of the 2005 Game Developer's Choice award for Community Contribution and is a founder and Steering Committee Chair of Women in Game International.

In my research so far, sexual content in games has been overwhelmingly aimed at men. Why is that?

Simply put, because the majority of game developers are male and the traditional target audience is male.

Have you seen an example of sexual content aimed at women?

No, but it would be interesting, because I think it would have to be different from the content aimed at men. In other words, you couldn't simply flip the gender on the characters and assume that now it would be sexually attractive for women. To do it right, you'd have to go to school on what is sexually arousing for females versus males. It's not just a case of making it the same for both genders.

In your book, you refer to "hypersexualized" avatars. Can you define "hypersexualized?"

Hypersexualized can be defined as the exaggeration of, and emphasis on, those traits on the human body that signal sexual receptivity. By that I mean exaggerating those physical traits that say "I'm ready for sex right now." When the human body becomes sexually aroused, several things happen.

The heart rate increases and there is a rush of blood to the face and genitals. This blood rush to the face results in a thickening and reddening of the lips. It also results in a thickening and darkening of the eyelids, which results in that heavy-lidded, "bedroom-eye" look.

The nipples become erect.

Respiration increases (which is often depicted in art by an open mouth).

The interesting fact is, these traits are the same on males as females, but it is only on our female game characters that we see any of them displayed. Not only do we depict these traits, but we emphasize and exaggerate them on the female characters.

For our female characters, we exaggerate the traits that indicate sexual receptivity, and then we dress them in clothing designed specifically to draw attention to these traits. We then pose them in provocative postures to give even more appearance that she is ready for sex "right now." We do none of that for our male characters.

Now, there are those who will argue that male characters are also exaggerated and, to be fair, to a certain extent they are. We do depict them as having exaggerated characteristics that indicate youth and strength such as big shoulders and arms, small waists and hips, and long thick hair, but we do not exaggerate the physical signs of sexual receptivity on our male characters. In fact, we rarely show any signs of sexuality at all on our males. In other words, the male characters are not hypersexualized.

What risks do developers face when they use hypersexualized avatars in games?

They risk alienating potential customers, regardless of gender.

After many months' break from RPGs, I started to play a popular one on the PS2 the other day. I happened to choose the female character. It was comical, odd, weird, to watch this woman walking through town in her "I've got to get to my stripping engagement" outfit. I mean, she may as well have been wearing a clown costume, she looked so out of place. Historically, how did we get to a point where that looks normal to people?

We all know that sex sells. Unfortunately, we have a marketing/advertising machine that has grabbed hold of that idea and doesn't seem willing to let go of it. I suppose they figure a little sex sold well, so a lot of sex will sell even better! It's not original or creative, but it seems to be selling.

It is this lack of creativity combined with a tremendous adversity to risk that has resulted in the continued use of the sexualized female as a marketing tool.

There is some validity to that reasoning. For instance, if your job depended on selling 100K units of a game and you had a choice between the next *GTA* or a new game for a new market, which would you pick? *GTA*, of course! You need to keep your job, so you're going to keep doing what you know works. If it doesn't seem to work, then you might use stuff that is even MORE sexually provocative, because by now the audience is jaded and you need to stimulate them more to get the same response.

While this may allow marketing people to keep their jobs for that fiscal quarter, it doesn't allow for any new game ideas or marketing methods to be tried. It also keeps the door firmly shut on some potentially lucrative markets.

Apart from the games we make, there's also a whole lot of "sex" in our industry, from booth babes to the infamous antics at tradeshows. How does that affect us as an industry?

I think we have to be very careful to define what we are talking about in this sense. Frankly, there isn't a lot of actual "sex"—as in the act of intercourse—in our games. However, there is a lot of sexual exploitation in our games, marketing, and advertising. By that, I mean the hypersexualization of female characters and the objectification of women.

It's really sad that we resort to this as an industry, because we are only hurting sales. This attitude essentially tells our potential female audience that we don't want their money.

I don't think there is another industry anywhere that goes so out of its way to actively and knowingly turn away a large and potentially very lucrative market the way this industry does with the female audience.

The automobile industry figured it out. When was the last time you saw a commercial for an SUV that featured bikini clad young girls hanging all over some macho dude as he gets into his SUV? Nope. You are more likely to see an ad featuring a man picking up the stroller as the woman puts the child in the car seat. That's because the auto industry figured out that the majority of car buying decisions were made by the female in the family.

Where do you see the "car babes?" They have a home in commercials about Hemis and trucks and so on. In other words, in the marketing collateral aimed at the same demographic that buys video games.

How do you create sexual content and have it be both necessary and tasteful (as opposed to gratuitous, one-sided and cheesy)?

Make sure your workforce contains both genders! Begin your work with focus groups and play tests of what is already available, and then use focus groups and play testing throughout the development of your product. And, most importantly, make sure you are using focus groups that are diverse in their population! Otherwise, your focus group results are meaningless.

One question the book asks is "What's appropriate?" Keeping in mind the broad defini-tion of "sexual content," what types of sexual content do you think are appropriate at the various rating levels—E, T, M, and AO? (If it's easier to say what's not appropriate, feel free to.) Please answer each individually.

I think our ratings should be mapped pretty closely to the movie industry, mostly be-cause this is the rating system most parents are familiar with. So, it would be easier to educate the public.

> E—Similar to the G rating, meaning little to no sexual content. I think this should probably have as much sexual content as an old *I Love Lucy* show.

> T—Similar to the PG rating, meaning a small amount of sexual content—more in line with some of the prime time television shows today. Kissing, light petting, light innuendo such as what you would find in *Friends* or *Grey's Anatomy*.

> M—This should be comparable to an R-rated movie: sexual elements, but no full frontal nudity.

> AO—Comparable to an X-rated movie. This could contain graphic depictions of sexual activity.

> Note that the criteria I list here have only to do with the sexual facet of the rating system. The film rating system also takes into account language, violence level, amount of blood (whether bullet hits are wet or dry is a primary concern), and so on.

I have a chapter on positive sexual inclusion in games. Can sexual content be used in a good way in a game? Has it? How?

You bet. Probably the best example of this is the original *Leisure Suit Larry* games. They were funny, risqué, and appealed to both males AND females. The trick, I believe, is to make sure your humor does not denigrate or "put down" women or men. The original *LSL* titles did a great job of avoiding this and yet were still very funny. I talked about this a bit in my book. After my editor read that chapter, she was very uncertain about it. She said she couldn't think of a "dirty" joke that didn't put down females. So she asked me to come up with one and put it in my book. Of course, I did!

Emergent sex is an alarming trend for some online games and PC/Xbox games that accept user created content. Prostitution rings have sprung up in MMOs, players in Anarchy Online and World of Warcraft cyber to their hearts' content using moves and animations initially meant for combat or relaxing. Some players love it. What are your thoughts on this?

This is a tough one. On one hand, I'm strongly against censorship of any sort. So long as there are profanity filters available and rules against sexual language used in "pub-lic" (meaning nonprivate) conversations, I don't think there is a problem, save with enforcement (another issue.)

On the other hand, I don't know how I'd feel about a child (meaning under the age of 18) being involved in that situation; i.e., "cybering." I certainly think that is a risk when you allow a child to play MMOs.

I think it may come down to the ratings. If a game is rated T, then it should be safe for kids, period. Although the current MMO boxes say, "game experience may change during online play," I'm not sure that's enough for a T rating, and may in fact be a huge cop out. Think about it. How upset would you be if you sent your 12-year-old child to a movie that was rated G, but since its release, several very graphic sexual scenes had been added? And how much would you trust the rating system after that?

Frankly, if we want our ratings guide to mean anything, then we have to stand by them and enforce them.

Now, I'm not saying I think all MMOs should be rated M, because at this point in this industry, that's a whole different market. But I am suggesting that we might need something in between the T and the M, something that indicates that sexual content could be encountered but is not the focus of the game.

The night elf and the succubus in *WoW* is another thing. We're back to the hypersexualized female characters. This type of objectification of the sexualized female character has no place in our MMOs, and while adolescent males may find it funny, it only serves to alienate a good portion of our potential female audience.

Should online developers support emergent sex or try to eradicate it? A bit of both?

I think that depends on the type of game they are developing and who their target audience is. If they are developing an adult AO title aimed at adults over the age of 21, then certainly it should be encouraged and should appeal to men and women. If they are developing a T-rated title aimed at 8- to 14-year-olds, then no, it shouldn't. It comes back to who your audience is and what it wants.

Oddly enough, the emergent sex found in games seems to be more gender inclusive than the sexual content developers intend to put in. Women cyberers really enjoy the emergent sexual component in games like Anarchy Online *and* Second Life. *What are your thoughts on this?*

This is something the romance book industry has known for quite a long while. In fact, the demand for "hot" romance, meaning those that contain more graphic sexual content, has exploded over the past five years and is now the fastest growing segment of that market!

And I say "Bravo!" We are well past the days when the prevailing thought was, "good girls don't enjoy sex" . . . and good riddance! But let's just make sure we label it appropriately so that parents can make smart choices about what their kids are playing.

A producer of an M-rated sexually themed game raised this question at my GDC roundtable on sexuality in games, "Do we as developers have an ethical responsibility? Do we need to think about what we might be teaching people who play these games?" What do you think?

This is a question that can be asked about all games in general. Do we have an ethical responsibility to all players of all our games? Do we need to think about what we are teaching people who play our FPSs or our RTSs or our RPGs or our Adult games? My belief is that it is entertainment. We do not have to "teach" anything.

However, we do have to ensure that we are harming no one through discrimination, exclusion, or perpetuation of derogatory representation or depiction. You wouldn't depict derogatory racial elements; you shouldn't depict derogatory gender or sexual elements either.

At a GDC party, you and I were talking. No fewer than a dozen people expressed their surprise to me and assumed there was an argument going on (or about to break out). Evidently, there's an assumption that being "gender inclusive" means "without sexual content." Would you care to set the record straight?

I think these are the same folks who think that my beliefs also preclude having attractive female characters in games! Believe me, neither idea could be further from the truth! I have *no problem* with sexual content in computer games as long as it is labeled clearly and appropriately, and no derogatory gender elements are depicted. By that I mean neither women nor men are depicted a way that would be construed to be a harmful, derogatory, or derisive manner.

I think it's about time we were able to produce sexy, fun, adult entertainment that appeals to both men and women!

REFERENCES

[Abram01] Abram, Brad, interview with Brenda Brathwaite, August 6, 2005.

[Bates01] Bates, Bob, interview with Brenda Brathwaite, August 4, 2005.

[Garriott01] Garriott, Richard, interview with Brenda Brathwaite, May 27, 2005.

[Graner Ray] Graner Ray, Sheri, interview with Brenda Brathwaite, March 7, 2006.

[Jonathan] "Jonathan," interview with Brenda Brathwaite, November 23, 2005.

[Kuehnel01] Kuehnel, Edward, interview with Brenda Brathwaite, August 4, 2005.

[Meretzky01] Meretzky, Steve, interview with Brenda Brathwaite, August 2, 2005.

Index